# THE BIBLE
## AND THE
# ANCIENT NEAR EAST

CYRUS H. GORDON received his professional training (B.A., M.A., Ph.D.) at the University of Pennsylvania. He is professor emeritus at both Brandeis University and New York University, where he taught Hebrew and other Near Eastern languages and literatures. Earlier in his career he taught at Smith College, Johns Hopkins University, and Dropsie College. In 1993 he served as visiting professor at Haifa University, and throughout his career he has served as visiting lecturer in many universities around the globe. From 1931 to 1935 he was a field archeologist on expeditions of the American Schools of Oriental Research in Jerusalem and Baghdad. Professor Gordon is the author of about six hundred publications, including over twenty books or monographs on the Mediterranean and the Near East. Among the most important are *Ugaritic Textbook* (1965), *The Common Background of Greek and Hebrew Civilizations* (1965), and *Evidence for the Minoan Language* (1966). He is a Fellow of the American Academy of Arts and Sciences and an Honorary Fellow of the Royal Asiatic Society.

GARY A. RENDSBURG was an undergraduate student at the University of North Carolina at Chapel Hill (B.A.) and received his graduate degrees at New York University (M.A., Ph.D.). Currently he serves as professor of Near Eastern Studies at Cornell University, specializing in the Hebrew Bible, West Semitic languages, and Egyptian. Previously he taught at Canisius College, he has served as visiting professor at the State University of New York at Binghamton, and twice he has held the post of visiting research professor at the Hebrew University in Jerusalem. Professor Rendsburg is the author of three books and dozens of articles on Hebrew language and literature, including *The Redaction of Genesis* (1986).

## BOOKS BY CYRUS H. GORDON

*Nouns in the Nuzi Tablets*
*Ugaritic Grammar*
*The Living Past*
*The Loves and Wars of Baal and Anat*
*Ugaritic Handbook*
*Lands of the Cross and Crescent*
*Ugaritic Literature*
*Smith College Tablets*
*Introduction to Old Testament Times*
*Ugaritic Manual*
*Adventures in the Nearest East*
*Hammurapi's Code*
*The World of the Old Testament*
*Before the Bible*
*The Ancient Near East*
*The Common Background of Greek and
Hebrew Civilizations*
*Ugaritic Textbook*
*Evidence for the Minoan Language*
*Ugarit and Minoan Crete*
*Homer and Bible*
*Forgotten Scripts*
*Before Columbus*
*Riddles in History*
*The Pennsylvania Tradition of Semitics*

## BOOKS BY GARY A. RENDSBURG

*The Redaction of Genesis*
*Diglossia in Ancient Hebrew*
*Linguistic Evidence for the Northern Origin
of Selected Psalms*

# THE BIBLE
## AND THE
# ANCIENT NEAR EAST

---

*Cyrus H. Gordon*
*and Gary A. Rendsburg*

FOURTH EDITION

W. W. NORTON & COMPANY
*New York • London*

Copyright © 1997 by Cyrus H. Gordon and Gary A. Rendsburg
Copyright © 1965, 1958 by Cyrus H. Gordon
Copyright © 1953 by Ventnor Publishers, Inc.

Previous editions of this book have been entitled
*Introduction to Old Testament Times* (1953)
*The World of the Old Testament* (1958)
*The Ancient Near East* (1965)

This edition first published as a Norton paperback by arrangement with Doubleday,
a division of Bantam Doubleday Dell Publishing Group, Inc.

The text of this book is composed in Bembo, with the display set in Copperplate Bold.
Composition and manufacturing by The Maple-Vail Book Manufacturing Group.
Book design by Charlotte Staub
Cartography by Jacques Chazaud

Library of Congress Cataloging-in-Publication Data

Gordon, Cyrus Herzl, 1908–
The Bible and the ancient Near East / by Cyrus H. Gordon and Gary
A. Rendsburg. — 4th ed.
p.   cm.
Rev. ed. of: The ancient Near East. 1965.
Includes bibliographical references and index.
ISBN 0-393-03942-0
1. Bible. O.T.—History of contemporary events, etc.
I. Rendsburg, Gary A.   II. Gordon, Cyrus Herzl, 1908–      Ancient Near
East.   III. Title.
BS635.G73   1997
221.9′5—dc21      96-37110      CIP

ISBN 0-393-31689-0 pbk

W. W. Norton & Company, Inc., 500 Fifth Avenue, New York, N.Y. 10110
http://www.wwnorton.com

W. W. Norton & Company Ltd., 10 Coptic Street, London WC1A 1PU

2 3 4 5 6 7 8 9 0

*To our wives*

CONSTANCE WALLACE GORDON
*and*
SUSAN L. RENDSBURG

*Who share with us our love
for the Bible and the world
whence it sprang*

# Contents

# List of Maps

# Foreword to the Fourth Edition

Thirty years have passed since the third edition of this book was published in 1965. New discoveries in the last three decades shedding light on the ancient Near East in general and on the Bible in particular made us keenly aware of the need for a new edition of this work. Among the most notable of these discoveries has been the recovery of ancient Ebla, which not only provides us with the oldest Semitic language attested (known to scholars as Eblaite), but which also radically alters our understanding of Syria in the third millennium B.C.E., about one thousand years before Abraham.

Closer to Israel there have been exciting developments as well. The most important discovery occurred in summer 1993, when an Aramaic stela inscription was found at Dan referring to both "the king of Israel" and "the house of David," with the two phrases referring clearly to the divided kingdoms of Israel and Judah. Then, in summer 1994 another fragment was found revealing the names of the two kings as Jehoram son of Ahab "the king of Israel" and Ahaziah son of Jehoram of "the house of David." This inscription is of singular importance, for while numerous kings of Israel and Judah are mentioned in contemporary inscriptions from Moab, Assyria, and Babylonia, this is the first time that David occurs in an extrabiblical text. And while the reference is not to King David himself, the text indicates that Judah was known to the nearby kingdom of Aram as "the house of David" about a century and a half after the reign of the founder of the dynastic line.

The reader will find reference to these and many other new finds in the pages that follow, synthesized with the older material from the earlier editions of this work.

In preparing this volume we have sought to understand the Bible on its own terms by situating it in the world of the ancient Near East. Too often nowadays scholars approach this classic text with preconceived notions based on social, political, religious, and/or ideological predilections reflecting the present, with little or no concern for how and what the past informs. The result is that much of what passes for scholarship is based not on facts "on the ground," but on theories suspended "on nothingness" (to use the expression in Job 26:7). We trust that the informed reader of this book will notice the difference, and, furthermore, that he or she will enjoy with us the exhilarating quest for uncovering the world of ancient Israel and its most remarkable achievement, the Bible.

—CYRUS H. GORDON
GARY A. RENDSBURG

# Foreword to the Third Edition

T he first edition of this book, under the title of *Introduction to Old Testament Times* in 1953, aimed at bridging the gap between ancient Mesopotamia and pharaonic Egypt via Palestine that lay in between and had connection with both. In the course of fulfilling that aim, a new factor emerged: the interrelation between Canaan and Greece during the second millennium B.C.E.

The second edition appeared in 1958 as *The World of the Old Testament*. By that time the decipherment of the Mycenaean Linear B inscriptions had made it possible to break into the Minoan Linear A texts and to determine that Minoan was some sort of Semitic language. It was not until 1962, however, that the specifically Northwest Semitic character of Minoan was established: a fact subsequently confirmed by two Eteocretan-Greek bilinguals from Dreros, Crete. A new chapter was thus opened in the history of western civilization and the numerous parallels between early Canaan and Greece could be attributed mainly to the spread of Northwest Semites over the entire East Mediterranean.

In 1964 a new development enabled us to focus on western origins more narrowly. The Phaistos Disc, from Minoan Crete of about 1600 B.C.E., has unmistakable affinities with Egypt and yet it is in the same Semitic language as the Minoan Linear A texts. Moreover, each sign is read as the opening "consonant + vowel" of the Northwest Semitic word depicted by the sign, showing that the script was devised for a Northwest Semitic language in Egypt. The Delta has generally had a large non-Egyptian population in Mediterranean people including Northwest Semites. It turns out that the Minoan palace builders came to Crete from the Delta around 1800 B.C.E, whereas the Hebrews left the Delta for Canaan around 1230 B.C.E. Accordingly, the earliest high civilization of Europe was founded by Northwest Semites from the Delta, like Hebrew civilization five and a half centuries later. It goes without saying that the Delta will assume a new importance in historical studies—an importance now visible in broad outline but yet to be delineated in detail.

The first edition of this book was published in the hope that it would open new vistas of history. The decade that followed fulfilled that hope and the second decade now bids fair to gain even further momentum in crowning with success the search to understand our past and ourselves.

—CYRUS H. GORDON

# The Bible
### and the
# Ancient Near East

———————

**CHAPTER I**

# Prolegomena

The most important area for the study of human antiquity is the Near East. There we find a cluster of ancient civilizations that are not only the oldest and among the greatest but are also well recorded. The Near East included notably Mesopotamia, Egypt, and Israel; Greece too, as we shall see, was closely related to it. The area is important not only for its own sake but also because it produced the origins of Western culture.

Mesopotamia gave birth to Sumer, Babylon, and Assyria, whose art and literature are being unearthed in our own time. But independent of archeological discovery, the Mesopotamian sexagesimal system of reckoning would live on in our sciences, ranging from the 360° circle (with degrees each of 60 minutes, and minutes each of 60 seconds) to our clocks on whose face the hour is divided into 60 minutes of 60 seconds each.

Egypt produced a civilization remarkable for its charm and continuity no less than for the massiveness of its pyramids and temples. Yet even if all the monuments should perish, Egyptian influence would live on in us through our calendar of nonlunar months. We still use the Egyptian calendar, albeit with Julian and Gregorian improvements.

Israel, unlike Mesopotamia and Egypt, was not among the great political powers of the ancient world. Nor did Israel excel in architecture, sculpture, painting, and the minor arts. But its genius in religion, ethics, literature, and historiography gave it an importance out of all proportion to its small population and land. Wherever Judaism and its daughters, Christianity and Islam, thrive, the influence of Israel lives on. Our most familiar names like David or John, Mary or Susan are Hebrew; our seven-day week stems from Genesis; our modern literature often enough follows biblical themes.

Since the study of the ancient Near East, or Bible World, is the study of the roots of Western civilization, it has a particular meaning for intellectuals in the West. For intellectuals in the Near East, it has additional significance; for the antiquity of the Near East, as it is being discovered through archeological excavations, has a growing effect on the nationalisms in the area today. The Egyptians associate their claim to superiority with their ancient past whose magnificent civilization is being steadily unfolded by archeologists and Egyptologists. The field of Egyptology was once the domain of Europeans and to a lesser extent Americans, but today Egypt produces native-born specialists in all areas of Egyptology. Iraq and Syria dedicate themselves to the rediscovery of the old cuneiform cultures that distinguish their lands from other Arab lands. Turkey associates itself with the Hittites about whom it knew nothing less than a century ago; the spectacular Hittite discoveries are now a source of national pride. Iran, which until the nineteenth century C.E. had lost all memory of its greatest period of history, the Achaemenian Age (sixth to fourth centuries B.C.E.), under the modern shahs turned back to that dynasty of Cyrus, Darius, and Xerxes for its inspiration. (The current Iranian regime of Muslim fundamentalists differs, however, in that it views the entire pre-Islamic past with contempt for its embrace of polytheism.) Lebanon distinguishes itself from the surrounding countries with an ideology whereby its people are the descendants of the Phoenicians and thus different from the other people around them. Just as the Phoenicians colonized the entire Mediterranean, so many modern Lebanese, in particular the Christian half of the population, have important ties with countries such as Greece, Italy, and France. Jordan cannot claim a great culture from antiquity, but still it takes pride in its Edomite, Moabite, and Ammonite past. The final example, and probably the best example, of a nation attaching itself to a glorious past is Israel. The momentum of Israel's long history, including notably the undying hope of biblical prophecy, is an indispensable factor in the shaping of the modern nation of Israel. Israel is also different from the other Middle Eastern countries, because its people not only live on the same land as their ancestors, but there is also an unbroken continuity of religion, culture, and language. Israeli devotion to its archeological antiquities has been evident since the birth of the modern state, even during the exigencies of its war for statehood.[1]

What sources have we with which to study the history of the ancient Near East? The most unequivocal are those in written form. The best known is the Hebrew Bible; next come numerous classic authors, in Greek and Latin. Though even the classical Greeks came on the scene rather late in Near Eastern history, they recorded many traditions that supplement more recently discovered native sources and so are of value not only as a window on their own times but also in that they enable us to work back into more remote antiquity.

In Asia the first literature is the Sumerian, written in cuneiform in Mesopotamia from about 3000 B.C.E. Sumerian became the classical language of the entire cuneiform world, embracing Mesopotamia and the surrounding areas. It died out as a spoken tongue a little after 1800 B.C.E., giving way to Akkadian, but remained the classical language of western Asia studied by cuneiform scribes for nearly 1900 years thereafter, until Akkadian cuneiform disappeared in the first century A.D. Thus Sumerian has had a history as a classical language comparable in length of time with Greek and Latin.[2]

The main cuneiform literature of the Bible World is Akkadian, sometimes called Babylonian or Assyrian after the two main dialects of the language. Akkadian is the standard Semitic language that gives us more written records of the ancient Near East than any other source.[3] The cuneiform script also was used by scribes in Syria as early as the third millennium B.C.E. to record their native Semitic language, known to scholars as Eblaite (after the site of Ebla, a large city in antiquity that has yielded an exceedingly large archive). Eventually cuneiform script spread to Anatolia where it was used to record non-Semitic languages such as Hurrian, Urartian, and Hittite. The former two languages are related to a group of languages still spoken

1. The most striking example is the manner in which the original Dead Sea Scrolls came into Israeli hands; see the personal account of Yigael Yadin, *The Message of the Scrolls,* London, 1957, pp. 15–52. For the patterns of cultural revivals in the modern Near East, see Cyrus H. Gordon, *Lands of the Cross and Crescent,* Ventnor, N.J., 1948; and Neil A. Silberman, *Between Past and Present: Archaeology, Ideology, and Nationalism in the Modern Middle East,* New York, 1989.

2. For a good introduction to the language, see Marie-Louise Thomsen, *The Sumerian Language,* Copenhagen, 1984. The best comprehensive grammar remains A. Falkenstein, *Grammatik der Sprache Gudeas,* Rome, 1949–50.

3. The best comprehensive grammar is Wolfram von Soden, *Grundriss der akkadischen Grammatik,* Rome, 1969.

in the Caucasus Mountains, while Hittite is the earliest attested Indo-European language.

Of the great ancient literatures, the one of most direct importance for the study of the Bible is the collection of texts unearthed at Ugarit, a city that flourished on the north coast of Syria in the fourteenth and thirteenth centuries B.C.E. Ugaritic is written in a cuneiform alphabet on clay tablets.[4] Although Ugarit is to the far north of Canaan and technically falls outside the geographical boundaries of Canaan, Ugaritic literature is a branch of the Canaanite literature. The Hebrews took over when they migrated to Canaan, so that they inherited a polished medium for giving their distinctive message to the world.

The Achaemenian kings of Iran, starting with the sixth century B.C.E., developed a cuneiform syllabary in which they carved their royal inscriptions on living rock or inscribed them on tablets of precious metal. The native language written in this script is called Old Persian.[5] Often the texts are trilingual, being written in Elamite and Babylonian as well as Old Persian. The most important of the Achaemenian texts is the long trilingual of Darius I, from around 520 B.C.E., at Behistun. The decipherment of Old Persian provided the key to the Babylonian version, which opened up the vast treasures of Akkadian, and ultimately of Sumerian, literature. The decipherment of Elamite has been slower because that language is not related to any well-known family.

Our sketchy survey of the cuneiform sources should at least show that there is no dearth of material, but rather so great a wealth of it that the historian is embarrassed and taxed because he has only one lifetime to devote to it.

Coming into Canaan (by which we mean approximately the modern boundaries of contemporary Israel, Lebanon, and Jordan), we find another series of native inscriptions written in an alphabet. The Phoenicians have left us a number of texts, often of a funerary or commemorative character. The basic vocabulary and grammar are intelligible to everyone interested in the subject who has a command

---

4. For the grammar, texts, and lexicon, see Cyrus H. Gordon, *Ugaritic Textbook,* Rome, 1967. For a complete translation of the main literary texts, see Cyrus H. Gordon, "Poetic Legends and Myths from Ugarit," *Berytus* 25, 1978, pp. 5–133. Virtually every year a new expedition at Ugarit (and at the neighboring site of Ras ibn Hani) brings to light important texts and monuments.

5. See R. G. Kent, *Old Persian: Grammar, Texts, Lexicon,* New Haven, 1950.

of Hebrew. Other close neighbors of the Hebrews, the Moabites east of the Dead Sea, have left one moderately long historic inscription of King Mesha, who is mentioned in the Hebrew Bible. Also from the region east of the Jordan valley come smaller inscriptions in Ammonite and Edomite. Of great interest to biblical scholars are the few texts discovered at Deir ʿAlla (perhaps biblical Succoth), in which the prophet Balaam (known to readers of Numbers 22–24) is mentioned.

The Israelites themselves, in addition to bequeathing to the world the Hebrew Bible, also have left some inscriptions that have been discovered in modern times. In the northern capital of Samaria were found ostraca, or inscriptions written in ink on pieces of pottery. The Samaria ostraca are wine and oil receipts. Though they are short and give us very little detail, they provide interesting insights into ninth–eighth century Israelite administration and tell us something about the northern Israelite dialect of Hebrew, as distinct from the Judean dialect that predominates in the Bible. From Judah in the south we have other texts such as the Siloam inscription commemorating the completion of the tunnel that Hezekiah built (in anticipation of the war with Assyria in 701 B.C.E.) to augment Jerusalem's supply of water within the city wall. Also from Judah are the Lachish ostraca, which are the most important historic inscriptions left by the Hebrews. These date from the early sixth century B.C.E. and tell of military operations and signals around the southern cities of Lachish and Azekah during Nebuchadnezzar's invasion.[6]

The language with the widest distribution in our study is Aramaic.[7] Although there is evidence of the Aramaic language in records of the second millennium B.C.E., the historic texts begin in the eighth century in the city-states of Aram (or inland Syria), when it displaced Phoenician as the lingua franca in Syria and nearby coastal Asia Minor. By the end of the century Aramaic had already won for itself the role of international language in official circles from at least Assyria to Judah (2 Kings 18:26; the date is 701 B.C.E.). The achievement is the more remarkable since the Arameans never forged a great empire but spread the language through relatively peaceful means,

---

6. For a survey of the distinguishing grammatical features of all these texts, as well as of Aramaic texts of the period, see W. Randall Garr, *Dialect Geography in Syria-Palestine, 1000–586 B.C.E.*, Philadelphia, 1985.

7. Stanislav Segert, *Altaramäische Gramamtik*, Leipzig, 1975.

notably tribal migrations and trade. The Achaemenians used Aramaic as their interprovincial tongue, at least for the areas west of Iran. Parts of the Bible are written in Aramaic, notably large sections of Daniel and Ezra. A military colony of Jews in the service of the Achaemenian kings at Elephantine in Upper Egypt have left a corpus of Aramaic papyri of prime importance. So great was Aramaic that it was destined to replace the native languages of all Semitic Asia outside of Arabia, and it remained unchallenged until the Islamic Conquest in the seventh century C.E.

From Egypt we have a host of inscriptions on stone, papyrus, leather, and other materials; in hieroglyphs, in a cursive simplification of hieroglyphs called Hieratic, and ultimately in a further cursive simplification known as Demotic. While Egyptology is full of difficulties, it is nonetheless simpler than cuneiform studies because it deals with only one language and one pre-Greek script, even though the language, and especially the script, underwent considerable evolution.[8]

The Aegean produced texts in native writing, starting with Cretan hieroglyphs around 1800 B.C.E. They are not yet deciphered, but the next stage of this script, called Linear A, has been deciphered. Most of the "A" texts are economic documents on clay tablets found at Hagia Triada, Crete. The most important group of texts, however, is the corpus of several dozen religious texts inscribed on cultic objects such as libation tables. These inscriptions come from a variety of places all over eastern and central Crete. Since they are written in one and the same Northwest Semitic language, the latter can only be the main language of Minoan Crete.[9]

The key to the identification of the Linear A language is a tablet on which pots are depicted with their names spelled out syllabically over them. Most of these words for pots were Semitic, making it likely that the language was Semitic; the highly civilized Minoans, who had been making pottery for many centuries, would not have had to borrow the majority of their ceramic terms from abroad. Then I [C. H. G.] discovered that *ü* was the conjunction "and," and that *kunnishu* was the word for "wheat," as in well-known Semitic lan-

---

8. The best entree to the study of Egyptian is Alan Gardiner, *Egyptian Grammar,* Oxford, 1957. The work deals mainly with Middle Egyptian (in use during the Middle Kingdom, i.e., the first half of the second millennium B.C.E.), the language of the classical Egyptian literary texts (Story of Sinuhe, Shipwrecked Sailor, etc.).

9. Cyrus H. Gordon, *Evidence for the Minoan Language,* Ventnor, N.J., 1966.

guages. However, the Semitic identification remained in question until 1962 when a dedication on a libation table was read with a distinctively Northwest Semitic formula: "so that the city may thrive." This formula at last provided not only isolated words but a whole phrase with syntax.

The Linear B tablets (in use from the fifteenth to twelfth centuries B.C.E.), from the Peloponnesus and from Knossos, continue the "A" script but in the Greek language.[10] Clay tablets are therefore the tangible link, witnessing the ancient Near Eastern backdrop of Mycenaean Greek civilization.

The Cypro-Minoan inscriptions (most of which come from Enkomi, on Cyprus) are roughly contemporary with Linear B but have not yet been deciphered. In later times, down to the third century B.C.E., Greek inscriptions on Cyprus were written not only in the familiar Greek alphabet but also in a development of the Minoan syllabary.

It would be impractical to try to exhaust the list of written sources from the ancient Near East. To enumerate the most important ones as we have done, and to convey an idea of the richness and variety of the written sources are all that need be done here.

The written sources are supplemented by numerous material remains.[11] Of the latter, the most important is architecture, including cities with huge walls, streets, and buildings that range from palaces to hovels. Connected with the buildings are installations of permanent and portable types. Permanent installations include ovens for baking bread or bricks, baths with drainage systems and bitumen waterproofing, cisterns for storing the seasonal rainfall, pits for the storage of food, and so forth. Then there are many movable objects, of which the most common is pottery. Pottery is often the most valuable archeological criterion because while it is easily broken, it is not readily destroyed. The abundance of ceramic remains thus provides a clue for establishing a relative chronology (and for indicating trade relations, if some of the pottery is imported) when epigraphical evidence is lacking.

10. For the results of Ventris's brilliant decipherment of Linear B, see M. Ventris and J. Chadwick, *Documents in Mycenaean Greek,* Cambridge, 1956.

11. For the material remains, see especially James B. Pritchard, *The Ancient Near East in Pictures,* Princeton, 1954.

The excavator also finds tools of more substantial materials, as the erection of cities and monuments required instruments of stone, copper, and eventually iron. After buildings were completed, they were supplied with furnishings, which under favorable conditions may be discovered. In dry areas like Upper Egypt, where organic matter is durable, we find wood and other perishable materials preserved. The same substances disintegrate in Asia where there is a seasonal rainfall that plays havoc with organic matter, so that all the excavator finds is a discoloration (often brown) in the soil.

Archeological finds also include the whole field of fine arts. There are reliefs and sculpture in the round, ranging from colossi to statuettes. Painting, unlike sculpture, is as a rule well preserved only in Egypt because of the accident of climate, though a few dry spots in western Asia have yielded painted frescoes. Then there is the work of the metalsmith and jeweler, constituting an attractive repertoire of the minor arts.

Sometimes when the original objects have partially or entirely disintegrated, their representations in art enable us to reconstruct them. For instance, in Ur crushed harps were found with all the wooden structure eaten away and only the metal, stone, and shell parts surviving. Yet because of durable stone and mother-of-pearl representations of scenes showing such harps being played, Sir C. Leonard Woolley, who discovered the harps, could restore the wooden and other organic materials, beat the crushed metal remnants back into shape, and reconstruct the instruments as they appeared in antiquity.[12]

The Egyptians frequently made models of servants at work on the whole gamut of arts, crafts, and economic activity.[13] Thus the excavator often discovers a model brewery or bakery, with men and women at work; or a model ship complete with busy crew, so that even where full-sized originals are lacking, these models plus other representations provide a vivid impression of modes of life, arts and crafts, professions, trades, household activity, and entertainment in those times.

Coins appeared on the scene rather late in history, in the seventh century B.C.E., and became common quite some time after that. Coins occupy an intermediate or conglomerate category. They are a form of art, but not quite fine art; the work of the metalsmith, but lacking the individuality of his special creations. Though coins are a

12. See C. L. Woolley, *Ur Excavations* II (plates): *The Royal Cemetery,* Oxford, 1934.

13. J. H. Breasted, Jr., *Egyptian Servant Statues,* New York, 1948.

useful source of general history, they play no role in this book until the last period of our investigation: the Achaemenian Age.[14]

Now that we have considered the sources, we turn to the question of how to use them in the study of history. Languages have a certain historic value in themselves. Thus the relation of Egyptian to the Semitic languages implies a degree of cultural history shared by the two groups of people. When we delve into the very remote past, we find that there are ultimate connections between the Indo-European and Afro-Asiatic families of languages. (Afro-Asiatic is the family of languages to which belong not only Semitic and Egyptian, but also Berber, Cushitic, and Chadic, whose various languages are used in different parts of North Africa to the present day). Research into the ultimate connections between Indo-European and Afro-Asiatic continues at a fast pace today. And although no two scholars agree on the specific details linking these two large language families, such disagreement in no way detracts from the potentially historic importance of the problem.

When languages share common features, they have either inherited them from a common origin or acquired them through borrowing. English "father" and German "Vater" come from a common Indo-European origin which both languages have inherited without borrowing from each other. Apparent phonetic discrepancies are normal in such cases and usually follow correspondences that have been (or can be) formulated precisely under the name of "phonetic law." However, English "kindergarten" is borrowed from German, while German "Sport" is borrowed from English; for words tend to be borrowed along with the cultural contributions they designate. When a community is mixed linguistically, it tends to produce a resultant speech that bears the stamp of one of the component languages, though the other component languages will leave some impression. The resultant speech will thus have features of its different component languages, which may be of totally unrelated stocks. This type of fusion is known as linguistic alliance—a phenomenon that the historian must bear in mind alongside the more generally known phenomenon of related languages evolving from a common stock. Attempts to reconstruct prehistory from linguistic interrelations are as a rule less reliable than history based directly on written sources.

---

14. See W. Wirgin and S. Mandel, *The History of Coins and Symbols in Ancient Israel,* New York, 1958; and Yaakov Meshorer, *Ancient Jewish Coinage,* 2 vols., Dix Hills, N.Y., 1982.

Linguistic arguments become far more cogent when they are used in addition to, not instead of, available written documents.

Though we are on firmer ground with texts, they have to be evaluated before they can be used to reconstruct history. Obviously the date and origin of a text have to be established before it can be applied to a historic context. It may also be desirable to establish some facts about the author. If his name cannot be determined, it is often essential to find out at least his viewpoint, his purpose, what other compositions he may have written, or to what group of people he may have belonged. Important, too, is the evaluation of the text's reliability. Is it completely reliable? Is it completely unreliable? Or, as is usually the case, is it somewhere in between? If so, which elements are reliable and which are not? The discipline of evaluating documents is known as philology and constitutes a basic aid to history. In fact the two overlap and it is often hard to tell where philology ends and history begins.

Texts can be used to build historical images of different types and magnitudes. For instance, the tablets from Nuzu, a town in Assyria during the fifteenth and fourteenth centuries B.C.E., constitute the private archives of leading citizens during four or five generations. The study of these texts enables us to show the social and economic development of the town in that time with a degree of detail and intimacy rarely matched in the study of the familiar cities of Europe or America of premodern times. But while a homogeneous group of texts coming from the same time and place may provide a detailed record of the society in that community at that time, it is possible to go further than that and here is where the subject becomes more intricate.

We can deal with interrelations. To take a simple example, we can study the thirteenth-century treaties made between the Hittites and Egyptians, comparing the Hittite version with the Egyptian version. Each will contain different elements depending on the respective viewpoints; and by correlating the two sets of treaties, we get a more exact historical picture than we could from examining only one or the other. Another example: we know that in the ninth century Israel had dealings with Moab that at times involved invasion and war. The biblical account is one of our independent sources; the Moabite inscription of King Mesha is another. By using the documents of both the Hebrews and Moabites, we arrive at a controlled history, in which one source can be checked against another. Sometimes the same episodes are recorded in different independent sources. Thus Sennacherib's invasion of Judah in 701 B.C.E. is recounted in the Bible and in the Assyrian annals. The general agreement between both sources fixes the historicity of the event, and each version fills in lacunae in the other. Naturally the war communiques from two enemy camps are not going to have the same tone or point of view, but it is precisely the difference in origin that enables us to reconstruct what we call controlled history.

Occasionally, controlled history enables us to put into context what had seemed to be an isolated phenomenon. As an example, let us consider the return of the Jews from the Exile in 538 B.C.E., during the reign of Cyrus the Great. From the biblical account one might imagine it was an isolated act of grace by a sovereign who was interested in the Jewish people and wanted to restore them to their home and revive their worship. All that is in general true, but taken out of context it gives a false impression. On reading the inscribed Cylinder of Cyrus, we learn that such grace was his policy toward minorities and cults in general. He prided himself on sending people back to their homes and on reviving their religions. Thus the return of the Jews was simply an application of the policy of that enlightened monarch. The historian must seek not only to discover facts but also to place facts in their proper perspective.

Now if we imagine the entire sweep of Near Eastern history from the beginning to, let us say, Alexander the Great, we have to reckon with a vast number of facts intricately connected. To one observer, a certain group of things will have an intimate relationship. To another person with a different background and point of view, those same things might seem totally unrelated. Usually he who can see relationships in a group of events has gotten closer to the heart of the matter than a person who sees only isolated phenomena; but ingenuity, without adequate judgment or knowledge, all too often leads to false combinations of unrelated facts. From the facts a controlled history can be derived. However, before that can be achieved, it is necessary to reduce the maze of facts to an intelligible whole by organizing what is important and suppressing what is not. To determine what is important presupposes a standard of values. It would be presumptuous to set up a universal standard of values. But a mature viewpoint, containing much if not all of the truth, might well include the following principle: in any period the important facts are those that determine subsequent history. In Hezekiah's reign it is likely that the construction of the Siloam Tunnel impressed the inhabitants of Jerusalem more than did Isaiah's Messianic prophecies. Yet the latter, which are infinitely more important, can be correctly evaluated on the principle set forth above, from our point of vantage. Incidentally, this principle also explains why it is hard to evaluate current events and the recent past.

Nonwritten archeological material also requires methodical evaluation. The individual object is not only of interest in itself, but when found in context, or when attributable to a definite context, it can throw light on the whole picture. Conversely, an object that cannot be associated with any context is not usable for historic purposes.

In addition to single objects, complete groups of objects may be found in context. The jewels of the royal tombs of Ur form a category of singular importance since they constitute the highest accomplishment of the Sumerians in fine art. Before the discovery of the royal tombs of Ur it was possible for the greatest historian of the ancient Near East to state that the Sumerians did not excel in any form of fine art and that if one compared their statuary with Egyptian statuary, he would find the Sumerian products primitive. Then the Ur excavations showed that we could not generalize from the statuary. We now know that in the field of metallurgy the Sumerians are unsurpassed in antiquity, while in the arts of the goldsmith and gem cutter, they are second to none in all history. Thus objects put in context and interpreted correctly may have wide implications.

It is also possible to examine a category of objects throughout a long history. Seal cylinders are quite numerous and constitute the most characteristic form of art in the cuneiform world.[15] These seals are small engraved cylinders (usually of stone) used to authenticate documents by pressing the seals on the soft clay. Such seals may be arranged according to type and period, and studied as a function of history, since, like all human products, they are a reflex of the historic process. First, they should be studied in themselves, and then integrated into the whole picture of history.

All human artifacts (by which is meant everything from great edifices to tiny pots) may be regarded as a part of history. We must be selective because the material is so abundant. It would be foolhardy to try to exhaust the evidence of ceramics in the Near East if we ever

15. See H. Frankfort, *Cylinder Seals,* London, 1939; and E. Porada, *Corpus of Ancient Near Eastern Seals in North American Collections,* 2 vols., Washington, 1948.

hope to study history as a whole, because the ceramics, if studied in detail, would take more than a lifetime. A knowledge of history helps the scholar put specialized material into perspective and evaluate it. A varied knowledge of specialized materials—written and archeological—enables the historian to control his subject by checking one type of evidence against the other. History without knowledge of source detail degenerates into groundless platitudes and false reconstructions; while concern with detail without historic perspective becomes cataloguing that, though important, is not history. One can take the evolution of the tomb in Egypt from a simple to a complex structure as an aspect or reflection of Egyptian history, particularly of the changes in religion and beliefs concerning the dead.[16] Just because something is specialized does not mean it lacks broader implications and human interest. The representation of Asiatics (particularly of the Semites) and African Negroes on Egyptian monuments could be studied and published as an illustrated catalogue; in such form it would be useful. However, if the physical types and costumes were analyzed, the study could become a key to the ethnology of the times and to the migrations of peoples and their historic roles.

One of the most interesting aspects of historical study is to compare texts with art objects reflecting the same phenomena. There is a passage in 2 Samuel 2:14–16 that tells of a battle fought between twelve champions of one army and twelve of another army around the year 1000 B.C.E. The fashion in which the twenty-four contestants fought is described as follows: "And each grasped the head of his opponent, with his sword in the side of his opponent, and they fell down together." This description is so brief and refers to such a strange type of combat that none of the interpreters of Scripture were able to make sense of the text. At last a scholar[17] pointed out that a relief from Tell Halaf in northwestern Mesopotamia shows two men engaged in exactly this type of combat, each grasping his opponent's head with one hand and with the other plunging a blade into his opponent's side. The relief illustrates the text graphically, and the text provides whatever commentary is necessary for understanding the relief.

16. G. Reisner, *The Development of the Egyptian Tomb down to the Accession of Cheops*, Cambridge, Mass., 1936.

17. Y. Yadin, "Let the Young Men, I Pray Thee, Arise and Play before Us," *Journal of the Palestine Oriental Society* 21, 1948, pp. 110–16.

Generally speaking, there are two methods of preparing material objects for historical study. Of basic importance is stratigraphy, which means that in excavating, the archeologist distinguishes the strata as sharply as possible and carefully records the provenance of all objects within their strata. Often, successive settlements were built one upon the other and formed a mound in which what lies below is earlier than what covers it.[18] If the objects of one stratum in one mound match those of another stratum in another mound, a synchronism is established between those two strata. The sum total of such synchronisms enables us to set up the relative chronology of the ancient Near East,[19] which is of paramount importance for periods before the introduction of writing around 3000 B.C.E. The stratigraphy of each mound provides the relative chronology of all the levels of that mound. The synchronisms between mounds make possible the establishment of comparative stratigraphy and a relative chronology for vast areas that form a cultural continuum. Stratigraphy must, however, be used with caution, for the altitude at which an object is found does not necessarily determine its stratum. Something that dropped into a well belongs not to the stratum of the bottom of the well, where it was found, but to the level from which it had been dropped. Archeologists must carefully note whether an object was found in a pit of some sort so as to enable the historian to ascribe the proper context. The soil and debris excavated by ancients digging a well will not belong to the level as found, but to the level from which the soil and debris were taken from the well pit. There are many such limitations to stratigraphy. Mastering them takes experience and reflection. The art of stratigraphic excavation is best learned in the archeological field, not from books and lectures. But our few remarks will suffice to indicate the nature of the problem and the snares it contains.

The second general method of handling material objects is according to their type. Anyone who observes styles in clothing appreciates the fact that they go through a definite evolution that enables the expert to date any characteristic specimen. The approximate dating of all manufacture is within the power of the specialist.

18. For an account of stratigraphic excavation, see Cyrus H. Gordon, *Adventures in the Nearest East,* London, 1957.

19. Cf. C. F. A. Schaeffer, *Stratigraphie comparée et chronologie de l'Asie occidentale,* London and Oxford, 1948.

Sometimes it is possible to assign exact dates, as in the case of automobile models that change from year to year. The evolution of any object follows a trend; and the typological arrangement of specimens will conform to the actual (or the reverse) chronological order. If two or more individual specimens in the series are datable (even relatively), the order of the series can be determined as to direction so that the possibility of reversing the order can be eliminated. Furthermore, any specimen that falls between two dated ones can be fixed in time between them. But like all other methods, typology must not be used blindly, for it, too, is subject to complications (e.g., recurrent cycles in style) that call for vigilance and common sense.

Another method used by historians of religion, art, and literature is that of motif. There are certain themes that tend to appear independently in different periods and areas. Sometimes we are able to understand the meaning of a historic phenomenon upon recognizing the general motif into which it fits. Yet this is often risky because while people in different periods and in different parts of the world have many things in common, profound differences also exist, and it is possible to read a false motif into source material that should be examined internally before we attempt to classify it. Furthermore, the search for universal motifs often results in the neglect of differences that reflect the evolutionary process of historic development. Here again common sense and awareness of the facts will enable us to use the motif method profitably. In the Ugaritic tablets a crown prince is said to suckle at the breasts of goddesses, while elsewhere a sick king threatened with death makes his family wonder whether a god can die. The motif of divine kingship explains such phenomena immediately; for the king attained divinity through claiming to have nursed at divine breasts, and the death of kings caused perplexity at the contradiction between their pretended godhood and actual mortality.

Despite all the foregoing (and there are still other methods with which the scholar should be acquainted), the material itself must dictate the method. There is no such thing as taking a course or reading a book on methodology and becoming thereby an expert in the field. The expert must master and understand his material. The only advantage in learning other methods and what has been done in the field is that it sometimes saves time and suggests things that are applicable to our new problems. We can apply established methods to new problems insofar as those methods are useful but not beyond.

Although objectivity is essential for the historian, the reconstruction of history will always have a personal element. The capacity to see implications and relationships, the judgment which decides that certain elements are more important than others, and the ability to reconstruct an evolving and continuous whole demand genuine creativity on the part of the historian.

This history focuses on the people of ancient Israel and the biblical literature that nation produced. But as the preceding pages already indicate, and as the following chapters will demonstrate clearly, the world of ancient Israel stretched far and wide. In its thousand-year history in antiquity, Israel's contacts stretched from the Mediterranean coastal regions in the west to the Iranian (and perhaps Indic) lands in the east. Accordingly, no one interested in the nation that produced the Bible can afford to be unfamiliar with the whole of "the Ancient Near East" (as we term this extensive area in the book title).

We are not the first to recognize this point. Indeed the great prophet Isaiah writing in the eighth century B.C.E. already recognized that Israel was part of a larger world that stretched to Egypt and beyond in one direction and to Mesopotamia (or Assyria, as he called it) and beyond in the other. His utopian vision is something we all can admire and strive for: "In that day, Israel shall be a third partner with Egypt and Assyria as a blessing in the center of the world. And the LORD of Hosts will bless them saying, 'Blessed be My people Egypt, My handiwork Assyria, and My special possession Israel' " (Isaiah 19:24–25).

Chapter II plunges into the Bible and sets the early stories of Genesis in their ancient Near Eastern context. Chapters III through VII follow with a presentation of general information on the individual Near Eastern societies whose impact on ancient Israel was greatest. Chapters VIII through XIX then return to the Bible and the history of Israel.

The emphases and omissions in this book are largely personal, for any other author or authors presumably would make different choices. The reader also should realize that this book, even in its fourth edition, will require additions and revisions with the further passing of time. This is true of many fields but especially of the ancient Near East where discoveries are constantly adding so much new source material that the subject is now the most dynamic aspect of the study of man's past.

## CHAPTER II

# In the Beginning

I n speaking of beginnings, there are several different subjects we can have in mind. One is actual beginnings as attested by material remains. We can speak of prehistoric men who lived tens of thousands of years ago, such as those whose skeletons have been found in northern Israel around the Carmel Ridge. We may speak of prehistoric migrations of people who introduced to the Near East the Egypto-Semitic languages. We may work back from the languages and talk about relations between the Indo-Europeans and Afro-Asiatics. From archeological discoveries we can trace the evolution of arts and crafts. We can see how the knife, the arrow, or pottery developed throughout the ages. From about 5000 to 3000 B.C.E. we have preliterate stratified towns, one on top of the other, each of which reflects organized society; for only an organized society can construct and maintain a complex social unit. In Mesopotamia we can trace the change between the earliest levels of civilization and those where Sumerian culture begins. That kind of evidence tells us that there was a population earlier than the first literate one, the Sumerian, of whom we have definite records.[1] In Babylonian mounds, a layer of silt separating two towns with sharply different cultures indicates that a flood destroyed the earlier settlement and that the newcomers who resettled the place represented another civilization. (River floods are characteristic of Babylonia but not of Canaan. It is therefore not sur-

---

1. Sumerian script was not devised for the Sumerian language, as incompatibilities between the script and language show. Accordingly, there was an earlier literate people from whom the Sumerians borrowed their system of writing. However, we so far have no clearly discernible texts in the language of that earlier people.

prising that the Hebrew Deluge is, as we shall see, derived from Mesopotamian sources.)

It is also possible, by extrapolating from the texts that preserve the traditions of a more remote antiquity and by studying the material remains unearthed by archaeologists, to trace the evolution of society in its main outlines. The texts and monuments reflect the early mode of hunting wild animals, the later mode of herding domesticated animals, then the settled agricultural life, and finally the development of commerce and industry. But the fact that people go into a new stage does not mean that the earlier stage disappears. We still have farming in America in spite of the fact that we also engage in commerce and industry. There is also extensive herding in certain areas. Hunting, of course, is now relegated almost entirely to the realm of sport in America but not so in the ancient Near East, where hunting sometimes appears as a means of subsistence in comparatively late periods (Genesis 25:27). With the development of writing about 3000 B.C.E. independently in both Mesopotamia and Egypt, we begin to enter upon the full light of history. What we can learn of times prior to that date is a subject in itself, which we may call prehistory but which does not concern us in our present investigation. It is rather another type of beginnings that concerns us: beginnings as the people of the Near East saw them. Their views of the origin of the universe are manifestations of their intellectual growth and of their outlook on life.

Several accounts of the beginnings have come down to us. The most extensive material comes from Mesopotamia. But the biblical material is by far the most familiar and best organized. How did the world come to be as it is? This is the first question taken up and answered in Scripture. The Hebrew answer is not the same as the latest scientific answer, but that is not our concern. Our concern at present is to understand how the Hebrews approached these problems and answered them. In fact, there are two accounts of creation at the beginning of the book of Genesis, though in their final redacted form they are artistically synthesized.[2]

---

2. We recognize the fact that the book of Genesis, like the whole of the Pentateuch, is composed of diverse sources. But we make no attempt to define or identify these sources. Instead we are much more impressed with the overall unity of the book of Genesis. See Gary A. Rendsburg, *The Redaction of Genesis,* Winona Lake, Ind., 1986. See further below, Chapter VIII, p. 123, n. 32.

According to the first version, before God began his creative activities, the world consisted of a dark, watery mass. God first introduced light into this world of darkness. After that, the waters had to be separated into orderly arrangement, so that there were two sets, one above and one below. Those above are the waters that provide us with rain, and are released for distribution on the earth by opening the windows of heaven. The waters below spring from wells and fountains and account for the rivers and seas. The next stage was to separate seas from dry land on the earth. Then comes vegetation, not chaotic vegetation, but an orderly vegetation in which each species produces seeds according to its own kind. Next come the luminaries of heaven: the sun, moon, and stars, which are intended not only to give light but also to mark time, ranging from day and night to months and years. Then come fish and fowl and beasts and finally, as the crowning accomplishment of creation, comes man in God's image to enjoy creation like no other creature (Genesis 1:1–28).

After this creation in six days God rested on the seventh, thus establishing the precedent for the day of rest that remains the most useful and enjoyed of social institutions for the working man in practically all of the world. Why we rest on the seventh day need not be answered in the same way by the modern critical historian, who is in a position to show on a comparative basis that the number seven permeated the thought of the ancient world. Thus there is not only the seven-day week but also the seven-year sabbatical cycle, and the jubilee year following seven sabbatical cycles.[3] But while we are able to explain "the seventh day" as a manifestation of the widespread "seven" motif, we are for present purposes interested in the biblical answer, according to which God's precedent sanctified the seventh day (which must therefore be kept hallowed as the day of rest by man and beast).

The second account of creation is more focused, narrowly concerned with man and with the fundamental questions of man and society. Why was woman created and why is there the institution of marriage? Because the Deity saw it was not good for man to be alone. He therefore created woman as a helpmate suitable for man. The type of marriage indicated is one whereby a man forsakes his parents[4]

---

3. Cf. R. North, *Sociology of the Biblical Jubilee,* Rome, 1954.

4. Note that this is not the marriage typical of patriarchal society, where the bride comes to live with the groom's family. However, it would be going beyond the evidence to insist that the verse presupposes matriarchy.

and cleaves unto his wife so that they become one flesh (Genesis 2:24).

It is apposite to note how the two different versions of creation are introduced. In Genesis 1:1 the expression "heaven and earth" is used, whereas in Genesis 2:4 the reverse phraseology "earth and heaven" appears. Since the first story of creation is more cosmocentric, the word "heaven" appears first in the word pair; but since the second story is more anthropocentric, the word "earth" occurs first. Moreover, simple translation may not convey all that the Hebrew text might signify to an ancient Hebrew. Pairs of antonyms, called merisms, often mean "everything" or "everyone,"[5] so that in Hebrew "heaven and earth" or "earth and heaven" might be such a pair, signifying "everything, the universe."[6]

The next crucial problem is why man is intelligent as distinct from the beasts of the field. Man is intelligent because (against the command of God) he obtained and ate magic fruit from the Tree of Knowledge, thus gaining knowledge that up to that time had been a monopoly of divinity, not intended for man. It is interesting to note that the knowledge imparted by the fruit of this tree is the "knowledge of good and evil," a much misunderstood phrase. Again we must reckon with the literary device of a merism. The antonyms "good and evil" mean "everything" here. (See also Genesis 24:50; Zephaniah 1:12; and Proverbs 15:3.) The same expression in inverted order occurs in Egyptian, where "evil-good" means everything,[7] and from Greek literature we may cite the words of Telemachus, "I know all things, the good and the evil" (Od. 20:309–10). The only reason that readers of the Bible have failed to grasp the proper understanding of "the Tree of Knowledge of good and evil" is that the traditional interpretation is so deeply entrenched.[8] Thus man obtained universal

---

5. Compare English "they came, great and small" = "everybody came."

6. The Hebrew language did not possess the abstract concept of "universe," so "heaven and earth" would be the best way to express this idea.

7. See Cyrus H. Gordon, "Samsi-Adad's Military Texts from Mari," *Archiv Orientalni* 18, 1950, p. 202, n. 7.

8. Note the absence of our phrase from A. M. Honeyman, "*Merismus* in Biblical Hebrew," *Journal of Biblical Literature* 71, 1952, pp. 11–18. It is listed in Jozy Krašovec, *Die Merismus im Biblisch-Hebräischen und Nordwestsemitischen*, Rome, 1977, p. 102, but without discussion of its significance.

knowledge, and to that extent shares with God a faculty that had been a divine prerogative.

Why are human beings, unlike animals, ashamed of nudity? Because man's newly won knowledge included a knowledge of decency, about which animals in their blissful ignorance know nothing. Why are snakes vile and why are snakes and men hostile to one another? It is because the snake induced Eve, who in turn induced Adam, to eat of the forbidden fruit; and as a divine punishment for this, the snake must crawl on its belly, eat dust, and bite at men's heels; with men, in retaliation, bruising snakes' heads. Why must men work for a living? This was Adam's punishment for his share in the transgression against divine will. And why does woman have disabilities such as being subject to her husband's authority, and to suffering pain in childbirth? This is her punishment for violating the divine decree. Why does mankind not live forever in a paradise? Mankind was driven out of paradise for all time because God saw that man could not be trusted to obey His will and to refrain from eating the magic fruit of another tree in the Garden of Eden that would give man immortality. God decided that man should not obtain immortality lest he become like the gods. Accordingly, if we examine the story in Genesis objectively, we see that, while many elements go into making up the whole picture, it is not so much an account of the "Fall of Man" but rather of the rise of man halfway to divinity. He obtained one of the two prerogatives or characteristics of the gods: intelligence; but he was checked by God from obtaining immortality, which would have made him quite divine.[9]

The next problems that confronted the Hebrews had to do with how Adam and Eve gave rise to the nations of the world. The Hebrew answer was that families and nations developed in a way that can be traced through genealogy: genealogy of actual people, from father to son, with certain individuals giving rise to groups and nations. Society originated, according to the Hebrews, through the contributions of individual historic characters. The first children of Adam and Eve were Cain and Abel, Cain being the farmer and Abel the herdsman, each representing different ways of life and reflecting

9. The element of disobedience is present in the story but only circumstantially. To stress the "evil" and overlook the "good" in the text would have no justification, even on the part of exegetes who are not familiar with the inclusive meaning of antonymic pairs.

the age-old hostility between the two pursuits. God liked the offering of the herdsman Abel better than that of the farmer; meat is preferable to vegetables as an offering. God's preference reflects a Semitic standard of values whereby the austere nomadic pattern represents the good life.[10] But Cain, the farmer, killed Abel, which may reflect the victory of stable societies depending upon agriculture over nomadic societies that depend on herding. Cain was the father of an Enoch associated with a city named Enoch: the first city in history according to Hebrew tradition. Later the genealogies take us to Lemech, who had two wives, Adah and Zillah. Adah gave birth to two sons. One was Jabal, who gets credit for founding the nomadic way of life; the other was Jubal, who instituted music, both on stringed instruments and on pipes. Zillah had two children who occupy a lower scale on the social ladder. Her son was Tubal-Cain, who founded the art of metallurgy. Among nomadic Semites the smith has a status inferior to those who own and tend the herds. Zillah's daughter Naamah should, according to some scholars, be fitted into the pattern as the founder of some way of life. It has been suggested that she is either the prototype of dancing or singing girls, and perhaps even of prostitutes. However, there is no textual evidence to support such a patternistic reconstruction. Another child of Adam and Eve was Seth, whose son was named Enosh, to whose time the worship of Yahwe is traced (Genesis 4:26). This tradition, to the extent that it relegates Yahwism to pre-Hebraic antiquity and ascribes Yahwism to non-Hebraic origins, is confirmed by early references to Yahwism outside the Hebrew sphere.[11]

There follows another set of genealogies, of heroes before the Flood. A few of them may be singled out because of particular interest. There is a second Enoch[12] who "walked with God and he was not, for God had taken him" (Genesis 5:24). This is the first recorded assumption, that is, where someone, instead of dying, is taken aloft into heaven. Another character, Methuselah, lived 969 years: not very much longer than some of his fellows in the genealogy; but because

10. The best statement in Scripture comes from late in Judean history (Jeremiah 35:1–19).

11. Yahwe occurs in Amorite names of Mesopotamia; and *yw* may stand for the same divine name in Ugarit. That Yahwe was known in Syria far north of Israel we shall see in Chapter XV, pp. 250–51.

12. Literary critics often identify the two Enochs, for it is possible that we are confronted with parallel traditions about the same antedeluvian hero.

he lived a bit longer, his name is a household term for longevity.[13] Then comes Noah, who is the father of Shem, Ham, and Japheth; each son being the ancestor of a major division of mankind.

Man and creation proved to be a disappointment to God, so that God regretted His work and decided to punish the world. Some steps were taken, like the reduction to 120 years of man's hitherto phenomenally long life span; but even that was not enough. Drastic punishment was called for, and God decided on a flood. Noah alone found grace because of his virtue, so God instructed him to build an ark according to exact specifications. He was told to take his family, including his sons and their wives, and a pair of each of the animals of creation, as well as supplies. Noah entered the ark at the appointed time and a flood destroyed all other living things. The ark eventually landed on the mountains of Ararat in Armenia, but Noah did not open the door of the ark until he was sure the earth was sufficiently dry. To determine this he sent out birds on four successive occasions: a raven on the first trip, and for the rest a dove. When, on the final trip, the dove did not return, Noah knew there was a place for birds to nest on dry land and it was safe to come out. Noah left the ark and sacrificed to God to show his gratitude. The sweet savor that rose was so pleasing to God that He promised never again to curse the land and the living because of man's innate evil. God realized by this time that man's imperfections were permanent and that the best would have to be made of a bad job. He promised man that the seasons would continue, that nature would not be upset, that there would be plowing time and harvest time. There would be cold and heat, summer and winter, day and night. Nowhere in Semitic ideology is the desire expressed that the best time of the year should prevail all the time.[14] Each thing is welcome in its season and when the seasons are regular there is a feeling of security in a world run properly according to rules by God. Then came a blessing for Noah and a

13. The longevity of ancient worthies harks back to an old tradition. The fantastically long lives of their Mesopotamian counterparts make these biblical life spans look quite brief.

14. This is overlooked by those who assume that in the ancient Near East the normal advent of the dry season was received with weeping for a god of fertility who died yearly at that season and who came back to life yearly with the return of the rains. It must be borne in mind that rain out of season was as disturbing as drought out of season (1 Samuel 12:17–20). Moreover, the god in control of life-giving water (Baal or Yahwe) is the god of summer dew no less than of winter rain.

code was laid down. The main article in this code regards blood. Man's blood must not be shed. If it is shed it will be sought not only from the hands of a man but even from an animal guilty of murder. Furthermore, since blood contains holy life, it must not be drunk but poured into the ground. This law, according to Hebrew tradition, is binding on all mankind. The obligations of Mosaic Law are binding only upon Jews; but God demands of both Jew and Gentile obedience to the Noachian Code. As a final touch, God put the rainbow in the sky to remind man He had made this covenant and would never again destroy the world by flood.[15]

To proceed with the next questions: Why is it that nations are unequal? Specifically, why were non-Hebrew inhabitants of Canaan, who are called Canaanites, inferior to the Hebrews? With what justification did the Hebrews dislike and subjugate the Canaanites? According to Scripture, Noah planted a vineyard and made wine after the Flood. One day, he was lying in a tent naked and drunk. Ham, quite by accident, came in and saw his father's nakedness, which is a sin, whether intentional or not. He informed his brothers, who walked in backward and covered their father.[16] When Noah woke up, he blessed his two sons who had covered his nakedness and cursed Ham who had seen it. But even more than Ham is Ham's son Canaan cursed. It will be noted that the story puts Ham, the ancestor of the Egyptians (with whom the Hebrews shared a reciprocal antipathy), in a bad light. Furthermore, it removes the Canaanites from the Semitic family, in which they properly belong, and classifies them as Hamites. Thus the story is used to explain a number of relationships of basic importance to the Hebrews.

We now turn to Genesis 10, which remains a great historic document. It is an attempt, containing considerable historicity, to put all the nations known to the Hebrews into an organic framework showing their interrelationships. There is much of technical interest worth noting. For instance, two cities well known from excavation are mentioned in verse 10: Babylon and Erech. But it is interesting to note that two other cities, Akkad and Calneh, have not been discovered

---

15. Such causal explanations of origins (like the origin of the rainbow) are common in the Bible; they are called "etiological."

16. In European art the scene is mistitled The Drunkenness of Noah. More nearly correct would be The Nakedness of Noah, for his being drunk is only circumstantial to his nakedness. According to the account in Genesis (9:20–27), not the intoxication of the father but only the son's beholding his naked father was the offense.

yet, though from other Mesopotamian sources we know that the former was the capital of the first Semitic empire. In verse 11, Assur (the envisaged ancestor of Assyria) is credited with building Nineveh and Calah, Assyrian capitals that have been excavated. But between them is Rehoboth-Ir about which nothing else is known. The following verse, 12, names Resen as "the great city" between Nineveh and Calah; the identity of Resen is still shrouded in obscurity. While we must always consider the possibility that the text is in error, we must do so with the knowledge that the trend of archeological discovery is to confirm even points that opinion had rejected as false.[17]

As we continue to read the genealogies, we note that the focus grows more and more narrow. The emphasis is now on Shem (verses 21–30), the ancestor of the Semites, including all the "sons of Eber" (verse 21) who embrace the Hebrews.

The next question (Genesis 11:1–9) is why mankind has so many mutually unintelligible languages. Man in his haughtiness aspired to power through the building of a great tower at Babel whose top would reach the heavens. God thwarted the plan by confounding human speech with a multitude of languages. Without a common language, men cannot engage in great cooperative enterprises; so the project was abandoned and men were scattered over the face of the earth.

We now come to the final narrowing of the genealogies with the descendants of Eber (Genesis 11:16–26) down to Nahor. Nahor begat Terah, who in turn begat Abram, the father of the Hebrew people, who are to occupy the center of the stage of biblical history, although they were encompassed by nations far greater than they. Terah, in keeping with his patriarchal authority, moved his family, which included Abram and the latter's wife Sarai, from Ur of the Chaldees to Haran in northwest Mesopotamia, en route to Canaan. But Terah died in Haran, whereupon Abram assumed the role of patriarch.

This brings us to the traditions of the first Hebrew about 1400 B.C.E. From now on the focus is on the evolution of Abram's seed in its relation to the God Who had chosen it as His people. However,

---

17. The confirmatory trend of archeology is applicable not only to Sacred Scripture but also to profane writing such as Herodotus, whose most amazing "yarns" have in a number of instances turned out to be sober truths. The absence of suitable mounds to account for lost cities near the Tigris may be due to the destructiveness of the river, which often overruns and devastates the countryside during the spring floods.

the Bible does not narrate the experience of the Chosen People as though isolated, but rather within the framework of world history.

The Mesopotamian accounts of the origin of the universe and of human institutions are more complex than the Hebrew account. Some of this complexity is due to the pluralistic attitude that goes with polytheism. But part of the complexity results from the fact that unlike Israel, which to some extent harmonized its traditions in the Bible, Mesopotamia never established one canonical recension of its traditions to the exclusion of all others. This is fortunate for the historian, whose ability to reconstruct the past is the greater when the sources are abundant and varied.

The chief Mesopotamian creation account is called *Enuma Elish* (When on High), the first words of the text. It tells of the creation of gods who, not surprisingly, became embroiled in plots and strife. One of the deities, the sea-god Apsu, was so bothered by the noisy young upstart gods that he wanted to wipe them out. But his wife Tiamat, the sea-goddess, was more moderate, and pleaded: "How could we destroy what we have created? Their way is grievous but let us act kindly!" (I:45–46). Apsu's resolution brought upon him the hostility of the gods, headed by the wise Ea, who lulled Apsu to sleep by magic and then attacked and slew him. This act of violence stirred Tiamat to rebel, with the aid of the god Kingu, which obliged the community of the gods to take action against her. To destroy her they created Marduk, who was beautiful and wise; so wise that he had four ears and four eyes the better to hear and see and accordingly to be more intelligent than other gods. Furthermore, to make him a king among gods, Marduk was suckled by goddesses, in keeping with a motif whereby kings (regularly in Egypt, sometimes in Mesopotamia, and often elsewhere, as in Ugarit) claimed divinity through the fiction that they had suckled divine breasts.[18] Marduk fulfilled his mission, slaying Tiamat and subduing her whole host of minor deities. Then Marduk proceeded to create the universe from Tiamat's corpse. Among his creations were three constellations of stars for each month, to fix the days of the year. The moon he created not only to shine by night but also to fix the monthly cycle and to maintain a relationship with the sun. Details of this sort reflect the scientific sophistication of the Babylonians as compared with the Hebrews,

---

18. Such notions may have been quite functional. The acceptance of the divinity of the king bolstered his authority and so contributed to law and order.

who were satisfied with less astronomical data. Marduk then proceeded to form a man, who bears the non-Semitic name "Lullu."[19] Marduk needed materials with which to create man, and it was decided that a guilty god would have to give up his life to provide them. Kingu was chosen because he had incited and helped Tiamat in her revolt. He was put to death[20] and his blood was used for creating man. Thus man was created out of divine stuff,[21] albeit from a rebellious god. This last item may suggest the source of man's troublesome qualities. The purpose in creating man was that he might serve the gods. The underlying idea is clear enough: there is no use being a god unless you have men to worship you. Mankind was created to make life agreeable for the pantheon; to perform work, to provide food and drink, and to practice religion for the benefit of the gods. The gods were so grateful that they awarded the great temple of Esagila to Marduk in Babylon. They made a housewarming for him there and offered him lavish praise.[22]

Although the mythology of the Creation Epic stems from Sumerian and perhaps earlier non-Semitic origins, the Babylonian recension that we have just outlined has been recast in such a manner as to show that Babylon is the chief of cities and the center of empire; that its shrine Esagila is foremost among shrines; that Marduk of Babylon is the greatest of the gods, the creator of the world, and the deity to worship above all others in the Babylonian Empire.[23] It is interesting to note that when Assyria made its version of the Creation Epic, it transferred some of the glory of Marduk to Assur (the patron god of the capital Assur and of the Assyrian Empire) in order to reshape the epic for its own political ends.

In addition to *Enuma Elish,* there are some lesser cuneiform creation accounts to which we may refer briefly. One of them is a text

---

19. This points to a non-Semitic origin of the Babylonian Creation Epic.

20. Note that a god can die. Nor is Kingu a god who was resurrected. We must avoid generalizing on the nature of divinity. Thus, far from being omniscient, the gods of Mesopotamia are often ignorant and error-prone. In the Egyptian pantheon, all the gods except Thoth are illiterate.

21. Compare the biblical creation of man "in the image of God" (Genesis 1:27).

22. For a good introduction to the *Enuma Elish* and to other Mesopotamian creation texts, see A. Heidel, *The Babylonian Genesis,* Chicago, 1951.

23. The Babylonian Creation Epic was recast in its basic classical form in the first half of the second millennium B.C.E., before the Hebrews appeared on the scene. The Hebrew accounts of creation, though later in date, drew (as a rule indirectly) upon the earlier traditions of other people including the Mesopotamians.

that tells of the creation of cities, gods, and man, the creation of the Tigris and Euphrates, the creation of plants and animals. According to another tablet, Ea creates out of clay the gods of the arts and crafts. Thus the creation is of gods, not of men, and it is gods that institute the arts, crafts, and sciences.[24] Another tablet tells of the creation of a divine man and a divine woman for serving the gods and performing the occupations of society such as herding, irrigation, and agriculture. The divinity of the pair may have been occasioned by the importance of the first ancestors of mankind or by the fact that they had been made with divine blood.

The greatest literary accomplishment of Mesopotamia is the Gilgamesh Epic, which was translated in antiquity into other languages of the Cuneiform World. The best preserved versions are in Akkadian, though the epic has Sumerian and perhaps earlier non-Semitic antecedents.[25] We have fragments of Hittite and Hurrian translations, and fragments of the Akkadian original have been found as far away as Megiddo in Israel and Tell el-Amarna in Egypt. Also, the heroes of the epics are frequently portrayed on works of art, such as seal cylinders, in ancient Mesopotamia.[26]

The epic starts out with praise for the city of Erech, with its wonderful brickwork, fine city plan, and magnificent walls. Gilgamesh, who is the tyrant of the city, is partly divine and partly human, for (like Achilles) his mother was a goddess. Gilgamesh was highhanded toward the populace; he forced young men to work and took girls for himself. At last the people of Erech cried out to the gods to rescue them. The gods accordingly designated one of their number to fashion a powerful creature out of clay, who was a bull from the waist down and human from the waist up, to oppose Gilgamesh and deflect him from his tyranny. Enkidu, as that creature was called, is placed in the fields where he lives among the animals, and is a lover of nature and an enemy of the hunter. He releases animals from traps

24. Contrast the Hebrew account where there is no theogony, and where crafts and sciences are traced back to men.

25. Scenes from the Gilgamesh Epic appear on seal cylinders prior to any written version. Popular and loosely connected episodes current in the fourth millennium B.C.E., were welded (apparently in the third millennium) into the literary masterpiece. The development is paralleled, on a grander scale, in the Homeric Epic, which imposed form and finesse on earlier episodic fragments current throughout the earlier East Mediterranean (e.g., at Ugarit).

26. On the growth of the Gilgamesh literary tradition, culminating in the canonical version, see Jeffrey M. Tigay, *The Evolution of the Gilgamesh Epic,* Philadelphia, 1982.

and thwarts all the devices of the hunters. A certain hunter, on seeing Enkidu, realizes why the hunters have not been catching any game. He goes home to tell his father of the sight he has beheld. The father sends the young hunter to Erech to fetch a girl named Shamhat who is to alienate Enkidu from nature, introduce him to society, and bring him to Erech where he will fulfill his mission by battling the tyrannical Gilgamesh. Shamhat has carnal relations with Enkidu, whereupon all of nature is alienated from him; the beasts no longer trust him, and he finds himself a changed but wiser creature. Enkidu comes back to the girl who tells him he is much too heroic a character to waste his time in the fields with the beasts and he should come to the big city where there is scope for his talents. She tells him of Erech where people wear festive garb, where every day is a holiday, and where he can meet Gilgamesh. Enkidu realizes that there is no more turning back to nature and that he must go to the big city where, as he tells Shamhat, he intends to shout (referring to heroic challenges and the war cry of victory).[27] But she warns him that he had better not plan on shouting because Gilgamesh outclasses him. Then Shamhat introduces Enkidu to other aspects of civilization such as eating bread, which he finds difficult because he had been grazing on grass until that time. He also has trouble learning to drink from vessels, for he had hitherto been lapping water from streams. Finally he learns of some of the joys of civilization like anointing himself with oil and putting on clothes. After becoming familiar with such facets of civilization, Enkidu is ready to go to the city where Gilgamesh has been behaving outrageously toward the people. The two heroes meet and Enkidu challenges Gilgamesh, who has been apprised of Enkidu in dreams. The two fight on a monumental scale and so impress each other with their might that they decide not to wear each other out but instead to practice heroic virtue, by slaying evil dragons and enabling uprightness to triumph.

Their first victory is against the dragon Humbaba in the cedar forest. The elders of the city, and Enkidu, do their best to dissuade Gilgamesh from undertaking the perilous mission, but Gilgamesh, preferring fame to security, resolves to go through with it. He obtains the blessing and good advice of everyone including his divine mother Ninsun, who is troubled by the restless spirit of her son. With the help of Enkidu, Gilgamesh makes the dangerous journey and locates

27. Discussed below in Chapter VII, p. 101.

the dragon. By hurling, through magic, eight winds into the wicked dragon's mouth, our two heroes overcome and capture it. Humbaba begs for mercy but in vain. They cut off his head and win immortal fame.

After that the handsome Gilgamesh, dresses himself so attractively that the goddess Ishtar proposes marriage to him. She offers him rich marriage gifts, but he points out that he is not prepared to give her food and drink and in general the standard of living to which a goddess is accustomed. He then reminds her of her long and shameful marital history: she had once loved a horse, but when she had tired of him, she treated him brutally and beat him to make him run. She had also loved a shepherd but tired of him and turned him into a wolf so that his own dogs drove him away. Gilgamesh enumerates all the instances of Ishtar's treachery to her mates, and rejects her proposal. His rebuff infuriates her and she determines to avenge the affront. She goes to her father, the great god Anu, and asks permission to have the Bull of Heaven placed at her disposal. The Bull of Heaven is a human-headed bull of great strength that she hopes will slay Gilgamesh. To extract permission from her unwilling father, she makes threats of violence. Anu, in granting permission, reminds her that the slaying of a hero will cause a seven-year famine. She had anticipated this dire consequence and assures Anu that she has laid up a seven-year supply of food.[28] Thereupon Anu commissions the goddess Aruru to make the Bull of Heaven. She obeys; but in the combat that ensues, Gilgamesh and Enkidu kill the Bull of Heaven.[29] Ishtar is dismayed at this and complains, but Enkidu cuts off a leg of the Bull of Heaven and flings it at Ishtar as a terrible insult.[30] She, in revenge, plans the death of Enkidu, for such an indignity to a goddess cannot go unpunished. Pathetically Enkidu perishes and vainly does Gilgamesh try to bring him back to life. He touches and talks to him but gets no answer. Finally, after watching his body with pious devotion, he notices a worm on the corpse and realizes that death takes

---

28. Two different motifs are combined here. One is the motif of a seven-year famine in sympathy for a slain hero; the other is the theme of anticipating a seven-year famine by laying up supplies. The first motif is matched in Ugarit where such a cycle of famine years follows the slaying of Aqhat; while the second is familiar from the biblical story of Joseph in Egypt.

29. Fighting the Bull of Heaven is one of the most frequent themes in Mesopotamian art, particularly on seal cylinders of the Akkad Dynasty.

30. That this symbolized, over a wide area, a serious affront, is demonstrated by its recurrence in Homer's Odyssey (see Chapter VII, p. 106).

its victims beyond recall. The awful reality of death fills Gilgamesh with fear for, since he is not completely divine, he too must die. Hence he becomes obsessed with the drive to obtain immortality.

Only one man had ever become immortal. That was the Babylonian "Noah," named Utnapishtim, who with his wife had become immortal after the Flood. Gilgamesh reasons that the way to get eternal life is to go to the immortal Utnapishtim and find out the secret from him. He knows the road is difficult, beset with many obstacles, but Gilgamesh cannot refrain from his quest. On the way he meets a divine barmaid, who is used to tales of woe and has observed personal frustrations. She gives him sensible advice:

> "Gilgamesh, whither runnest thou?
> The life which thou seekest thou wilt not find.
> When the gods created mankind,
> They allotted death to mankind;
> Life they retained in their own keeping.
> O Gilgamesh, let thy belly be full,
> Day and night be thou merry!
> Make every day one of rejoicing,
> Day and night, dance and play!
> Let thy clothes be clean,
> Thy head washed
> And thy self bathed in water.
> Cherish the little one holding thy hand
> Let (thy) wife rejoice in thy bosom.
> This is the lot of [mankind]." (X:iii:1–14.)[31]

But Gilgamesh cannot get himself to make the most of mortal reality and persists on his dangerous mission to far-off Utnaphistim. When he at long last beholds the old man, he is surprised. Gilgamesh, who thought he was going to see a mighty hero different from other men, looks at him and says:

> "I look upon thee, Utnapishtim.
> Thine appearance is not different
> Thou art like me.

31. R. Campbell Thompson, *The Epic of Gilgamesh: Text, Transliteration and Notes;* Oxford, 1930, pp. 53–54.

Yea, thou art not different
Thou art like me.
My heart had fancied thee as one perfect for waging battle
[But] thou liest idly on thy back.
[Tell me!]
How didst thou enter the company of the gods
And obtain immortality?" (XI:2–7.)

At this point Utnapishtim decides to tell him the whole story, which includes the flood epic of Babylonia. While the Hebrew and Babylonian creation accounts are radically different, their flood epics are quite similar and come from a common source.[32]

Gilgamesh is told that Utnapishtim lived before the Flood in the city of Shuruppak. The gods had decided to destroy mankind. One god, Ea, was friendly to Utnapishtim and determined to give him the information necessary for saving him. Ea did not venture to talk to him directly but instead went to the reed hut of Utnapishtim and addressed the hut.[33] Utnapishtim was there to hear the message, which instructed him to disregard his possessions, to construct an ark according to exact specifications, to take the seed of all living aboard, to include his wife, and to secure adequate supplies and a crew. The Babylonian account is more detailed and realistic than the biblical version because the Mesopotamians were more advanced than the Hebrews in material civilization in general and specifically in the arts of naval construction and operation. It is interesting to note that the wall of the reed hut was to be converted into the ark. This was a well-known technique in ancient Mesopotamia, where the reed wall of a house could be converted into a boat.[34]

The rains came and, as in the biblical narrative, the ark landed on a mountain from which Utnapishtim sends out first a dove, then a swallow, and finally a raven before he determines, much like Noah, that the earth was dry. Again like Noah, he gets out and sacrifices to

---

32. This becomes especially clear upon contrasting these accounts with the Egyptian myth of the Destruction of Mankind.

33. The device of addressing an inanimate object with a message meant to be heard by people, occurs also in 1 Kings 13:2, where a prophet, whose message is to be heard by Jeroboam and the public, addresses the altar.

34. The consonantal text of Genesis 6:14 has *qnym*, which should be read *qanim*, "reeds," not *qinnim*, "nests" (which does not mean "compartments of a ship"). The Hebrew word for the "ark" occurs elsewhere only in the story of Moses, who as a baby was exposed in such a vessel, which is explicitly described as constructed of reeds (Exodus 2:3).

the gods, who hover over the sweet-smelling sacrifice like flies. One particularly malicious god, Enlil, is angry because the flood secret has been divulged, and a man and his wife have been spared. Enlil wants to destroy all life out of sheer malevolence. But Ea appeases him and counsels moderation so successfully that Enlil puts his hand on the forehead of the man and woman and confers immortality upon them. Utnapishtim, as he closes his narration, reminds Gilgamesh that special circumstances had accounted for the conferring of immortality after the Flood, but that no such circumstances are at hand to secure a similar favor from the gods for Gilgamesh. The latter is dismayed by his shattered hopes.

Utnapishtim then asks Gilgamesh to try to stay awake for seven days and seven nights. Apparently the idea was that if a man aspires to immortality, he ought first to be able to overcome sleep. If one cannot fight off ordinary sleep, how can he hope to escape from the sleep of death? But Gilgamesh, unable to stay awake, falls asleep, whereupon Utnapishtim tells his wife to bake bread, a loaf each day, for Gilgamesh. She does so day after day until the seventh day, when he wakes up and claims he had only been dozing a little. But the loaves of bread, each in a different stage of mold, prove he had been asleep for a week; and so Gilgamesh who could not resist sleep is hardly a candidate for immortality.

Just before Gilgamesh is to leave Utnapishtim and his wife, the latter tells her husband to give Gilgamesh a parting gift: the secret of how to find the elixir of youth, which happens to be a plant at the bottom of the sea. By putting stones on one's feet and diving to the ocean floor, one can obtain the plant that restores the aged to vigorous youth. Gilgamesh gratefully goes off with Utnapishtim's boatman and together they get the plant; but instead of eating it right away, Gilgamesh keeps it against the time when he will be old and decrepit, and when eating it will rejuvenate him. On the way back to Erech, Gilgamesh stops at a pool to refresh himself, leaves the plant there, and a snake steals it and eats it—which explains why the snake sloughs off its old skin and thus, as it was believed, is rejuvenated in a new skin every year. Disconsolate, Gilgamesh goes into a bitter complaint, for he had gone through countless woes, not for himself, but for the serpent; and his quest had ended in utter failure.

Gilgamesh asks the boatman to go on to Erech with him. The two visit that great city and behold its wonderful brickwork, its fine city plan, and its magnificent walls. Thus the epic repeats the note on which it began. For though men cannot win immortality, they can at least appreciate their earthly abode. The fact that it is not our lot to share eternal life with the distant Utnapishtim need not prevent us from enjoying the advantages of our native city.

Here we need to say a special word about the relationship between the flood accounts as preserved in the Bible and in the Gilgamesh Epic. It is obvious that the two versions are strikingly similar and must be related to one another in some way. The consensus of scholars is that the Babylonian version influenced the Israelite version. The reasons for this are manifold. First, all things being equal, a greater society is more likely to influence a lesser society than vice versa. Babylonia was the dominant culture of the Asiatic Near East and Israel represented a backwater of sorts. Secondly, the manner of destruction, i.e., by flood, is typical of Mesopotamia, where the great Tigris and Euphrates Rivers regularly flood their banks and cause havoc and destruction. Israel, by contrast, is very arid; it is unlikely that anyone in that part of the Near East would conceive of a divine destruction of the people through flooding. Third, the geography of the biblical account points to a Mesopotamian origin. Noah's ark lands on the mountains of Ararat, at the headwaters of the Tigris and Euphrates; if the story had originated in Canaan we would expect Mount Hermon (c. 7,500 feet high), for example, as the locale of the ark's resting place. Fourth, as we have seen, the Gilgamesh Epic was the literary masterpiece of antiquity, and one fragment even has been found in the land of Israel (at Megiddo). Fifth, the earliest Hebrews come from Mesopotamia, and it is unlikely that Abraham and his entourage would have been unfamiliar with the story.

There is also a sixth point to be made. The biblical version has some significant additions lacking in the Babylonian version. We refer to (1) the importance placed upon morality and immorality, and (2) the issue of covenant. In the Mesopotamian story, the gods decide to destroy the world capriciously, and we are not told why Utnapishtim was selected to survive, other than the fact that he was Ea's favorite. In the Bible, by contrast, the world is to be destroyed because of people's depravity, and Noah is chosen to survive the Flood because of his righteousness. Further, in the Babylonian version, there is a great distance between the gods and man, but in the Bible there is a closeness between God and man as indicated by the establishment of the covenant.

Accordingly, there can be no doubt that the Israelite flood story has Mesopotamian precursors (either the Gilgamesh Epic itself, or parallel, less well-known, flood traditions). This demonstrates very clearly that Israel did not live in a vacuum, but rather was part and parcel of the ancient Near Eastern cultural world. At the same time, the relationship between the two stories points to the manner in which ancient Israel incorporated polytheistic literary traditions. The basic outline of the story is accepted, but the underlying theology is altered to conform to Israelite religion.

There are numerous other Mesopotamian mythological texts dealing with similar and other problems. An important text, with its own creation and flood traditions, is the Atrahasis Epic.[35] We conclude our survey with a brief discussion of one text that deals with the quest for immortality. It is about a wise hero called Adapa, who while fishing was infuriated by the South Wind that upset his boat. He retaliated by breaking the South Wind's wings and was consequently summoned before the gods. Ea instructed him to refuse the water of death and the food of death that the gods would offer him. As things turned out, he was offered the water of life and the food of life; yet, following Ea's advice, he refused them. Thus again is sounded the sad note of man's aspiring in vain to immortality, which the gods withhold as their own prerogative. Like the biblical Adam, Adapa acquired wisdom but not eternal life. The theme of the gods' preventing mankind from attaining immortality is accordingly widespread throughout the Bible World.

35. W. G. Lambert and A. R. Millard, *Atra-Hasis: The Babylonian Story of the Flood,* Oxford, 1969. See also Tikva Frymer-Kensky, "The Atrahasis Epic and Its Significance for Our Understanding of Genesis 1–9," *Biblical Archaeologist* 40, 1977, pp. 147–55.

# CHAPTER III

# Egypt to
# the Amarna Age

O ur discussion of the biblical account brought us down to about
1400 B.C.E., by which time the Near East had experienced
considerable development both in the Nile Valley and in Asia. In this
and the next chapter we shall summarize the historical experience of
the Near East down to that time, starting with Egypt.

Inhabitable Egypt was the long river valley divided into districts
called nomes, each with a capital city that contained a temple dedicated to the local god. The division into nomes remained a factor in
Egyptian history long after the country had attained unity. The
nomes tended to be divided into two groups—those in the north and
those in the south. The final development was the unification of
Upper (=south) Egypt and Lower (=north) Egypt around 3000
B.C.E. From about that time, a predynastic king named Narmer has
left us a monument, on which he is shown wearing on one occasion
the flat red crown of Lower Egypt and on another occasion the elon-
gated white crown of Upper Egypt, indicating that he was in a position to claim sovereignty over both halves of the country. Shortly
after his time, Menes, the first king of the first official dynasty, ruled
over the two Egypts and he, according to the tradition of the country,[1] was credited with the achievement of uniting the two Egypts,
and with him begins the full light of actual Egyptian history around

---

1. The authority for the accepted division of Egyptian rulers into dynasties is Manetho, an
Egyptian who wrote a history of his nation in Greek during the third century B.C.E.

3000 B.C.E.[2] His personal monuments and relics, inscribed with his name in hieroglyphs, have been found; so that he is not a shadowy king known only from late tradition but fully attested by contemporary evidence. By his time Egypt had already developed a well-defined and distinctive civilization with an art (and system of writing)[3] whose basic canons were in large measure established.[4]

Egypt had a strong love of tradition. The marks of its civilization rarely died out. Other elements could be added but this resulted in an accumulation of mixed traditions, because the Egyptians could learn new things more readily than forget old ones. Thus, along with the development of hieroglyphic writing was included an alphabet. Each consonant in the language could be represented by a separate hieroglyph, but the Egyptians were not systematic enough to see the advantages in writing in a purely alphabetic way. Instead they combined three different systems of writing: (1) the logographic, whereby each sign stands for a word; (2) the syllabic, whereby each sign stands for a syllable; and (3) the alphabetic, whereby each sign stands for a single sound. Often a word is written in two or even in all three systems simultaneously and there might be in addition a "determinative," which is a hieroglyph that places the word in a semantic category.[5] Script is not the only manifestation of the Egyptians' inability conveniently to forget during the process of accretion. In religion, gods were added but not dropped from the pantheon, with the result that the growing host of deities became an unwieldy clutter. So, too, myths were added to myths, with the sum total growing ever more complicated.

Early in the third millennium the Egyptians began to exploit the

---

2. The difference between Narmer's and Menes's work may have been that Narmer's unification was ephemeral, whereas Menes's endured. For the problems involved in identifying Narmer with Menes, see E. Drioton and J. Vandier, *L'Egypte,* 3d ed., Paris, 1952, pp. 161–62; and W. Helck, "Gab es ein König 'Menes'?" *Zeitschrift der Deutschen Morgenländischen Gesellschaft* 103, 1953, pp. 354–59.

3. Egyptian hieroglyphic writing remained, to the end, a branch of the graphic arts.

4. Standard works on Egyptian history are the following: James H. Breasted, *A History of Egypt,* 3d ed., New York, 1943; Drioton and Vandier, *L'Egypte;* Alan Gardiner, *Egypt of the Pharaohs,* London, 1961; and John A. Wilson, *The Culture of Ancient Egypt,* Chicago, 1956. The best collection of Egyptian historical documents remains James H. Breasted, *Ancient Records of Egypt,* 5 vols., Chicago, 1906–7.

5. A determinative tells, so to speak, whether a consonantal combination like *ct* means "cut," "cute," or "cat."

mineral resources of the Sinai Peninsula. It is characteristic of Egyptian history that whenever Egypt was strong, she left traces of her activities, including inscriptions, in Sinai. Thus, although compared with Mesopotamia, Egypt was relatively isolated, it had contacts with the outside world, not only at the north and south ends of the long Nile Valley, but also through conquest and trade with the continent of Asia and with the islands and coasts of the Mediterranean and Red Seas.

After the first two Early Dynasties, the period of the Old Kingdom was ushered in by the Third Dynasty. The most important king of that dynasty was Joser, whose adviser Imhotep was a remarkable man later to be deified and appear in Egyptian history as a giant in the development of civilization. He was a physician, sage, counselor, and the architect of the imposing Step Pyramid (the first monumental stone building, still standing, in the world) that still amazes the traveler at Saqqara, near Cairo. The king at the beginning of the Fourth Dynasty, Senefru, had contacts with Western Asia, so that already in the third millennium Egyptian influence was felt in Canaan.

The Old Kingdom (around the middle of the third millennium) was in many ways the most noteworthy of all the periods of Egyptian history. It has left us the greatest monuments and the finest art of Egypt, and it embraced the essential pattern that Egyptian civilization was to follow for almost three millennia. Already in this early period there was the tendency to place Re, the Sun, as the foremost god in the Egyptian pantheon; and in Old Kingdom times temples were built for his worship. This ran against another current in Egypt, whereby the deities were local gods rather than the personifications of natural, universal phenomena. Nomic deities are more numerous than those with claim to universality. In spite of the early beginnings of the cult of Re, it took over a thousand years for Egyptian solar worship to gain enough momentum to produce one of the most amazing revolutions in world history.[6]

The fact that the gods varied from nome to nome did not mean that real religious differences existed between nome and nome. The underlying ideas were the same for all the nomes. But Egyptians, depending on which was their nome, worshiped at different shrines and had gods with different attributes. The different gods might be represented each by a different animal, and each might have different

---

6. The revolution culminated after 1400 B.C.E., during the Amarna Age (see Chapter V).

festivals. But an Egyptian who changed his residence from one nome to another had little difficulty, emotionally or intellectually, in getting used to the change. The differences between the cults were as a rule only externally varying expressions of the same religious character that prevailed from one end of Egypt to the other.

The Egyptians visualized the universe as divided into three parts: (1) the land of the gods was located in the east where the sun rises; (2) in the middle was the Nile Valley, the land of the living; (3) to the west lay the land of the dead. Such was their universe. They were not particularly concerned with foreign lands, for which no Egyptian cared to leave Egypt; nor with foreign nations, which the Egyptians viewed with contempt. The common man was not interested in foreign contacts nor in conquests, however much his sovereign might embark upon them.[7]

Egyptians lived in a rich country, where they developed their own homogeneous civilization in spite of changes partly brought about by periodic infiltrations from the north or south. They were ideally situated to develop their own distinctive culture, which far excelled anything that men had achieved anywhere else. The Egyptians knew this; whence their national pride and disdain for other civilizations and other people.

They believed in the existence of an otherworldly paradise—in fields where the dead could enter if they had lived meritorious lives in this world. In paradise no chores had to be done by the blessed, who enjoyed plenty and happiness.

The king was considered divine, as was perhaps indicated in a country where vital projects of nationwide scope had to be correlated, particularly in irrigation. The whole length of the river valley had to be under one "Nile Valley Authority"; and the best way to get the people to cooperate throughout the vast length of the land was to have them respect the king as divine and follow his authority unquestioningly. The cult of the dead during Old Kingdom times was reserved for the king and eventually extended to the nobles (but not to the common people), and so the magnificent funerary structures and the elaborate rituals and sacrifices in them—all of which necessitated onerous taxation and forced labor—were just for the

---

7. The modern Egyptian Arab feels much the same way and rarely wants to go abroad. In this he is unlike the Lebanese Arab who gladly goes to the ends of the earth in quest of opportunity, much like his Phoenician predecessors.

king and his immediate circle. The pharaoh was a busy, enlightened administrator, who kept the country united by holding his governors in check.

In family life, women had a peculiarly important position, for inheritance passed through the mother rather than through the father. Accordingly, the oldest daughter was normally the heir; and the chief protector of a person was not his own father but his mother's oldest brother. This system may well hark back to prehistoric times when only the obvious relationship between mother and child was recognized, but not the less apparent relationship between father and child.

A wisdom literature grew up, whose authors warned the reader against vice, admonishing him to live the good life and to shun evil. But the evils that the sages refer to are described so graphically that we can see the corrupt social usages that evoked this wisdom literature.

The royal circle maintained a standard of luxury that almost defies imagination, while the peasants, as always in Egypt, lived in abject poverty. Yet there was no caste system and it was possible for a talented lad of humble birth to attain the circle of officialdom by getting an education. The motive to learn to read and write was to qualify for government work. Any boy, by excelling first in his studies and then in government service, had just as much chance to rise to the prime ministry as an American boy has to become president.

In spite of such ideas as the divinity of kings and the cult of the dead,[8] the mentality of the Egyptians was basically materialistic and practical. Even the cult of the dead was quite materialistic. The body was mummified because corporeal existence was the only existence acceptable to the Egyptian. Offerings of bread and of beer figure prominently because an afterlife without food and drink would be no life for an Egyptian.

Included among the practical arts, however misguided it may have been, was magic, which was designed, as it is all over the world, to produce practical effects: to restore or ensure health, and to obtain things that otherwise seem out of reach. Naturally magic was not

---

8. Superficially an Egyptian custom like writing letters to the dead might convey an impractical and spiritual outlook. But such a conclusion would be just as false as it would be to conclude that American messages addressed in the second person to the dead (such messages can be found nearly every day on the obituary page of *The New York Times* under the title "In Memoriam") indicate that the United States is an impractical, spiritual nation.

used where the Egyptians could accomplish their ends scientifically. Only when science and rational technique broke down would magic be invoked. For example, Egyptians might resort to magic in an attempt to cure a disease they did not understand; but they would never depend on magic for the construction of a pyramid, which they did understand.

Already in Old Kingdom times sculptured portraits are often superb likenesses. This again was practical. The identity of the dead had to go on and this could best be achieved through an exact portrait likeness, which explains why such statues as the one known as Sheikh el-Beled[9] are superb portraits of definite individuals; in that particular case, of a man of the upper classes, well fed, sure of himself, used to exerting authority, self-satisfied. It is not an idealized portrait but one calculated to fulfill a purpose that called for faithful individuality.

Old Kingdom reliefs already show the canons that were to remain in Egyptian art throughout antiquity. The eye and shoulders had to be front-view. The feet and trunk, however, are in profile. This is a strange combination for us until we get used to it, but once we accept it as the standard, as the Egyptians did, it becomes quite acceptable.[10] All art has its conventions; and Egyptian conventions in no way detract from the greatness of Egyptian art. Another difference between our art and Egyptian is that while we like to have only one moment represented in an artistic composition, the Egyptians felt free to combine a number of different moments in the same composition. One part of a scene may represent one stage of the action, while another part of the same scene represents a later stage. Thus in battle scenes of the Empire Period,[11] one and the same scene can show a number of operations ranging in time from the launching of an attack upon a city to leading off captives and booty after the victory.

The temples had only straight lines, upright and horizontal. The arch was already known; it was reserved for vaults in funerary build-

9. Good comprehensive volumes on the art of ancient Egypt are H. Ranke, *Meisterwerke der ägyptischen Kunst,* Basel, 1948 (see plate 53 for the Sheikh el-Beled); and W. Stevenson Smith, *The Art and Archaeology of Ancient Egypt,* Harmondsworth, 1958.

10. The ancients never developed a science of perspective such as the artists of the Renaissance created.

11. This is not limited to Egyptian art; it is also common in Mesopotamia and elsewhere. For an example from the art of Mesopotamia, correlated with a text from Ugarit, see Gary A. Rendsburg, "*UT* 68 and the Tell Asmar Seal," *Orientalia* 53, 1984, pp. 448–52.

ings, but was not used in temples because the Egyptians did not know how to buttress walls sufficiently for taking the thrust of an arch. In thick-walled tombs the thrust offers no problem.

Cheops, a king of the Fourth Dynasty, was the builder of the greatest of all pyramids, the first one at Giza containing 2,300,000 blocks. The average weight of the blocks is two and a half tons. The height of the pyramid is 481 feet; the base has sides 755 feet long. The margin of error in construction is for all intents and purposes nil. Precision, organized labor, planning, varied personnel (from drudges to masons and up to the master architect) and the backing of an entire economy were necessary for accomplishing the greatest of the Seven Wonders. And it may be worth noting that of all the Seven Wonders, the pyramids alone survive.

The governors were strong men who inherited their position. Other officials, too, increased their power as time went on. After the great pyramid of Cheops, the subsequent Old Kingdom pyramids progressively diminished in size, because the resources of the kingdom were being exhausted and power was passing from the pharaohs to the governors and officials. Decentralization was setting in. However, it was in this period, when the process of disintegration had begun, that the finest artistic work (as in painting) and the finest texts of the Old Kingdom were produced, during the Fifth and Sixth Dynasties. As is often the case, the arts flowered most as power began to decline. With the fall of the Sixth Dynasty, the Old Kingdom comes to an end. Not only has the Old Kingdom left some of the greatest monuments ever put up by men, but it was an age that had seen the building of ships for sailing and exploring lands and seas, and, more than that, an age that had seen the beginning of a concept of personal judgment based on character and merit in this world.

The intermediate period that followed (toward the close of the third millennium) is not one of glory. For the Eighth Dynasty we have little or no trace of activity in the fine arts. No monuments were then erected by the pharaohs. There are texts of local governors, in which the pharaoh is disregarded, indicating that he had become more or less a figurehead. The Ninth and Tenth Dynasties need not delay us. For present purposes we may note in passing that their center was Heracleopolis in the nome where the crocodile was worshiped. The rulers are known as the Heracleopolitans.

With the Eleventh Dynasty, however, the rulers of the ancient city of Thebes asserted themselves, first locally and later uniting the two

Egypts to inaugurate the Middle Kingdom. The ruling family formed a succession of kings, some called Intef and some called Mentuhotep. Expeditions were resumed and a Mentuhotep put up a mortuary temple that was the prototype of one of the greatest temples in the Nile Valley; namely, the one built at Deir el-Bahri by Queen Hatshepsut, whom we shall discuss later. Out of the Theban ruling family came a leader, around 1950 B.C.E., who founded the great Twelfth Dynasty. His name was Amenemhet I. He emerged from Thebes, got control of all of Egypt, and checked the nomarchs (as the heads of the nomes are called). However, in his rise to power he had to depend on friendly nomarchs, so that feudalism was a foregone conclusion. The Twelfth Dynasty, which marked the height of the classical age of the Middle Kingdom, is characterized by feudalism. Yet the king was able to control the nomarchs so that the country could function efficiently as a whole, though at the same time local sensibilities and local initiative were not crushed. Because Thebes was in Upper Egypt, and therefore not in a central position, the capital was moved north, to a point south of Memphis in Middle Egypt, where control could be better kept over the northern and southern parts of the land. The king was able to exert authority through his treasury, for all taxes had to filter through from the nomes into a central treasury. Another unifying factor was the palace schools, where reading and writing were taught for the training of officials. The officials thus had contact with the royal circle and felt allegiance to the divine king. The masses were in abject poverty as usual. But again there was always the opportunity for the individual, regardless of the station in which he was born, to rise by showing his ability, to get an education, and enter government service.

The local gods continued, but their cults, to survive, had to be associated with, or subordinated to, Re. For example, the god of Thebes, the royal city, was Amon who became so important that his priests were the most powerful in the land. Yet Amon was combined with Re into "Amon-Re," in order to fit in with the trend whereby gods had to be connected with Re in order that their cults might continue.

Egyptian religion developed a kind of Passion Play concerning Osiris, the god of the dead, showing his suffering, death, and revival.[12]

12. Osiris died and rose from the dead once. The idea that he died and rose annually has no foundation in the ancient Egyptian sources.

Each dead person was identified with Osiris on the assumption that the deceased would undergo, but emerge triumphant like Osiris from, a trial full of vicissitudes to qualify for the life eternal.

This fully developed concept of a personal judgment, whereby each man enters paradise if his character and life on earth warrant it, appears quite remarkable when we consider that centuries later there was still no such idea in Mesopotamia and Israel. The Babylonians and Assyrians never developed it. And in Israel, throughout nearly all of the Bible, the afterworld was considered a dreary underground place called Sheol, where the good and bad alike led an eventless existence. Indeed the later Jewish, Christian, and Islamic concept of the afterlife, as one in which the individual is rewarded or punished depending on his earthly record, is more akin to Egyptian views than to those of the Hebrew Bible.[13]

The aggressive and progressive Amenemhet I organized the realm and brought Egypt into its second era of splendor. A palace plot on his life convinced him that his throne was not secure, so he made his son, Sesostris I, coregent, a precedent that was followed throughout the Middle Kingdom. That is, each king at some point in his reign associated the crown prince with him so that when the father died, the son was already enthroned. (This was to happen in Hebrew history; e.g., when David made Solomon coregent before his own death.)[14]

The most charming piece of Egyptian literature comes from this period. While Sesostris I was performing military service in the field, news came secretly of Amenemhet's death, whereupon Sesostris hastened to the capital to forestall trouble and to make sure of the throne. One of Sesostris's courtiers was a man named Sinuhe, the hero of the Romance of Sinuhe. This story relates that when Sinuhe got wind of Amenemhet's death, he feared that evil consequences might befall him, as so often happens to courtiers in times of political change. Sinuhe therefore fled from the camp of his master and went stealthily from Egypt to Asia as a fugitive. In the desert, around the Isthmus of Suez, he was saved by hospitable Semitic Bedouins. He had nearly died of thirst and they gave him water and then cooked milk, like the

---

13. As we shall see in subsequent chapters, it is only toward the close of the Hebrew Bible that the concept of personal salvation comes in.

14. I Kings 1:32–40. Also Jotham was regent of Judah before his father's death (cf. 2 Chronicles 26:21 with verse 23).

modern Bedouins who regale their guests with *leben*. Thence, Sinuhe wandered north into Canaan where he fell in with a sheikh, or local ruler, who respected him because of his Egyptian origin and his experience in Pharaonic circles. He offered him a frontier post to be defended against invading Semitic Bedouins. Sinuhe accepted the position as well as the ruler's eldest daughter in marriage and soon attained wealth and success. The Bedouins made attacks on him but he got the best of them. His orchards and vineyards yielded rich harvests of figs, olives, and grapes. His sons had grown strong and were helping him. He had everything an Asiatic could want. But to an Egyptian, even an Asiatic paradise was bitter exile. All Sinuhe's prosperity was vain because of his longing to return to his native land. At last he got in touch with emissaries on diplomatic missions of Sesostris, and after many years of waiting and growing old, he received in writing from the pharaoh a clean bill of health and a welcome home. Without any hesitation, he liquidated his Asiatic interests, turned his power over to his sons, and apparently felt no qualms about leaving the wife who had borne them. He put his affairs in order, as an upstanding administrator should, and wended his way back to Egypt, going through the frontier posts, and then boarding a Nile boat provided by the king. Sinuhe tells us about the wonderful service aboard the Egyptian boat, on which every member of the crew knew his job and performed it smoothly. What a change from "barbaric" Asia! As he sailed up the Nile to the palace, his heart rejoiced, for he was glad to be back in his homeland, and on his way to the court where he belonged. The king received him well and summoned the queen and royal children. When they came into the court and saw Sinuhe, about whom they had heard so much, they screamed on seeing him clad like an Asiatic. They could not believe that the exotic person before them was Sinuhe, but the king assured them it was he. Then Sinuhe was clad in fine linen, perfumed, shaved, and given an estate and royal support. The king also gave him a funeral endowment and a statue covered with gold to perpetuate his existence in the world to come. Gratefully Sinuhe put behind him all the years of exile, and settled down to enjoy the rest of his life in honor, as a favorite in the court of his sovereign, with the prospect of proper burial indispensable for securing immortality.

The Romance of Sinuhe is literature composed for enjoyment, without any religious or political motive. It is of some special interest to Bible students because in the course of the narrative conditions in

Canaan are reflected, such as the fertility of the land, Bedouin raids, and Egyptian influence. Sinuhe's geography includes Qedem ("East"), where Bedouins were commonly seen. The land of the tent-dwelling Job (1:3) is also designated as Qedem ("East"). But from the Egyptian viewpoint, the text was literature written for the sake of entertainment. Papyri inscribed with the story have been found in tombs; they were placed there so that the dead might have good reading matter in the future world.[15]

The greatest conqueror of the Middle Kingdom was Sesostris III, who made the first real Egyptian invasion of Canaan. Among the towns he encountered there was Sekmem, which is either the biblical Shechem in central Israel or another Canaanite town of the same name.

Middle Kingdom art does not have the originality and genius of Old Kingdom masters. The figures now begin to get bigger. More effort was spent on size than artistic merit. However, the best portraits of this period are still excellent.

Another phenomenon of this period is prophecy. There is for example a prophet called Ipuwer; Neferrohu is the name of another. A prophet, according to the Egyptian pattern, appears before the king and gives him sad news. He tells him that because of evil, the land is going to suffer. An enemy will invade Egypt and inflict upon it all kinds of misery including the inversion of all social relationships, until a righteous king will arise as a savior, drive out the destructive invader, and institute a godly order. Egyptian prophecy may have had an influence on Israelite prophecy, though Israel added further religious and ethical content.[16]

One of the literary masterpieces of the Middle Kingdom is the Song of the Harper, in which the minstrel appears before a banquet, where he sings to the guests that everything in life is vain, that we cannot take our possessions with us after death, and that the only thing to do is to eat, drink, and be merry because the future holds nothing certain in store for us; nor have the dead ever come back to tell of the future life. This represents an inquiring, skeptical attitude of oriental origin that may have eventually influenced (centuries

15. Magical and religious compositions such as the Book of the Dead were for the grim business of securing salvation. The Sinuhe story and other Middle Egyptian pieces of literature are the world's first secular literature composed for reading enjoyment.

16. For extensive translations (with bibliography on the originals) of Egyptian literature, cf. Miriam Lichtheim, *Ancient Egyptian Literature,* 3 vols., Berkeley, 1973–80.

later) the author of Ecclesiastes,[17] whose musings run the gamut of thoughts expressed by the Harper; although in good Hebrew fashion, the biblical book concludes that after all is said and done, the best course is to fear God.[18]

As the Harper shows, there were Egyptians who doubted the make-believe future world, where the blessed eat, drink, and play, with no work to do. Thinking people, even in Egypt, questioned the widely accepted tenets of the cult of the dead, which should warn us against the temptation to generalize.

The splendor of the Middle Kingdom was not to last. It ended with usurpers seizing the throne one after the other. Finally, foreign invaders called the Hyksos entered the country from Asia, imposing their rule that was intolerable to the Egyptians. However, the Hyksos introduced the horse-drawn chariot and modernized warfare to the degree that made possible the next step of Egyptian history: the Empire Period. The Hyksos ruled an empire, not merely an Egyptian kingdom. They chose as their capital the city of Avaris in the Delta from which to govern their holdings on two continents. A capital in Upper or Middle Egypt would not have been sufficiently central. That the Hyksos ruled not only over Egypt but also over some of Western Asia paved the way for the Egyptian Empire that was to see Egypt's maximum expansion beyond her own natural borders. Since the capital of the Hyksos was in the far north, the rulers were not in a position to control the far south; and it was from there that Egyptian nationalism, as has always been the case, rose again, finally to drive the invader out and establish the New Kingdom (as the Empire Period is also called).

The Hyksos consisted of a mixed multitude, including many Semites along with other Asiatic elements. With their expulsion around the year 1550 B.C.E. by Ahmose I (about 1550–25 B.C.E.) of Thebes, the founder of the Eighteenth Dynasty, the New Kingdom begins.

The Middle Kingdom had been an age of feudalism. The New Kingdom (coinciding approximately with the second half of the second millennium B.C.E.) was to be an age of royal ownership of the land, as is depicted in Genesis 47:19–20, where the system is attrib-

17. Some attribute the skeptical outlook in Ecclesiastes to Greek sources. The Song of the Harper shows that notions such as "you can't take it with you" (etc.) need not have been borrowed from Greece.

18. The Hebrew language has no word for "religion." The true religion is designated as "the fear of God (or Yahwe)."

uted to Joseph's planning. The people were nearly all serfs bound to the king who owned the land. The taxes included one fifth of the crops that the serfs had to pay into the royal treasury. This, too, is attributed to Joseph's administration in Genesis 47:23–27. The Joseph story shows the biblical writer's familiarity with New Kingdom government, national economy, and society. The only tax exemptions were those of the priesthood, again specified in the Joseph story. The priests received their maintenance from the crown and, being tax exempt, were able to hold on to their lands.

The state was military and the Egyptians were now able to accomplish feats of warfare that they had never been able to do before. Both in tactics and in the strategic distribution of troops, new features were added. The world's first well-documented accounts of strategically conducted campaigns come from the New Kingdom. The new branch of the army was the chariotry, whose charioteers formed the uppermost military class. Members of the old nobility who wished to retain a privileged position sought their way into the circle of charioteers, because caring for horses and serving the king in his chariotry constituted the most important source of New Kingdom power.

Public opinion was of no consequence. Egypt was an absolute dictatorship. Accordingly, the king had to be strong. Thus, as long as there was a succession of strong Pharaohs, the New Kingdom was able to survive. When able leadership was lacking on the throne, the doom of the New Kingdom was sealed.

The old nobility, as we have mentioned, disappeared as such, but in its place came an officialdom. The king always needed an able prime minister, who in turn needed able civil servants to administer the land. There was thus opportunity for talented common people. As was typical throughout Egyptian history, a young man able to show his merit and to rise first in school and then in civil service could aspire to the highest positions. Accordingly, the rise of Joseph from a slave to the highest position next to the king fits in with the picture of Egypt as we know it from native sources.

The name Thutmose figures prominently in the Eighteenth Dynasty. Thutmose I invaded Syria and his records are consequently important for the study of Canaan. The complicated succession to the throne at this time forms one of the most interesting chapters of history. There were three kings named Thutmose whose careers and succession to the throne were complicated by a woman, Queen Hatshepsut (about 1479–57 B.C.E.). She assumed not only queenship but kingship, and she even wore a false beard to simulate masculinity in posing for some of her monuments. The able woman sent expeditions abroad and built edifices at home. The man of her confidence was Senmut, the architect who built at Deir el-Bahri her funerary temple, which, as we have observed, was copied from the older neighboring temple of Mentuhotep. The ambitious men in her family naturally hated her. Thutmose III (about 1479–25 B.C.E.), the ablest monarch of the dynasty, was related to her by marriage as well as through other family ties. She suppressed him, obliging him to wait until she died before he could rule by himself and carry out his grandiose plans. When she died, male resentment expressed itself in defacing her monuments, erasing her name, and trying to obliterate her memory from history.

Thutmose III invaded Canaan against a coalition headed by the king of Kadesh, a city by the Orontes River in central Syria. Thutmose III's account of the way he conducted his battle at Megiddo (around 1455 B.C.E.), in the course of the war, is now classical. There were three routes by which he could go. The shortest, now known as Wadi Ara, happened to be the most dangerous because it was so narrow in places that men had to march in single file. Accordingly, if the enemy had intelligence of his passage through the narrow wadi, they could attack him with relatively few troops and wipe out his forces. Against the advice of all his counselors, he insisted on taking this daring, shortest, and least expected route. The gamble turned out to be a complete success and he vanquished the coalition of kings near Megiddo. In defeat, Megiddo shut its doors on its defenders so that the men who saved their own lives and got back into the city had to be hauled up over the wall. In those days strongly walled cities were rarely captured. The Egyptians did not yet know the science of effective siege warfare, for the Assyrians were yet to invent such basic techniques as mining under city walls. Accordingly, expedition after expedition was necessary to win control over Canaan. The walled cities provided refuge and perpetuated the resistance. In this particular case, although gifts were offered to Thutmose in recognition of his "conquest," Megiddo's gates remained closed to him. Moreover, the king of Kadesh escaped so that another battle had to be fought in the vicinity of Kadesh, where again Thutmose was victorious, though none of his victories had permanence for the reason already given.

Thutmose III introduced naval adjuncts to supplement his land movements. His ships landed troops to help in the attack on North Syrian points.

Thutmose III reached the Euphrates River, which was the natural Syrian boundary of the Egyptian Empire at its greatest extent. On the other bank was the Mitanni Kingdom. The river surprised the Egyptians who had not realized that nature permitted a great stream to flow south, instead of north like the Nile. To the Egyptians (to whom "upstream" and "south" were indentical), the Euphrates was the river that paradoxically flowed "upstream."

Biographies of generals that served under Thutmose III are interesting compositions of the period. One of them tells how an elephant broke loose and menaced the king near Carchemish on the Euphrates, until the general slashed off its trunk with a sword. The story incidentally shows that elephants were still known in the area.

Another of his generals, Thutiy by name, tells in his biography how he captured the Canaanite city of Jaffa, by hiding his soldiers and their equipment in baskets. These were gotten into the city stealthily as goods, and once they were behind the fortifications, captured the city of Jaffa. The tale is thus a forerunner of Ali Baba and the Forty Thieves. In any case, deception could lead to the capture of walled cities that were invulnerable to the force of arms.[19]

Year after year the great conquering pharaohs of the New Kingdom returned to Canaan, ravaged the countryside, carried off all the booty and tribute they could get, and kept the land within the empire. Yet the conquest was never complete because of the impregnability of the walled cities.

It is interesting to note that two of Thutmose III's obelisks from Heliopolis are now in the English-speaking world. One is on the Thames Embankment in London; the other is in Central Park, New York. They are reminders in our midst of Egypt's greatest conqueror.

Thutmose IV (around 1400–1390 B.C.E.) married Mutemuya, a Mitanni princess, and thereby inaugurated an era of close diplomatic contacts between Egypt and Asia. It is true that such princesses did not become the official queens in the royal harem, but nevertheless they were wives of the king and cemented friendships with Asiatic royalty. Mutemuya and Thutmose IV were the parents of Amenhotep III (about 1390–52 B.C.E.), the first of the two Amenhoteps who

19. The most famous example of this in literature is, of course, the Trojan Horse.

ruled Egypt during the Amarna Age (see Chapter V). The favorite wife of Amenhotep III was Tiy, a commoner but an Egyptian. The queen at this time could not be anyone except an Egyptian. However, we observe a certain breaking down of old traditions, in that he married the daughter of a commoner. Amenhotep III also married a number of princesses from Asia, one of them a Mitanni princess named Giluhepa. He also obtained in marriage for his son Amenhotep IV (about 1352–36 B.C.E.) another Mitanni princess named Taduhepa. The prestige of Egypt stood higher than that of any other country of the day. Egypt would take princesses into the royal harem but would never give an Egyptian princess, or for that matter any Egyptian woman, in marriage to any of the Asiatics.

With Amenhotep III and IV the political decline of the New Kingdom had begun. But in their time internal and international developments combined to make the period one of the most fascinating in the pages of history. The Egyptian Empire had come into direct contact with the Cuneiform World. To understand the events, we must now turn back to Mesopotamia and follow its course down to the Amarna Age.

# CHAPTER IV

# Mesopotamia to the Amarna Age

The physical geography of Mesopotamia is important for understanding the history of the country.[1] The converging of the Tigris and Euphrates Rivers made it possible for a network of canals to be dug and maintained, giving the land a productivity unheard of in any other area.[2] Accordingly, enterprising invaders in early times were able to settle down and by their industry establish the agricultural basis for a stable, civilized society, and eventually to conquer and rule over a vast empire.

When written history dawns in Mesopotamia (around 3000 B.C.E.), Semites and Sumerians are both in the land.[3] But it is the Sumerians who predominate in warfare, politics, and culture. It is they who have first left us numerous business records that give us a detailed insight into their economic life. They also produced a classical and religious literature that was translated into Semitic Akkadian and then into other languages. As long as the Babylonians and Assyrians perpetuated a culture of their own, they regarded Sumerian as their classical language and studied it as such. There was no cultural

1. Note that far southern Mesopotamia has been formed by silt brought down by the two rivers and that the land is still in the course of expanding southward into the Persian Gulf. Many southern cities that are now inland were at or near the water's edge in antiquity.

2. Herodotus, who describes both lands, found Mesopotamia more productive than Egypt in the fifth century B.C.E.

3. Basic treatments of ancient Mesopotamia are Samuel Noah Kramer, *The Sumerians: Their History, Culture, and Character,* Chicago, 1963; H. W. F. Saggs, *The Greatness that Was Babylon,* New York, 1962; A. Leo Oppenheim, *Ancient Mesopotamia,* Chicago, 1977; and George Roux, *Ancient Iraq,* Harmondsworth, 1992.

hostility between the Sumerians and their Semitic contemporaries and successors. The Semitic inhabitants of Mesopotamia recognized their debt to Sumer and cherished its cultural heritage.

Sumer was divided politically into city-states, each with its own cult. The city of Ur was a center for the worship of the moon-god Nanna (who was called Sin by the Semites). Nippur was the center of the cult of Enlil. Gods like Nanna and Enlil formed part of the pantheon known and revered throughout Mesopotamia. But some cities had cults dedicated to the worship of local gods. Thus Lagash was the center for the worship of Ningirsu, the patron god of the little city-state, that in more than one period reached high levels of culture. By the happy accident of discovery, many outstanding records of Lagash—both written and artistic—are in our possession.

One of the rulers of early Lagash (shortly after the middle of the third millennium) was Ur-Nanshe, who has left us a number of monuments including a relief of the royal family, on which various members are named. The sculpture is undeniably crude; but it is so "literal" in detail that it is a valuable factual source of information. The last ruler of this early period was the remarkable Urukagina, who like other heads of Sumerian city-states in the standard tradition, bore the title *ensi*. An *ensi* was not a king (for "king" is *lugal* in Sumerian), but the human agent of the city god appointed to look after the population as a shepherd takes care of his master's flocks. In other words, the city god was viewed as the actual ruler; the *ensi* was merely his executor. Government in the name of gods is theocracy. The human executor was regarded as relaying and implementing the god's commands, which could be conveyed by the god directly to the *ensi* in a dream, or as an oracle through a priest.[4] As Urukagina rose in power, he assumed more ambitious titles. Though he began as *ensi,* he later became the king of Lagash and finally through conquest, he was able to call himself King of Lagash and Sumer. He is most famous, however, not for his conquests, but for his reforms, of which we have the written record. He reduced the fees extorted by a rapa-

4. The clearest description of the process is provided by two long inscribed cylinders of Gudea, a later *ensi* at Lagash, who relates in detail how he received and fulfilled the commands that the gods revealed to him. In a community where theocratic ideals are fostered, there is no difficulty in accepting the necessary assumptions and techniques, however exotic the latter may appear to the modern reader. Forms of theocracy appear in the Bible. The clearest example is perhaps the period of Samuel's ministry (1 Samuel 3–16). The simplest formulation is Samuel's "Yahwe, your God, is your king" (1 Samuel 12:12). Samuel's granting the people a human king could only be justified by God's order to do so (1 Samuel 8:22).

cious priesthood, and reduced prices in general in the interest of the common man. The modern idea of a prosperity that consists of high prices and scarcity of goods is unknown in antiquity. Thus, in the Bible World, material prosperity implied abundant goods and low prices.

Urukagina's reform is the first evidence we have of an attempt by a ruler to improve society by lightening the economic strains on the citizens, although it remains a possibility that some Sumerian mound may yet reveal an earlier one.

Near Lagash was situated the rival city of Umma, and the rivalry between them often waxed to friction, which in turn sometimes burst into the flames of war. In Urukagina's time, Umma was ruled by an able conqueror named Lugalzaggisi, who vanquished Urukagina and destroyed Lagash. The catastrophe is lamented bitterly in a poem that has survived on clay. This type of composition is one of the characteristic forms of literature in the ancient Near East. The classic example in the Bible is the Book of Lamentations about the destruction of Jerusalem in 586 B.C.E.

Lugalzaggisi not only conquered all of Sumer but extended his conquests far beyond and laid the foundation for the first empire emanating from Mesopotamia. However, his success was of short duration because in his reign there arose the first Semitic conqueror in history: Sargon of Akkad (around 2251–2196).[5] Since Sargon's establishment of Semitic supremacy, which was to be eclipsed only for short periods by the Sumerians, the Semites have remained the dominant ethnic element through the Assyro-Babylonian, Aramean, and Arabic periods down to the present.

Before presenting the history of Sargon and his successors, we need to diverge for a moment and turn our attention to Ebla, the large city-state of north Syria. Strictly speaking, Ebla lies outside the traditional boundaries of Mesopotamia, but since much of its culture was closely linked with Mesopotamia, we include our discussion of this important site in the present chapter. By at least the twenty-fourth century B.C.E., Sumerian culture had spread from its homeland in southern Mesopotamia to an area 700 miles to the northwest, no longer within Mesopotamia proper, but in the neighboring region of

---

5. Scholars continue to debate the absolute chronology of the ancient Near East. The dates presented herein often are approximate, especially for the earlier periods. Readers can follow the debate about chronology in Paul Astrom, ed., *High, Middle or Low? Acts of the International Conference on Absolute Chronology*, 3 vols., Göteborg, 1987–89.

northern Syria. The thousands of cuneiform documents discovered at Ebla attest to numerous professional scribes proficient both in Sumerian and in the native Semitic language called by scholars Eblaite. These scribes produced lengthy bilingual dictionaries, the earliest such works in world history; the largest of them contains several hundred entries listing Sumerian words and their Eblaite equivalents. Nor is there a single exemplar of this important text; rather, there are several dozen copies of it, pointing to a well-established academy. On one occasion, the academy of Ebla imported a mathematics expert from Kish in southern Mesopotamia. The economic base of Ebla was its textile production; wool and fabrics were traded throughout the region. There were also contacts with Egypt, attested to by the discovery of a stone lamp fragment bearing the cartouche of Pharaoh Pepi I (Sixth Dynasty) at Ebla.[6] Before the discovery of the Ebla tablets in the 1970s, scholars had assumed that Syria was a backwater in the third millennium, populated largely by illiterate nomads. The evidence from Ebla, of course, shows that just the opposite was the case. A major cosmopolitan center existed there in the century prior to the reign of Sargon of Akkad.

Eblaite is the earliest attested Semitic language; texts in Eblaite antedate Akkadian documents by about a century or so. Scholars continue to debate the classification of the language; suffice it to comment that it has connections both with Akkadian in the East Semitic branch and with Hebrew, Aramaic, etc., in the West Semitic branch. The biblical scholar needs to have a control over the wide variety of sources from the ancient Near East, no matter how temporally or geographically removed those may be from ancient Israel. For example, Isaiah 26:20 and Habakkuk 3:4 refer to a demon of some sort known as Haby(on). The same word with the same connotation is attested not only in Ugaritic from the Late Bronze Age, but also in Eblaite from the Early Bronze Age. Similarly, there exists in biblical Hebrew a construction in which the conjunction *w*- is followed by an enclitic *m*, thus producing an emphasizing conjunction *wm*-. This usage is known from no other Semitic language, except for Eblaite. These and many other examples that could be put forward demonstrate a cultural and linguistic continuity in the West Semitic world

6. On Ebla in general, see Giovanni Pettinato, *The Archives of Ebla*, Garden City, N.Y., 1981 (though many conclusions reached in this book have been questioned upon further analysis of the Ebla material); and Giovanni Pettinato, *Ebla: A New Look at History*, Baltimore, 1991.

from Ebla in the third millennium B.C.E. to Israel in the first millennium B.C.E.[7]

We return now to our discussion of Sargon of Akkad. According to legendary tradition, Sargon was born of obscure parents and was exposed as a baby in a basket set afloat on a stream. An irrigator found the child and took care of him. The goddess Ishtar loved him and facilitated his stellar rise to the throne. The tale has features typical of a number of stories about the birth and career of famous men, among them, of course, Moses. Being the favorite of some deity is a frequent motif in the legendary biographies of ancient characters.

Kings in Sargon's Dynasty (about 2251–2071) sometimes put the star for divinity in front of their names showing that the idea of divine kingship had made its appearance in Mesopotamia. This had not previously been typical of Sumerian rulers, who governed *for* gods but not *as* gods.

Sargon calls himself King of the Universe, a claim that rested on his conquests extending from the Persian Gulf to the Mediterranean Sea, even up into Asia Minor. For Sargon's period, the meager historic records must be supplemented by the epic and omen traditions that have preserved the record of events (often containing some historic truth) in his reign. The King of Battle epic tells of his exploits in Asia Minor. Quite popular among future Mesopotamian kings were omens, whereby observations of livers and other innards of animals were interpreted as implying such and such, even as such and such had taken place during Sargon's career when a similar observation had been made.[8]

Sargon's life came to a violent end through an upheaval in his own palace. Though he perished, his Akkad Dynasty continued. Ever since his time, Babylonia could be referred to as "Sumer and Akkad," Sumer being the more Sumerian south; and Akkad, the more Semitic north.

Sargon's greatest successor was Naram-Sin (about 2171–2135).

---

7. For details on these and other examples, consult the on-going series of collected studies edited by the authors of the present volume: Cyrus H. Gordon and Gary A. Rendsburg, eds., *Eblaitica: Essays on the Ebla Archives and Eblaite Language,* Winona Lake, Ind., vol. 1, 1987; vol. 2, 1990; vol. 3, 1992.

8. This analogic type of reasoning is characteristic of thought in ancient Mesopotamia; cf. G. Contenau, *Everyday Life in Babylon and Assyria,* London, 1954, pp. 158ff. Inductive, deductive, and syllogistic ways of reasoning were not typical of Mesopotamia (or of the ancient Near East in general).

This ruler set out to expand Akkadian rule over large areas of the ancient Near East. Naram-Sin was successful in his military endeavors, and among his conquests was Ebla. Only after his defeat of the great city-state of northern Syria did Naram-Sin claim his rule over the four quarters of the world. His stone stela of victory is the most remarkable composition in the early history of art. Like so many masterpieces, it stands isolated as a peak, and was not equaled anywhere in the world for centuries to come.[9]

The seal cylinders of the Akkad Dynasty are often large and well cut. They include a great number of mythological scenes, which in many cases can be correlated with texts of later date, though the seals prove the early existence of the myths in question. Akkad glyptic art is much more vigorous and realistic than the earlier Sumerian glyptics; the musculature becomes more pronounced and the scenes are more convincing.

Under the impact of invaders from the mountains of the northeast, the Akkad Dynasty collapsed. The principal invaders were from the land of Gutium in mountainous Iran. The Guti, as they are called, were looked upon as destructive barbarians. Their invasion was part of a recurrent pattern in Mesopotamian history: the hostility between the hardy men of the hills against the more civilized men of the plains. Wave after wave of mountaineers have descended on the plains, lured by agricultural and urban wealth, only to become plainsmen whose descendants would be menaced by further invaders from the highlands.

With the passing of the Akkad Empire, Sumer and Akkad split into their component city-states, among which Lagash is outstanding culturally. Under the *ensi* Gudea, after the Guti conquest,[10] the city rose to unprecedented heights of artistic achievement. Gudea speaks neither of aggressive wars nor of any human overlord. He apparently lived in an era when central authority was either weak or nonexistent, and when small city states could once more come into their own. His statues are the apex of Sumerian sculpture in the round. While the bodies are somewhat dwarflike, the faces are superb. His two great cylinders mark the zenith of Sumerian literature; and his

---

9. Cf. C. Zervos, *L'Art de la Mésopotamie*, Paris, 1935, p. 164; and Anton Moortgat, *The Art of Ancient Mesopotamia*, London, 1969, pl. 155–56.

10. The Guti seem to have introduced a turban with a short, heavy brim. Gudea, who wears this type of headgear, must follow the time of its introduction to Mesopotamia.

literary compositions form the basis of the standard textbook on the Sumerian language.[11] In keeping with the best traditions of Sumer, he was an *ensi* concerned with piety and construction. He obtained by trade and peaceful expeditions the materials he needed for his greatest undertaking, the Eninnu temple of Ningirsu in Lagash.

Gudea's cylinders are leading sources for ideas and institutions in the Bible World. For instance, Gudea gives names to parts of, or furnishings in, Eninnu. Thus a pillar or a divine emblem will have a name given to, and inscribed on, it. This is in keeping with "Jachin" and "Boaz": the names ascribed to pillars in Solomon's temple (1 Kings 7:21).

Gudea's dreams were accepted as oracles delivered through a regular channel used by gods in giving instructions to men (as often in the Bible; see 1 Samuel 28:6). Dreams, to be sure, have meanings that need not be clear to ordinary people, not even to rulers of cultured cities.[12] An *ensi* might have to go to priests or priestesses, skilled as interpreters, for the meaning. But once the dreams are interpreted, the ruler knows what the god wants, and if the *ensi* is virtuous, he proceeds to fulfill the divine wish. Gudea's dreams conveyed to him divine orders to build a temple. The fact that dreams figure in the authentic records of Mesopotamian rulers is important for biblical studies, as for example in the case of Solomon's dreams (1 Kings 3:5–15; 9:2–9) which need not be taken as late additions to the biblical text on a priori grounds. For against the background of royal inscriptions from the Bible World, we know that dreams formed an integral part of kings' actual accounts of their own reigns. The difference between ancient and modern attitudes toward dreams obliges us to evaluate dreams in Scripture in proper historic context. To write off all dreams as apocryphal accretions is unhistoric. The fact that a number of dreams in historic inscriptions might have been invented by the ancient rulers who claimed to have dreamed them does not affect the case. Since dreams—even invented ones—could be accepted by

11. See the reference to A. Falkenstein's grammar in chapter I, p. 19, n. 2.

12. The biblical Hebrews never need interpreters to explain their dreams, although individual Hebrews (like Joseph or Daniel) may interpret dreams for foreigners. Were it not for texts like Gudea's, showing that Gentile rulers admitted their need for interpreters, we might suspect the Hebrews of prejudice (for Gudea's dreams, like pharaoh's, seem too obvious to require interpretation). It may be that the undeniable religious genius of the Hebrews included a greater and more popular exercise of psychic qualities than characterized the other people of the Bible World.

the public as divinely inspired, they would be included in pronounce-
ments and texts concerning current events.

The foreign yoke of Gutium was thrown off by Utuhegal (about
2041–34), a ruler of Erech in Sumer. The expulsion of the invaders
made possible a Sumerian revival that culminated about 2000 B.C.E.
under the Third Dynasty of Ur (about 2028–1920), whose first king
was Urnammu (about 2028–11). He united the land, extended his
conquests beyond Sumer and Akkad and promulgated (in Sumerian)
the first code of laws so far known anywhere in the world. His son,
Shulgi (about 2010–1963), who reigned for almost half a century, not
only claimed divine kingship but had a religious cult established to
adore him. The events of the dynasty are known largely from the
date formulae on the countless business documents of the period.
Instead of numbering years, the Sumerians (and Akkadians) named
each year after some event of a military, religious, or commemorative
character. Thus the names of the years provide us with a list of military operations, ecclesiastical developments, and building projects.

The tablets are frequently dated even to the month and day. The
month is of considerable importance for the host of Third Dynasty
tablets whose provenience is unrecorded. Because each town had its
own set of month names, it is usually possible to identify the town in
which the tablet was written.

Most of the tablets deal with economic transactions regarding
grain, fruit, vegetables, large and small cattle, slaves, employment,
family life, and the whole gamut of business contracts. Business dealings were concentrated in the town temple in keeping with the tendency for the temple to be the social and economic, as well as
religious, center. No transaction was too small to be recorded. If an
obscure shepherd had a single sheep assigned to him, it was recorded
on a tablet. Accurate ledgers were kept for daily, monthly, and yearly
totals. Sumerian life was meticulously recorded, especially from the
bookkeeper's standpoint.

The courts of law made decisions in keeping with the accepted
standards and accumulated social experience of the land. Thus the
law was more akin to the common law of the Anglo-Saxons than the
code law of continental Europe. The idea of codified law existed in
the Bible World after Sumerian times. However, the codes were not
followed by the people or the law courts, as we know from the
numerous contracts and lawsuits. The contracts often violate the law
codes promulgated in their respective periods; and the decisions of

the judges regularly omit any reference to the codes. The real law was thus the common law, representing custom and public opinion. The concept of a written law whose statutes should be consulted for the definite answer to every conceivable dispute[13] was a different institution, emanating not from the people or the courts but from the crown.[14] The first law code to be accepted[15] as permanently binding was the part of the Bible known as the Law of Moses. The latter did not win chronologically unbroken adherence until 621 B.C.E., an event we shall take up later. Among the nations of the Cuneiform World, none before the Medes and the Persians (starting in the sixth century B.C.E.) had in practice accepted the idea of absolute law.

The oldest known law code is that of Urnammu (in Sumerian). That earlier Sumerian law codes existed is quite probable. The oldest known law code written in Babylonian comes from Tell Abu Harmal (near Baghdad), which in antiquity formed part of the Kingdom of Eshnunna. These Laws of Eshnunna show that Hammurapi (about 1704–1662) was not the first to promulgate a code in the Semitic language of the land, even though Hammurapi's formulation is by far the best organized and most comprehensive of antiquity. Fragments of a law code in Sumerian have also survived from a ruler named Lipit-Ishtar (about 1850–40).

From time immemorial, but especially from the time of the Akkad Dynasty, the Semites kept pouring into Mesopotamia from the desert that lies to the west. As the Semites grew more numerous, their Akkadian language became the predominant speech, while Sumerian, though persisting as a classical written medium, was dying out as a spoken language. Although the Third Dynasty of Ur was a Sumerian revival, the land of Sumer, as well as Akkad, was linguistically Semitized; and even the names of the later kings of the dynasty are Semitic. Thus Shu-Sin (about 1953–45) meaning "He of the Moon-god" and Ibbi-Sin (about 1944–20), generally taken to mean "The Moon-god has called," are Semitic. The latter monarch, who was the last of the dynasty, was carried off in chains as his empire was

---

13. We adhere to this ideal, though common sense tells us that it is impossible. Changing conditions constantly render the best of law codes inadequate.

14. To be sure, code law was studied, as we know from Neo-Babylonian copies of parts of Hammurapi's Code. However, code law remained essentially a theoretical subject, while the actual law practiced in courts was at the discretion of judges who respected custom and opinion but did not cite codes.

15. Earlier codes, such as Hammurapi's, claimed but did not win permanent validity.

destroyed. For the hapless king and his destroyed city, a lament, in the tradition of lamentation literature, has survived.

The breakdown in central authority resulted in the splitting up of Sumer and Akkad into the older system of city-states. The period is known as the Isin-Larsa Age, because the leading city states that emerged from the ruins of the Third Dynasty of Ur were Isin (about 1934–1709) and Larsa (about 1937–1675). By this time, the western Semites, known as Amorites, who were pouring in from the desert, had established the Semitic element as the definite majority. However, in cultural and official circles the Sumerian pattern continued. Thus the law code of Lipit-Ishtar of Isin, to which we have referred, is written in Sumerian.

By now (nineteenth century B.C.E.) the influence of Mesopotamia was felt far and wide. Assyria, though politically independent of Sumer and Akkad, adhered to the same cultural complex that included language, script, religion, and art. There were differences between Assyria in the north and Babylonia in the south, but they were not great. Assyrian merchants had penetrated Cappadocia, where they established communities that maintained trading relations with the Assyrian homeland. The Cappadocian tablets—as the abundant documents of those Old Assyrian colonists are called—constitute a major branch of Assyriology.

Virtually all of Mesopotamia fell into the hands of Amorite rulers during the Isin-Larsa Period. Assyria was governed by an Amorite king, Shamshi-Adad I (about 1727–1695): an able monarch who established his sons as the rulers of a realm along the middle Euphrates. Their capital was Mari, where French archeologists unearthed about 20,000 tablets of military, administrative, and diplomatic contents. One of the interesting features of the tablets is the clear picture of how Shamshi-Adad trained his sons for leadership by giving them reasons as well as orders so that they might understand as well as act.

The Mari Age was one of numerous kinglets entering ever shifting coalitions in the struggle for power or to avert ruin. The interrelated terrain of those kinglets included several sites in Canaan, most prominently Hazor. One of the city-states in Akkad was Babylon, now ruled by its First Dynasty (around 1806–1507), whose greatest king, Hammurapi (about 1704–1662), was a junior contemporary of Shamshi-Adad. Both monarchs were fine civil administrators and military commanders. Of the two, Hammurapi emerged triumphant, by shifting adroitly from coalition to coalition, in the course of his long reign and eliminating his rivals, one by one, until he achieved the unification of Babylonia and adjacent areas. Babylonian unity is reflected by the spread throughout the land of a single calendar, whose month names persisted to the end of Babylonian history, and which live on in the religious calendar of the Jews, who adopted it during the Babylonian Exile.

Numerous business documents, lawsuits, and letters attest the activity of the land during the First Dynasty of Babylon. The normal language is now the Semitic, Old Babylonian, though Sumerian ideograms and technical formulae appear commonly enough. The years are still dated by formulae, usually in Sumerian, alluding to events. Many tablets deal with Hammurapi's personal interest in the administrative details of his empire. His crowning achievement was the law code, never to be to surpassed in scope or quality in the ancient Near East. On the top of the stone stela is carved a relief of Hammurapi alongside the sun-god Shamash.

The society reflected in the law of Hammurapi is divided into three classes: (1) an upper class, whose members have the greatest rights but also the greatest responsibilities; (2) an intermediate class; and (3) slaves.[16] Society was carefully regulated. Prices were pegged at fixed levels. Fees varied according to the social class of the client or patient. Laws for all situations in society, ranging from marriage and the care of children to river traffic regulations and a Veterans' Bill of Rights, are worked out in detail and lucidly phrased in language devoid of obscure legalistic jargon. Hammurapi's stated aim was to enable the average citizen with a legal problem to go to the stela and have the appropriate section read to him so that he would understand the law.[17]

Hammurapi's Code has a comprehensive literary form. The prologue and epilogue are in poetry, whose form is parallelistic[18] and whose language is archaic. The laws in the middle, however, are in

16. In Babylonian, the members of the three classes are called, in descending order: *awilum, mushkenum,* and *wardum.* For a more detailed breakdown, see Cyrus H. Gordon, "Stratification of Society in Hammurapi's Code," *The Joshua Starr Memorial Volume,* New York, 1953, pp. 17–28.

17. For a general introduction to the document, see Cyrus H. Gordon, *Hammurapi's Code,* New York, 1957.

18. The essence of pre-Greek poetic form is parallelism. Exact meter was introduced by Indo-Europeans; see C. Watkins, "Indo-European Metrics and Archaic Irish Verse," *Celtica* 6, pp. 194–249.

prose, so that the whole composition has a pattern, which we call ABA; A being poetry, B being prose. This has an important bearing upon other oriental compositions including the Bible. Thus the Book of Job starts out with a prose prologue; but the main body of the book is poetry with parallelism and archaic language; and the epilogue is in prose. Some scholars are inclined to detach the prologue and epilogue because they are in prose, whereas the rest of the book is in poetry. Such an argument fails to reckon with the literary composition as a whole, which, like Hammurapi's Code, has the architectural form ABA. Although in the Book of Job the prose and poetry are reversed, the architectural balance remains the same. Similarly the biblical Book of Daniel begins and ends in Hebrew, though the middle is in Aramaic. The possibility of an intentional ABA structure deserves earnest consideration and should deter us from hastily dissecting the text.

In the poetic sections of the Code stela, Hammurapi tells of the pious deeds he performed for the various city gods and their shrines. However, Marduk as the god of Babylon the capital attained a preeminent position as the god of the empire. It is probable that the version of the Creation Epic (and other literary compositions) in which Marduk figures as the supreme god, came from the time that the First Dynasty of Babylon reached its zenith under Hammurapi.

Strong as it was, the First Dynasty of Babylon eventually fell to foreign invaders. A people called the Kassites invaded the land, and divided the rule of the land with Hammurapi's successors. The First Dynasty of Babylon ended with the fall of the capital around 1507 B.C.E. Then the Kassites ruled the country from Babylon for some centuries without adding luster to the nation's history. Art went into decline and Kassite texts are relatively few, though there are some sculptured and inscribed boundary stones to indicate the limits of land grants.

In Asia Minor, from about 1800 to 1200 B.C.E., the Hittites[19] were in power and have left many texts behind them. They brought about, in 1507 B.C.E., the destruction of Babylon that ended the First Dynasty there. The Hittites politically absorbed a varied population, including people that had long been in Anatolia. However, the offi-

---

19. They probably came from Central Asia, which is the most likely home of the Indo-Europeans. See A. Goetze, *Kleinasien,* 2d ed., Munich, 1957, for the standard study of ancient Asia Minor.

cial language, the ruling class, and a number of cultural elements were Indo-European. Hittite documents are our earliest written records related to Sanskrit, Greek, Latin, English, and the other languages with which we are familiar. Like so many other Indo-Europeans, the Hittites reared horses. The earlier Near East knew of the donkey (for both riding and drawing chariots) and, in the case of the nomads, knew also of the camel. The Indo-Europeans introduced to the Near East the horse for pulling chariots, thus revolutionizing the art of war and the economy of the area. The aristocracy of charioteers, called *maryannu,* spread from the Indo-Europeans throughout the civilized Near East in the second millennium B.C.E.[20]

The Hittites were important in several ways. They were geographically situated so as to constitute the land bridge between the Semitic World and the Greeks (cf. Chapter VII). Moreover, their imperial interests carried their influence into Canaan, so that Canaan came to be called Hattu ("Hittite Land") by the Assyrians and Heth by the Hebrews. In Chapter VIII we shall see that Genesis 23 hinges on Hittite law, and that intermarriage between Hebrews and Hittites occurred from the earliest period of Hebrew history. The ethnological contribution of the Hittites to the makeup of the Hebrews is stated clearly by Ezekiel (16:3), who says of Jerusalem: "Thy father is the Amorite, and thy mother is the Hittite."

Another great cultural center that flourished throughout the second millennium B.C.E. was the Aegean and Minoan sphere, including Crete (Caphtor).[21] The civilization of that sphere was closely connected by trade and migration with the Asiatic and Egyptian mainland.[22]

As we shall see in the ensuing chapters of this book, "Caphtor" played an important role in the international order. One of its major

---

20. However, on a limited basis horses were known in the Near East even as early as the late third millennium B.C.E. See David I. Owen, "The 'First' Equestrians: An Ur III Glyptic Scene," *Acta Sumerologica* 13, 1991, pp. 259–73.

21. The area is called Caphtor in the Bible and Ugaritic tablets. Actually Caphtorian (Minoan) culture goes back to the third millennium and should be considered a major cradle of Near East and European civilization, contemporary and parallel with the Old Sumerian and Old Egyptian civilizations. The most important effect of Caphtor was its impact on both Greeks and Canaanites, with the result that the earliest Greek and Hebrew literatures have in Caphtor one of their common denominators.

22. The reader will now want to consult the multivolume work of Martin Bernal, *Black Athena,* New Brunswick, N.J., vol. 1, 1987; vol. 2, 1991; vols. 3–4, forthcoming.

contributions to Near Eastern civilization is its artwork.[23] Minoan art is remarkable for its vivacity and it injected a notable degree of liveliness into the art of the Near East (including Egypt) of the Amarna Age.[24]

23. See the illustrations in C. Zervos, *L'art de la Crete,* Paris, 1956.

24. For example, beautiful Minoan-style friezes were discovered recently at Avaris in the Egyptian Delta.

## CHAPTER V

# The Amarna Age

The Amarna Age (when Amenhotep III and IV ruled Egypt in the fourteenth century B.C.E.) derives its name from Tell el-Amarna, the capital built in Upper Egypt by Amenhotep IV, where nearly four hundred documents of singular interest were discovered. The texts are written in Babylonian on clay, for Babylonian cuneiform had become the medium for international correspondence and there was a school to train Egyptian scribes to write it in Tell el-Amarna.

The Amarna Age is the focal period of the ancient Near East, when extensive and unprecedented international contacts produced a fusion of cultures from Babylonia in the east to Egypt in the west, and from Anatolia and the Aegean in the north to the Arabian border and the Upper Nile in the south. Into the Amarna Age flowed the cultural resources of the Babylonians, Assyrians, Hittites, Hurrians, Caphtorians, Canaanites, Egyptians, and numerous other ethnic elements of pre-Amarna antiquity. Out of their synthesis emerged, first and foremost, the historical Greeks and Hebrews: two primary fountainheads of Western civilization; and also the post-Amarna Phoenicians, Arameans, Neo-Assyrians, Neo-Babylonians, Late Egyptians, and many others. The hub of the Amarna Age was Canaan, so that the Hebrews appeared at the right time and in the best place to fall heir to the maximum cultural legacy of the ancient Near East. Between the international Amarna Age in the fourteenth century and the international Hellenistic Age in the fourth century B.C.E. fell a period of nationalism during which the distinctive course of

Hebrew nationhood was historically possible. The Hebrews of the
Bible ran their entire course between the Amarna and Hellenistic
Ages.

The Amarna tablets are mostly letters exchanged between the pharaohs and the rulers of the Near East, and Cyprus, including among
the latter the kings of Kassite Babylonia, Assyria, Mitanni, the Hittites, and especially the kinglets of Canaanite city-states. The documents from Canaan have nothing to do with the Hebrew Conquest,
for they come from the earlier period when the Hebrew Patriarchs
flourished. There is but little in the patriarchal narratives that can be
expected to fit into the political or military history of the Near East,
with the one great exception of Genesis 14, which supplies the names
of nine kings and their realms. That chapter tells of a coalition of four
kings against five, who fought near the Dead Sea. The invaders were
from the Mesopotamian sphere. The forces were small, as is shown
by Abraham's ability to defeat the victors, although his men numbered only 318[1] (Genesis 14:14). The incident fits into the Amarna
Age, when Canaan was the scene of petty strife, foreign infiltration,
and restless folk. Typical of the period was small-scale Mesopotamian
interference. Until the actual personages of Genesis 14 are encountered in other documents, we cannot be sure of the situation. Meanwhile that chapter will remain the most tantalizing historic problem
of the Bible.

Canaan was divided into two spheres of influence, Egyptian and
Hittite.[2] Many a little city-state tried to pit those major powers against
each other in the hope of bettering its own position locally. Thus the
real hostility in the land was among rival city-states whose kinglets
engaged in international intrigue and fought petty local wars. The
belligerents would pretend loyalty to an imperialistic power, such as
Egypt, in the hope of getting assistance against local enemies. Roving

1. The number 318 is conventional, to judge from the fact that Princess Giluhepa of Mitanni,
with her 317 maids, was in a party of 318. The number was apparently proper in the Amarna
Age for groups of people, such as a company of troops, or a bevy of maidens. The scarab of
Amenhotep III, recording the arrival of Giluhepa, is conveniently reproduced in A. de Buck,
*Egyptian Readingbook* I, Leiden, 1948, p. 67. See further Stanley Gevirtz, "Abraham's 318,"
*Israel Exploration Journal* 19, 1969, pp. 110–13.

2. The Mitanni Empire was the leading power of Western Asia at the start of the Amarna Age
but it was gradually eclipsed by the Hittites in the fourteenth century and conquered by the
Assyrians in the thirteenth.

bands of 'Apîru[3] infested the country and menaced the settled communities, thus adding to the general insecurity.

Egypt was still capable of cultural achievement, and still enjoyed international prestige, but its actual power was a thing of the past.

The outstanding personality of the Amarna Age was Amenhotep IV: a sensitive intellectual, married to the beautiful Queen Nefertiti. He was at the head of a group of religious revolutionaries dissatisfied with the crass and complicated polytheism of Egypt. His theology had developed among a circle of priests at Heliopolis, where the sun-god was worshiped. As the Amarna Letters show us, he neglected his empire so that Egypt lost its grip on Canaan. Instead he dedicated himself to a religious revolution whereby all the gods were suppressed except the Sun, called Aton (or Aton-Re), which was elevated to the position of the one and only god of the universe—thus culminating the trend toward solar monotheism that had begun back in Old Kingdom times. The change was thoroughgoing. Art was revolutionized as well as religion, with the breaking down of old canons, and the introduction of new trends. Modernistic realism and distortion suddenly appear in the art of what had been the world's most conservative country. Up to this time the Egyptian written language remained that of the classical Middle Kingdom texts. With the Aton revolution came a break with the classical past, and new forms were allowed to penetrate the written language from the spoken, thus inaugurating the New Egyptian stage of the language.

So thoroughgoing was the pharaoh's fanaticism that he changed his own name, because "Amenhotep" contained the name of the god "Amen" (or "Amon"; the vowels are unexpressed in Egyptian writing). Instead he called himself "Akhenaton" containing the name of the sun-god "Aton." The names of Amon and of other gods were eradicated from monuments, even where they only formed part of the names of royalty or commoners.[4]

---

3. The 'Apîru (in Mesopotamian cuneiform Ḫa-bí-ru) often have been equated with the 'Ibrim "Hebrews." The 'Apîru appear all over Mesopotamia, Anatolia, Canaan, and Egypt. For surveys and discussions of the relevant material, see Moshe H. Greenberg, *The Hab/piru,* New Haven, 1955; and Jean Bottéro, ed., *Le problème des Habiru,* 4th Rencontre Assyriologique Internationale, Paris, 1954.

4. This trend has a counterpart in Hebrew tradition, where the name of Saul's son Eshbaal (1 Chronicles 8:33; 9:39) is changed to Ish-bosheth (2 Samuel 2:8, 10), where *boshet,* "shame," is substituted for the pagan deity Baal; and a still closer parallel in the name of the Judean king Abijam (1 Kings 15:1, 7, 8), where the last element Yam, "Sea-god," is changed to Yah (= Yahwe) so that the royal name is altered to Abijah in 2 Chronicles 13:1, 4.

Akhenaton founded a new capital, Akhetaton ("The Horizon of Aton"), whose site is today called Tell el-Amarna. But neither his capital nor his religious revolution was to endure. The resentment stirred up through his religious persecution, particularly among the priests and devotees of the powerful Amon cult, was profound. Shortly after Akhenaton's rather early death, a counterrevolution burst loose, destroying his fanatical reforms. Akhenaton was for all time abandoned. The Amon cult was restored in all its glory and Akhenaton's memory was held in bitter hate. But the Amon counter-revolution could not wipe out all the traces of Akhenaton's reform. The New Egyptian language was there to stay. And while the old canons of art were reinstated, the modernistic effects of Akhenaton's school occasionally peer through later works in some of the details.

Akhenaton is certainly to be ranked as a genius in the history of religion. Aton monotheism, although it had behind it the long history of Re theology and worship, owed much to the fanatical planning and implementation of the pharaoh. The purity of the monotheism far exceeded that in biblical Hebrew circles for centuries to come. The hymns to Aton reach heights of beauty eclipsed only by much later Hebrew Psalms. Yet we must recognize that Akhenaton's reform was stamped out so thoroughly that it had no influence on the subsequent history of religion. Akhenaton's son-in-law Tutankhaton ("The Living Image of Aton") changed his name to Tutankhamon[5] ("The Living Image of Amon"). Aton monotheism was quickly and thoroughly obliterated from official Egyptian life, including the royal circle. Accordingly, it is out of the question to assume that Moses (whose career falls a century and a half later) could have shaped Hebrew monotheism directly on the inspiration of Akhenaton's reform. Nor is chronology the only reason for dissociating Mosaic monotheism from Akhenaton's.[6] Typologically the two are unrelated. Aton was the sun disc, representing a single phenomenon in nature, and elevated to sole god of the universe through the suppression of the other deities of Egypt. Yahwe was never a specialized phenomenon of nature, such as the sun. Yahwe is represented in the patriarchal narratives as being the supreme God, Who created heaven and earth

5. The minor pharaoh who has won modern fame because of his rich and virtually unrifled tomb discovered by archeologists.

6. In the preceding discussion we use the term "monotheism," without necessarily making the distinction between this brand of religion and the type known as "monolatry." On the difference between these two terms, see below Chapter IX, p. 149.

(Genesis 14:22). As His name indicates, He is, the One Who "Calls into Being," or the Creator.[7]

In the Amarna Age, Egypt ranked as the aristocrat among the nations. She had attained this status through the spread of her culture and commercial enterprise in the wake of her conquests under the pharaohs of the Eighteenth Dynasty, notably Thutmose III. But a true internationalism cannot flourish if one nation exercises a monopoly of power; and the Amarna Age was no exception. Egypt could no longer control Canaan up to the Euphrates, as she had done in the days of Thutmose III. There were other nations that shared in varying degree the control of the Near East.

Babylonia under the non-Semitic Kassites, who supplanted Hammurapi's Dynasty, had more pretension than power. It could claim to be the successor of Sumer and Akkad, and of the Hammurapi Age, but genuine cultural attainment and military prowess were lacking. The Kassite king of Babylonia would send his daughters and other ladies of his family as gifts to the pharaoh; but in vain would he beg for the daughter of the pharaoh or for any other Egyptian woman— beautiful albeit picked from the common people—to be sent as the pharaoh's daughter to save face for the Kassite. The latter also repeatedly begged for gold because Egypt, unlike Mesopotamia, was rich in the precious metal. The stated purpose for seeking the gold was for the adornment of temples and similar cultic embellishment.

Assyria was a rising power, soon to be ruled by Assuruballit (about 1362–27), who made encroachments on Babylon and Mitanni.

The Mitanni Kingdom was the leading power in Asia during the early part of the Amarna Age. We have already mentioned its close alliances through marriage with the Pharaonic House. The Mitanni King Dushratta sought the brotherly love of the pharaoh, but he wanted that love to be expressed in terms of gold.

In Anatolia the Hittites were rising at the expense of Mitanni and Egypt. Although relations in the diplomatic correspondence are cordial, the Hittites were making encroachments in Syria to the detriment of Egypt. North Canaan fell into the Hittite sphere of influence and the little kingdoms of the area became vassal states. A tablet from

---

7. Such is the meaning that "Yahwe" came to have (though secondarily) in Hebrew (for it has taken on the appearance of the causative of the verb "to be"). However, the name may be an expansion of a shorter form (cf. Yo-, Yeho-, Yah, and -Yahu, which also occur).

Ugarit records the tribute sent by Niqmad, king of Ugarit, to his master, Suppiluliuma (around 1355–1321), king of the Hittites.

Canaan is a country chopped up by mountain ranges and, in the north, also by rivers. The geographical barriers worked against the unity of the land, which was fragmentized along the coast and inland into little city-states that might join into coalitions against a common enemy but otherwise remained rivals. However, the fact that the influence of Egypt from the south, of the Cuneiform World from the north, and of Caphtor from the west, converged in Canaan, preconditioned the land of Israel as the land in which the Hebrews could grow and make contributions of momentous effect on world history. Canaan was the crossroads of all the great cultures of the day, so that the Hebrews had the richest possible international background on which to draw before adding the contributions of their own distinctive Semitic genius.

While the Amarna Letters do not give us any evidence about the Hebrews as a people, they do provide important data on the language of Canaan, which the Hebrews adopted as their own. In the letters, Babylonian words are sometimes translated into Canaanite, showing that what was later known as Hebrew was already spoken in the country. Inasmuch as these Canaanite words are written in the Babylonian syllabary, the vowels are indicated. This is of considerable linguistic interest because the inscriptions of the Hebrews, Phoenicians, Moabites, and other Canaanites are written in a consonantal alphabet so that scholars have to infer what the vowels might have been by working back from later tradition and by theoretical deductions from comparative linguistics.[8]

The Amarna Age is richly documented from several other sources, notably the texts from Ugarit (which illuminate the origins of Hebrew literature) and Nuzu (which clarify the social institutions of the Hebrew Patriarchs). In the following chapters we shall investigate those sources.

---

8. The Amarna evidence, and cognate material from Ugarit, Alalakh, and Taanakh, is collected in Daniel Sivan, *Grammatical Analysis and Glossary of the Northwest Semitic Vocables in Akkadian Texts of the 15–13th C.B.C. from Canaan and Syria,* Neukirchen-Vluyn, 1984. A work devoted to a detailed study of the texts from one site is Shlomo Izre'el, *Amurru Akkadian: A Linguistic Study,* 2 vols., Atlanta, 1991.

# CHAPTER VI

# *Ugarit*

The most important corpus of ancient Near Eastern literature for the study of the Bible is the group of texts discovered at the north Syrian port of Ugarit. The documents date to the Amarna Age, during which time the city of Ugarit emerged as a major cosmopolitan center. The texts are written by stylus on clay in the fashion of the Mesopotamian scribes; but the system of spelling is alphabetic: each sign stands for a single sound, which is a Canaanite contribution. As we have noted above, the Egyptians had already invented alphabetic values, but since the ancient Egyptians never got themselves to use alphabetic signs without syllabic signs, logograms, and determinatives, they did not reap the benefits of pure alphabetism. Pure alphabetism goes back to Canaan, whence one of the groups (the Phoenicians) passed it on to Greece. Among the texts found at Ugarit were copies of the ABCs taught in the Ugaritic schools; their fixed order of the letters is the one from which our own English ABCs are ultimately derived.[1]

The Ugaritic language belongs to the northwest branch of Semitic, along with Hebrew, the other Canaanite dialects, and Aramaic. No student of the Bible today can progress far without a working knowledge of the Ugaritic language and literature. The literature of Ugarit is mostly mythological and concerns the pagan gods of Canaan, such as the male Baal and female Asherah, whose worship is forbidden in the Hebrew Bible. El, whom the Bible identifies with Yahwe, appears as the head of the Ugaritic pantheon. The Ugaritic tablets confront

---

1. Cyrus H. Gordon, "The Ugaritic ABC," *Orientalia* 19, 1950, pp. 374–76.

us with so many striking literary parallels to the Hebrew Bible that it is universally recognized that the two literatures are variants of one Canaanite tradition. To the Hebrew writers, however, the mythology is often little more than a literary background on which to draw for poetic imagery. Just as John Milton was a good Christian in spite of his profuse allusions to pagan mythology, the Hebrew poets were monotheists who worshiped Yahwe and Yahwe alone.

The prose as well as poetic documents from Ugarit enable us to describe the society and ideas of the times in considerable detail. The king was considered divine by dint of being suckled by the goddesses Anat and Asherah. The king's duty was to exercise justice and benevolence in the land. His virtuous deeds include help to the widow, fatherless, and other unfortunates.

The army is rather prominent in the numerous administrative documents that have been found in the archives of Ugarit. It consisted of infantry, including bowmen and slingers. The pride of the army was, however, the chariotry.

The chiefs of the army and the priesthood were sometimes selected from the tribes of the ruling class, including the king's own family. By planting members of trusted families in the priesthood and army, the king could exercise better control over the realm. Some of the priests were assigned on regular duty with the army. This resulted from a theocratic ideal that permeated society. Not only in Ugarit but also among the Mesopotamians and Hebrews the army on occasion would have on its staff, in the field, a seer or priest to give oracles. Thus not only were wars embarked upon in accordance with divine will as revealed by oracles, but even tactics in the midst of military campaigns were frequently undertaken only after the will of the god(s) had been consulted.

Taxation, conscription, and other government functions were exercised through three channels: tribes, towns, and professional guilds. The tribe, the oldest of these classifications, still functioned in Ugarit.[2] However, as throughout Near East history, the town was encroaching upon tribal organization, so that in many cases men were no longer known as members of such and such a tribe but rather as citizens of such and such a town.[3] Furthermore, the guilds of various

---

2. Indeed, in the Near East today, tribalism is still an important element in society, government, and economy.

3. The agricultural population was dealt with through the provincial towns.

professions, and of the arts and crafts, were organized to such a degree that a guild member could be related to the state, not through tribe or town, but through the guild.[4]

The family had at its head a man who possessed one or more wives. The children owed filial obligations to their parents in return for which they had inheritance rights. A model son was one who looked after his father's needs, such as the performance of religious rites, washing his father's stained clothes, plastering his father's roof against leaks, and holding up his father when the latter was in his cups.[5] The ideal daughter was one who looked after the food supply, fetched water, and was gifted with the art of divination. She was thus possessed of both domestic and psychic qualities.

The oldest son of the favorite wife would normally inherit the chief share. However, the father had considerable latitude in such matters. One man of Ugarit wrote a will whereby his future widow had full charge of the estate, which she could bequeath to the son that treated her best. Thus the father puts the widow in control of the purse strings, so as to place a premium on good filial conduct toward her by the children, after he is no longer alive to provide for her. So while the widow did not have the right to dispose of the estate to an outsider, she did have the power to select the heir from among the children.[6]

Of course, slavery existed. However, the plight of the slaves was not always hopeless. We have one document that tells of how a man in consideration of twenty shekels of silver married off one of his slave girls so that as far as we know, she became the mistress of her own home. Slaves could be freed.

Education was complicated because it consisted of scribal training in a cosmopolitan community where not only Ugaritic but also Babylonian, Hurrian, Sumerian, and still other languages were in use. As in all ancient communities, education was not popular but professional. Only scribes learned to read and write. In order to facilitate scribal education in so polyglot a community, vocabularies in two,

---

4. The guilds represented the latest and most advanced aspect of society, for industry and art follow agricultural development, which in turn represents a more advanced stage than nomadism.

5. The desirability of children for holding up drunken parents is also reflected in Isaiah 51:17–18.

6. Cf. A. van Selms, *Marriage and Family Life in Ugaritic Literature,* London, 1954.

three, and four languages were prepared for training scribes to translate.[7]

The literary texts include legends primarily about men, and myths
dealing entirely with gods. One of the legends is about a king called
Kret, who feared that his line might die out because his wife had left
him. He prayed to the god El, who tells him how to regain his wife
who will bear him eight sons, the youngest of whom will be suckled
at divine breasts so as to qualify to rule after him. Among the children
will also be a daughter (whose name means "Eighth" =) Octavia,
who although the eighth will be elevated to the place of firstborn.
These facts constitute interesting literary themes. The announcing of
children yet to be born is a recurring feature in the Bible, starting
with Hagar, who receives an annunciation from an angel predicting
the birth of Ishmael. This repeated characteristic of Hebrew literature
thus harks back to an ancient tradition. Also the idea of a younger
child eclipsing the older one(s) is a recurrent theme in Scripture,
which we shall have occasion to discuss, particularly in the Patriarchal
Period. More specifically, it is interesting to note that the elevation of
a seventh or an eighth child over his elder siblings is paralleled in the
account of David, whom Samuel anoints as king after looking over
and rejecting the seven older brothers (1 Samuel 16:6–13). In the
Legend of Kret it is not the oldest son who succeeds to the throne
(at least as far as the story goes) but apparently the youngest who
eclipses the elder siblings, as so often happens in biblical literature.[8]

Another legend concerns Aqhat, the son of the heroic king Daniel,
who ruled his people justly and protected the widowed and fatherless.
Daniel had only a daughter as the story opens, but he longed for a
son. He therefore prayed to the gods and performed the necessary
rituals, so that he was blessed by the birth of a model son Aqhat. To
celebrate that event, he summoned songstresses to sing joyously for
seven days. The songstresses were called the Kosharot, who appear
also in Psalm 68:7, where they celebrate the happy occasion of pris-
oners being released by God. Like so many passages in the Bible, this
one was not understood until the discoveries at Ugarit.

The god of arts and crafts, Kothar-and-Hasis, who hails from

7. The polyglot dictionaries now may be studied in John Huehnergard, *Ugaritic Vocabulary in
Syllabic Transcription,* Atlanta, 1987.

8. Thus Jacob eclipses Esau, his senior; similarly Ephraim eclipses Manasseh; etc. This feature
is singled out as worthy of saga precisely because it runs counter to the norm of primogeni-
ture. "Man bites dog" is more newsworthy than "dog bites man."

Caphtor, fashions a wondrous bow for Aqhat, who uses it effectively in the hunt. The impetuous goddess Anat covets the bow, which Aqhat refuses to give her, in spite of her promises not only to make him wealthy but even immortal. His persistent refusal impels her to go to her father El, from whom, by threats of violence, she wrings permission to assassinate Aqhat and thereby get his bow. Even though it may have been her intention to bring him back to life (the defective state of the tablets precludes certainty), Aqhat is slain so that the area is cursed with a seven-year (or, climactically, eight-year) drought by Daniel, who retrieves for burial his son's remains from the crop of an eagle.

One of the epithets of Daniel is "The Man of Repha," referring to his tribe. Some scholars have taken the references to people called the "Rephaim" (in Genesis 14:5, etc.) as mythological because the word also means "shades of the dead." However, that the name was borne by real people in the Amarna Age is indicated not only by the Legend of Aqhat and the biblical account of the Patriarchs (e.g., Genesis 14:5), but also by the occurrences of the name in administrative texts from Ugarit,[9] where legend and myth are out of the question. To be sure, there are some tablets that contain references to divine chariot-riding Rephaim, who may be "shades of the dead" associated legendarily with Daniel.[10] Their attachment to the legend may have been facilitated by verbal identity; resemblance in the sound of names often accounts for the association of elements that would otherwise not be placed together.

The end of the story of Aqhat and Daniel is not extant. But scholars are in agreement that the legend ended happily with the return of Aqhat to life. The reasons for this will be discussed below, in conjunction with the mention of Daniel in the book of Ezekiel.[11]

Most of the mythological texts concern the god Baal and his beloved Anat. Baal seized kingship by vanquishing the sea-god Yamm and then petitioned for a palace in which to live up to his newly won position. The fact that Kothar-and-Hasis from Caphtor fashioned the palace shows that Caphtor was already recognized in Canaan as the center par excellence for arts and crafts. The saga of Baal's palace is a

9. See Cyrus H. Gordon, *Ugaritic Textbook,* Rome, 1967, texts 91:7, 119:24, 300:rev. 14.

10. Ibid., texts 121 to 124. For a mythological reference, see 62:45.

11. See Chapter XVII, p. 289.

mythological forerunner of the historical account of building Yahwe's Temple in Solomon's reign. After Baal wins his palace, he is challenged by Mot, the god of death, who kills him. On another occasion Baal killed Mot for seven years. Since Mot remains dead for seven years, this cannot be seasonal conflict. The significance of the fighting between Fertile Baal and Lethal Mot, leading to the death of one or the other for seven years, can have nothing to do with the seasons, but ties in rather with the sabbatical cycle of seven years appearing in the Bible. In any event, we know from Hebrew[12] and Egyptian[13] sources that seven years of famine was the most feared scourge that could befall a nation. The Canaanites accepted the dry summer as an inescapable aspect of nature and wished only to get rain in its season. Moreover, the dry summer, far from being sterile, is precisely the season when many prized fruits ripen to the joy of the populace. What the Canaanites feared was a succession of famine years due to drought, locusts, or other sources of calamity. It is possible that the Hebrews let the earth lie fallow in the seventh year of the sabbatical cycle in the hope that it would induce the next cycle to be fertile in accordance with an assumed principle of alternation. The problem was so important to the Ugariteans that it transcended the myths and cult of Baal. Indeed the main Ugaritic text (number 52) touching on the problem is a myth wherein the spirit of privation is banished and the great god El begets auspicious deities for whom a cycle of abundant food and drink is inaugurated. The theme of "seven" permeates the text. Baal is not even mentioned, which shows that the question went beyond Baalism.

That Ugaritic is the greatest literary discovery from antiquity since the decipherment of the Egyptian hieroglyphs and Mesopotamian cuneiform is generally recognized. That it lies closer than any other literature to the Hebrew Bible is also well known. This does not mean that the ethical and moral heights reached in the Bible are to be found in Ugarit. The analogies are literary rather than spiritual. Indeed the Hebrew view is to a great extent a conscious reaction against the Canaanite milieu. This is illustrated by the fact that bestiality, far from being looked at askance in Ugarit, was practiced by the adored Baal, who copulates with a heifer as is celebrated in the reli-

12. 2 Samuel 24:13.

13. See James B. Pritchard, ed., *Ancient Near Eastern Texts,* Princeton, 1955, p. 31.

gious texts (67:v:17–22).[14] If it be argued[15] that Baal assumes the shape of a bull for the act, the same cannot be said for his priests who reenacted his mythological career, cultically. The Bible, in forbidding bestiality, expressly states that it was an abomination wherewith the Canaanites had defiled themselves (Leviticus 18:24). Other illustrations of the consciousness of the Hebrews' reaction against Canaanite usage can be found in the Bible and corroborated in Ugarit. We will return this issue in greater detail below in Chapter X.

The impact of Ugarit on biblical studies is growing constantly as new organic parallels are being pointed out by many scholars active in the field.[16] Our sketch here has been brief, but not due to any dearth of evidence. Rather, this chapter merely touches the tip of the iceberg. The reader will notice that in the chapters ahead the evidence from Ugarit plays a prominent role in manifold ways.

---

14. Apparently no moral issue was made of bestiality in Ugarit. Or to state it differently, bestiality had no significance in Ugaritic criminology. In Israel (whose attitude we inherit), however, it was a heinous crime.

15. See A. Kapelrud, *Baal in the Ras Shamra Texts,* Copenhagen, 1952, p. 20, n. 7.

16. The annual *Ugarit-Forschungen,* published in Neukirchen-Vluyn, Germany, is the best publication for readers of the Bible to keep abreast of the impact of Ugaritic studies.

# CHAPTER VII

# Homer and the
# Ancient East

Ｔhat the Bible must be understood in its ancient Near East context is generally recognized. But the origins of Greek culture
also lie to an appreciable extent in the ancient Near East.

At no time during the broad sweep of ancient Near Eastern history
were Greece and the Near East not in contact. We may begin our
discussion with the early third millennium B.C.E., during which era
the Sumerians apparently had reached the Balkan peninsula (specifically Tartaria in present-day Romania) in search of precious metals.
From later in the third millennium and from the early second millennium there are attestations of Egyptian and Akkadian artifacts and
inscriptions from Cythera in the Aegean. The major civilization in
the Aegean during the greater part of the second millennium B.C.E.
was the Minoan one. The Minoans were Northwest Semitic sea
lords, and most likely they had arrived on Crete after leaving the
Egyptian Delta around 1800 B.C.E. The art, architecture, and script of
the Minoans have unmistakable Egyptian roots.[1] At Ugarit we have
evidence of extensive contact with Crete, and from Amarna we know
that Cyprus was part of the international order. A recent discovery
that points to the elaborate trade relations of the period is the Ulu
Burun shipwreck.[2] The Hittite factor also needs to be considered, for
Anatolia served as the overland route that connected the Semitic and
Greek worlds.

1. This is discussed in detail by Sir Arthur Evans, *The Palace of Minos at Knossos,* 4 vols.,
London, 1921–36.

2. See George F. Bass, "Oldest Known Shipwreck Reveals Splendors of the Bronze Age,"
*National Geographic* 172:6, 1987, pp. 693–733.

In time, when the Mycenean Greeks began to pressure the Minoans in the Aegean, the peoples of Crete and elsewhere left the region for the mainland Near East. In this regard they appear as the Sea Peoples, including the Philistines.[3] As we shall see later on, the Israelites left Egypt at approximately the same time, i.e., the twelfth century B.C.E. In time, one of the Sea Peoples, the group known as the Danuna, became one of the tribes of Israel, namely, Dan.

Out of this interaction in the East Mediterranean came the heroic ages that inspired the early literatures of both the Hebrews and the Greeks. During this period peoples from Caphtor (i.e., Crete and other East Mediterranean islands and coastal areas) came to dominate the two main centers, mainland Greece and the land of Canaan. The Myceneans from Caphtor dominated southern Greece, and their impact on Greece is universally recognized. The Philistines meanwhile came to dominate much of Canaan; during the period of the Judges (1140–1000 B.C.E.), the Philistines were the overlords and the Hebrews were frequently their subjects. Later, around 1000 B.C.E., David's sojourn in the Philistine city of Gath provided him with the military experience to shake the Philistine domination.

The events leading to the establishment of the Davidic monarchy and the memories of the Trojan War provided the material for the epics and sagas of both Hebrews and Greeks. Besides, there was considerable international give and take among the poets and minstrels who composed and recited the epics and sagas that underlie Homer and the early parts of the Bible. For all these chronological, geographical, and historical reasons, it is not surprising that early Greek and Hebrew literatures—far from belonging to different watertight compartments—are related branches of one and the same ancient East Mediterranean complex of literatures.[4]

---

3. This is not to say that the Philistines of the Bible are the exact equivalent or the descendants of the Minoans of the Middle Bronze Age. Future evidence well may show this to be the case, but it would be premature to make such connections uncategorically. However, we may say that the Minoans and Philistines are part of the same cultural phenomenon: Semitic sea lords of the East Mediterranean. On the Semitic identity of the Minoan language, see Cyrus H. Gordon, *Evidence for the Minoan Language,* Ventnor, N.J., 1966. Little can be said about the language of the Philistines, but note that Philistines and Israelites do not require translators and that many Philistines bear Semitic names. By the same token, certain presumably Philistine words, such as *seren* "lord" and *koba'/qoba'* "helmet," are not Semitic. Only future discovery will resolve this dilemma.

4. See Cyrus H. Gordon, *The Common Background of Greek and Hebrew Civilizations,* New York, 1965.

A look at the map of the Ancient Near East will indicate that the strongest contacts between Homer and the East are to be found at Ugarit.[5] This city is the largest and closest seaport on the mainland Near East (i.e., Western Asia and Egypt) to the Greek-speaking world. A specific textual link is the Phoenician port city of Sidon. In the Iliad (6:290) we read that the Trojan Queen Hecuba wears embroidered robes from Sidon. In the Ugaritic texts, Sidon figures prominently in the Kret epic.[6]

That general concepts are shared between Homer and the ancient Near East does not prove much, though it is of some interest. Thus Zeus's epithet of "Father of Men" (Iliad 1:544; 11:182; 22:167) is the same as El's at Ugarit. The full Homeric epithet for Zeus is "Father of Men and of Gods," which is at least implied in Ugarit where El "The Father of Man" is also the consort of Asherah who bore the "seventy[7] gods."

In the following discussion there are many such points that have a general character so that individually they prove little or nothing. Collectively, they have a cumulative value; but without supporting evidence they would add up to something less than a proof. However, the specific and striking parallels in the paragraphs below establish the relationship between Homer and the earlier East. The reader should therefore first view the evidence as a whole. Then, if one wishes to test individual points, one should remember that the cogency of the thesis rests on the parallels of a specific nature and not on those of a general character that are given only to round out the picture.

There is a common atmosphere shared between Homer and Ugarit as is attested in a number of typical situations. For example, Calypso asks Hermes why he came and then offers him refreshments (Odyssey 5:87–91). Similarly El greets Asherah thus:

> "Why has Lady Asherah of the Sea come?
> Why came the Creatress of the Gods?
> Art thou hungry?

5. It is always possible that future discoveries in Phoenicia, Cyprus, or on the coast of Asia Minor will provide still stronger contacts with Homer. But we can only base our discussion on the material now available.

6. Cyrus H. Gordon, *Ugaritic Textbook,* Rome, 1967, p. 472, no. 2145.

7. The number is a literary cliché for a large brood; it is not to be taken literally. It occurs in the Bible as well (see Exodus 1:5; Judges 8:30; 2 Kings 10:1) and in the postbiblical tradition of the seventy sons of Noah (the Bible does not use this number in Genesis 10, and to arrive at this figure one must do so some juggling; see Gary A. Rendsburg, *The Redaction of Genesis,* Winona Lake, Ind., 1986, pp. 17–18).

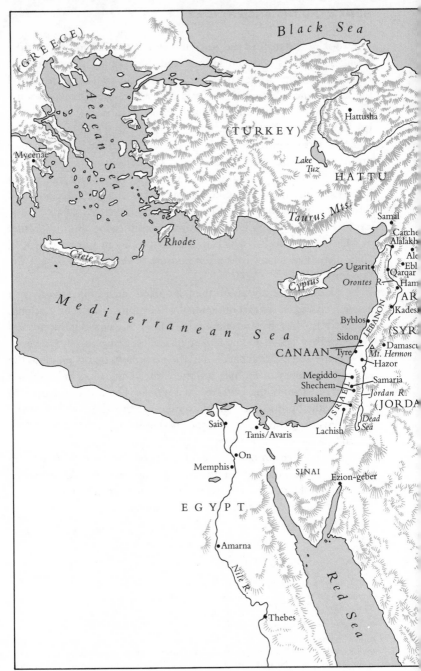

MAP 1: THE ANCIENT NEAR EAST

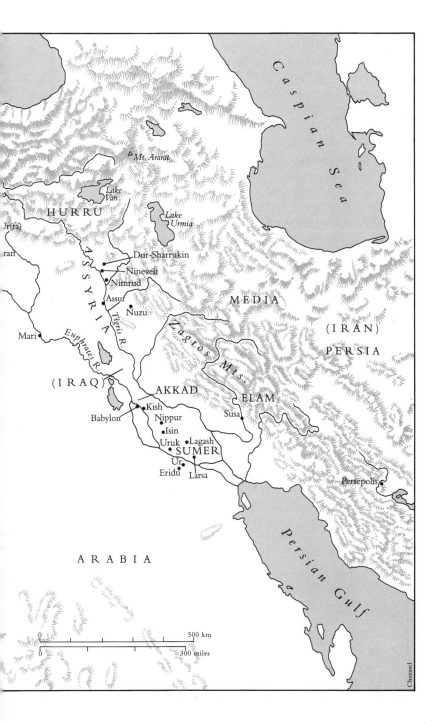

Caspian Sea

Mt. Ararat

Lake Van

HURRU

Lake Urmia

Ur(fa)

ran

ASSYRIA

Dur-Sharrukin

Nineveh

Nimrud

Assur

Nuzu

MEDIA

(IRAN)

PERSIA

Mari

Euphrates R.

Tigris R.

Zagros Mts.

(IRAQ)

AKKAD

Kish

Babylon

Nippur

Isin

ELAM

Susa

Uruk

Lagash

SUMER

Ur

Eridu

Larsa

Persepolis

ARABIA

Persian Gulf

0                    500 km

0                    300 miles

Chazaud

99

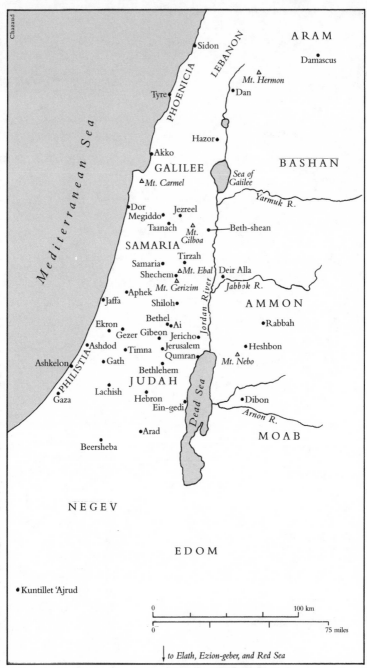

MAP 2: ISRAEL AND ENVIRONS

> Then have a [morsel]!
> Or art thou thirsty?
> Then have a [drink]!
> Eat or drink!
> Eat bread from the tables
> Drink wine from the goblets
> From a cup of gold the blood of vines!"
>                                    (51:IV:31–38)

This parallel looks general enough but it takes on a more specific character when combined with other passages. The Ugaritic emphasis on serving wine in a golden cup is shared with Homer; e.g., "bearing in his right hand honey-hearted wine in a cup of gold" (Od. 15:148–49). The frequent Homeric epithet "honey-hearted" (as also in Od. 13:53, etc.), or its variant "honey-sweet" (Od. 14:78), for wine recalls the frequent parallelism between "wine" and "honey" in Ugaritic (Kret:72, 165). Moreover, the mixing of wine is common to Homer (Od. 7: 179, 183, etc.) and Ugarit (Anat:I:17; etc.). The theme of entertaining guests brings up still another parallel: In Ugarit the word for "soul" includes the idea of "appetite." The Homeric "when he had dined and satisfied his soul [=appetite] with food" (Od. 5:95) is paralleled in Ugarit where the guest's "soul" is satisfied with food and drink (127:11; etc.).

While such general parallels to Homeric expressions are most abundant in Ugarit, there are also some in other Near East texts. For example, the Homeric notion that gods may assume the guise of human strangers in order to check on men's behavior (Od. 17:483–87) is paralleled in the Bible, where divine beings in human form are entertained by Abraham and then proceed to Sodom, where they observe firsthand the iniquity of the people there (Genesis 18: 1–19:25).

"Good at the [war] cry" is a Homeric epithet, applied in Od. 15:14, 67 to Menelaus. The war cry is a heroic feature that appears in ancient Near East sources. Thus in the Story of Sinuhe, the hero Sinuhe slays his foe and then stands upon him and yells. Also, when Enkidu tells Shamhat that he intends to shout in Erech, he means that he will vanquish Gilgamesh. That is why Shamhat informs him that Gilgamesh is the stronger so that Enkidu should not be sanguine.

Elements of everyday life often appear in the epics. In such an instance in Homer, the oriental parallel may come from business documents rather than literature. The offending guests (in the words of Eurymachus) try to appease Odysseus by promising: "We shall each bring you the worth of twenty oxen and pay you back in bronze and gold until your heart is warmed" (Od. 22:57–59). In Mesopotamian business documents such as the Nuzu tablets, there are standard equivalents of fixed sums stated in terms of animals or metal.[8] Furthermore, "until one's heart is warmed" has numerous parallels in the Sumerian, Akkadian, Aramaic, and Egyptian business formula "his heart is good" = "he is paid in full to his complete satisfaction."[9]

Idiomatic clichés are shared by Ugarit and Homer. The Homeric "not yet was the word fully uttered" (Il. 10:540; Od. 16:11 etc.)—when such and such happened—is not only paralleled in Ugarit but also clarifies a grammatical obscurity in the Ugaritic texts. A repeated formula "from his mouth the word verily / not went forth" (1 Aqhat:113, 141)—when such and such happened—has been erroneously translated with "verily" instead of "not," for both meanings can be expressed by the prefix *l-* before verbs in Ugaritic. However, the Homeric parallel provides the meaning for the Ugaritic, which improves the interpretation, because "the word had not [yet] gone out of his mouth" is more vivid than "verily had gone out"; and in a lush literature like Ugaritic, vividness is more in character than restraint. A further cliché shared by Homer and Ugarit is "another thing will I tell you" (Il. 1:297; Od. 16:299; 17:548; etc.; Ugaritic text 51:I:20; etc.).

Concern for someone is expressed as far back as Gudea (Cylinder A:19:24) by the simile "like a cow that looks toward her calf." However in both Homer and Ugarit the simile is specifically applied before violent and vengeful action. We may thus compare "as a bitch stands over her tender whelps growling when she sees a man she does not know and is eager to fight, so his heart growled within him in his wrath at their evil deeds" (Od. 20:14–16) with

> "As with the heart of a cow toward her calf,
> As with the heart of a ewe toward her lamb,
> So is the heart of Anat toward Baal" (49:II:6–9)

said of Anat before she wreaked vengeance on Mot for Baal.

8. Cyrus H. Gordon, "Nuzi Tablets Relating to Theft," *Orientalia* 5, 1936, p. 312.

9. See Raymond Westbrook, "The Phrase 'His Heart is Satisfied' in Ancient Near Eastern Legal Sources," *Journal of the American Oriental Society* 111, 1991, pp. 219–24.

A literary device characteristic of the entire area under consideration is the one whereby one or more digits in a number are increased by 1 for climactic effect. Thus Homer describes loudness "as when 9,000 warriors or 10,000 cry in battle" (Il. 5:860–61). Compare Ugaritic "he took 66 towns, yea 77 cities; 80, Baal—90, Baal—" (51:VII:9–12). Here we may also point to a Hittite parallel "77 I slew; 88 I slew"[10] although Hebrew, Akkadian and other oriental examples are common, too.

Social attitudes often span Homer and the Semitic East. Neither Homer (Il. 1:348–63) nor the bards of Ugarit (Kret:30) saw any shame in great heroes weeping copiously.

The Homeric shame of one's corpse being devoured by dogs (Il. 22:75–76) or vultures (Od. 22:30) on the surface seems universal to us, who share the tradition of decent burial. However, consideration of Zoroastrian customs, which call for the exposing of the dead to be devoured by vultures, and which prohibit burial as a pollution of the land, disabuses us of the illusion of universal accord in such matters. Hence it is not altogether idle to recall that (among other biblical examples) the abominable Jezebel's corpse was devoured by dogs (1 Kings 21:23; 2 Kings 9:36). Also the curse of one's body being eaten by the fowl of heaven is common in the Bible (Genesis 40:19; 1 Samuel 17:46). In the Ugaritic Legend of Aqhat, the hero is slain for the sake of his wondrous bow and is devoured by an eagle to climax the tragedy. While the relationship, if any, is distorted, it is at least interesting to note that in Od. 22:30 the penalty for slaying a man with bow and arrow is to be devoured by vultures.

All through the Odyssey, wisdom and guile are equated. The hero Odysseus himself is "he of many wiles." Od. 13:294–99 shows that wisdom and guile are identified, to the credit of the goddess Athene no less than the mortal Odysseus. This standard of values pervades the patriarchal narratives in Genesis (particularly as concerns Jacob and Laban) and still persists among the Bedouins. To be sure, many people in America today actually accept the identification; but our mores are officially against it, which was not the case with the milieu of Jacob or of Odysseus.

That guile even on the part of God was thinkable in Israel down to at least Ahab's time is reflected in 1 Kings 12:23, where a true

10. See Cyrus H. Gordon, *Ugaritic Manual,* Rome, 1955, p. 41, n. 3.

prophet of Yahwe, Micaiah, states that Yahwe had sent deceptive dreams. Similarly Zeus sends a false dream to Agamemnon (Il. 2:1–15). Not only is this of interest for the history of ideas, but it brings up an important question of literary style. The dream is related with verbal variation in Il. 2:23–34 and again in 2:60–70. Compare also a similar repetition with differences in 2:157–65 and 2:173–81. Among many examples of this phenomenon is Priam's message concerning the ransom of Hector's body in Il. 24:144–58 repeated in a slightly longer version in 24:171–87. Nowhere throughout ancient literature (Homeric, cuneiform, Egyptian, Hebrew, etc.) did the authors reproduce a text with verbal exactness. Instead, almost always there are literary or stylistic reasons for slightly altering the repeated section of a text.[11]

The structure of ancient Near East poetry differs considerably from that of Homer. In the ancient Near East, parallelistic repetition is the poetic form. The following is a Ugaritic example but the poetic structure of the whole ancient Near East follows the same pattern:

> "The mountains will bring thee much silver
> The hills, the choicest of gold" (51:V:77–78).

The parallelism is in thought rather than in syllables or stresses.

The position of Ugarit as the known ancient Near Eastern culture closest to the Homeric World is brought out by a clear parallel: Dogs are accepted in the Homeric household; thus they are in Priam's palace (see especially Il. 22:69), while Argos is the pet dog of Odysseus (Od. 17:291–319). The Semites have a general aversion to dogs, which they regarded as useful for watching sheep, but not fit for admission to the home.[12] Therefore dogs do not figure as pets in the Bible or cuneiform literature. The great exception is Ugarit, where in the Legend of Kret (:123, 226; 125:2, 100), dogs are present in the royal residences of Kings Pebel and Kret.

Situations that in themselves are common enough may constitute organic parallels because of the emphasis on those situations as wor-

---

11. The whole gamut of ancient literature is covered by G. Douglas Young, "Ugaritic Prosody," *Journal of Near Eastern Studies* 9, 1950, pp. 124–33. On repetition in biblical literature, see especially Meir Sternberg, *The Poetics of Biblical Narrative*, Bloomington, Ind., 1985, pp. 365–440.

12. This is still true in the Arab World. It is interesting to note (at least in northeast Iraq, where I [C. H. G.] observed it, but probably over a wide area) that an exception is made in the case of the saluki, which is not considered a dog in Arabic terminology.

thy of saga. Hephaistus's making armor for Achilles (Il. 18:478–613) is paralleled by Kothar-and-Hasis's making the bow for Aqhat (2 Aqhat:V:12–13; cf.:VI:24). Thetis, coming for Achilles' armor, finds Hephaistus at his bellows working on other artistic creations (Il. 18:372–79) much as the delegation approaching Kothar-and-Hasis to construct Baal's palace finds the divine artisan busy at his bellows on other works of cunning craftsmanship (51:I:24–44).

Telemachus, after ordering his mother to return to feminine affairs, tells her "the bow shall be for all men but most of all for me" (Od. 21:352–53). Aqhat brought on his own doom by telling the goddess Anat that the bow is for men and not for females (2 Aqhat:VI:39–40). Aqhat thus refused to give her the bow though she tried to persuade him by offering him immortality (2 Aqhat:VI:26–30); even as Calypso offered immortality to Odysseus, who, like Aqhat, refused it (Od. 23:335–37).

Among the abominations hated by Baal is the "abuse of hand-maids" at banquets. The word for "abuse" is *tdmm,* which is often mistranslated as "murmuring," though the correct Arabic cognate confirms the meaning "abuse."[13] The same conclusion is indicated by Homer, who singles out the abuse of one's host's handmaids at banquets as a most grievous offense committed by Penelope's suitors in Odysseus's halls (Od. 20:318–19 and 22:37). Another Ugaritic obscurity is clarified by a Homeric parallel: In Kret (:128, 285) it has been a question as to whether one of the gifts offered by Pebel to Kret should be translated "charioteers of horses and a chariot" or "three horses and a chariot," because the same consonants express "three" and "charioteer" in the related Hebrew language. But that "three" is correct is indicated by the Homeric "three horses and a well-polished chariot" (Od. 4:590–91) specified as a lavish gift, quite as in Ugaritic.

In Homer as in Ugarit,[14] horses were used only to draw chariots. "Charioteers (and infantry)" (Il. 11:529, 720, 745; 12:66, etc.) should not be translated "horsemen" as is sometimes done in the widely used Loeb Classics edition (e.g., for Il. 11:529), for there was no cavalry in the Homeric World. Besides the charioteers, there are spearmen, bowmen, and slingers (Il. 13:716) in the Homeric armies

13. I. Yasin, *The Lexical Relation between Ugaritic and Arabic,* New York, 1952, p. 148, no. 71.

14. There are no references to horses in the myths of Ugarit but only in the Legends of Aqhat (in the so-called Rephaim texts = numbers 121–24) and Kret (and of course in certain prose texts). The translation of *lsmm* (49: VI:21) as "horses" should be abandoned. The myths reflect a culture before the introduction of the horse. The legends are of later origin.

as in the Ugaritic.[15] The Trojan soldiers were grouped in fifties (Il. 8:563) precisely as the Hebrews (2 Kings 2:16–17; Isaiah 3:3; etc.). Moreover, there may have been a predilection for grouping companies in fifties (Od. 20:49). The fair distribution of spoils among the troops is attributed to the precedent of Odysseus (Od. 9:40–42, 548–49) in Homer just as it is ascribed to David's precedent in Israel (1 Samuel 30:23–25).

When Telemachus insists that he has come of age and knows everything, he says "I know all things, the good and the evil" (Od. 20:309–10). Here the pair of antonyms indicate totality and mean "everything," exactly as Egyptian "evil-good" and Hebrew "good and evil" in such passages as the so-called "Fall of Man" in Genesis.[16]

Now we may consider a more striking and specific parallel between Homer and the ancient Near East. In the Gilgamesh Epic, Enkidu sealed his fate through affronting Ishtar by hurling a bull's leg at her. In Homer (Od. 20:299) Ctesippus commits a terrible affront by hurling a bull's foot (mistranslated "hoof" in the Loeb Classics edition). The deed is avenged in Homer (Od. 22:287–91) even as in the Gilgamesh Epic. Surely the singling out for epic celebration of so specialized a phenomenon is not fortuitous. A cultural common denominator must be assumed.

The curse that a herdsman be attacked or devoured by his own dogs (Od. 21:362–65) is reminiscent of Ishtar's cruelty whereby she changed a shepherd into a wolf so his own dogs menaced him.

The speech of Xanthus (Il. 19:404–17), the horse of Achilles, is of a piece with the talking of Balaam's ass in the Bible (Numbers 22:28–30). The ability of Balaam's ass to see things (verse 27) invisible to Balaam is matched by Athene's invisibility to Telemachus, while the dogs perceive her (Od. 16:159–63).

Jacob's besting an angel in physical combat (Genesis 32:29) is paralleled in Homer's account of woes inflicted by men on gods (Il. 5:382–404).

The heroes mentioned in the Catalogue of the Ships (Il. 2) are to be compared with the catalogue of David's heroes (2 Samuel 23:8–39). Both lists are of a similar character and may well rest on authentic originals with the result that such catalogues have more historicity than the saga that flanks them.

15. Cyrus H. Gordon, *Ugaritic Literature,* Rome, 1949, p. 124.

16. See above, Chapter II, pp. 36–37.

Definitions of a good woman have considerable variety. One of the repeated virtues of womanhood in Homer is skill at fine handiwork (Od. 16:158; 24:128). This is matched in the account of the model woman in Proverbs 31:10–31, which is unique in the literature of the ancient Near East and may be of Mediterranean rather than inland Judean origin.

The idea that there is "a proper time for each thing upon the earth" (Od. 19:592–93) is expressed more fully in Ecclesiastes (3:1–8). However, the early date of the Homeric formulation shows how risky it is to view the ideas in Ecclesiastes as necessarily of very late origin; indeed his ideas are in most cases very old.

Another common bond between the Homeric World and the ancient Near East is the regular custom of sending messengers in pairs; thus Il. 1:320 ff. (etc.), 2 Kings 5:23 (etc.), and at every turn in Ugaritic.

Above we have seen how passages from Homer have clarified some ambiguities in Semitic (especially Ugaritic) texts. The opposite can also occur, as the following one little illustration demonstrates. In Hebrew the combination "yesterday + day-before-yesterday" is a regular idiom for "formerly." There is no doubt that the same idiom occurs in Homer (e.g., Il. 2:303), where we should translate "formerly" and not "it was as yesterday or the day before" (as is done in the Loeb Classics and elsewhere).

The value of grasping that Israel and Greece are both part of the same complex of East Mediterranean nations is considerable. The conventional Jewish and Christian reader of the Bible may find it relatively easy to understand the postexilic periods (after 538 B.C.E.). Men like Ezra and Nehemiah (who backed a program that called for enforcing Scripture, for returning to Zion, for rebuilding the Temple, for reviving the Hebrew language, for discouraging mixed marriages, etc.)[17] are fairly comprehensible to the Bible reader today. But the modern reader will be at a loss to understand the Patriarchs or David or for that matter most of preexilic biblical history. David has more in common with the heroes of the Iliad than with Ezra and Nehemiah. His command of a band of rough men, his impetuousness, his winning of a princess by slaying Philistines instead of paying a brideprice, his amours, his intimate love of Jonathan (2 Samuel 1:26)—all of these and other features fit rather into the milieu of Homer's heroic

17. See Chapter XVII, p. 290.

age than into the framework of synagogue and church. To take a clear and specific illustration that should give no offense: When the men of Jabesh-gilead confer final honors on the corpses of Saul and his sons, they burn the bodies before burying them (1 Samuel 31:12–13) exactly in the Homeric manner of honoring heroes like Patroclus and Hector. Scholars who read back Jewish and Christian burial customs into the Books of Samuel have found the text incomprehensible, corrupt, and in need of emendation. Yet the very strangeness of the text shows that it cannot be a product of later Jewish times; it is obviously an ancient statement that has not been modified in keeping with later customs. The historic context leaves no doubt as to what happened: Saul was killed by the Philistines, who were of the same East Mediterranean origin as the Myceneans in the Trojan War. Both Troy and Beth-shan (where Saul was slain) were cities in the same cultural continuum during the same heroic age. The early histories of the Hebrews and Greeks were intricately interrelated, and neither can be understood in isolation from the other.[18]

18. For numerous parallels between the Homeric and biblical corpora, see Cyrus H. Gordon, "Homer and Bible," *Hebrew Union College Annual* 26, 1955, pp. 43–108 (published in monograph form as *Homer and Bible,* Ventnor, N.J., 1967).

# CHAPTER VIII

# The Patriarchal Age

The Israelites traced their origins back to three individuals: Abraham, Isaac, and Jacob, known as the Patriarchs. Their story is told in the book of Genesis, and in a moment we will consider this material. But first we need to discuss a group of documents from the Amarna Age that has revolutionized our knowledge of the Patriarchal Period. The texts were unearthed at the town of Nuzu[1] in northeastern Mesopotamia and they provide us with a more complete picture of the community than we have for any other town of antiquity. The tablets, dating from the fifteenth and fourteenth centuries B.C.E., come from private archives and are written in a clumsy Babylonian, because the native speech of the people was Hurrian. Those Babylonian texts have a number of Hurrian loanwords that are a source for reconstructing the language of the Hurrians.

Among the Nuzu texts is a series of tablets recording the lawsuit filed by the citizens against the mayor, who was guilty of complicity with a kidnaping ring, of accepting bribes, and stealing wood and misappropriating workers from public projects for his own purposes, and of shady dealings with a woman of the community. The interesting thing is that the people were able to appeal to the courts of law

1. For accounts of life in Nuzu, see Edward Chiera, *They Wrote on Clay,* Chicago, 1938; and Cyrus H. Gordon, *Adventures in the Nearest East,* London, 1957, pp. 105–20. For on-going research into the Nuzu tablets, consult the series edited by David I. Owen and Gernot Wilhelm, eds., *Studies on the Civilization and Culture of Nuzi and the Hurrians* (Winona Lake, Ind., 1981–). Many scholars refer to the name of city as Nuzi (in the genitive case), but we opt for the form Nuzu (in the nominative case).

and present their case against the mayor himself and bring him to justice.

Most of the archives, however, are private documents pertaining to personal and family affairs. Some tablets are about the ʿApîru who enter into servitude, not en masse like the Israelites in Egypt, but individually contract to remain enslaved for life in the house of some wealthy person in the community. Their goal was simply economic security, for being a permanent slave in a wealthy household guaranteed food, clothing, and shelter for life, whereas freedom was often precarious for the poor. These ʿApîru, however, show no trace of Hebrew names or Hebrew religion.

Most of the archives dealing with private affairs hinge on the institution of adoption. Inasmuch as land could not be sold legally, sale of land was often masked as adoption. In other words, a man would ostensibly adopt a son in order to pass on property to him, and the "son" would in exchange give the adopter a "filial gift." A rich man might be the adopted son of hundreds of less fortunate neighbors, whose lands he thus snapped up. Playing such a game of make-believe adoption certainly fooled no one in Nuzu; but, being within the law, it was acceptable. Since the archives of Nuzu extend over a period of four to five generations, it is possible to trace the fortunes of various families, as well as of individuals, amassed mainly through acquiring land by fictive adoptions.[2]

There are also real adoptions in Nuzu, especially in the case of people without a son, who adopt one in order to keep the continuity of the family and estate, to perform filial service during the lifetime of the parents and the mourning rites after their death. Even a slave might be adopted as a son in Nuzu. However, there is normally a clause stating that if, after an adopted son comes into the family, a real son is born to the parents, the real son shall become the chief heir and the adopted son shall be relegated to a secondary position in the family. Very sacred is the possession of the household gods. Hence when a man is adopted, there may be the proviso that if a real son is born to become the chief heir, the adopted son shall not have title to the gods of the father. Perhaps possessing the gods was in some way connected with being head of the family.

---

2. The prohibition against alienating land outside the family held also in ancient Israel, whose law (Leviticus 25:8–17) calls for the return of land to the original owners every fiftieth (=jubilee) year.

Adoption is sometimes tied in with marriage in Nuzu. A father without sons may adopt his son-in-law, thus at least making the grandchildren his by blood.

The purpose of marriage in these documents is not companionship but an heir. As a result, if a woman who is bought as a wife does not produce an heir, she may be obliged by clauses in her marriage contract to supply her husband with another woman. The wife's position could be protected by a clause to keep the second woman in a servile status to her. The children of the second woman could be protected by a clause forbidding the wife to expel them.[3]

The analogies to be pointed out presently, between the society of Nuzu and of the Hebrew Patriarchs are so numerous and striking that many scholars agree that the patriarchal narratives in Genesis portray a genuine social picture. Because some of the phenomena are known from other cuneiform records, some scholars have denied any relevance of the Nuzu tablets for the study of the Bible.[4] But the fact remains that no set of known texts offers as many parallels to the patriarchal narratives as do the Nuzu tablets. Clearly the society at Nuzu is the single society closest to the life of the patriarchs. We shall look soon into the various aspects of the narratives and see that some of the reputed anachronisms and legendary features are correct historically. But before comparing the Genesis narratives and the Nuzu tablets, first we must comment on issues of chronology, geography, and socioeconomic background.

As noted above, the three generations of the Patriarchal Age are represented by Abraham, Isaac, and Jacob.[5] Jacob, in turn, is repre-

3. For a selection of Nuzu texts translated into English, see James B. Pritchard, ed., *Ancient Near Eastern Texts,* Princeton, 1955, pp. 219–20.

4. See most importantly Thomas L. Thompson, *The Historicity of the Patriarchal Narratives* (Berlin, 1974); and John Van Seters, *Abraham in History and Tradition* (New Haven, 1975). The entire issue is treated thoughtfully, and with balance, by Barry L. Eichler, "Nuzi and the Bible: A Retrospective," in H. Behrens, D. Loding, and M. T. Roth, eds., *Dumu-e₂-dub-ba-a: Studies in Honor of Ake W. Sjöberg,* Philadelphia, 1989, pp. 107–19.

5. The following discussion is not meant to rule out schematic and artificial elements. The settlement of the Patriarchs in Canaan, their treaties with the natives, and the Divine Promise were reshaped and used to justify the Conquest. Moreover, the origin of the "twelve" tribes, each from a son (or grandson) of Jacob, is certainly paternistic and calculated to instill a feeling of close kinship among the tribes of the Israelite amphictyony. But all this does not mean that the traditions are entirely fictional. The Age of Discovery in which we live has, to the contrary, shown that the traditions fit into genuine historic contexts that cannot possibly have been created out of thin air. We must avoid overskepticism as much as gullibility. Critical evaluation against the background of the available facts is the only course for us to follow.

sented as the father of twelve sons, the most famous of whom is
Joseph. Through another of his sons, Levi, Jacob is the great-great-
grandfather of Moses (Exodus 6:16–20). As demonstrated below (see
Chapter IX, pp. 149–52), the Exodus from Egypt occurred c. 1175
B.C.E. under the leadership of Moses. The story makes it clear that
Moses already was advanced in years and that he had grown children
of his own, namely, Gershom and Eliezer. If we assume that a generation spans approximately thirty years,[6] we are able to calculate a relative chronology for the events of the period. Thus, if we fix the date
of adulthood of Gershom and Eliezer at 1175 and of Moses at 1205,
we can work back to an approximate date of 1295 B.C.E. for Joseph,
Levi, and the other ten brothers. Working still further back, we arrive
at approximate dates of 1325 for Jacob, 1355 for Isaac, and 1385 for
Abraham. This date for Abraham puts him firmly in the Amarna
Age, and thus makes the evidence from Nuzu all the more relevant.[7]

As has been shown, the above conclusions are compatible with the
biblical genealogies, but not with the biblical figures in terms of
actual years. The latter, as is well known, point to a far longer span
of time. One passage (Genesis 15:13) predicts that Abraham's descendants will be afflicted in a foreign land for four hundred years.[8] In
another passage (Exodus 12:40–41), the stay of the Hebrews in Egypt
is given as 430 years. But it is obvious that these numbers are not to
be taken literally, for they are idealized figures very typical of the epic
tradition.

In accepting the evidence of the genealogies and rejecting the year
reckonings presented in the Bible, we base our conclusion on addi-

---

6. Many scholars assume a lower figure, such as twenty-five years or even twenty years per
generation. But the evidence of ancient Near Eastern king lists and the evidence extracted
from ancient marriage documents suggests that thirty years per generation is a much more
accurate figure. See David P. Henige, *The Chronology of Oral Tradition,* Oxford, 1974; and
Martha T. Roth, "Age at Marriage and the Household: A Study of Neo-Babylonian and
Neo-Assyrian Forms," *Comparative Studies in Society and History* 29, 1987, pp. 715–47. In our
survey of standard works by biblical scholars, we have found only one individual who utilized
the figure of thirty years, namely K. A. Kitchen, *Ancient Orient and Old Testament,* Downers
Grove, Ill., 1966, p. 72.

7. We hasten to emphasize, of course, that these dates are in no way to be taken as an absolute
chronology, rather they are a rough guide to fixing the relative chronology of the period. Not
until datable texts, with unambiguous mention of any of the Patriarchs or their descendants
(such as Joseph), are found will we be in a position to speak more accurately.

8. For the conventional status of "400 years" in Ramesside Egypt, cf. "The Era of the City of
Tanis," in Pritchard, *Ancient Near Eastern Texts,* pp. 252–53.

tional evidence as well. Among the tribal Semites, such as Arab nomads down to the present day, there is a great feeling for genealogy, and it is not unusual for an Arab to be able accurately to recite the names of his ancestors for ten or fifteen generations covering several hundred years. Yet that nomadic Arab will not know how old he is. Tribal Semites have no birth certificates, and while they memorize genealogies, they keep no track of birthdays. Accordingly, when we choose between the two conflicting chronological schemes of the Patriarchal Period, we are forced by the nature of that type of Semitic society to lean more on the genealogies than on the reckoning in terms of years.[9]

From the above discussion of chronology, we move now to a consideration of the geography involved. Abraham was born in a place called Ur of the Chaldeans (Genesis 11:28, 31) and then lived for some time in Haran as well. The latter is a well known site in northern Mesoptomia. The former is most likely to be identified with present day Urfa, also in northern Mesopotamia.[10] The general area of northern Mesopotamia was a meeting ground of various peoples, most importantly the Amorites, the Arameans, and the Hurrians.

The personal names of the Patriarchs are of an Amorite type, and as noted earlier (see Chapter II, p. 38, n. 11), the divine name Yahwe appears in Amorite personal names.[11] Abraham's family in Mesopotamia is Aramean (note Deuteronomy 26:5); his kinsmen who stayed on in Mesopotamia are called Arameans (Genesis 25:20; 28:5; 31:20, 24) and they speak Aramaic (Genesis 31:47). The customs reflected

9. On the general accuracy of the genealogical records preserved in the Bible, see in detail Gary A. Rendsburg, "The Internal Consistency and Historical Validity of the Biblical Genealogies," *Vetus Testamentum* 40, 1990, pp. 185–206. More skeptical is Robert R. Wilson, *Genealogy and History in the Biblical World,* New Haven, 1977, who noted that "genealogies seem to have been created and preserved for domestic, politico-jural, and religious purposes," yet he also admitted that they "may contain accurate information" and that for a given genealogy we often "have no reason to question its accuracy" (pp. 199–200).

10. Since the time of Woolley (see above, Chapter I, p. 24), many scholars have identified Abraham's Ur with the famous Ur in southern Mesopotamia. But this identification is incorrect. For details, see Cyrus H. Gordon, "Abraham and the Merchants of Ura," *Journal of Near Eastern Studies* 17, 1958, pp. 28–31. In all probability, however, Ur of the Chaldeans was established as a commercial colony of the famous Ur of Sumer in southern Mesopotamia.

11. The best studies of Amorite names are H. B. Huffmon, *Amorite Personal Names in the Mari Texts,* Baltimore, 1965; and I. J. Gelb, *Computer-Aided Analysis of Amorite,* Chicago, 1980. On the Amorites in general, see M. Liverani, "The Amorites," in D. J. Wiseman, ed., *Peoples of Old Testament Times,* Oxford, 1973, pp. 100–133.

in the Patriarchal stories, meanwhile, are of a piece with the practices of the Hurrians as known from Nuzu. Thus, while it would be unwise to label the Patriarchs as specifically Amorite or Aramean or Hurrian, it is clear that the cultural world of Abraham before he migrated to Canaan included elements of all three peoples in northern Mesopotamia.

Abram (only later was his name changed to Abraham) left this Amorite-Aramean-Hurrian world of northern Mesopotamia and came to the land of Canaan. The Bible explains this migration as Abram's acceptance of the divine command (Genesis 12:1–2). The historian who seeks another explanation for Abram's movement from Mesopotamia to Canaan can point to the evidence of merchants from Ur who plied their trade in Canaan. The Patriarchs, far from being desert nomads (as is commonly assumed), gravitate around cities such as Shechem, Gerar, and Beersheba; they have contacts with kings in Canaan as well as with the pharaoh of Egypt; and the Bible repeatedly states that the Patriarchs were rich in gold and silver, as well as in cattle. Aside from the intrinsic worth of herds and flocks, we must remember that they served as a common medium of exchange in the Near East. Moreover, unlike precious metal, they have advantages of great service to wandering traders: They are a form of wealth that increases naturally, and are capable of locomotion. The Bible, then, portrays the Patriarchs not as shepherds, but rather as wealthy individuals of prestige. Note, moreover, that generally they are portrayed as possessing servants who care for the animals (Genesis 13:7, 26:20). Also, when they do utilize their silver for purchase, it is in shekels "current to the merchant" (Genesis 23:16).

The collateral evidence that supports this picture of the Patriarchs comes from Ugarit, where there is reference to foreign merchants from Ur outpacing the local businessmen of Ugarit. The men of Ugarit eventually complained to the king of the Hittites, whose territory included both Ur and Ugarit, and a deal was struck. The deal was that the merchants of Ur could trade in Ugarit, but they could not own real estate there and they could not settle there permanently. Apparently, such traveling merchants normally were prevented from settling down and acquiring real estate in Canaan. The Bible is therefore at pains to tell how the Patriarchs, by treaty and purchase, overcame these disabilities and gained the right to live on their own land in Canaan. A striking parallel to the aforementioned case from Ugarit is the offer that the prince of Shechem presents to Jacob and his family (Genesis 34:10). The same three rights are referred to, though in this case, the Hebrews gain all three rights (trading, settling, and acquiring real estate).[12]

In Genesis 14:13 Abram is called a Hebrew, marking a clean break with his Mesopotamian past. He had already collected a group of followers so that he was able to muster a company of armed men in the field and, as small wandering sheikhs went, hold his own in reputable fashion. He met a Canaanite priest of El Elyon "God the Most High," whom Abram, and subsequent Hebrew tradition, identified with Yahwe.

Since Abram had no child of his own, he adopted his slave Eliezer as his heir (Genesis 15:2–3) but, as in the Nuzu tablets, with the proviso that if a real son should be born, the real son would be the heir (Genesis 15:4). The text does not use any word meaning "adopt[ion]" but the interpretation of the passage is no longer in any doubt since the Nuzu tablets have come to light.[13]

In the patriarchal narratives (Genesis 14:5) it is stated that among the inhabitants of Canaan are the Rephaim, whose mention is often misconstrued as a mythological allusion. However, as we have observed, the references to the Rephaim in Ugaritic administrative documents show that real people bore that name in Canaan of the Amarna Age.

Inasmuch as Sarai, the wife of Abram, was childless, she gave Hagar as a concubine to Abram for the purpose of producing an heir (Genesis 16:2). This is not an isolated instance of unfeminine generosity, but in accordance with the laws and customs of the times as we know from the Nuzu and other cuneiform tablets. It is interesting to note that Hagar later receives an annunciation that she is to bear a child (Genesis 16:11). As noted above, such annunciations are typical of Canaanite literature and we find them in the Ugaritic documents as well as the Bible. The angel predicting Ishmael's birth tells Hagar that the lad will be "a wild ass of a man" (Genesis 16:12). This is not an insult but a compliment because the wild ass was then to be

12. See Cyrus H. Gordon, "Abraham of Ur," in D. W. Thomas and W. D. McHardy, eds., *Hebrew and Semitic Studies Presented to Godfrey Rolles Driver,* Oxford, 1963, pp. 77–84.

13. The Nuzu evidence is collected in Cyrus H. Gordon, "Biblical Customs and the Nuzu Tablets," *Biblical Archaeologist* 3, 1940, pp. 1–12.

found in the desert and it was the choicest beast of the hunt.

Abram entered into an eternal covenant[14] with God, whereby, on the one hand, God agreed to be the God of Abram and his descendants and, on the other hand, Abram and his descendants agreed to be God's own people; and whereby the land of Canaan would be forever associated with this people and with this God; in token whereof, the family of Abram would for all time practice the rite of circumcision. To commemorate the covenant, Abram's name was changed to Abraham, and Sarai's name to Sarah. Ishmael was thirteen years old when he was circumcised and since he is recognized as the father of the Arabs, the Muslim custom is to circumcise at about thirteen years of age. By contrast, the Jews circumcise at the age of eight days, following the precedent of their ancestor Isaac, the second son of Abraham.

In due time Sarah, the chief wife, bore a son Isaac, whose name means "laughs." The Bible explains it as referring to either the laughter of Abraham (Genesis 17:17) or Sarah (Genesis 18:12) because they were so advanced in years that it seemed ridiculous for them to expect a child. Scholars have been more inclined to explain the name as referring to the laughter of God, which is plausible in that God (expressed or understood) figures frequently in Hebrew names. Formerly, scholars thought the divine laughter was that of terrifying scorn (Psalms 2:4). But now that the Ugaritic texts refer to the good-natured laughter of El, scholars are beginning to feel the laughter implied by the name Isaac is kindly. In the Homeric poems the laughter of the gods is jovial, not scornful. So comparative evidence, outside as well as inside Canaan, points to God's kindly laughter, which is better suited for a congenial personal name.

The closeness of men to gods in this period is a social[15] phenomenon for which we must develop a feeling if we are to understand the

---

14. Covenants between a man and a god are attested repeatedly in ancient Near Eastern literatures, including Homeric Greek. Many a man, in exchange for divine protection, promised to worship the god; for the gods required human worship even as men needed divine help. The importance of the biblical Covenant is therefore not its structure, but what it led to through Judaism, Christianity, and Islam. In general (and this holds for India or Greece as well as Israel), the importance of epic saga (such as the patriarchal narratives) lies not so much in the historic kernel as in the ideas and institutions, which through the epic saga have become part of subsequent culture.

15. To what extent the patriarchal institutions are those of actual life, and to what extent they reflect epic tradition, can now be outlined by the Nuzu (for real society) and Ugaritic (for epic) parallels, respectively. Cf. Chapter XIX, pp. 317–18.

biblical texts. In our society if a man claims to have divine visions, most likely he would be considered in need of psychological help. In Hebrew society it was not abnormal for people to experience theophanies, that is, to see divine manifestations, and converse with the apparition. Nor would it be odd to attribute divinity to strangers, whose behavior might be appropriate to angels on divine missions. From the biblical viewpoint, it was nothing supernatural for three divine beings, in the form of men, to visit Abraham, who entertained them in good Bedouin fashion with water for washing before a meal of bread, milk curds, and meat (Genesis 18:1–8).[16] Far from being overawed, Sarah engaged in some eavesdropping and is reported to have been amused at the annunciation of her son (verse 12). Certainly such a reaction would be unthinkable among a people who regarded divine manifestations as supernatural. For the ancient Hebrews, the human and divine communicated freely. Abraham was intimate enough with Yahwe to bargain with him and influence His policies. Abraham's reverence does not prevent him from dealing with God as a personal friend. They discuss a problem, finish speaking, and part (Genesis 18:23–33) until their next meeting, without any unnatural event or circumstance, from the Hebrew point of view. It is not easy for every modern reader to understand the atmosphere of Hebrew society. Background is necessary, but the most important single element in obtaining the background is to read and reread the biblical text until it becomes familiar and real. Nearly always we can know that we understand a biblical passage correctly when its literal[17] meaning fits smoothly into the general context.

Abraham's bargaining with God was on behalf of the people of Sodom and Gomorrah, which God had decided to destroy on

16. Like the Bedouin today, Abraham waited on his guests instead of eating with them. The best sources for understanding the society of the Patriarchs are: (1) the Ugaritic legends, especially where they tie in with Bedouin life among the Arabs, and (2) cuneiform texts (especially from Nuzu) pertaining to law and custom. We hasten to add, however, that the "Bedouin" factor in the patriarchal narratives should not be identified with modern nomadism in Arabia. The Bedouin now in the Near East hinterland are quite unsophisticated compared with the Hebrew Patriarchs, who had dealings with aristocratic and royal Canaanites, Hittites, Egyptians, etc. Today's Bedouin are relatively detached from current history, in sharp contrast with the Patriarchs whose careers unfolded in the hub of the highly cosmopolitan Amarna Age.

17. It cannot be overemphasized that the discoveries of archeology tend to justify the literal meaning of the text as against scholarly and traditional interpretation. This holds not only for the Bible but for ancient texts in general.

account of the cities' evil. Abraham persuaded God to reduce from fifty to ten the number of righteous men that would have to be found there for God to abandon His plan to demolish the cities. Two angels (Genesis 19) proceeded to Sodom where Abraham's nephew Lot received them well but where the mob of townsmen behaved abominably without respect either for strangers or for sexual decency. Sodom and Gomorrah were therefore destroyed, but only after Lot and his family were given a chance to escape. Through their own folly, his wife and sons-in-law perished, leaving Lot and his two daughters as the only survivors. To forestall the extermination of their family, the daughters got their father drunk on successive nights when he unwittingly impregnated them. The elder gave birth to the ancestor of the Moabites; the younger, to the ancestor of the Ammonites (Genesis 19:31–38). Such narratives have a purpose. On the one hand, the story brings out the kinship of Israel with the Transjordanian nations of Moab and Ammon. On the other hand, it illustrates the emphasis on tales that are "worthy of saga" concerning aristocrats in a heroic literature.

Abraham and Isaac are said to have had dealings with Abimelech of Gerar, a king of the Philistines (Genesis 20 and 26). This is generally regarded as an anachronism, because it is held that the Philistines first migrated from Caphtor to Canaan around 1200 B.C.E. However, the fact is that the wave of Sea Peoples, which included Philistines, around 1200 B.C.E. was only a late migration in a long series of migrations that had established various Aegean folk in Canaan long before 1500 B.C.E.[18] By the Amarna Age their settlements had become linguistically Canaanitized so that interpreters are never needed to facilitate relations between Hebrews and Philistines. To be sure, the Philistines left linguistic traces behind them. Indeed the name of "Palestine" (which means "Philistia") recalls their role in Canaan. The rulers of the five major Philistine cities[19] are each called in the

18. The early "Philistines" of the Patriarchal Period are peaceful folk living around Gerar and Beersheba. The later Philistines of the Pentapolis are warlike. It is impossible to regard the earlier Philistines as an anachronistic retrojection of the later ones. If we were dealing with an anachronism, the locale and character of the earlier Philistines would not have been changed. Cf. Y. M. Grintz, "The Philistines of Gerar and the Philistines of the Coast" (written in Hebrew) in *Studies in Memory of Moses Schorr 1874–1941*, New York, 1944, pp. 96–112 (see pp. 108ff.); and Yehezkel Kaufmann, *The Biblical Account of the Conquest of Palestine*, Jerusalem, 1953, p. 50.

19. Gaza, Ashkelon, Ashdod, Gath, and Ekron.

Hebrew Bible, a *seren*—the native Philistine term. Furthermore, the warlike Philistines introduced the helmet to the Levant, so that their word *koba*[20] appears in the Hebrew Bible and persists in modern Hebrew as the ordinary word for "hat." In some regards, the Philistines resisted acculturation to Canaanite culture, for the Philistines, of all the nations in Canaan, are singled out in the Bible as "the uncircumcised." In material civilization they excelled the other inhabitants of Canaan, specifically in the arts and crafts. Aegean-type pottery has been found not only on the Philistine plain of southern Canaan, but throughout the country. As late as the time of Saul, about 1000 B.C.E. the Philistines held a monopoly on metalwork in the region, and thereby were able to keep the Hebrews disarmed. That the Caphtorians were already recognized in Canaan as the masters par excellence of the arts and crafts, including metallurgy, is reflected by the fact that the divine artisan (Kothar-and-Hasis) in the Ugaritic pantheon comes from Caphtor, where his workshop is located. In the light of this many-sided evidence, the presence of Caphtorians in Canaan during the time of Abraham is not anachronistic. Furthermore, the general historicity of the incident is favored by the fact that the social institutions exhibited are not those of later Hebrew times.

Biblical law forbids the marriage of all half brothers and sisters (Leviticus 18:9; Deuteronomy 27:22). When, however, Abraham in self-defense had stated that Sarah was his sister, and Abimelech had discovered that she was in reality Abraham's wife, Abraham defended himself by asserting that she was not only his wife but also his half sister: the daughter of his father but not of his mother. We have no reason to doubt the veracity of Abraham's claim; thus the Bible account was not revamped to make it conform to the later Hebrew legislation that became binding on the Jews.

In accordance with divine promise,[21] Isaac was born to Sarah and Abraham. Once Isaac was born, Sarah resented the presence of Hagar's son Ishmael. Custom did not favor Sarah's wish to expel

20. The initial Philistine sound was intermediate between Semitic *k* and *q;* hence the word is written either *qoba*ᶜ (1 Samuel 17:38) or *koba*ᶜ (1 Samuel 17:5) in the Bible. In Ugaritic, *Ḫkpt* (a term used in parallelism with "Caphtor") is once written *Ḫqkpt,* showing that the Semitic scribe vacillated between *q* and *k* in representing the same foreign sound.

21. From the Hebrew viewpoint, childbirth required not only biological conditions but also divine will. The Hebrews shared this attitude with their pagan neighbors; e.g., in Ugarit, where the Legends of Aqhat and Kret bring out the same point.

Hagar and her child, as is suggested by the prohibition in the Nuzu tablets.[22] Sarah's request that Abraham drive them out to prevent Ishmael from inheriting along with Isaac therefore required a divine dispensation to justify Abraham's acquiescence (Genesis 21:1–14).

The "sacrifice" of Isaac (Genesis 22:1–13) reflects a transition from human sacrifice to the vicarious sacrifice of some animal. Since Isaac was the firstborn of Sarah, he would have to be sacrificed according to the old principle of giving to the gods the firstborn. Thus at the dawn of Hebrew history the barbaric custom of sacrificing the firstborn child was eliminated, though the redemption of the firstborn, whereby parents buy back their firstborn from God, attests to the existence of the earlier savage custom.[23]

We may also note that in Genesis 22:3 when Abraham took Isaac to be sacrificed, the caravan included an ass and the two errand lads of Abraham. This fits in exactly with the picture in Ugaritic literature where missions move on donkey back and where two lads are regularly in attendance.

Later, Abraham, to bury his dead, wanted to buy a parcel of land near the city of Hebron (Genesis 23). The lot, which included the Cave of Machpelah, belonged to a Hittite named Ephron. According to the Hittite law code, levies on real estate were borne by the original owner as long as he held on to any part of the estate. Abraham, to sidestep such obligations, tried to buy only the corner of the field containing the cave (verse 9). But Ephron wanted to unburden himself of the entire field (verse 11) so that Abraham should bear the obligations (corresponding to our real estate tax, though they may have included liability to military service or corvée). With a corpse on his hands requiring prompt burial, Abraham was in no position to hold out, and so he had to buy the whole field to get the cave.[24]

Abraham did not want his son to marry a Canaanite, so he sent his servant[25] to Paddan Aram (as the Haran region of north Mesopotamia

22. Be it noted, however, that according to the Sumerian Code of Lipit-Ishtar (section 25), the expulsion would be legal in exchange for the freedom which Hagar and Ishmael thereby won.

23. That human sacrifice was practiced by neighbors of the Hebrews, and even by isolated Judean kings, will be pointed out below.

24. See Manfred R. Lehmann, "Abraham's Purchase of Machpelah and Hittite Law," *Bulletin of the American Schools of Oriental Research* 129, 1953, pp. 15–18.

25. In Jewish tradition this servant is identified with Eliezer.

is called) to secure a bride for Isaac. With ten camels and adequate personnel, the servant heads the caravan toward his master's Aramean kinsmen. The mention of camels here and elsewhere in the patriarchal narratives often is considered anachronistic. However, the correctness of the Bible is supported by the representation of camel riding on seal cylinders of precisely this period from northern Mesopotamia.[26]

Although Bethuel (the father of the prospective bride Rebekah) was alive, Rebekah's brother Laban figures as the head of the family and does most of the talking and negotiating about the marriage. This is to be connected with fratriarchal elements in family life, which are particularly common in the Nuzu tablets but also are present to some extent in Hebrew society.[27] After Rebekah personally consents to go with Abraham's servant to Canaan, where she is to wed her kinsman whom she had never seen, the caravan returns with its mission successfully accomplished.

A gift she had received from the servant was a nose ring of gold weighing a *beqa*ᶜ. Stone weights marked *beqa*ᶜ have been found in excavations in the land of Israel.[28] While this is not of great importance in interpreting the text, it illustrates quite clearly the way archeology can supply exact meanings of hitherto vague words.

Laban had recognized Yahwe as the God of Abraham's household to judge from Laban's greeting Abraham's servant with "Come, thou blessed one of Yahwe!" (Genesis 24:31). As we shall see later, the Mesopotamian and Canaanite branches of the family had different ancestral gods.

The children resulting from the marriage of Isaac and Rebecca were the twins Esau and Jacob, Esau coming into the world first and therefore the firstborn. It is said that he was *admoni*, "ruddy" (Genesis 25:25), which again has a purpose. Whether or not he was particularly ruddy is of little importance. The etiological character of the statement is the interesting thing: Esau's connection with the nation

---

26. The best of several illustrations is in the journal *Iraq* 6, 1939, pl. II, 9. In general, see J. P. Free, "Abraham's Camels," *Journal of Near Eastern Studies* 3, 1944, pp. 187–93.

27. See Cyrus H. Gordon, "Fratriarchy in the Old Testament," *Journal of Biblical Literature* 54, 1935, pp. 223–31.

28. Their average weight is about 6.1 grams. See further Roland de Vaux, *Ancient Israel*, New York, 1961, pp. 204–6.

of Edom prompted the story that the lad was *admoni* at birth; for the Semitic ear, "Edom" and *admoni* are derived from the same root.[29]

Jacob purchased from Esau the "birthright," which means the title to the position of firstborn. This is no longer a peculiar incident without parallel. In the Nuzu tablets, inheritance prospects are negotiable (though only from brother to brother) much as stocks and bonds are today. One Nuzu tablet records how a man in need of food sold his inheritance portion to his own brother[30] in exchange for livestock, even as the hungry Esau had sold his to Jacob for a "mess of potage."[31]

A famine sent Isaac to the same King Abimelech of the Philistines, at Gerar. There Isaac tried his hand successfully at a season of farming, and his yield was a hundredfold (Genesis 26:12), a statement worth recording because in the heroic age the aristocratic leaders are landowners, who personally excel in agriculture between military campaigns. Greek epic portrays Laertes tending plants, and Odysseus plowing with oxen; even as the Bible tells of Isaac the farmer, and Saul the plowman (1 Samuel 11:5). Genesis represents Abraham and Jacob as acquiring land, as well as Isaac cultivating it. The bellicose side of the Patriarchs comes out in Genesis 14, in Jacob's vanquishing a supernatural being (even as Homeric heroes are sometimes more than a match for gods) (Genesis 32:25–30), and in the swordsmanship of Simeon and Levi (Genesis 34).

Esau married two "Hittite" (i.e., native) girls to the chagrin of his parents. The name of the one is Judith, daughter of Beeri, which is quite Semitic; that of the other is Basemath, daughter of Elon, again

---

29. This story has yet another interesting aspect. Frequently in Cretan and Egyptian art, the men (but not the women) are colored reddish brown. In the Legend of Kret, the hero is told by El to redden himself to become ceremonially fit. Obviously such was the color that males assumed for heroic or ceremonial purposes. Esau's being born red presaged his heroic stature. The only other person in the Bible who was of that color by nature is David (1 Samuel 16:12): significantly the hero par excellence. The custom whereby men painted themselves red, and women yellow, was widespread geographically and chronologically. At several different sites in the Near East, I (C. H. G.) have excavated pieces of red and yellow ocher in ancient private houses as well as in sacred areas. It is likely that men used the red, and women the yellow, to prepare themselves for formal occasions.

30. Both the biblical and Nuzu examples are sales of a birthright from brother to brother. The patrimony could not be sold to a total stranger.

31. The Hebrew text specifies the dish as lentils.

Semitic (Genesis 26:34). To appease his parents he married a kins-woman, the daughter of Ishmael (Genesis 28:8–9).[32]

Before Isaac died it was his wish to confer a blessing on his favorite and elder son Esau. Through deception, Jacob obtained the blessing and the blessing stood as binding. In patriarchal society, in which the ancient equation of "intelligence" and "trickery" was accepted,[33] a man nevertheless felt obliged to abide by his word, though it might be to his disadvantage and might have been extorted from him under false pretenses. A Nuzu tablet tells of a man repeating in court the blessing his father had given him on the deathbed, willing to him a wife. Since the terms of such a blessing could be upheld by a court, it is in keeping with the times that an oral blessing on a father's death-bed was legally binding. However, unlike the Nuzu tablets that deal primarily with material things, the patriarchal narratives are more concerned with future leadership.

Repeatedly throughout the patriarchal account, but especially in Jacob's career, a premium is placed on a kind of cleverness, which if practiced in our society would be condemned as cheating. The Bible does not confront us with a static code but rather with a historic evolution whereby religion and morals grew from humble beginnings to the loftiest heights. The miracle of Israel is that it grew and gave an ever increasing message to the world; not one that remained static from Abraham's time on.

The mother, Rebekah, fearing that Esau would take revenge and kill Jacob, told her favorite Jacob to flee to her people in Mesopota-mia, and asked the rhetorical question: "Why should I be bereft of the two of you in a single day?" (Genesis 27:45). The implication is

---

32. For the variant traditions of the names of Esau's wives, compare these passages with Gene-sis 36:2–3. The fact that the Bible contains such variants often has been used by scholars to argue for multiple sources underlying the finished product. We do not disagree with the main point; clearly there were earlier sources upon which the book of Genesis and the entire Torah were based. But the enterprise of uncovering these earlier sources is a misguided one. The fact remains that all we possess is the final product, and all analysis of biblical literature should work from that real text, not from hypothesized and reconstructed sources. Moreover, as recent studies have shown, there is much more unity to biblical narrative, especially in the book of Genesis, than there is disunity. See Gary A. Rendsburg, *The Redaction of Genesis,* Winona Lake, Ind., 1986.

33. Thus in Arabic *shaṭâra* means either. Yet the danger of drawing sweeping conclusions in distinguishing Bedouin from ourselves will be evident if we note that a similar range of meaning is inherent in English "shrewd" and "smart."

that the laws of blood revenge would have it that if Esau in his anger killed Jacob, the tribe in turn would have to kill Esau so that the mother would lose both of them.[34] Jacob heeded her advice and fled. On the way Jacob beheld a theophany, wherein God reaffirmed His covenant. On waking up Jacob was filled with awe, but in no way mystified, by the experience. He anointed with oil the stone that lay under his head during the theophany; for the Deity, that in some way resided in it, could thus be gratified. The place, previously known as Luz, was renamed Bethel ("House of God") by Jacob. (Such topographical equations are of considerable value in historical geography.) Jacob furthermore vowed that if Yahwe, who had appeared to him, would guard him on his journey and supply him with food and clothing, and bring him back safely, Jacob would keep Him as his God. (Thus the relationship between man and God was still on a contractual basis, and the individual man could still lay down conditions that would affect that relationship.)[35] Jacob furthermore vowed that he would pay God tithes on all God would give him (Genesis 28:10–22). The theophany, and Jacob's response to it, thus confirm the covenant, justify the sanctuary at Bethel, and set the precedent for the paying of tithes.

After reaching his mother's people in Mesopotamia, Jacob agreed to serve his uncle Laban for seven years for the hand of Rachel. Entering into a contract whereby a man pays in labor for his wife is again attested in the Nuzu tablets. But there is much more to the affair than that. No sons of Laban are mentioned and Jacob enters into this bargain for the purpose of being heir of the household, not only as the son-in-law of Laban but as his adopted son, as we shall demonstrate in due course. Laban deceived Jacob and palmed off Leah on him instead of Rachel. So far Laban has gotten the better of Jacob, and in this period (as we have noted) getting the better of the other fellow was a sign of intelligence.

In this case, the deception carried out by Laban against Jacob is of extra special interest. First we should note how brilliantly the author has conveyed his message. When Jacob awoke the morning after the wedding and realized that he had married Leah, and not Rachel, he asked Laban, "What have you done to me? Was it not for Rachel that

34. Compare 2 Samuel 14:5–7.

35. The freedom of the individual man in such matters became more and more curtailed as Israel grew from simple origins into nationhood.

I worked for you? Why have you deceived me?" (Genesis 29:25).
Laban's response was "It is not the custom in our place to put the
younger before the firstborn" (verse 26). In other words, Laban was
telling Jacob: I know what you did in placing yourself (the younger)
before Esau (the firstborn), but that is not how we do things here. In
this way, Jacob was punished for having deceived his father Isaac in
procuring the blessing intended for his older brother Esau. As we
have stated, yes, there is a premium placed on cleverness, but on the
other hand God eventually will see to it that deceivers receive their
just desserts. But punishment need not be carried out by God himself; rather, human agents take care of matters. Moreover, note that
the author of the narrative nowhere informs the reader that Laban's
deception of Jacob is the latter's punishment for having deceived Isaac
(i.e., in contrast to Aesop, there is no statement such as the moral of
the story is: do not deceive your old blind father). Instead, the narrative demands the reader's input in reaching the conclusion that
deception, even in a society where cleverness is appreciated, will be
requited.

The second point to note here is the legal consequences. Jacob
was now married to Leah, but he agreed to work another seven years
in order to marry Rachel. Among the Nuzu tablets is a combination
adoption-marriage contract that provides the necessary legal background to understanding the relationship between Jacob and Laban.
In this tablet, a man named Wullu agrees to labor for a man named
Nashwi, and in exchange Nashwi gives his daughter to Wullu. Furthermore, upon Nashwi's death, Wullu will inherit his estate.
Accordingly, Wullu becomes both adopted son and son-in-law of
Nashwi. However, there are several additional clauses in this contract.
One states that if Wullu should take a second wife, then he subsequently surrenders all ownership rights (i.e., even over his wife) and
future inheritance rights. If we assume that Jacob became Laban's
adopted son and his son-in-law at the same, i.e., when he married
Leah, the trickery carried out by Laban against Jacob has even further
ramifications. Laban knew that Jacob would still want to marry
Rachel, which is exactly what transpired, but in so doing Jacob took
a second wife and thus he sacrificed numerous rights. Another clause
in this Nuzu tablet states that if in the future a natural son is born to
Nashwi, then Wullu must share any future inheritance (see also the
case of Eliezer; above, p. 115). As we shall see, only at a later point in
the narrative are sons of Laban mentioned, leading to the conclusion

that they were born after the marriages of Jacob to Leah and Rachel.[36]

In short, by tricking Jacob into marrying Leah instead of Rachel, Laban masterminded the plot from several angles. From the literary perspective, we see how Jacob was punished for his having deceived Isaac. From the legal perspective, especially upon Jacob's subsequent marriage to Rachel, we see how Laban has forced Jacob into losing various rights. Still further, once sons were born to Laban, Jacob's losses were even more manifold.

The Nuzu material is relevant to the Jacob and Laban story in still another detail as well. Thus Leah and Rachel each brought a handmaid as a marriage gift from their father (their names are Zilpah and Bilhah, respectively). The paternal wedding gift of a handmaid to his daughter is again attested in the Nuzu tablets.

But Jacob was not one to be placed in a desperate position due to this set of circumstances. After his two wives and his two handmaidens had borne him a large family, Jacob decided the time had come to return to the land of Canaan. He requested from Laban the permission to leave with his wives and children. Laban agrees, but only after settling the monetary matter that in that society meant dividing the flocks. Laban attempted to manipulate Jacob on this issue, but because of his superior knowledge of the animals, in the end Jacob succeeded in producing a large flock for himself. This additional piece of cleverness ended with Jacob's becoming wealthy to the dissatisfaction of Laban's sons. Then Laban's daughters, siding with their husband, agreed that home is no place for them. Since Jacob's inheritance prospects had deteriorated (through both his having married a second wife and through the subsequent birth of natural sons to Laban) Rachel and Leah agreed that they no longer had any portion in the house of their father. Laban had gone off to shear his flocks, so Jacob took advantage of the occasion to escape with his wives, children, and flocks. Rachel, without telling her husband, stole Laban's household gods, which, as we know from the Nuzu tablets, were to go to a real son and not the adopted son. Rachel's motive was the securing of some prized advantage in family affairs for her husband and children. Since they were bound for Canaan and were leaving Mesopotamia for good, it is not likely that the gods conveyed valu-

---

36. We know nothing about Laban's wife or wives, but in a polygamous society it would not be impossible for a man with grown daughters (i.e., Leah and Rachel) to have a newborn son or sons.

able property rights. The possession of the gods may rather have betokened clan leadership and spiritual power to an extent that made possessing them of paramount importance.[37]

When Laban overtook them, he expressed his claim that the daughters and their children, and the flocks, indeed everything belonged to him, and that Jacob should have asked his permission before leaving. But what bothered Laban most was the theft of his gods. Obviously Laban was in the legal right, for his claims went uncontested. And as noted above, we now possess via the Nuzu tablets the legal background to fully understand the passage. Indeed everything did belong to Laban! Furthermore, Jacob remained his adopted son and thus still would be under Laban's jurisdiction. As far as the gods were concerned, Laban searched in vain for them. Rachel had hidden them under her saddle and told her father that her menstrual period was upon her and thus she could not descend from the camel. Courtesy prevented Laban from forcing his daughter off the saddle, so the theft remained unexposed. Note once more how deception plays a role in the story.

Nevertheless, in a magnanimous forgiving way, Laban allowed Jacob's household to depart. Jacob and Laban exchanged blessings and made a treaty and all Laban required of him was to swear he would treat his girls well and not marry other women. They furthermore set up a monolith and swore that neither would transgress the boundary to harm the other. Their respective ancestral gods—"the God of Abraham" and "the god of Nahor"—were invoked to judge between them. Jacob also swore by "the Fear of his father Isaac," God's special epithet with reference to Isaac. The devotion to the god of one's father is a feature of Hebrew religion that stemmed from the pre-Hebraic East. The covenant between Jacob and Laban was solemnized by a sacrificial feast and on the morrow they parted company and each went with his followers toward his native land.

En route to the land of Canaan, Jacob effected a reconciliation with Esau, who graciously pardoned his brother. Jacob bowed down to the earth seven times before his brother (Genesis 33:3); the sevenfold prostration is a widespread custom attested also in epistles from Amarna and Ugarit.

Jacob proceeded with his wives and children to Shechem, where

---

37. See also Moshe Greenberg, "Another Look at Rachel's Theft of the Teraphim," *Journal of Biblical Literature* 81, 1962, pp. 239–48.

he bought some land from the local residents. However, because the prince of the city seduced Dinah, the daughter of Jacob, her brothers Simeon and Levi resort to treachery against the inhabitants. This story is the setting of the aforementioned offer of the Shechemites to allow the family of Jacob to settle, trade, and acquire real estate. The Shechemites further suggested that they and the Israelites intermarry. Jacob's sons agreed to this proposal, but only with the proviso that the Shechemites circumcise themselves before the two people become one. The Shechemites agreed, but while they still were recovering from the procedure, Simeon and Levi attacked and killed all the males of the city. This action displeased Jacob, the more so since he had few supporters and was a stranger who could ill afford to have enemies.[38] But again this episode, particularly the treachery of Simeon and Levi, is purposeful; and we must remember it to understand part of the blessing that Jacob is eventually to make on his deathbed (Genesis 49, in particular verses 5–6).[39]

In Genesis 35:2–3 we read: "And Jacob said to his household and to all with him, 'Remove the foreign gods which are in your midst and purify yourselves and change your garments, that we may arise and go to Bethel, where I may make an altar to the God who answered me in the day of my distress and was with me on the road I walked.' " Whereupon Jacob and his household buried their gods under a tree near the city of Shechem (Genesis 35:4), which clearly shows that foreign idols were still in the midst of the people, although Jacob recognized that his allegiance was not to them but to Yahwe, who claimed his sole devotion by being with him when he was in trouble, and bringing him back safely to the land of Canaan. Thus, while the covenant between God and Israel was established and recognized, pagan survivals clung on, and, as we shall see, did not end until the destruction of Jerusalem in 586 B.C.E., when Judaism was purged of its idolatrous vestiges. The contractual nature of the rela-

---

38. For a brilliant literary analysis of the entire episode, see Meir Sternberg, *The Poetics of Biblical Narrative,* Bloomington, Ind., 1985, pp. 441–81.

39. The Hebrew text of this passage includes one of the outstanding examples of polysemy, indeed double polysemy, in the Bible. Polysemy refers to multiple meanings inherent in the same word. In Genesis 49:6, the poet used two words that are synonyms of each other in two different ways (thus the term double polysemy). The first verb in this passage means both "enter" and "desire"; the second verb parallels both meanings as "be united" and "rejoice." For details, see Gary A. Rendsburg, "Double Polysemy in Genesis 49:6 and Job 3:6," *Catholic Biblical Quarterly* 44, 1982, pp. 48–51.

tion between God and His people stems from the Patriarchal Period and remains a cornerstone of biblical religion.

The command to change garments, meanwhile, is a key to understanding another aspect of the text. Jacob's return to Bethel is an example of the homecoming, or *nostos*, motif common in ancient Near Eastern literature. In the Odyssey, Odysseus changes his clothes upon returning home to Ithaca; Sinuhe does likewise in the Egyptian tale bearing his name; and Gilgamesh also changes his clothes upon returning to his home in Uruk. In short, this small detail in the story is a clue to the reader that Jacob has come home to Canaan, the land of the Israelites.[40]

The narrative in Genesis continues with the birth of Benjamin, the second and last child of Rachel, for she died in bearing him. The family was moving from Bethel to Ephrathah, which is in the vicinity of Bethlehem. She was buried with a monolith to mark the grave. A little tomb, still frequented by pilgrims, now stands on the traditional site of Rachel's resting place.

Genesis 35:22 records Reuben's scandalous affair, with his father's concubine Bilhah,[41] with characteristic Hebrew conciseness. The incident is "worthy of saga" precisely because it is a shocking story about a famous man. The incident is necessary for understanding Jacob's last blessing to his sons, the tribal fathers, that lies ahead in Genesis 49 (note verse 4).

In our treatment of the history of the Patriarchs, we have relied to a great extent on the material from Nuzu. But the literature dealing with the Patriarchs, that is, the book of Genesis, is illuminated mainly by the literary texts from Ugarit. In the Bible the major themes that carry through the Patriarchal narratives are a) the barren wife and b) the younger son. Both of these occur as motifs in Ugaritic literature. As noted earlier (Chapter VI, pp. 91–92), Daniel is described as being childless, though eventually a model son is born; and Kret bears seven sons, though it is the eighth child (a daughter no less!) who is to be

---

40. See further Gary A. Rendsburg, "Notes on Genesis XXXV," *Vetus Testamentum* 34, 1984, pp. 361–66.

41. This motif is part of the repertoire of East Mediterranean Epic; cf. Iliad 9:447–57 in which Phoenix (like Reuben) received a paternal curse instead of blessing for seducing his father's concubine. Both Reuben and Phoenix were not motivated by lust, but acted in their mothers' interests. All of the many *Frauengeschichten* in the historic books of the Bible, from Genesis through Kings, stop with the end of David's career. This is due to the heavy epic antecedents of the biblical account through, but not beyond, David's reign.

elevated to firstborn. Though we lack a complete picture of Canaanite (including Ugaritic and Hebrew) literary expression for the Late Bronze and Early Iron Ages, we reconstruct a situation in which these motifs were popular among the reading public. The Ugaritic epic poets incorporated them into their great stories, and the biblical writers utilized them to the utmost in their narratives about the Patriarchs. Thus, not only Sarah, but also Rebekah and Rachel are barren until eventually they, too, bear sons. The younger son motif is apparent in the Isaac-Ishamel and Jacob-Esau relationships, and, as we shall see in the next chapter, it occurs in the stories of Joseph and his brothers, Judah's sons Perez and Zerah, and Joseph's sons Ephraim and Manasseh.

In the Bible these motifs have an additional value; they gain a theological overlay. The Patriarchs represent a microcosm of Israel. God's intervention in their personal lives is akin to the role He plays in the life of Israel. Moreover, Israel is not a powerful nation like Egypt or Babylonia; instead it is a "barren" country, and a "younger son" among the nations of the world. God has made Israel prolific and He has made it His firstborn (Exodus 4:22), ideas reflected in the Patriarchal narratives.

There are also other themes shared by Ugarit and the book of Genesis. The most important of these is the "Helen of Troy" motif. Just as Agamemnon had to rescue Helen from the Trojans, so did Kret have to rescue his wife Hurrai from the people of Udm, and on numerous occasions the Patriachs needed to resort to the same. Abraham twice needs to recover Sarah from foreign palaces, Isaac does so with Rebekah, and, in a variant on the theme, Dinah's brothers need to rescue her from the city of Shechem. This, too, must have been a popular motif in its day, one that readers throughout the East Mediterranean enjoyed.

The more we study the Bible against the background of the ancient Near East, the more we learn its true message, both in large strokes and in small details.

# Israel and
# the Ramesside Age

With Genesis 37 we come to the saga of Joseph, which is one of the most appealing narratives in world literature; for in it are blended the spirits of Israel and Egypt.

Joseph, the son of Rachel, was the favorite of his father. He was accordingly hated by his half brothers; the more so because of his conceit. He had two dreams that are really duplicates of one another, as is typical in ancient Near East literature. In one dream he saw the family binding each a sheaf in the field; and everyone's sheaf got in circle around Joseph's sheaf and bowed down to it. In his second dream the sun, moon, and eleven stars bowed down to him. On this occasion, as regularly when the Hebrews were confronted with dreams, no interpretation is necessary; the meaning of the dream is obvious to them. Without more ado, Jacob scolded Joseph and asked rhetorically: "Must I, your mother, and your brothers come to bow down to you unto the earth?" (Genesis 37:10). The offended brothers succeeded in expressing their resentment more drastically. They laid hands on him and sold him as a slave but deceived their father into believing Joseph had been devoured by a wild beast. Jacob, disconsolate on losing his favorite son, summed up his grief thus: "I shall go down mourning into Sheol to my son" (Genesis 37:35); indicating that there was as yet no concept of a heaven among the Hebrews but simply a belief in an underworld where everyone went to spend a dreary, inactive eternity.

The cycle of Joseph is a success story. Many ills befall him but everything turns out well in the long run because God is with him and a kindly Providence sees to it that he overcomes every obstacle and rises in station. He was sold as a slave into the house of Potiphar, an Egyptian official, but before long he was made the majordomo in Potiphar's house.

With Genesis 38, the narrative changes abruptly, interrupting the story of Joseph. There are two reasons why this chapter may have been injected. First, the incident it relates is necessary for the genealogies of the fathers in Israel. Second, the Joseph story is told with exquisite artistry, including the element of suspense that is frequently introduced. In this particular case, where an entirely different tale is interposed, may it not be that the biblical author or editor purposely inserted this long chapter for suspense? For, while Joseph is left behind as a slave in Potiphar's house, we must go through all of Chapter 38 before we get back to the fate of the hero.

In Genesis 38, Judah, the son of Jacob, went to an Adullamite friend of his, to live with him. This shows that toward the end of the Patriarchal Period, the Hebrews, in spite of their apparent clannishness, did not live to themselves but mingled freely with the natives of the land. Furthermore, Judah married a Canaanite woman who bore him three sons: Er, Onan, and Shelah. A girl named Tamar was obtained as a wife for the firstborn, Er, who died without progeny. Thus Tamar was automatically married to the next brother, Onan, because no children had been born of the first union, and according to the Hebrew law of levirate marriage,[1] it was incumbent upon the deceased's next of kin (usually the next brother in line) to marry the widow of a childless man in Israel, so that the first child of the second union may be reckoned as the son of the deceased to carry on the latter's name in Israel. Onan selfishly did not want to raise a child for his dead brother, so he practiced birth control, which was displeasing in the eyes of God, who killed him for it.

The next son, Shelah, still a minor, was too young to become Tamar's mate immediately; yet the law of levirate marriage entitled her to have him automatically upon his growing up. Pending his

---

1. Levirate marriage goes back to crass beginnings, when a woman purchased in marriage belonged permanently to the family of the man that bought her. Nuzu marriage contracts sometimes specify that the woman purchased by a man for his son, shall, if later widowed, pass on to a second, and if necessary to a third, fourth (etc.) son of the purchaser. Levirate marriage appears in the Middle Assyrian and Hittite law codes as well as in the Bible. It does not appear in Hammurapi's Code. Since it is well attested in ancient India, and crops up in the Near East only in the wake of the Indo-European invasions, it was apparently introduced, or at least popularized, by the Indo-Europeans.

maturity, Tamar was sent away to wait in the home of her father. But when she heard that Shelah, who was still being withheld from her, had reached maturity, she resorted to a drastic subterfuge to obtain her right to be the mother of the family's heir. Her father-in-law Judah was coming to attend the shearing of his flocks. Tamar, seizing the opportunity, put off the clothes of her widowhood, and disguised herself as a veiled prostitute. Sitting by the wayside, she attracted the attention of her father-in-law Judah, who did not realize who she really was. Inasmuch as he did not have the hire with which to pay her, he left as security, at her request, his three articles of identification,[2] including his personal seal and staff. After this incident Tamar took off her disguise, donned her widow's weeds, and returned to the house of her father. Judah, wishing to pay his debt and redeem his security, sent a kid as payment for what he owed her. However, no prostitute could be found in the locality. Presently news of Tamar's pregnancy was spread abroad. Judah, not knowing that he was the father of her child, indignantly insisted that she be ousted from her father's house and burned alive for her sins. For even though she was residing with her father, she was legally Judah's daughter-in-law, belonging to his family and subject to his patriarchal jurisdiction. Tamar was brought forward, but she turned the tables on Judah by showing the three incriminating articles of identification and declaring that their owner had impregnated her. She, after all, had been wronged by Judah, who had deprived her of her rightful husband Shelah. Since she was prevented from bearing the heir to the latter, she made the best of her plight by tricking Judah into siring the heir out of her. The fact that she was in the right and he in the wrong is confessed by Judah, who admits "She is more in the right than I" (verse 26). The twins that were born, far from being illegitimate, included the ancestor of King David (Genesis 38:29; Ruth 4:18–22). The fact that Judah and Tamar were father- and daughter-in-law would offend ancient Near Easterners less than might appear on the surface. In the Hittite law code, not only the deceased's brothers, but also his father, could marry the widow.

The Joseph story, then, begins with two deceptions, and these in turn relate to the deceptions discussed in the previous chapter. In

---

2. In the Ugaritic myths, the gods each have three articles of personal identification. Since Judah's three were probably the standard articles possessed by every solid citizen, whereas the Ugaritic gods each have a different three, the parallel is subject to qualification.

each case, it is through the means of a goat and clothing that the deceptions are carried out. Jacob began the series with his deception of Isaac, having worn his brother Esau's clothes, using a goatskin to cover his otherwise smooth skin, and preparing a goat for his father to eat. Laban tricked Jacob by having the veiled Leah take the place of Rachel on the wedding night, and of course the goats that Jacob tends for Laban are a major part of their interfacing as well. When Jacob's sons plot to sell Joseph as a slave and then inform Jacob that he is dead, their means is a piece of clothing, specifically Joseph's "coat of many colors,"[3] and a goat that they kill and whose blood they use to stain Joseph's garment. It is noteworthy that Judah was the mastermind of this plot, and while it is true that his plan was at least more humane than the majority of his brothers who sought to kill Joseph, still Judah's action requires punishment. Finally, Judah was in turn deceived when his daughter-in-law Tamar used clothing (prostitute's garb for widow's garb) and a goat (the payment to be made) in order to dupe Judah. All of this, of course, is a well-interconnected plot,[4] and once more shows how the ancient readers delighted in seeing how the deceiver would in turn be deceived. Furthermore, as noted earlier, it is not God who exacts revenge for the sins committed; rather, it is always human agents. According to bibical theology, God has a master plan for the history of the world in general and for the history of Israel in particular, but it is His human agents who more often than not carry out His desires.

The twin boys born to Judah were Zerah and Perez. Zerah, though the firstborn, was eclipsed by the younger Perez. The superiority of the latter was evident from quaint obstetrical circumstances attending the birth (Genesis 38:27–30). The motif of the younger eclipsing the elder, and the narration of it being worthy of saga, are, as we have observed, characteristic of Canaanite literature, both biblical and Ugaritic.

There is another side to such epic saga. The individual is supposed to be led to proper action, through the lapses, as well as the virtues, of the great. We thus learn that God's will, that men shall perform their levirate obligations, must be done. Judah himself could not

3. The exact sense of the Hebrew term is unknown; a more appropriate translation may be "ornamented tunic."

4. Again, this argues for the essential unity of the book of Genesis, regardless of what disparate sources may lie beneath it.

evade his duty. For his negligence, he suffered disgrace, but God's will was done. To the ancient Hebrew, Genesis 38 conveyed this warning: "Fulfill your levirate duties, no matter how high the cost! If the great Judah couldn't avoid them, don't you try to!"

That the early traditions of Israel are frequently aimed at inducing right action is so important for the student of the Bible World that we ought to note at least one more striking illustration. Yahwe was about to kill Moses for not circumcising his son. Luckily the mother of the lad had the wit to pick up a flint and circumcise him then and there to avert Moses' doom (Exodus 4:24–26). Such a tale makes no sense to the modern reader until he understands its function. It is designed to warn the Hebrews of every generation: "Don't fail to circumcise your sons! If Moses couldn't get away with it, how can you?"

We return now to the narrative of Joseph in Chapter 39. One of the striking features of the story, as we shall detail in the pages below, is its strong Egyptian coloration. At every stroke the author accurately portrays life in Egypt, mixing his narrative with Egyptian literary motifs and introducing a few Egyptian words and names into his Hebrew text. Thus, while cuneiform documents are in general more important than Egyptian records for illuminating most of the Hebrew Bible, the reverse is true for the Joseph story at the end of the book of Genesis and for the account of the Exodus in the beginning of the book of Exodus.

Joseph rose to the top of Potiphar's household, but because of the machinations of his master's wife, he fell out of grace and was sent to jail. This is the first motif that is paralleled in Egyptian literature. In the Tale of Two Brothers (written about 1225 B.C.E., during the Nineteenth Dynasty), as in Genesis 39:7–20, a married woman attempts to seduce a virtuous youth and, on failing, falsely accuses him of rape.[5]

Even in prison, however, Joseph rose in station, so that when the king's cupbearer and baker fell out of favor and were sent to prison (Genesis 40), it was Joseph who was commissioned to look after them. The cupbearer had a dream in which he saw a vine with three branches and grapes growing. He squeezed the grapes into a cup,

---

5. The same motif occurs also in the story of Bellerophon (Iliad 6:155–65), showing that it is common to the repertoire of East Mediterranean Epic, spread, as it is, over Egypt, Israel, and the Aegean.

which he put into the pharaoh's hand. He was troubled by this dream, which Joseph interpreted for him thus: The three branches mean three days, whereupon the pharaoh will forgive and restore him to his former office. As a reward, Joseph asked the cupbearer to recommend him to pharaoh and thus rescue him from prison.

The baker dreamed there were three baskets on his head; in the topmost there was baking for the pharaoh, but birds descended and ate it. Encouraged by the favorable interpretation of the cupbearer's dream, the baker turned to Joseph who gave him a gloomy prediction: In three days the pharaoh will remove the baker's head and hang his corpse, so that the birds will devour his flesh.

Both interpretations came true, but the lucky cupbearer forgot to help Joseph, who therefore had to wait two years for the pharaoh to have a dream that would require Joseph's talents to explain, and so raise him from an inmate of a prison to the highest position under the pharaoh.

Pharaoh characteristically had his dreams in duplicate. First he dreamt of seven fat cows that were devoured by seven skinny cows, then he dreamt of seven healthy ears of grain that were devoured by seven poor ears of grain (Genesis 41:1–7). None of his professional dream interpreters was able to advise pharaoh as to the meaning of these dreams. Only at this point did the cupbearer remember Joseph, who then was brought from prison to interpret pharaoh's dreams. The emphasis placed on dream interpretation in the Joseph story is another aspect of the Egyptian background of the account. Peoples in all societies dream; it is merely a question of how we deal with our dreams. In Egypt, as the story itself implies, there was a class of professional dream interpreters whose job it was to explain people's dreams. We even possess a rather lengthy dream interpretation textbook from ancient Egypt, listing various things dreamt and the appropriate meanings thereof.[6] Accordingly, it is not surprising that the author of the Joseph story made a major motif out of dream interpretation.[7] Furthermore, we may note that the content of pha-

6. For an English translation of excerpts of this work, see James B. Pritchard, ed., *Ancient Near Eastern Texts,* Princeton, 1955, p. 495.

7. In stories set in the land of Israel there is never any dream interpretation necessary. Dreams are referred to, but their understanding is prima facie. The only other place in the Bible where dream interpretation plays a role is Daniel 2, set in Babylon. This is consistent with the evidence from Babylonian, where there also existed classes of professional dream interpreters, omen givers, etc.

raoh's dreams befits a resident of the Nile Valley, where cows and grain are the major products. The corresponding items in the land of Canaan would be sheep and goats, olives, dates, and grapes.[8]

In Genesis 41:14 we read how Joseph was prepared for his first royal audience. He shaved and changed his clothes. The Semites did not shave themselves clean, but Egyptians did. When he came before pharaoh, Joseph explained that the duplication of the dreams was merely to show that God had determined to fulfill their message quickly (Genesis 41:32). Joseph explained to pharaoh that the dreams portend seven years of plenty to be followed by seven years of famine. Joseph wisely suggested that the government should gather and store grain during the seven years of plenty in anticipation of the seven years of famine.[9] He also advised that a competent director be put in charge of the national program, with officials to assist in collecting a fifth of the produce of the land so that the granaries would be sufficiently filled before the bad years began. Pharaoh decided that no man was better qualified for the job than Joseph himself. So he appointed Joseph to the highest position in Egypt (except for the pharaoh himself) as majordomo of the palace, and food administrator of all the land; in token whereof His Majesty gave his signet ring to Joseph, clad him in robes of honor, and placed a golden necklace on him. This is characteristically Egyptian and we compare Sinuhe's elevation in rank together with royal gifts of robes and other honors. As Joseph was paraded through town, the people yelled "Abrek!" an Egyptian expression that means literally "heart to you," or in more idiomatic language "hail!" (Genesis 41:43).

Pharaoh confered upon Joseph an Egyptian name Zaphenath-panenah, which means "The god speaks, he lives." Since pharaoh was considered divine in Egyptian religion, "the god" here refers to pharaoh, through whose decree Joseph lives, i.e., has gained a new life (Genesis 41:45).

Joseph married the daughter of a priest of On or Heliopolis, the

8. This difference is based on topography. The flat Nile Valley can be the home to large cattle herds and grain grows nicely in such an environment. In the hills and mountains of Canaan, sheep and goats are much more effective at traversing the terrain, and olives, dates, and grapes can grow on the rocky slopes.

9. Although there is nothing mythological in the Joseph story, the motif of seven-year cycles both of plenty and of famine runs through Near East mythology. As we have already observed, the Gilgamesh Epic even contains the element of laying up a seven-year supply in anticipation of the famine.

major center in Egypt for the worship of Re. Both his wife's name
Asenath and his father-in-law's name Potiphera are good Egyptian
names. The latter, moreover, means "he who is given by the god
Re," a most appropriate name for a priest of the city of On.[10] Asenath
bore him the firstborn Manasseh, and Ephraim the younger.

Famine forced Joseph's brothers down to Egypt to secure food.
Semites coming to Egypt for food in famine years were familiar
enough throughout Egyptian history. For Canaan depended on precarious rain, while Egypt could always count on the Nile. The Semites of Asia knew this and turned to the breadbasket of Egypt when
starvation faced them in Canaan.

The story proceeds with characteristic suspense and denouement.
Joseph recognized his brothers, but they did not recognize him. He
accused them of espionage. They protested their innocence and
related that they were a family of twelve sons, the youngest of whom
had been left behind with their father in Canaan. They added that
one of their brothers was no more. Joseph declared that their veracity
would be tested by their producing the brother left at home. The
reader will find the intricate but charming story in Genesis 42–45.
The way Joseph worried his brothers over a long period, and yet
surreptitiously supplied the needs of their family, has an unmistakable
resemblance to the Egyptian classic called the Eloquent Peasant,
where the peasant was kept worried, so as to amuse his peers, who,
though teasing him, saw to it that his family was looked after.

At long last the whole family, including the aged Patriarch Israel,[11]
came to Egypt, as the relatives of the famous Joseph (Genesis 46).
Together with Joseph's children the family numbered seventy souls
(verse 27), in keeping with epic tradition. The newcomers were settled in the Goshen region of the Delta, where they raised flocks as
their ancestors had done. A historical parallel to this settlement of the
Hebrews in the Delta is to be found in an Egyptian text that tells of
people from Edom coming to Egypt to graze their animals.[12]

---

10. However, this point should not be pushed too far, since the name of Joseph's former
master, Potiphar, is a variant of the same name.

11. Jacob was renamed Israel (Genesis 32:29). "Israel" appears as the name of a *maryannu*
warrior in a tablet from Ugarit. In another Ugaritic text, the name "Abram" is associated
once with Egypt and once with Cyprus. See text 2095:2, 4 in Cyrus H. Gordon, *Ugaritic
Textbook,* Rome, 1967, p. 25°.

12. The text may be found in Pritchard, *Ancient Near Eastern Texts,* p. 259.

The pharaoh treated the Israelites well. One incident (regardless of its historicity) is a tradition reflecting an important trait of the nomadic Semites. Pharaoh asked Jacob his age. The reply was the unrealistic "130 years; few and evil have been the days of the years of my life, nor have they attained the days of the years of the lives of my fathers" (Genesis 47:9). If this is compared with the specific genealogy in Genesis 46:8–27, we have further evidence that, while the genealogies were transmitted with care,[13] the Hebrews had not yet begun to reckon realistically with time in terms of years. An understanding of the facts explains how a document, so reliable in so many ways, can ascribe to Jacob the unreasonable life span of 147 years (Genesis 47:28).

Stripping the above events of unhistoric romance, we date the historic migration of the Israelites to Egypt in the early part of the thirteenth century B.C.E., the period of the Nineteenth Dynasty, which followed upon the age of Akhenaton. The reference to the Land of Ramses (Genesis 47:11) fits in perfectly, for it is during the Nineteenth Dynasty that we first encounter the royal name Ramses. However, if we had to select a particular pharaoh under whom Joseph served, our choice would be Seti I (1308–1291).[14]

The account goes on to tell how through Joseph's planning, the silver, the livestock, the very persons, and the land of the people were step by step converted into royal property. The priests alone, through government support, saved their land. The people, now royal peasants, were to cultivate the king's land and pay one fifth of the yield to the crown. The biblical author is not concerned with the social implications of the national economy ascribed to Joseph's administration. For the author, Joseph was a clever man who served his sovereign brilliantly. The later Prophets, such as Amos, might have objected to such treatment of the general population, but we need not expect the later ethical standard in early Hebrew history and tradition.

Jacob expressed a wish to be buried in Canaan, not in a foreign land. He fell ill and called for Joseph and the latter's two sons. For the aged Patriarch's blessing, Joseph properly stationed Manasseh at

---

13. See above, Chapter VIII, pp. 109–113.

14. We reach this conclusion because Ramses I ruled for only one year and because Ramses II is the most likely candidate for the pharaoh who first enslaved the Israelites. On these first three rulers of the Nineteenth Dynasty, see below, pp. 141–43.

Jacob's right and the younger Ephraim at his left, but the old man crossed his hands so that the right touched the younger, and the left the older. Here again is the theme of the younger child eclipsing the elder, a theme worthy of Canaanite saga in both the Bible and Ugarit. The historic fact that the tribe of Ephraim was more important than that of Manasseh is thus explained etiologically by a circumstance in Jacob's blessing.[15]

Then follows the blessing of the tribes in which twelve actual sons are singled out as the ancestors of the future tribes (Genesis 49). Reuben, destined for a history full of trouble, had his misfortunes attributed to his misbehavior with his father's concubine. Simeon and Levi,[16] who also came to grief, are reproached with their treachery at Shechem. But Judah, who is not an older son, was designated as a leader over his brothers, reflecting the emergence of Judah under the House of David.

After the blessing of the tribes, the last wish of Jacob was to be buried in the cave of Machpelah, that Abraham had purchased from Ephron. Subsequent to Jacob's death and his burial in Canaan, the brothers still felt that Joseph might seek revenge on them for what they did to him years before. So they invented the white lie that their father had expressed a wish to them before he died that Joseph should forgive them. Joseph gladly did so. This telling a falsehood was not considered reprehensible when it was prompted by self-defense; we have noted other examples of such deception in the patriarchal cycle.

Genesis closes with Joseph's request that when God remembers His people and brings them back to the Promised Land, that Joseph's bones be carried as well. The last verse of the book tells us that Joseph died at the age of 110 years and was then mummified and placed in a sarcophagus in Egypt (Genesis 50:26). In like fashion Jacob, too, had been mummified (Genesis 50:2). These details once more add to the Egyptian coloration of the story. Mummification, as is well known, was a ritual unique to Egypt in the ancient world. Elsewhere in the Near East, especially in Canaan, much simpler burials were the custom. Finally, the age of 110 years is what scholars call the ideal life

---

15. Furthermore, Jacob's actions and words represent a formal adoption of his two grandsons. For a roughly contemporary parallel, see Isaac Mendelsohn, "A Ugaritic Parallel to the Adoption of Ephraim and Manasseh," *Israel Exploration Journal* 9, 1959, pp. 180–83.

16. The Levites, however, by being scattered throughout the tribal territories as a sacerdotal class, have survived down to the present among the Jews.

span of an Egyptian. There are about two dozen references in Egyptian literature to people, typically wise men, living to exactly the age of 110.[17]

We now return to the events of Egyptian history. Tutankhaton, husband of Akhenaton's third daughter, succeeded to the throne and went to Thebes; his name, as we have stated, was changed to Tutankhamon (around 1336–1327), in keeping with the anti-Aton reaction. After the death of Tutankhamon his widow Ankhesenamon offered to wed a son of Suppiluliuma, the great Hittite monarch. Suppiluliuma wrote back for confirmation, for never had Egypt accepted a foreign prince as the husband of an Egyptian queen. Since Egypt was weak and the Hittites were strong, the match would have been tantamount to making the Hittite prince the pharaoh. Yet confirmation was received from the queen and Suppiluliuma sent his son. But Egyptian opposition was organized and the prince was slain on his way into Egypt, which was a sufficient cause for war. The situation was so bad that, in order to save Egypt from Hittite domination and from internal disintegration a leader arose in the person of General Haremhab (end of the fourteenth century), who founded the Nineteenth Dynasty, saved Egypt from the Hittites and established the basis for peace. Egypt was able to salvage its hold on Canaan during the period.

In spite of the Amon counterrevolution, Akhenaton's reform left some permanent effects on Egypt. For the intellectuals, all the gods were merely manifestations of one true god. Thus in the much later composition of the Wisdom of Amenemope, "the god" is often referred to. To be sure, it is not unknown in pagan cultures[18] to find a trend toward monotheism in the midst of a polytheistic milieu. Along with religion, there remained as always the practice of magic on a popular plane.

Ramses I (about 1309–8), the first king of the Nineteenth Dynasty, embarked on gigantic building operations, including huge temples and colossal statues, that eventually exhausted the resources of the land. His successor Seti I (about 1308–1291) invaded Canaan against both the Bedouins and the Hittites. Though the Hittites had conquered Mitanni and got North Syria into their sphere, Egypt main-

---

17. J. M. A. Janssen, "On the Ideal Lifetime of the Egyptian," *Oudheidkundige Mededeelingen uit het Rijksmuseum van Oudheden te Leiden* 31, 1950, pp. 33–44.

18. Many pagan Greek authors often speak of "the god" in the singular.

tained its domination over southern Canaan. Ramses II (about 1291–1224) put up vigorous opposition to the Hittites. His well-documented battles, particularly the one at Kadesh (around 1285), culminated in treaties and a century of peace with the Hittites. It was about 1270 that Hattusil III, king of the Hittites, and Ramses II made treaties in keeping with the peace allegedly established of old by the Egyptian god Re and the Hittite god Teshub. The kings made nonaggression and mutual-assistance pacts; and cordial relations continued between members of the royal families. Thus the Egyptian Queen Naptera corresponded affectionately with the Hittite Queen Puduhepa. Around 1255 B.C.E., the Hittite king sent his eldest daughter with gifts to become the queen of Egypt by wedding Ramses II. This might superficially convey the impression that Egypt won a diplomatic triumph in the match. Historic perspective, however, points in the opposite direction. Never before had an Asiatic been accepted as the official queen in the land of the pharaohs.

The reign of Ramses II brings us to the beginning of the book of Exodus. Although there is no sure proof associating him with the enslavement of the Hebrews, there are several pieces of evidence that point to this conclusion. First, we know that he began or continued several massive building projects in the eastern Delta, the location of the cities Pithom and Ramses constructed by the enslaved Israelites (Exodus 1:11).[19] Second, and more specifically, two texts from the time of Ramses II refers to the ʿApîru slaves engaged in the building campaign.[20] Again, the exact relationship between the ʿApîru and the biblical Hebrews is subject to debate, but in this specific case the correspondence may be quite close.

Accordingly, Ramses II is the most likely candidate for the pharaoh who enslaved the Israelites. Since above (p. 139) we suggested that Seti I was the pharaoh who elevated Joseph, we interpret Exodus 1:8 to refer to immediate succession.[21] The Israelites, at least from the

19. The exact location of these two cities is still debated by scholars. Pithom, or Egyptian Per-Atum ("House of Atum"), may be Tell el-Maskuta, and Ramses is identified with either Tanis or Qantur.

20. John Wilson, "The ʿEperu of the Egyptian Inscriptions," *American Journal of Semitic Languages and Literatures* 49, 1933, pp. 275–80.

21. Many scholars place Joseph in the Hyksos period and explain the new king "who knew not Joseph" as any one of the numerous pharaohs of the Eighteenth or Nineteenth Dynasty who held the Hyksos in low regard. Moses typically is placed in the time of Ramses II, for the same reasons we have indicated. But such a scheme is forced to assume that the Bible is

pharaoh's perspective, were becoming too numerous for the Egyptians, and thus the king decreed that Israelite newborn males were to be drowned in the Nile.

This proclamation sets the scene for the famous story of Moses' birth in Exodus 2:1–10, an episode that fits into a widespread literary motif from antiquity called the exposed-infant motif.[22] Most familiar to readers will be the examples of Oedipus from Greek legend and Romulus and Remus from Roman lore. The closest parallel to the Moses birth story is the Legend of Sargon, as noted above (p. 72). In the Exodus story, as in the story of Joseph, we expect and we find numerous elements familiar to us from ancient Egypt, but in the present instance the evidence comes from Mesopotamia. This reminds us that the scholar of the Bible always needs to have the broadest perspective.

The legendary nature of the Moses account is indicated in another way as well. Although the biblical tradition records for us the name of Moses' parents (Amram and Jochebed in Exodus 6:20) and of his sister (Miriam in Exodus 15:20), the birth story opts not to use these names and instead calls the characters "man," "woman," and "lass." From a literary perspective, there is an additional reason for the lack of names in the story: There is a secrecy factor involved in the salvation of Moses and the omission of the names feeds into this aspect of the narrative. Only at the end is the name of the hero Moses given.

Most likely Moses grew up in a symbiotic manner, that is, he could travel with equal ease in both Egyptian and Hebrew circles. As a young adult, he came to the defense of an Israelite who was being beaten by an Egyptian. Moses came to the defense of the former and slew the latter. This made Moses a wanted criminal in Egypt and he was forced to flee the country eastward into the desert. There he settled among the locals, living with a Midianite priest named Reuel[23] whose daughter Zipporah he married.[24]

---

silent concerning several hundred years of Israelite history. This is most unlikely, and, as demonstrated above (pp. 112–13), the genealogies do not bear out such a time span.

22. Donald B. Redford, "The Literary Motif of the Exposed Child," *Numen* 14, 1967, pp. 209–18.

23. Alternatively called Jethro, but this most probably is a title meaning "His Excellency."

24. The exact location of Midian, and thus of Mount Sinai as well, is unknown. The large tract of arid land called the Sinai Desert by modern cartographers is the general location, but we cannot be more specific than this.

One of the authentic Egyptian elements in the story is the afore-mentioned beating. This is referred to again later in the narrative when the Hebrew taskmasters go to pharaoh and say: "Behold, thy slaves [i.e., we] are beaten" (Exodus 5:16). The expression is not idiomatic in Hebrew but it rings true for Egypt, where beating was not so much a matter of brutality as it was a normal expression of relationship between men of unequal status in their daily work. Collecting taxes, educating scribes, or getting any work done without beating was rare in Egypt.

In Midian, Moses received a theophany (the famous episode of the Burning Bush, for which see Exodus 3:1–5), in which God recalled the covenant and ordered Moses back to Egypt to save his brethren from distress.[25] God empowers Moses with the powers befitting an Egyptian magician. Magic in ancient Egypt was the most respected of the arts and sciences. So if anyone was to impress the Egyptians, as Moses would have to do in order to secure the freedom of the Israelites, he would have to "show his stuff" in the manner of an Egyptian magician. Thus, for example, we possess an Egyptian story called "The Wax Crocodile," in which a magician (or lector-priest as the term often is translated) turns an inanimate wax crocodile into a real crocodile. This recalls Moses' ability to turn his staff into a snake. In fact, although Exodus 4:3 uses the regular Hebrew word for "snake," in Exodus 7:10 we encounter the Hebrew word for "crocodile."[26]

In like fashion, if Moses is to appear before pharaoh, his mission would be most effective if he did so as an equal. This will explain the rather surprising statement in Exodus 4:16, 7:1, that Moses is elevated to a god vis-à-vis pharaoh. For a man to achieve the role of the divine is heretical in the Hebrew Bible, but in the present case the promotion (temporary though it may be) is accomplished because pharaoh was viewed by the Egyptians as divine. Moreover, just as Moses is elevated from prophet to a deity, so is Aaron elevated from the role of priest to prophet.[27]

Exodus 6:3 records for us a precious piece of information regarding the name of Israel's deity. The passage informs us that the patri-

---

25. The stories of Moses and of Sinuhe have much in common. They are both men of consequence in pharaonic circles; they both get into trouble and have to flee to Semitic territory to the east, where they marry, each to a local girl, before returning to Egypt.

26. English translations typically render the word "serpent," but in truth it means "crocodile."

27. The priesthood of Aaron will be discussed later, Chapter X, pp. 164–65.

archs referred to God as El Shaddai,[28] but that the name Yahwe was unknown to them. Most likely this is historically accurate. Probably Moses learned about the god Yahwe during his residence in the desert. Numerous biblical texts associate Yahwe specifically with the desert region (referred to in different terms: Sinai, Paran, Seir, Edom, Teman; see especially Deuteronomy 33:2; Judges 5:4–5; Habakkuk 3:3). Furthermore, several Egyptian texts refer to "Yhw in the land of the nomads" in the same general region. These facts permit us to conclude that Yhw = Yahwe was a deity associated with the desert region separating Egypt and Canaan. Furthermore, they allow us to understand one of Moses' important contributions to Israelite religion: It was he who introduced the people of Israel to the worship of the desert deity Yahwe, who then was fused with the older deity El or Elohim associated with the land of Canaan.

Moses returned to Egypt, was reunited with his brother Aaron, and the two of them now were ready to bring on the ten plagues. There are various ways of understanding the plagues, none of them mutually exclusive. The first approach is to view them as natural phenomena that strike the land of Egypt. The first plague is not to be taken literally as blood, rather it refers to the reddening of the Nile that occurs periodically due to erosion of the clay banks. To this day Egypt is burdened by insects, skin diseases, locusts, etc., so that these elements add to the Egyptian coloration of the story.[29]

The second approach views the plagues as a magic contest. As noted above, magic played an important role in ancient Egypt, and indeed Moses and Aaron are pitted against the Egyptian magicians in the contest of turning staffs into snakes or crocodiles, as well as in the first three plagues. It is important to note, however, that the biblical tradition considers magic to be a pagan practice. Accordingly, the author makes a distinction between Moses and Aaron, on the one hand, and the Egyptian wise men, on the other. When the former bring frogs about the land, for example, it is because they have been empowered by God to do so. When the Egyptian magicians do likewise, they accomplish this feat through their incantations and spells.

Finally, the plagues may be understood as attacks on the Egyptian

28. The exact meaning of Shaddai still is unknown (though traditionally it has been translated as "Almighty").

29. See the detailed study by Greta Hort, "The Plagues of Egypt," *Zeitschrift für die alttestamentliche Wissenschaft* 69, 1957, pp. 84–103; 70, 1958, pp. 48–59.

gods. The early plagues are more nuisances than anything else, and they attack minor deities of the Egyptian pantheon. These would include Hapi, the Nile River god, and Heqet, the frog-goddess of life. The later plagues not only are more intensive, they also are an attack on the chief god Re. Thus the eighth plague of locusts blots out the sun in midday, and the ninth plague of darkness (most likely to be understood as a severe sandstorm) darkens the skies for three days.[30] The Bible itself recognizes that the plagues struck the Egyptian deities (Exodus 12:12; Numbers 33:4).

The story of the plagues is one of the classic instances in the Bible of the combination of history and epic. Our prose account probably is derived from poetic precursors (and the same goes for much of biblical narrative down to the introduction of annals in the tenth century B.C.E.).[31] Thus, we cannot regard our account as "history" in the accepted modern sense of the word. But we can identify historic elements through the use of collateral information. While we should try to place epic traditions in a historic context, we cannot succeed in doing so comprehensively because they are the products of many generations. In the course of transmission there are changes, including many accretions and some deletions. A historic kernel may have a precise historic context in time and place, but the problem of extracting a historic kernel from an epic is always difficult and often impossible. Applying this view of biblical narrative to the specific case of the ten plagues, we content ourselves with the opinion that in some way a series of natural disorders struck the land of Egypt. To the Israelites, these events were interpreted as Yahwe's bringing salvation to His people. To the Egyptians, they were viewed as bad omens that forced them to expel the Israelites from their country.

The plagues account culminates with the killing of the firstborn, an act that leads pharaoh to allow the Israelites to leave. This event occurred in the spring, at the time of the joint holidays of Pesah (Passover) and Matzot (Unleavened Bread), agricultural feasts celebrating the lambing of the flocks and the first harvest of the year

---

30. See further Gary A. Rendsburg, "The Egyptian Sun-God Ra in the Pentateuch," *Henoch* 10, 1988, pp. 3–15.

31. In fact, poetic versions of the ten plagues, with important differences in detail, are preserved in Psalms 78 and 105.

(barley in particular).[32] The Israelites, who viewed their God as one who interacts in human affairs, that is, as a God of history (unlike the pagan concept of the divine, which equated gods with various aspects of nature without any direct influence on human affairs), connected the Exodus from Egypt with this joint festival. In this way, Passover came to commemorate a historical event, the Exodus from Egypt.[33]

The account of the Exodus itself is filled with epic features. The baking of bread is such a feature, as is the greatly exaggerated numbers of Israelites, 600,000 adult males to be specific (Exodus 12:37). A parallel to the entire narrative is to be found in the Ugaritic Legend of Kret. In the Kret story, the hero performs a ritual sacrifice, bakes bread as provisions for his troops, embarks with his 3 million soldiers on a military expedition, marches for three days, rests at a shrine to the deities, then marches for three more days to reach his target, remains silent for six additional days, and then on the seventh day the action commences with the successful completion of his mission. All these features are present in the biblical story. The Israelites perform the Passover sacrifice, bake bread (specifically unleavened bread) for the journey, march forward with a large army (note the use of military terms in Exodus 12:37, 41, 51; 13:18), progress to Mount Sinai, worship Yahwe at this site, march farther to the land of Canaan, remain silent for six days in their encirclement of Jericho, and then attack on the seventh day.[34] Again, these features do not lessen the historical fact that in some way the Israelites left Egypt and made the trek to Canaan. But they do make the task of the historian more difficult, because the narrative as we have it combines historical and epic features into one unified account.

The biblical account continues by informing us that pharaoh regretted granting permission for the Israelites to leave Egypt, and thus he sent his troops to pursue them into the wilderness. It is apposite to cite an Egyptian document that relates to this story. From

32. On the background of these holidays, see Roland de Vaux, *Ancient Israel,* New York, 1961, pp. 484–93.

33. In a world full of dislocations, the Exodus theme was international. For Amos (9:7), God was equally the sponsor of the Exodus of Israel from Egypt, the exodus of the Philistines from Caphtor, and the exodus of the Arameans from Kir.

34. See Cyrus H. Gordon, "Notes on the Legend of Keret," *Journal of Near Eastern Studies* 11, 1952, pp. 212–13; and G. Del Olmo Lete, "La conquista de Jericó y la leyenda ugarítica de *KRT,*" *Sefarad* 25, 1965, pp. 1–15.

approximately the same period we possess a letter from an Egyptian border patrolman to two of his colleagues concerning the pursuit of two escaped slaves. He writes, "Who found their tracks? Which watch found their tracks? What people are after them? Write to me about all that has happened to them and how many people you sent out after them."[35] Now, if the Egyptians exerted the effort to track down two escaped slaves, it is not unlikely that they would have pursued a larger group, i.e., the Israelites, as well. A striking similarity between the biblical story and the Egyptian document is that both texts mention the place Migdol (Exodus 14:2). Is it possible that the route the Israelites used to leave Egypt was a type of "underground railway" known to slaves fleeing the regime?

The Egyptian force caught up to the Israelites at the Sea of Reeds (a body of water to be identified with one of the marshy lakes separating Egypt and the Sinai Desert).[36] It was here that the final encounter between the two peoples occurred; the highlight of the story is the well-known episode of the parting of the waters.

Regardless of what actually happened at the Sea of Reeds, we are fortunate to possess a striking Egyptian literary parallel to the episode. One of the tales of wonder that the Egyptians told about their magicians was the case of the lector-priest Djadja-em-ankh who saved the day on the occasion of a royal yachting party. When one of the princesses lost her pendant, which fell into the water, the day was almost ruined. But the hero said his say of magic, parted the waters, recovered the lost pendant on dry land, returned it to the princess, and then brought the waters back together again so that the party could continue.[37] This comparable story allows us to see what the author of Exodus is doing in relating the story of the Sea of Reeds. Moses, empowered by God, saves his last and greatest act to the end. He defeats the Egyptians on their own terms using their rules.

The story is told not only in prose (Exodus 14), but it is celebrated in song as well (Exodus 15). It is important to note that at this time God is recognized as the supreme but not the only god. The query in the Song of the Sea, "Who is like You among the gods, O Yahwe?" (Exodus 15:11), indicates that God is beyond compare but is not the only deity. Also in the Ten Commandments (Exodus 20:2–

---

35. For the full text see Pritchard, *Ancient Near Eastern Texts,* p. 259.

36. Today the Suez Canal runs through this region.

37. Miriam Lichtheim, *Ancient Egyptian Literature,* vol. 1, Berkeley, 1973, pp. 216–17.

17) it is said, "You shall not have other gods before Me. . . . You shall not bow down to them or worship them because I, Yahwe, your God, am a jealous God." And above we noted that the Bible understands the ten plagues as attacks on Egyptian deities. Throughout most of the Hebrew Bible, the existence of other gods is recognized, but their worship is forbidden. This type of religion is called a monolatry, etymologically "the worship of one." Eventually, as we shall see (Chapter XVII, pp. 291–92), the religion shifted to a pure monotheism, etymologically "the belief in one," when the very existence of other gods was laughed at as ridiculous. But this development was still hundreds of years away (it would occur in the sixth century B.C.E.).

With the Egyptians now behind them, the Israelites embarked on their trek through the Sinai region en route to Canaan. The Bible describes various events that occur along the way, but for the most part the remainder of the Pentateuch is concerned with the law and the cult of ancient Israel (to be discussed in detail in the next chapter). The period of the Wandering in the desert before the entrance to the Promised Land via Transjordan is given the round number of forty years, which, in accordance with Hebrew idiom, need not be taken exactly, and in this case was probably shorter than that figure. The story comes to its conclusion with the recording of the death of Moses at the very end of the Torah (Deuteronomy 34).

We conclude this chapter with a discussion of the chronology involved. In truth the date of the Exodus can only be discussed in conjunction with the date of the Conquest / Settlement of the Israelites in the land of the Canaan. This topic will be the subject of a subsequent chapter, but here we can say a few words relevant to the issue of chronology.[38]

Recent surveys of the land of Israel demonstrate the arrival of the Israelites in the twelfth century B.C.E. The central hill country was largely unoccupied in the Late Bronze Age, but from the beginning of the Iron Age, i.e., the twelfth century, onward, there are dozens, even hundreds, of new settlements in the region. The pattern of these settlements, moreover, indicates the arrival of a seminomadic people and its transition to a sedentary lifestyle. There can be little doubt

---

38. The cumbersome term Conquest/Settlement refers to the manner in which the Israelites emerged in the land of the Canaan. In some cases military action was necessary and in other cases peaceful settlement was the method. For details see Chapter XI, pp. 168–73.

that the archeological record bespeaks the arrival of the Israelites.[39]

Furthermore, several cities that the Israelites encountered either did not exist until the 1100s B.C.E., or there is clear evidence of their destruction at this time. Examples of the former are Heshbon in Transjordan and Ai in the territory of Benjamin. The most important example of the latter is Lachish, whose destruction can now be dated to about 1160 B.C.E., thanks to the discovery there of a metal object bearing the cartouche of Pharaoh Ramses III (1182–51).

If the Israelites emerge in Canaan only in the twelfth century, and if we agree that the period of the Wandering was not a long one (see above, p. 149), then the Exodus from Egypt must have occurred in the twelfth century as well. There are several lines of evidence that point to this conclusion.

We have already discussed the importance of genealogies for establishing a relative chronology. What we need, therefore, is a genealogy that links an individual whose dating is fixed with an individual whose dating is still in flux. Fortunately, we have one such genealogy that fits the bill, namely, the lineage of King David, dated by all scholars to c. 1000 B.C.E. In Ruth 4:18–22 and in 1 Chronicles 2:5–15, his lineage is traced back to Nahshon. Nahshon is a member of the Exodus generation; Exodus 6:23 mentions him as the brother-in-law of Aaron, and Numbers 1:7 lists him as the tribal leader of Judah at this time. Now Nahshon is five generations before David, which according to our system would place him c. 1150 B.C.E.

We still need to discuss what is perhaps the most important piece of evidence, namely, the Merneptah Stela. This inscription commemorates the military conquests of Pharaoh Merneptah (1224–1214), first boasting of his victory over Libya and then ending with several lines about Canaan.[40] The text mentions Israel; in fact this is the only reference to Israel in all of Egyptian literature. Earlier we discussed the Egyptian writing system, which not only spelled out words phonologically, but also included determinatives to allow the reader easier comprehension. When the Merneptah Stela refers to other conquered peoples and places, it uses the foreign land determinative to mark them. Such is the case, for example, with larger enti-

---

39. For details see the important book by Israel Finkelstein, *The Archaeology of the Israelite Settlement,* Jerusalem, 1988.

40. For the text see Pritchard, *Ancient Near Eastern Texts,* pp. 376–78.

ties such as Canaan and Hurru and with individual cities such as Gezer and Ashkelon. But when Israel is mentioned, the people determinative is used (i.e., a man, a woman, and the plural marker). We interpret this orthography to refer to the Israelites as a people without a land, a situation that matches their condition as slaves in the land of Egypt. The scribe knew they originated in Canaan, and thus he included them in his listing of Merneptah's enemies from that region, but he distinguished the Israelites by marking them as a people, not a foreign land. If this interpretation is correct, then the Israelites still were slaves under Merneptah, that is, late in the thirteenth century B.C.E.

The question still remains: Can we pinpoint the date of the Exodus? A clue that helps us answer this question comes from a series of texts from the reign of Ramses III. This pharaoh was under attack from the Sea Peoples c. 1175 B.C.E. The coalition, led by the Philistines, sailed across the Mediterranean and attempted a marine invasion of Egypt in the area of the Delta. Ramses III successfully repelled the invaders, and the Sea Peoples were forced to move up the coast to settle along the Canaanite plain. On the other hand, however, we know they inflicted great damage on Egypt. In fact, the Egyptian empire, which had included Canaan for much of the Bronze Age, was so weakened that within a few decades of the Sea Peoples invasion it withdrew from Canaan for the final time in its glorious history.[41] The attack of the Sea Peoples would have been a propitious time for the Israelites to leave Egypt. The Bible, furthermore, hints at a correlation between the Exodus and the Sea Peoples invasion in Exodus 13:17. This passage states that when the Israelites left Egypt, "God did not lead them by way of the land of Philistines though it was near, for God said, 'Lest the people change their minds when they see the fighting and then return to Egypt.' " In other words, the Israelites left Egypt when the Philistines were attacking along the coast, and thus they took a longer exit route through the desert to the south.

The sum of all these arguments is that the Exodus from Egypt

---

41. Egypt was not to produce a fourth flowering of her splendid native civilization. There had been the Old, Middle, and New Kingdoms with their cultural brilliance, but now the end had come. Later revivals, despite finesse or monumentality, fall short of the three great periods now passed.

occurred c. 1175 B.C.E., during the reign of Ramses III. The Israelites arrived in Canaan sometime shortly thereafter, let us say, c. 1150 B.C.E.[42]

42. For a more detailed version of the above arguments, see Gary A. Rendsburg, "The Date of the Exodus and the Conquest/Settlement: The Case for the 1100's," *Vetus Testamentum* 42, 1992, pp. 510–27.

## CHAPTER X

# Israelite Law and Cult

W e interrupt our telling of Israel's history to discuss two subjects that dominate the latter books of the Pentateuch: law and cult. The story line, which begins in Genesis 1 with creation and culminates in Exodus 15 with the crossing of the Sea of Reeds, continues in only selected chapters of the remainder of the Pentateuch (mostly the Wandering period is described, see above Chapter IX, pp. 147–49). The majority of the remaining material (most of Exodus 20–40, all of Leviticus, portions of Numbers, and the majority of Deuteronomy) is devoted to law and cult.

But the dichotomy between law and cult, on the one hand, and narrative, on the other hand, is not so sharp in the canonical version of the Torah.[1] They are meshed in the following way. After the Israelites leave Egypt, Moses brings them to Mt. Sinai (Exodus 19). At this point he ascends the mountaintop where he receives from God the Ten Commandments (Exodus 20:2–14; see also Deuteronomy 5:6–18). All the legal and cultic material of the Pentateuch will follow in the succeeding chapters and books. Accordingly, from this layout it is clear that the Ten Commandments (or Decalogue) is the foundational statement of ancient Israel. That is to say, it is not only later generations of Jews and Christians that ascribed to this document

1. Torah and Pentateuch are the two terms used to describe the books of Genesis through Deuteronomy. The former derives from Hebrew and means "teaching" (because the basic teachings of ancient Judaism are to be found in these five books); the latter derives from Greek and means "five scrolls" (because in antiquity the five books were written on five separate scrolls, unlike today when all five are bound together in one very large scroll for liturgical use in the synagogue).

such great importance; from its placement in the Pentateuch it is quite obvious that the Decalogue was viewed as fundamental already in ancient times.

Accordingly, the question may be asked: What makes this document so foundational? And the answer is readily forthcoming: Whereas other laws and cultic details depend on individual circumstances (e.g., whether one is a farmer or a shepherd, a priest or a layman, etc.), the proclamations in the Decalogue are directed to all Israelites regardless of circumstances. This universality is indicated not only by the content of the Ten Commandments (e.g., the worship of only one God, the prohibition against idols, no murder, no adultery, etc.), but also by their concise wording. The legal material found elsewhere in the Torah is couched in more complex language, often with technical legal terms (compare English "legalese"). Not so the Ten Commandments, which are characterized by a remarkable conciseness (in some cases, only two words in the Hebrew, e.g., *lo' tirṣaḥ* "you shall not murder"). From these and other factors it is clear that already in ancient Israel the Decalogue was viewed as a unique text.[2]

We turn now to a more detailed look at Israelite law. There are three legal collections imbedded in the Torah; they are known to scholars as the Covenant Code (Exodus 21:1–23:19), the Holiness Code (Leviticus 17–26), and the Deuteronomic Code (Deuteronomy 12–28). Experts debate the relationship among the three, though there is at least a consensus that the Covenant Code is the oldest. What is striking about this collection (though it is true to some extent of the others as well) is the high number of parallels between its individual laws and laws found in Mesopotamian legal collections.[3] If we compare only the most famous of the Mesopotamian legal texts, namely, Hammurapi's Code (HC) (c. 1700 B.C.E.), we note a goodly number of close parallels.

For example, both HC 14 and Exodus 21:16 outlaw kidnapping; both HC 209 and Exodus 21:22 deal with the case of a woman who miscarries when accidentally injured during a scuffle between two

2. See further Moshe Weinfeld, "The Decalogue: Its Significance, Uniqueness, and Place in Israel's Tradition," in E. R. Firmage, *et al.*, eds., *Religion and Law: Biblical-Judaic and Islamic Perspectives,* Winona Lake, Ind., 1990, pp. 3–47; and for a less detailed treatment, Moshe Weinfeld, "Israelite Religion," *The Encyclopedia of Religion,* vol. 7, New York, 1987, pp. 481–97.

3. See Shalom Paul, *Studies in the Book of the Covenant in the Light of Cuneiform and Biblical Law,* Leiden, 1970.

men; both HC 250–251 and Exodus 21:28–29 treat the famous case of the goring bull;[4] and both HC 266 and Exodus 22:9–12 consider the issue of a sheep that had been entrusted with another man for care, but that now has been killed by a lion at prey. Such examples could easily be multiplied, especially if we were to extend the boundaries of the discussion beyond Hammurapi's Code and into other Mesopotamian legal collections.

The closeness of these and other parallels, both in content and in wording, demonstrates a clear relationship between individual laws in the Bible (especially in the Covenant Code) and in Mesopotamian collections. The best way to explain this phenomenon is to assume that ancient Israel participated in what may be called the ancient Near Eastern legal tradition. There is no need to posit direct borrowing. Instead, we simply may conclude that the various peoples of the ancient Near East had a common understanding as to what constituted crime and how particular crimes should be punished.[5]

Thus, for example, in the last of the instances cited above, in the case of a sheep that had been entrusted for care with a shepherd, but that now has been killed by a lion at prey, Israelites and Babylonians and presumably others agreed that the shepherd could not be held responsible. He could not be expected to ward off every wild animal on the hunt and to protect what must have been dozens if not hundreds of sheep from the attacker. At the same time, however, both the Bible and Hammurapi's Code make it clear that the shepherd had to clear himself of any suspicion of theft by bringing the mangled carcass as testimony. The similar judgment in both biblical and cuneiform law in this case should be attributed to the common approach to law mentioned above, and the same holds for all such parallels that have or can be adduced.

But just as biblical law has much in common with the laws of

---

4. Most ancient Near Eastern languages, Hebrew and Akkadian among them, do not distinguish between "bull" and "ox." Accordingly, many scholars call this case "the goring ox." But oxen (who, because they have been castrated, are quite docile) are much less likely to gore than bulls (whose strength and virility are well known).

5. As an analogy, compare the Western legal tradition shared by the United States, Canada, England, France, etc. Similar laws will be found in the law codes of all these countries, but this does not mean that a Canadian legislator was reading the French code and decided that a particular law would be good for his country as well. Rather, as we all recognize, the aforementioned nations share a common approach to law—that is, by and large they agree as to what constitutes crime and punishment—and so a comparison of their law codes will reveal close parallels.

Israel's neighbors, so does it differ in important respects. Dozens of laws in the Torah reveal a uniquely Israelite viewpoint. The distinctively Israelite laws fall into either one of two groups: (1) those laws that were promulgated because of Israel's greater concern for human life, and (2) those laws that were promulgated as a reaction to the practices of Israel's immediate neighbors in Canaan. Both of these issues require further elucidation.

The first of the above points can be illustrated by pointing out the differences between the laws of the Torah and the laws of Hammurapi's Code (the similarities between these two corpora notwithstanding). The differences that occur generally are attributable to the greater concern for human life in ancient Israel. For example, slavery in Israel undoubtedly was not as cruel a fate as it was in Babylonia. In HC 15 we learn that harboring a runaway slave was punishable by death. In Deuteronomy 23:16–17, by contrast, we read that the Israelites were commanded to give refuge to a runaway slave. Similarly, in Babylonia (and elsewhere presumably) slavery appears to have been an open-ended proposition, that is, there was no time limit to the condition (though slaves could buy their freedom, if possible). In Israel, by contrast, slavery was limited to six years and in the seventh year the slave went free without payment (Exodus 21:2). Moreover, in Hammurapi's Code, there is reference only to the slave who denies the mastery of his master (HC 282), whereas in the Bible there is reference only to the slave who is so committed to his master that he wishes to remain his slave forever (Exodus 21:5). The general picture that emerges from these and other considerations is that the lot of a slave in ancient Israel was far better than that of a slave elsewhere. So, while Israel admitted slavery as a natural aspect of society, the culture recognized that slaves were human beings worthy of the basic decencies.

Another example of this process may be cited. The death penalty is mentioned throughout all of the legal collections of the ancient Near East. Outside of Israel, there is no reason not to assume that the death penalty was carried out with relative frequency. In Israel, however, other laws, called rules of evidence, were developed that made the implementation of the death penalty quite rare. The most important of these laws required the testimony of at least two witnesses before the death penalty could be enforced (Numbers 35:30, Deuteronomy 17:6). When one considers that most crimes that carry capital punishment are not committed in broad daylight, it must have been difficult to find two witnesses who could testify to such an offense. Furthermore, in ancient Israel, women, minors, and slaves were disqualified from serving as legal witnesses.[6] This made it all the more difficult to find two witnesses (who thus could be only free adult males). All of this goes to show that, notwithstanding the numerous mentions of the death penalty in the Torah, criminals must have been put to death very rarely in ancient Israel.[7]

One last example of the greater concern for human life will suffice. But this example differs from the above two. In the instances of slavery and the death penalty, the greater concern for human life in Israel led to a more lenient attitude. But this principle is a two-edged sword, because when a life is lost, the same concern will ensure retribution for the lost life. The example we can use is that of the goring bull. Above we addressed the remarkable similarity between HC 250–251 and Exodus 21:28–29, but an important difference needs to be stressed as well. In the case of a bull that gores someone to death the first time, according to HC 250 the case is not subject to claim. Exodus 21:28 agrees to the extent that the owner of the bull goes unpunished, but at the same time the law states that the bull must be stoned to death. The point is that a human life was lost, and while no human being will pay for the loss of life with his own life, retribution is necessary, so the bull receives the death penalty. In the case of a bull that gores a second time, according to HC 251, the bull still is not punished, and the owner simply pays a fine. In Exodus 21:29, not only is the repeat-offending bull to be stoned to death, but the owner of the animal suffers the death penalty, too.[8] In these instances, we can see that the greater concern for human life leads to a harsher position in ancient Israel. Regardless of the circumstances, a human life was lost and that life needs to be recompensed by loss of life; not so in Babylonia where monetary payment suffices.

A second group of laws bears a distinctively Israelite outlook

6. We learn this from the postbiblical Jewish legal collection called the Mishna, edited c. 220 C.E. by Rabbi Judah ha-Nasi.

7. The still later postbiblical Jewish collection called the Gemara (c. 400 C.E.) states that a court that implemented the death penalty once in seven years (a climactic variant says seventy years!) was considered a "hanging court." We may wish to compare the situation in the United States today. The death penalty is "on the books" in most jurisdictions. But only rarely is it carried out; so rarely, in fact, that when a criminal is electrocuted or killed by other means, the event still makes the evening newscasts.

8. One must assume that this repeat-offending bull previously gored someone, but not to death, and thus was permitted to live.

because of their reaction to Canaanite practices (we touched upon this subject ever so briefly in Chapter VI, p. 94). While it is useful to compare and contrast the laws of the Pentateuch with Mesopotamian legal collections such as Hammurapi's Code, in the end we must keep in mind, as noted above, that no direct contact can be proved between Israelite law and Babylonian law. However, when we turn to Israelite laws that were promulgated as a reaction to Canaanite practices, here we are dealing with very real and very direct contact. For the Israelites shared the land of Canaan with the peoples called collectively the Canaanites. This does not mean that Israelites and Canaanites lived side by side in the same cities. Instead, we assume that there were separate towns and villages for each. But these locales lay in close proximity to each other, so that contact between the groups was common.[9]

The picture that emerges from a look at a relatively large number of biblical laws is that the Israelites found much of Canaanite society to be abhorrent and depraved. Moreover, because Canaanite religion was attractive to segments of the Israelite population (this theme will recur repeatedly in the books of the Prophets), the Israelite leaders saw as part of their calling the need to separate the Israelites from the Canaanites. The way to do this was to drive a legal wedge between Israelites and Canaanites by outlawing for the former many of the practices of the latter.

As we saw earlier in Chapter VI, our knowledge of the Canaanites comes mainly from Ugarit. While it is true that this site lies far to the north of the region settled by the Hebrews, scholars are in agreement that the society reflected in the Ugaritic texts is not unlike that of Canaanite cities farther south. The epics themselves refer to Canaanite cities closer to the area inhabited by the Israelites (such as Tyre and Sidon). Accordingly, in the analysis that follows, we will be comparing specific customs reflected in the Ugaritic texts with individual laws appearing in the Pentateuch. The pattern is clear: Many biblical laws originate as a reaction to Canaanite practices.

9. We can compare the situation in the modern Middle East. In Lebanon, for example, there are Christian villages and there are Muslim villages. The latter often are either solely Sunnite or Shiite. In Israel, to take another example, there are Jewish settlements alongside Arab villages. Only in the big cities such as Beirut and Jerusalem do the groups mix, and even here they are divided geographically into different sectors. This pattern is unlike the American system, in which peoples of different ethnic and religious backgrounds may all live in the same neighborhood, on the same street, or in the same building.

We may begin with two passages in the mythological texts that depict Baal, the god of fertility, engaged in sexual intercourse. In one passage he makes love to the goddess Anat, who is both his consort and his sister, and in another passage he copulates with a heifer (the latter was discussed earlier; see Chapter VI, pp. 93–94). There exists a doctrine in the study of religion called *imitatio dei,* by which scholars refer to the fact that the actions and passions of deities in the mythological texts are often a reflection of human society; then, through a circular process, the humans justify their actions because the gods and goddesses act in those ways. Thus, although we have only Canaanite deities involved in incest and bestiality, there can be no doubt that Canaanite people engaged in these acts as well. We hasten to add that in the normal course of things, we can be quite sure that the average Canaanite husband and wife had normal relations with each other, and that the farmer returning from a hard day of work did not seek out his cow as a sexual partner. But that such practices occurred, no matter how regularly or irregularly, can be determined by reading about the amours of Baal.

In light of this, we come to an understanding of the biblical laws that prohibit these actions. Leviticus 18 is devoted to all types of illicit sexual relations; incest involving a brother and a sister is referred to specifically in Leviticus 18:9, and bestiality is referred to specifically in Leviticus 18:23. It is also important to look closely at Leviticus 18:24, which attributes these practices to the Canaanite people themselves, in line with our above conclusion based on the doctrine of *imitatio dei.*

In the Epic of Aqhat we read how the goddess of war Anat desired the special bow and arrows manufactured for the hero Aqhat by the craftsman god Kothar-and-Hasis (see Chapter VI, pp. 91–92). When Aqhat refused to part with his equipment, Anat simply killed him and took the bow and arrows. In a section of the Baal cycle, we read of this deity: "Baal goes on the roam, he draws near to the plains, he reaches and finds the great creatures, Baal verily covets and desires them." Exactly what is intended by the great creatures we do not know; for our present concern this point is unimportant. What is significant is that once more a Canaanite deity is portrayed as covetous. These passages, therefore, supply us with the background of the Tenth Commandment in the Decalogue "you shall not covet" (Exodus 20:14; Deuteronomy 5:18). Coveting, of course, is no more than a thought process, against which it is difficult to legislate. But the

Israelites realized that from one's thoughts follow one's actions. Thus they outlawed not only the acts themselves (murder, adultery, stealing, etc.), but also the thought (coveting) that precedes these actions. In Canaanite society, if one had the power, one exercised it, first by coveting and then by putting these thoughts into action. Later on, we shall see that the Canaanite princess Jezebel acts in exactly this manner when she engineers her husband Ahab's seizing the vineyard of Naboth (Chapter XIV, p. 228).

Another biblical law that now can be explained through recourse to the Ugaritic texts is the prohibition against transvestism in Deuteronomy 22:5. This act is described in the Epic of Aqhat as well. After the hero is slain, his sister Pughat seeks revenge against Anat for the murder. To do so, Pughat disguises herself as a male, replete with rouge (the coloration of males, especially warrior heroes), man's clothing, and weaponry. The Israelite reaction is to forbid transvestism, another aspect of Canaanite society that they found reprehensible. Again, one needs to place this in its proper context. No doubt the average Canaanite male or female dressed in proper fashion throughout most of his or her life. But since Canaanite epic literature describes transvestism in a noble manner, we may conclude that this act not only was practiced but also was countenanced. A close reading of the biblical prohibition reveals that the female is referred to first and then the male follows. This runs counter to most laws in the Pentateuch, which either are addressed to the male solely, or are addressed to the male first and the female second. This is not coincidental; rather it suggests an even closer connection with Pughat's action detailed in the Epic of Aqhat.

There existed in Ugarit a group of temple functionaries known as qedeshim. We do not know their exact role, but they and their female counterparts qedeshot specifically are outlawed in the Bible, particularly in connection with temple ritual (Deuteronomy 23:18). Various theories concerning these individuals have been put forth; the most commonly held one identifies them with temple prostitutes whose function was to engage in ritual orgies. While the priests offered the sacrifices to the gods, these temple prostitutes (so the theory goes) committed acts of sexual intercourse in order to elicit the rain of Baal. In the Canaanite fertility cult, the relationship of Baal to the earth was compared to that of a human couple having intercourse. Just as the male supplies the liquid semen that impregnates the female, so does Baal supply the liquid rain that causes Mother Earth to be fertile and reproductive. Thus, in a type of ritual drama these temple prostitutes would perform the very act that Baal was to perform. This also will explain why Baal is portrayed as sexually active in the mythological texts (see above concerning his relationships with Anat and with the heifer). Unfortunately, none of this can be proved to the extent that would satisfy most scholars. Regardless of details, however, it remains true that *qedeshim* were functionaries in the Canaanite temples, and that they and their female counterparts were unacceptable to the Israelites.

In the above examples, from our subjective viewpoint three thousand years later, we can see that the Israelites found various Canaanite practices (incest, bestiality, coveting, transvestism, temple prostitution) to be abhorrent. But the need for driving a wedge between Canaanite and Israelite society was so great, that even in cases where nothing so morally upsetting was at stake, the Hebrews likewise outlawed some of their neighbors' practices. An example of such a law is the prohibition against sacrificing honey in Leviticus 2:11. Clearly, there is nothing so repugnant about such an act. But in the Legend of Kret (see Chapter VI, p. 91), the hero performs a sacrifice of wine and honey. Wine was too dear to the Israelites (it was the leading produce of the country) and thus could not be excluded. But honey was expendable, and thus it was not permitted to be sacrificed. The sole reason for this prohibition can only be that honey was used in Canaanite sacrifices, and thus to distinguish Israelite ritual from pagan ritual this practice was outlawed.[10]

Still other examples of this pattern could be presented, but the five instances discussed here make it perfectly clear that a good portion of biblical law originates as a reaction to Canaanite practices.

Next we must consider the date of the legal portions of the Pentateuch. Although the entirety of the law is presented against the backdrop of the life of Moses, and in many cases the laws actually are placed in the mouth of Moses (see, for example, Leviticus 18:1, where God speaks to Moses, who is then to convey the message to the Israelite people), for a variety of reasons we are forced to con-

---

10. The greatest of all medieval Jewish legal scholars, Maimonides (1135–1204), already made this point. Driven by Aristotelian principles, he sought to uncover the reasons for the laws in the Bible. While he did not have access to ancient Canaanite literature, he intuitively realized that the prohibition against the sacrifice of honey must be due to its having been a pagan practice. His view was substantiated with the discovery of the Ugaritic texts in this century.

clude that this picture is a fiction created by the Israelite literati responsible for the Torah in its final form.

To begin, if all that we said above about Israelite laws as reactions to Canaanite practices is correct, then certainly Moses could have nothing to do with such laws. A point made quite clear in the Bible at various spots is that Moses did not enter the Promised Land (e.g., Deuteronomy 34:4). For the Israelite legalists to have promulgated laws in reaction to Canaanite practices, the setting must have been the land of Canaan. Indeed, once the Hebrews settled the land of Canaan, we begin to read how many among them were attracted to the worship of Canaanite deities and to intermingling with the Canaanite population (Judges 2:11–13, 3:5–7; etc.). It is against this backdrop that the laws discussed above must have developed.

Furthermore, during Moses' time, the Israelites were wandering in the desert. The laws of the Pentateuch, by contrast, reflect a settled population with fields and vineyards (see, for example, Exodus 22:4; Leviticus 19:9; etc.). And while it is possible that the Israelites in the desert engaged in some seasonal agriculture (this would be possible at a large oasis such as Kadesh-Barnea), the constant reference to vineyards in the laws of the Bible can point only to Canaan, where, as noted above, wine production was a major component of the economic life of the people.

There are other laws in the Bible that reflect a post-Moses society. Foremost among them is the law of the king in Deuteronomy 17:14–20. No society develops laws until they are required by particular societal needs. Not until 1020 B.C.E. did the Israelites appoint their first king (Saul), so that this section of the Deuteronomic Code cannot antedate that period. In this case, we can be even more specific, because Deuteronomy 17:16–17 refers to actions associated specifically with Solomon (engaging in horse trade, having too many wives, and amassing too much wealth). Below we shall discuss the reign of Solomon in greater detail (see Chapter XIII). For now, it is important to note that the excesses of his reign led to much discontent among the people. Without doubt the restrictions placed upon the king in Deuteronomy 17 are a direct reaction to Solomon, and these laws may be dated confidently to c. 930, near the end of his reign.[11]

11. Compare the Twenty-second Amendment to the United States Constitution, which limits a president to two terms. This amendment was proposed in 1947 and ratified in 1951 to prevent another situation like that of Franklin D. Roosevelt who was elected to four terms

In short, the laws of the Pentateuch derive from the period of Israel's early settlement of the land through the united monarchy. There are references to the promulgation of law in post-Moses contexts (e.g., Joshua 24:25) and these should be viewed as essentially historically accurate. But if this is correct, then still we need to answer the question: Why does the Bible portray Moses' active involvement in Israelite law? The answer lies in the uniquely Israelite view that law is divine in origin. Unlike other societies in the ancient Near East, which had kings as the promulgators of law (Hammurapi emphasizes this point repeatedly in the prologue and epilogue to his law code), in Israel God was seen as the lawgiver. The attribution of law to Yahwe obviously is related to Israel's unique understanding of Yahwe as a God of history who interacts in human affairs, in contrast to the polytheistic view of nature gods (this point was noted earlier, Chapter IX, p. 147). Thus, if God is the one who generates the laws, they need to be transmitted to the people through His greatest prophet, namely Moses (see Deuteronomy 34:10). In this manner Israelite literati invented the notion of Moses' involvement in the transmission of Yahwe's law to the people of Israel. For the Hebrews this became a theological trusim; but historically it is inaccurate, for as we demonstrated above, the legal portions of the Torah are the result of generations of development.

The fact that the Bible portrays the law as divine in origin leads us to our next discussion: the relationship of law and covenant. Until now we have concentrated on the content of the legal portions of the Torah. But the form in which the legal portions are presented is of extreme importance for understanding another unique aspect of Israelite thought. Simply stated, the laws are depicted as stipulations that Israel must adhere to under its covenant with God. The form used to express this thought is the treaty format that was widely circulated in the ancient Near East. We possess numerous treaty documents from the Hittites, the Assyrians, and others, and typically these texts are written in the same format. They begin with a preamble identifying the speaker, then move to a historical prologue, the stipulations that are to be adhered to, a list of curses and blessings that will occur if the treaty either is broken or followed, a description of the

(1932, 1936, 1940, 1944). Similarly, compare the campaign financing reforms that were instituted in the United States in the 1970s and 1980s in direct reaction to the excesses of Richard M. Nixon.

deposition of the treaty and its public reading, and finally a list of witnesses, specifically the gods of the nations involved.

All of these elements are to be found in the Torah, both in the Exodus version of the covenant and in its repetition in Deuteronomy.[12] Preambles may be found in Exodus 20:1a and Deuteronomy 1:1–5; historical prologues in Exodus 20:1b and Deuteronomy 1:6–3:29; the stipulations or laws in Exodus 20:2–14, etc., and Deuteronomy 4:1–26:19; the curses and blessings in Leviticus 26 and Deuteronomy 28; and the deposition and public reading in Exodus 24:7, 25:16, and Deuteronomy 31:9–13. Because Yahwe Himself is a party to the agreement between Him and the Israelites, the inclusion of witnesses to the treaty or covenant presents a problem. In the Exodus version, this element is not present; in the Deuteronomy version, the problem is solved by invoking the testimony of the written document itself or the ark in which it is to be housed (Deuteronomy 31:26). In sum, the covenant established between God and Israel is expressed in terms understandable to the human partners of the covenant.[13] The wording is exactly that of the ancient treaty formula, a format well known in antiquity (note that Hebrew *berit* means both "covenant" as between deity and man, and "treaty" as between two humans [e.g., Genesis 14:13]).

The covenant, of course, was established originally with Abraham, Isaac, and Jacob (we have mentioned this on several occasions in Chapter VIII). But it is in the books of Exodus and Deuteronomy where the covenant takes on its greatest expression, in particular in its relationship with divine law.

We move now to our treatment of the cult of ancient Israel, to which a significant portion of the Pentateuch is devoted. Three components of the cult need to be discussed: the priests, the sacrifices, and the Tabernacle.[14]

The administrators of the Israelite cult were the priests, who according to the Bible were limited to the tribe of Levi (e.g., Num-

---

12. For a standard treatment see Dennis J. McCarthy, *Treaty and Covenant,* Rome, 1963. On Deuteronomy in particular, see also Moshe Weinfeld, *Deuteronomy and the Deuteronomic School,* Oxford, 1972.

13. Note the maxim of the rabbis of the postbiblical era, recorded in several places in the Gemara: "the language of the Torah is the language of man" ( = ordinary human language).

14. Our discussion attempts only to summarize a vast amount of material. A great amount of detail may be garnered from Menahem Haran, *Temples and Temple-Service in Ancient Israel,* Oxford, 1978.

bers 3:5–10). Among them one would serve as high priest, the first of whom was Aaron, the brother of Moses. Priesthood was hereditary, to be handed down from father to son, and the high priesthood likewise was retained in the same family.[15]

The main function of the priests was the offering of the sacrifices, which was the dominant form of public worship in ancient times (both in Israel and throughout the Near East).[16] The first seven chapters of the book of Leviticus present the different kinds of sacrifices in great detail; among these are daily sacrifices and sacrifices for a variety of special occasions. The sacrificial system goes back to a very primitive notion that holds that the gods, like people, must eat and drink, and that it is man's responsibility to supply them with their food and drink. Thus various solid foods (animals, birds, grains, etc.) are offered, as are liquid sacrifices, called libations, of wine and other beverages. The gods want their food to smell good as well, and so incense accompanies the sacrifices. Similarly, musical accompaniment is desirable for fine dining, so liturgical music develops as part of the cult.

Most probably the Israelites did not conceive of Yahwe partaking of a meal during the sacrificial service. Their understanding of the deity was very different than that of their polytheistic neighbors. But since religious rituals are the most conservative aspect of society, the Israelites continued the system of sacrifices, even though it may have run counter to their theology to some degree.[17] Thus solid and liquid sacrifices, replete with incense and music, formed the core of Israelite ritual, no less than it did the cult of Canaanites and others.

The locus of the cult was the Tabernacle, a portable tent shrine constructed in the desert by the Israelites (Exodus 25–30, 35–40).[18] A permanently settled population would have a temple as its shrine, but

15. This would have been true of many professions in antiquity, not unlike the guild system of the Middle Ages. Note that the later Christian concept of a celibate priesthood has no origins in the priestly system of the Hebrew Bible.

16. Prayer existed, but only as a private matter (e.g., Genesis 25:21, 1 Samuel 1:12–13). Only in exilic and postexilic times did prayer develop as a public system (e.g., Nehemiah 9:4ff.). Once the Second Temple was destroyed in 70 C.E., the prayer system became more formalized; it remains the dominant form in Judaism to the present day. Similarly, Christianity and Islam developed as religions greatly devoted to prayer.

17. As we shall see later on, in time the whole enterprise was questioned, specifically by the Prophets.

18. On these chapters see Victor Hurowitz, "The Priestly Account of the Building of the Tabernacle," *Journal of the American Oriental Society* 105, 1985, pp. 21–30. On the Tabernacle

for a people moving through the desert, the Tabernacle served this purpose. Among the polytheists in antiquity, an idol of the god stood in the center of the temple, so that the temple was viewed as the dwelling place of that deity. The Israelites, of course, could not make physical representations of Yahwe. Moreover, their unique understanding of God precluded the idea that He could have a dwelling place in a single spot. So, at the center of the Tabernacle was the ark of the covenant, in which were housed the two tablets of the Ten Commandments (Exodus 25:16), representing not God Himself but God's presence among the people (Exodus 25:8) and His covenant with them.

Attached to the Tabernacle were a variety of paraphernalia, including the main altar on which the sacrifices were performed, a smaller altar for burning incense, the lampstand or menorah, and other items. This entire complex was portable. When the Israelites encamped for any period, it was constructed. When they marched, the Tabernacle was taken apart and carried. In the past, scholars have doubted the historicity of the Tabernacle, but there is no need for such questioning. We possess sufficient archeological and historical evidence for such portable tent shrines, including one discovered at Timna, not far from where the Israelites trekked through the desert.[19] To look ahead just a bit, the Tabernacle remained the center of Israel's religious life even after the Hebrews settled in Canaan. In time, however, it came to replaced by a more permanent structure, namely, the Temple in Jerusalem constructed by Solomon in 960 B.C.E. At that point, the ark was transferred to the Temple and the other components of the Tabernacle were replaced by newly built items.

The description of the cult just given is based on the system detailed in the Torah itself, with the tacit assumption that the entirety goes back to Moses' time. But just as the legal portions of the Torah were seen to be the culmination of several centuries of development, so, too, should the material devoted to the cult be seen as developing over time. For when one reads further in the Bible, one encounters information that contradicts some of the information conveyed in the Pentateuch.

in general see the excellent discussion by Nahum M. Sarna, *Exploring Exodus*, New York, 1986, pp. 190–220.

19. Suzanne Singer, " 'From These Hills . . .'," *Biblical Archaeology Review* 4:2, 1978, pp. 16–25. For additional evidence, see Sarna, *Exploring Exodus*, pp. 196–200.

For example, non-Levites served as priests in Israel in the period up to the early monarchy. Samuel is the most important of such individuals; he was of the tribe of Ephraim (1 Samuel 1:1), nonetheless his sacrifices to God were accepted (1 Samuel 7:9; etc.). Not until the reign of Jeroboam I late in the tenth century B.C.E. do we hear our first condemnation of non-Levites serving as priests (1 Kings 12:31). Apparently, it was desirable to have a Levite serving as priest (see Judges 17), but non-Levites could have a role in the cult as well. The watershed may have been Solomon's construction of the Temple, an outgrowth of which may have been the solidification of the Levite monopoly on the priesthood.

The whole notion that sacrifices were offered in the desert also needs to be questioned. In the very least, there was another tradition in ancient Israel that sacrifices were not offered in Moses' time. Two later prophets, Amos (5:25) and Jeremiah (7:22), contended that there were no sacrifices in Moses' day, and utilized this viewpoint to argue for the fruitlessness of the whole sacrificial cult.

In light of this, we must see the Torah's description of the cult in a manner similar to its legal portions. Just as most of the law is post-Moses but was retrojected to the great prophet, parts of the cult as described in the Torah must also be later developments but were retrojected to Moses for the same reason discussed above. This conclusion must be viewed cautiously, however, for at the same time we accept the fact that the Tabernacle (minus the altars perhaps) is very much a product of the wilderness period.

## CHAPTER XI

# Israel as a Tribal League

A s indicated at the end of Chapter IX, the emergence of the
Israelites in the land of Canaan is to be dated to the twelfth
century B.C.E. Moses brought the Israelites to the doorstep of Canaan,
and already during his lifetime the Hebrew tribes had taken possession of part of Transjordan. Toward the end of his life, Moses selected
Joshua to be his successor (Numbers 27:18–23; Deuteronomy 31:7–
8), and it is the latter who led the Israelites into Canaan proper.

In their journeys and battles, the people were accompanied by the
Holy Ark; even as in late historic times, Arab tribes carried sacred
cult objects with them during their wanderings and wars. So the
Israelites crossed the river Jordan[1] and entered "the land flowing with
milk and honey." These two terms refer to the great abundance of
milk-producing sheep and goats in the country, and to the large
amount of date palms in the land. The fruit of the latter were pressed
to extract a sweet substance, the commonest form of "honey" mentioned in the Bible.[2] Israel is a land of milk and honey only from the
standpoint of people entering from the east. It is almost impossible to
describe the beauty and richness of the land after you have been in
the desert, but from the standpoint of people from really fertile areas
like the Nile Valley or ancient Babylonia, Israel was hardly a land of

1. "Jordan" is an East Mediterranean word for "river" (cf. the "Iardanos" in Crete mentioned
by Homer). That "Jordan" is a common noun meaning "river" is evident from such expressions as "this Jordan" (Joshua 4:22) and "the Jordan of Jericho" (Numbers 26:3, 63) and from
the fact that the Mandeans apply "Jordan" to rivers in general.

2. The Hebrew word is *debash,* whose Arabic cognate *dibs* refers only to the sweet extracts
(saps, molasses, syrups, etc.) of fruit (dates especially).

outstanding productivity, even in Joshua's time when soil erosion and the denudation of forests had not reduced the country to the wretched state it was in prior to the modern revival.

As noted earlier, the Hebrew tribes escaped from a weakened Egypt. They entered Canaan at a time when the world had no strong empire. The absence of great powers was a necessary factor in Israel's conquest and settlement of Canaan and subsequent rise to nationhood, which could only have happened in a prolonged period when small states had a chance to come into being and evolve their own way of life. As stated previously, the Egyptian empire in Canaan had come to an end,[3] and the traditional power to the north, the Hittites, had also crumbled in the wake of the Sea Peoples invasion.

A local factor that permitted the Israelites to establish themselves in the land of Canaan was the lack of a unified front opposing the new arrivals. Canaan was governed by a series of city-states; there were literally dozens of them dotting the landscape. The Amarna letters attest to traditional rivalries among the cities, so that military cooperation to stop the advance of the Israelites was not to be expected. Moreover, after centuries of Egyptian rule in the country, the cities clearly were weakened and were in no position to deal with a new force. The Bible may allude to this with the statement that God had sent the ṣirʿah, or hornet, in advance to crush the enemy (Exodus 23:28; Deuteronomy 7:20). The hieroglyphic sign used for the pharaoh was a bee, so that the ṣirʿah would refer to the Egyptian king having weakened the Canaanites during years of military occupation of their land. It is true that the hornet and the bee are different species, but we need not press the ancients too hard for entomological sophistication, or, alternatively, our identifications and translations may be slightly incorrect. Moreover, we should note that the size of the armies referred to in the Amarna letters is very small, and there is no reason to assume any change in this condition two centuries later when the Israelites arrived in Canaan. In sum, conditions were good for the Israelites to gain a foothold in the country and to expand their base of power.

Another factor of prime importance is the religious imperative. As the Bible makes abundantly clear, the Israelites believed that the land of Canaan was a gift from God to the people of Israel. In addition,

3. See James M. Weinstein, "The Egyptian Empire in Palestine: A Reassessment," *Bulletin of the American Schools of Oriental Research* 241, 1981, pp. 1–28.

they had a strong faith that Yahwe was fighting on their side. Western readers of today may have difficulty understanding the importance of this factor, but it was a real one that no doubt motivated the Israelite fighters to the utmost.

But not everything was in Israel's favor. All things being equal, the attacker is at a disadvantage because it is easier to defend a city than to attack it. The Canaanites lived in fortified cities, and even though they were not necessarily large cities, nonetheless they had defense walls surrounding them. The Canaanites armies may not have been large, but they possessed one weapon that the Israelites lacked, namely, chariots. In light of all this, Joshua had to use specific military tactics to neutralize certain Canaanite advantages.[4] First, the overall strategy was to attack in the mountains, not in the coastal plain and valleys, for in the former, the chariot is of no use. Secondly, when attacking cities, the direct method of siege warfare was not utilized. Instead, Joshua employed tactics subsumed under the category of indirect warfare (more or less the same as our modern term guerilla warfare).

In the first battle, at Jericho, Joshua used psychological warfare to allow the enemy soldiers to let their guard down. This is the best way to explain the circling of the city. When the Israelites finally attacked, they shouted and blasted their horns, and it is quite possible that the sound waves created by these actions would have weakened the walls to force them to collapse.

In the second battle, at Ai, Joshua used an ambush to defeat the local Canaanites. First he feigned weakness and started retreating from Ai, thus enticing the soldiers of Ai to leave their city and to pursue Joshua's troops. Once the city was vacant, the ambush force came in and conquered it. Such a tactic could not have worked on the coastal plain, where an ambush force would easily be spotted from a watchtower. But in the mountains, replete with good hiding places, such a guerilla-type tactic can succeed with relative ease. In conquering Ai, the Bible implies that the Israelites gained control of its neighboring city Bethel as well.

Between campaigns Joshua (8:30–35) constructed a shrine on Mount Ebal near Shechem, with some of the people standing for the

4. A much more detailed discussion of the military situation and the tactics employed by the Israelites may be found in Abraham Malamat, "Israelite Conduct of War in the Conquest of Canaan," in F. M. Cross, ed., *Symposia Celebrating the Seventy-Fifth Anniversary of the Founding of the American School of Oriental Research (1900–1975)*, Cambridge, Mass., 1979, pp. 35–56.

ceremony on Mount Ebal and others on the opposite Mount Gerizim. It is stated that no iron was used in constructing the shrine and
its altar. This reflects the conservatism of religion; for though the Iron
Age had begun, the innovations of the age were characteristically
shunned (see also Exodus 20:22). Several years ago a fascinating discovery was made directly related to the biblical account. In an excavation atop Mount Ebal an installation was found, which, according
to its excavator, is a sanctuary site with an altar. The site dates from
the Early Iron Age, i.e., the time of Joshua, and around the altar were
burnt sheep, goat, cattle, and deer bones, evidently the remains of
sacrifices.[5]

After the fall of Jericho and Ai (and Bethel), the people of the
nearby city of Gibeon decided it was better to ally with the Israelites
than to fight them. Accordingly, they entered into a treaty with the
Israelites (Joshua 9). By this time the Israelites now had a secure foothold in the land of Canaan, having gained control of most if not all
of the territory of Benjamin.

Only at this point did a group of Canaanite cities form a coalition
to halt the Israelite advance. The alliance included the kings of Jerusalem, Hebron, and Lachish, i.e., the area to the south and southwest
of the Israelite center. The coalition attacked Gibeon and the Israelites came to the rescue of their treaty partner. Joshua's troops
marched all night to surprise the enemy by attacking them at dawn.
Since the Israelites were attacking from the east, they were able to
use the sun for military advantage. The sun was at their back, but it
blinded the coalition forces who had to face eastward as the sun rose
over the horizon. This set of circumstances explains the famous biblical statement that "the sun stood still" at Gibeon (Joshua 10:13).

The biblical text quotes some of its written sources. At this point
(Joshua 10:13) we read that additional material can be found in the
Book of Jashar, now lost—a fate that has befallen all the sources
named in the Bible. If we had those lost books, the extent of Israel's
literature would be considerably bigger than the Bible. The Book of
Jashar is mentioned once more, in 2 Samuel 1:18. Both quotations
from it are in poetry and both deal with wars. It is likely that this
composition was the poetic epic that told of the Hebrew Conquest

5. Adam Zertal, "Has Joshua's Altar Been Found on Mt. Ebal?" *Biblical Archaeology Review*
11:1, 1985, pp. 26–45. For a different interpretation, however, see Aharon Kempinski, "Joshua's Altar: An Iron Age Watchtower," *Biblical Archaeology Review* 12:1, 1986, pp. 42–49.

culminating in David's reign. When Israelite historiography turned to prose writing, as in most of Genesis through Kings, the earlier poetic texts eventually were lost. But the two surviving excerpts of the Book of Jashar indicate that it would have ranked high in world literature.

It is only for the first three battles of Jericho, Ai, and Gibeon that the Bible presents for us the details necessary to reconstruct Israelite military conduct. After describing these three conflicts, the narrative shifts to a simple survey of the land. Israelite forces moved both northward and southward from their base in the mountains of Benjamin. Most of the captured cities were not destroyed. In fact, Hazor is singled out as the only city burned out of quite a number captured in the north. The Hebrews did not come to destroy but to occupy the land and keep it in as good a condition as possible. The few exceptions of destroyed cities (e.g., Jericho, Ai, and Hazor) do not invalidate the general rule.

The process we have just described is one of military conquest of the land. Scholars continue to debate whether or not there is sufficient archeological evidence to confirm the picture presented in the Bible. In some cases, such as at Hazor and Lachish, there is clear evidence of Canaanite sites being destroyed. But even at these sites, archeologists cannot prove that it is the Israelites who are responsible for these destructions. Other causes may be equally at play: internecine warfare between rival Canaanite city-states, Sea Peoples invasion, campaigns of Egyptian pharaohs, etc. In other cases, such as those of Jericho and Ai, the picture is ambiguous at best; most archeologists find no evidence for the Israelite conquest at these sites.

Because of the lack of evidence in strong support of a conquest of the land, an alternative model to explain the emergence of Israel in Canaan has been proposed by scholars. This reconstruction of Israelite history calls for a peaceful settlement of the land. According to this theory, the Israelites came out of the desert but did not forcibly conquer the land; instead they peacefully infiltrated the country and settled in regions previously uninhabited. For this model there is in fact significant archeological evidence. As noted earlier (Chapter IX, pp. 149–50), the central hill country of Canaan reveals literally hundreds of new settlements in an area previously sparsely inhabited.[6]

6. The latest and most important discussion of all the evidence is Israel Finkelstein, *The Archaeology of the Israelite Settlement,* Jerusalem, 1988.

We accept the fact that the Israelites peacefully settled the land. Nevertheless, there is a strong counterargument regarding the silence of the archeological record vis-à-vis the Conquest. Other known conquests in world history, well attested in historical documentation, also have little archeological evidence to substantiate them. These include the Anglo-Saxon invasion of Britain, the Norman conquest of England, and the Arab conquest of Palestine.[7] And yet, of course, no one would deny the authenticity of these events.

A pleasant compromise is intended by the term Conquest / Settlement introduced earlier. The Israelites conquered those areas where military means were necessary, and settled peacefully those areas where military action was unnecessary. The biblical tradition recalls mainly the former because military heroics lend themselves to national epic storytelling more so than peaceful infiltration.

Joshua then proceeded to parcel out the land to the twelve tribes, some of whom settled in Transjordan though the majority settled west of the Jordan. The number "twelve" given to the tribes involves quite a bit of manipulation throughout biblical history, and yet that number is adhered to even though the facts in specific situations are against it. The reason for the insistence on the twelveness of the tribes[8] is that the tribes had a function within the nation as a whole. The function meant, as we shall see later in Solomon's time, discharging national obligations governmentally, militarily, and religiously; each tribe, one month per year. Hence the twelveness of the tribes is a deep-seated institution pervading Hebrew history.

The boundaries represented by the allotment of the land in Joshua 13–19 are ideal ones. In many cases the tribes did not possess all the land allotted to them. Pockets of Canaanites remained in the mountainous regions; the most famous example being the city-state of Jerusalem that retained its independence. More significantly, the Canaanites remained in firm control of the coastal plain and the Jezreel Valley (the largest valley in the country). Along the southern coastal plain the newly arrived Philistines were dominant. Not until the time of King David (tenth century B.C.E.) did the Israelites approach the reality suggested by the ideal boundaries detailed in the book of Joshua.

7. B. S. J. Isserlin, "The Israelite Conquest of Canaan: A Comparative Review of the Arguments Applicable," *Palestine Exploration Quarterly* 115, 1983, pp. 85–94.

8. Not only in Israel but among other tribal confederacies in antiquity. Cf. Martin Noth, *The History of Israel,* London, 1960, pp. 85–108.

**MAP 3: THE TWELVE TRIBES**

Of all the place-names mentioned in the detailed lists of Joshua 13–19, we single out the locale named "the spring of Me(r)-neptah" (Joshua 15:9, 18:15) for special consideration.[9] This place, located not far from Jerusalem,[10] bears testimony to the fact that Merneptah's armies marched near Jerusalem as well, a fact not stated in his own stela referred to above. Furthermore, it confirms our dating of the Exodus to the twelfth century B.C.E. For the Israelites to have found a toponym bearing the name of Merneptah upon their arrival in Canaan, they must have come to the land only after the reign of this pharaoh.

The story we have outlined thus far is essentially the one given by the Bible. But an objection must be entered here, because, as is quite obvious, the Bible presents the history of Israel in an idealized fashion. Nations simply do not descend from the offspring of one man (in this case Jacob/Israel). Instead, nations typically develop from the coming together of a variety of peoples over time.[11] The history of Israel presumably is no different, and there is, in fact, some evidence to support this claim.

One tribe, Asher, is mentioned as an entity in Canaan in a text dating to the period of Ramses II,[12] that is, at the very time when almost all scholars believe the Israelites were enslaved in Egypt. If Asher existed in Canaan during the reign of Ramses II, then it could not have been part of Israel enslaved in Egypt or coming out of Egypt in the Exodus.

More documentation is available concerning the tribe of Dan.

9. On this site see Gary A. Rendsburg, "Merneptah in Canaan," *Journal of the Society for the Study of Egyptian Antiquities* 11, 1981, pp. 171–72.

10. Its modern name is Lifta, located just west of Jerusalem on the main road to Tel Aviv.

11. Compare the formation of Britain, with a basically Celtic native population joined by invading Angles, Saxons, Vikings, Normans, etc.

12. See James B. Pritchard, ed., *Ancient Near Eastern Texts,* Princeton, 1955, p. 477.

*(facing page)* The concept of political boundaries in the modern sense did not exist in ancient Israel. Instead, the tribal territories most likely were amorphous regions with variable or overlapping boundaries. Accordingly, this map does not indicate the exact boundaries between the tribes. Note that Manasseh is divided into an eastern half and a western half. Note further that Dan, due to pressure from the Philistines, had to surrender its territory in the south and migrated to the north where it inhabited the region of the city of Dan (formerly called Laish).

Among the Sea Peoples was a group called the Danuna, associated by many scholars with the people called the Danaoi by Homer. This group, like the Philistines, settled on the coast of Canaan, but in time joined the Israelites as the tribe of Dan. Their tribal allotment is on the seacoast, immediately adjacent to Philistine territory. Judges 5:17 refers to their dwelling in ships; Genesis 49:16 suggests that Dan is joining the Israelite tribal league at a rather late date; and Judges 18:1 notes that Dan did not have an allotment of land like the other tribes. All of these factors combine to support the theory that the tribe of Dan originated as one of the Sea Peoples.

Of the origin of the other tribes very little can be said, though there may be an ultimate connection between Benjamin and the Bani-yamina mentioned in the Mari texts.[13] Regardless, the evidence of Asher and in particular Dan is enough to demonstrate that the tribes of Israel had diverse origins. Not all of the Israelites experienced the Slavery, the Exodus, the Wandering, etc. However, when the biblical tradition was formed, it created a national epic in which all of Israel fictively underwent the same historical experience, regardless of actual origins. Presumably a certain segment of the population could trace its ancestry back to the Patriarchs Abraham, Isaac, and Jacob, but the story of Jacob's sons has been cast in a light to give every tribe a tribal father, each the son of Jacob/Israel.

The unified national epic probably included the traditions embodied in the book of Joshua. In that book we read of a united Israelite military front in the conquest of Canaan, led by Joshua, after which the land is parceled out to the individual tribes. The picture is complicated, however, by the opening of the book of Judges (1:1). Here we read that after the death of Joshua, individual tribes campaigned against the Canaanites to gain control of the territories already allotted to them. The prevailing view considers Judges to be more historically accurate and views Joshua as a later attempt to present a unified picture.

The main topic of the book of Judges is the disorganized tribalism (as opposed to united nationhood) that prevailed among the Israelites at this time. This lack of unity contributed to Israel's susceptibility to subjugation by foreign rulers, both from within Canaan and without.

---

13. The evidence is presented by Abraham Malamat, *Mari and the Early Israelite Experience*, Oxford, 1989, pp. 31, 35, though Malamat concludes that he sees "no connection between the two entities beyond the similarity of name."

The Bible also talks at this point about the problem of Canaanite worship tainting the true worship of Yahwe. Specific mention is made of the worship of Baal, Astarte, and Asherah (Judges 2:11, 13; 3:7) and of intermarriage between Israelites and Canaanites (Judges 3:6). The Bible connects these two facets of Israelite life. Because they sinned by engaging in pagan practices, God punished them by bringing foreign oppressors upon them.

Archeological evidence illustrative of Israel's attraction to paganism is forthcoming from a site called by scholars "the bull site." On a hilltop in the territory of Manasseh, archeologists revealed an early Israelite sanctuary site, replete with a five-inch high bronze figurine of a bull.[14] The iconography is reminiscent of purely Canaanite artistic representations of bulls, both in statuary and in artwork, and recalls that in the Ugaritic texts the chief god El is called "Bull."

Even though God was responsible for bringing the oppressors to subjugate Israel, it was also He who insured that in each instance a ruler or "judge" arose to lead the Hebrews into battle to lift the subjugation.[15] Actually, these submissions to foreign rule did not effect the nation as a whole; typically they were localized subjugations effecting one or several tribes. The first of the judges was Othñiel, on whom the spirit of the Lord descended[16] so that he vanquished the foe, and characteristically established the peace for "forty" years. Then Eglon, king of Moab, afflicted Israel and invaded the territory west of the Jordan. But another judge arose, Ehud, who assassinated Eglon and gave the land peace for "eighty" years, again a multiple of forty. Shamgar (whose name is Hurrian and whose reputed[17] mother was the Canaanite goddess Anat) slew six hundred

14. Amihai Mazar, "The 'Bull Site': An Iron Age I Open Cult Place," *Bulletin of the American Schools of Oriental Research* 247, 1982, pp. 27–42; and Amihai Mazar, "Bronze Bull Found in Israelite 'High Place' from the Time of the Judges," *Biblical Archaeology Review* 9:5, 1983, pp. 34–40.

15. The Hebrew word *shofeṭ* can mean either "ruler" in general or "judge" in particular. The heroes of the book of Judges are of the former type, for their leadership typically is military and social, not judicial. But after centuries of calling these people "judges" and of calling the book "Judges," we are stuck with the term.

16. Prior to the accession of King Solomon, Hebrew leadership was inspired, not hereditary, though it was limited to the aristocracy.

17. The warlike Anat is an appropriate mother for a hero in Canaan. Similarly, the great conqueror Thutmose III is called the son of the bellicose goddess Sekhmet in the story of The Taking of Jaffa 1:13 (Alan H. Gardiner, *Late-Egyptian Stories*, Brussels, 1932, p. 83, l. 5).

Philistines single-handed as the story goes. While such round numbers are not to be taken literally, this does not mean that all the other elements are unhistorical.

The tribes were confronted with a succession of enemies from many quarters, but the most formidable of the foes was King Jabin from the northern city of Hazor. His general Sisera, who could put nine hundred iron chariots into the field, terrorized the northern tribes. A savior arose in the person of Deborah, a prophetess and a judge of her people. She chose a man, Barak, as her general. But inasmuch as he was uninspired and insisted that she come along into the fray, the glory for the victory went to a woman according to Deborah's own prophecy. The woman was not Deborah, but Jael, as the story later brings out. According to the prose account in Judges 4, the battle was fought and Sisera, who fled to a nomad's tent, was craftily slain by Jael, a nomad woman, and the Israelites gradually gained strength against Jabin until ultimately they eliminated him.

There is also a poetic account of the same historic events[18] in Judges 5, containing the famous Song of Deborah of genuine antiquity.[19] The God of Sinai is pictured as coming out of His holy mountain and using all of nature, especially the storm to rout the enemies of His people. He emerges from Edom amid earthquake and storm to bring salvation to His tribes. The poem describes how the highways of the land had become so insecure that people had to go by devious means along the byways until Deborah arose to restore security. The Israelites were so disarmed that among thousands there was not a single weapon. Not all the tribes responded to the call, but many of them did and are praised in the poem. Those that remained aloof are jeered at. As the poem tells us, even the stars in their courses took part in the battle and the dismay of the enemy was enhanced by a cloudburst filling the River Kishon (which might have been an insignificant stream just before it became a raging torrent). The town of Meroz is singled out for particular contempt in that its people did not participate in the battle. Sisera's mother, who is waiting in vain

18. It is not unusual for history to be recorded in both prose and poetic versions almost simultaneously. In the New Kingdom, pharaohs sometimes celebrated their compositions in three versions: poetry, prose, and pictures.

19. Semitic tribesmen are quick to celebrate important local events in poetry and song. Such compositions may be handed down for many generations with little significant change.

for her son to come back with spoil taken from Israel, is also the object of scorn.[20]

Deborah's career marks a milestone in the transition from individual tribalism to united nationhood.

Among the enemies of the Hebrews in this period were the Midianites: camel-riding nomads, who would make raids particularly at harvest time, stealing and destroying crops and making the people of the sown so miserable that they would seek refuge in caves. The hero who arose on one occasion to redeem his people from Midianite oppression was Gideon, who in his zeal for God destroyed an altar of Baal and the adjacent Asherah,[21] belonging to his father. The local populace were indignant but his father defended him from them, pointing out that gods can take care of themselves; and if Baal is a real god, he will avenge himself.

Gideon, who belonged to the tribe of Manasseh,[22] also assembled the other northern tribes of Asher, Zebulun, and Naphtali to rid the Hebrews of their Midianite foes. Rivalry resulted so that Ephraim was offended. Gideon appeased the Ephraimite tribesmen by flattering them on their capture of the two Midianite chiefs, Zeeb and Oreb. According to Judges 7:25, the heads of those chiefs were cut off and sent on as evidence and trophies of the success. Naturally it is difficult to transport whole corpses around; so to count the foe or establish his identity the head was cut off, for the sake of convenience, and shipped to headquarters. This was a routine procedure all through the ancient Near East. There was another way of counting the slain foe in order to facilitate statistics and avoid too much bulk, that is, by cutting off a palm (really the whole hand from the wrist down) of the victim's arm. In Ugarit, Mesopotamia, and Egypt cutting off either palms or heads, and even heaping them up in triumph, is referred to repeatedly.[23] Also in art, heads and hands are depicted to

20. There is another side to the poet's description of the enemy's mother back home. This may be the same feature that in Homer's Iliad is developed into the touching scenes where the heroic enemy Hector is at home in Troy with his mother, wife, or other relatives.

21. In the Bible, an "Asherah" is an idol or symbol of the Canaanite mother-goddess Asherah.

22. Gideon claims to be from the poorest clan in Manasseh and the youngest in his family (Judges 6:15). The elevation of the less eminent and of juniors (among the nobility) to leadership is a frequent theme.

23. See also below, p. 187, n. 6.

symbolize victory in battle.[24] When Gideon proceeded to march against two other chiefs named Zebah and Zalmunna, he came to a town where he asked for supplies and help. The townsmen asked him sarcastically: "Is the palm of Zebah and Zalmunna already in your hand that we should give bread to your army?" (Judges 8:6). The meaning need not be "Are you now leading them by their hand as captives?" More likely it is "Have you already slain them with their amputated palms as proof?" The word for "palm" is *kaf* (as distinct from the "hand" of the victor, which is *yad*), precisely as in the Ugaritic tablets, where the same word designates the "palms" to commemorate Anat's victory. Gideon saw the cogency of their argument, but told them that after capturing the two chiefs he would come back and punish them with physical torture for their lack of cooperation in his hour of need. On his victorious return he carried out his threat.

The movement toward hereditary kingship was already making itself felt in Hebrew society. Gideon was offered hereditary rule but he refused it, expressing his reaction in the standard formula of theocracy that God alone was the ruler, and not men. However, when he died his seventy[25] sons, who were dividing the rule, fell out with their half brother Abimelech, born to Gideon by a concubine from Shechem. Abimelech was able to muster the citizenry of Shechem behind him because of his mother's connections; and, through treachery, butchered all his brothers except the youngest, Jotham, who escaped and prophesied Abimelech's downfall, which in fact followed.

Next, the Transjordanian nation of Ammon molested Israel. The Hebrew chiefs in the Gilead region of Transjordan decided that the first man who would arise to fight the Ammonites would be made the leader of Gilead. The Gileadite Jephthah (the son of a prostitute), whose half brothers expelled him from his father's house, was chosen as the leader because of his ability and initiative. (Jephthah belonged to the nobility through his father. His mother's social inferiority makes his elevation "worthy of saga.") His message to the enemy is consistent with what was stated earlier (Chapter IX, pp. 148–49) about monolatry. "Is it not that you should inherit what your god,

24. See Cyrus H. Gordon, "Near Eastern Seals in Princeton and Philadelphia," *Orientalia* 22, 1953, p. 249 (no. 32), pl. LXVII (no. 32).

25. This number is the familiar epic cliché. Compare "the seventy sons of Asherah" in Ugaritic literature.

Chemosh, has caused you to inherit? But we shall inherit all which Yahwe, our God has driven out from before us?" (Judges 11:24). Thus Jephthah did not deny that the enemy had its national god, just as Israel had Yahwe.

Jephthah was successful and again the tribe of Ephraim was angry because it had been left out of things. Because of insults that Ephraim heaped on Jephthah, the latter warred on Ephraim and won. Intertribal war was one of the manifestations of disunity that weakened Israel in the Period of the Judges. During the war on Ephraim, Jephthah's forces were able to detect Ephraimite fugitives by their inability to pronounce the word *thibbolet* (spelled *shibbolet,* since the Hebrew alphabet does not include a letter to mark the *th* phoneme), which instead they pronounced *sibbolet:* a valuable fact for the Hebraist concerned with early dialectal differentiation.[26]

The enemy that next appears in the Book of Judges is the one destined to become the most serious of all: the Philistines. The hero to combat them is Samson, whose entertaining narrative is replete with folklore. Of greater historicity in detail is the story of Micah, a well-to-do Hebrew citizen, who makes for himself an idol, with ephod[27] and teraphim[28] with a view to setting up a private chapel for himself. So simple it was for a wealthy individual to establish his own cultic center! His own son was available to serve as a priest because in those days priests did not have to come from a special class.[29] However, he was later delighted upon securing a genuine Levite to take over as his priest. Shortly thereafter, the tribe of Dan, located precariously on the Philistine border in the south, and unable to get land of its own, sent spies to go north in search of a place where the population was weak enough to be conquered and so make room for the Danites to settle. On the way, they happened to come across Micah's household, where the Levite was serving as priest. They secured a favorable oracle from the Levite; and later when the Danite army came north, the Danites forced the Levite to accompany them with his ephod, idols, and other cultic equipment of his master. The prop-

---

26. For details see Gary A. Rendsburg, "The Ammonite Phoneme / $\underline{T}$ /," *Bulletin of the American Schools of Oriental Research* 269, 1988, pp. 73–79; and Gary A. Rendsburg, "More on Hebrew *Šibbōlet,*" *Journal of Semitic Studies* 33, 1988, pp. 255–58.

27. A cult object used for securing oracles.

28. Household gods.

29. The ideal of limiting priests to the tribe of Levi was not rigidly observed until much later. Even King David appointed sons of his own as priests.

osition was appealing to the Levite, in that he would be priest not for just a family but for an entire tribe. Micah's objections were silenced by Danite desperadoes, who convinced him that, right or wrong, they were not to be trifled with. The Danites proceeded (with their newly acquired Levite and cultic equipment)[30] to the tranquil and unsuspecting town of Laish that was enjoying peace within the Sidonian[31] sphere of influence in northern Canaan. They easily conquered Laish and changed its name to Dan, which became the northernmost town in Israel. The story shows us not only how tribes might move at this time but also the religious usages and the way new cults might be set up. The incident explains the origin of the Danite cult that became quite important after the northern Kingdom of Israel was established.

There follows the story of an atrocious crime in Gibeah of Benjamin, where a concubine belonging to a Hebrew was abused and killed. The Hebrews stirred up the tribes to concerted action by dismembering the woman's corpse into twelve parts, sending one part to each of the tribes to rouse them to avenge the injustice that had been perpetrated. So strong a sense of right and wrong prevailed among the tribes that they united against Benjamin and almost wiped it out. However, there followed a feeling of remorse, in that a tribe was on the verge of extinction[32] in Israel. To provide wives for the decimated Benjaminites, girls were secured from the town of Jabesh-gilead, according to Judges 21:6–15; and to round out the required number of women (Judges 21:16–24) the men of Benjamin were instructed to capture the girls of Shiloh as brides during a religious festival. Thus the extermination of the tribe was averted. The episode is the last in the Book of Judges, which adds only one revealing verse: "In those days, there was no king in Israel. Everybody did what was right in his own eyes" (Judges 21:25). Such freedom is not far removed from anarchy.

---

30. The reason a band of warriors in the midst of a military campaign required a cultically equipped priest was that oracles were needed not only to know whether or not wars should be launched but even whether or not tactical steps should be taken in the course of a war.

31. "The Sidonians" are not necessarily the people of Sidon; the term can also refer to the south Phoenicians including, for example, those of Tyre.

32. The desire to prevent the extinction of groups—even disliked groups—is widespread. The Flood story thus records the urge to perpetuate unclean as well as clean animals. In our own time, the sentimentality in preventing the extinction of any species (human, animal, or plant) is a manifestation of the same phenomenon.

## CHAPTER XII

# The Transition to Kingship

The Israelites and the Philistines, it will be recalled, had arrived in the land of Canaan at approximately the same time. Probably, as long as the Israelites held to the mountains and the Philistines held to the southern coastal plain, there were no major problems between the two newcomers to the land. But as both began to expand their territory, it was only natural for the two to challenge each other militarily. The Philistines had the upper hand, one of the reasons being their technological advantage. In one passage, the Bible informs us that the Israelites even had to go to the Philistines for as simple a procedure as sharpening a tool (1 Samuel 13:19–22).

The system of the judges had worked in the past when Israel was threatened, but with the continual dominance of the Philistines, the Israelite populace realized that a more permanent mode of government was necessary. At one point even the ark had been captured by the enemy. This catastrophe impressed upon the people the necessity of union and kingship, because only through kingship (despite the tyranny that goes with it) could the nation be united for concerted action in any emergency that may arise.

The elders of Israel approached Samuel with the idea of appointing a king. Samuel was a many-faceted individual, who had served in his career as priest, prophet, and judge (apparently in the true sense of the word, i.e., in adjudicating legal cases). Because of his many public roles, Samuel was the most respected man in Israelite society, so it was only natural for the elders of the people to approach him. Samuel was theoretically opposed to establishing a kingdom, because he adhered to the theocratic ideal whereby God alone is king. Yet he had to yield to circumstances and to the insistence of the people, with the revealed permission of God that was required to legitimize any step taken in a theocracy such as Israel. On principle, the kingdom was not relished; as God's reluctant authorization and Samuel's reluctant consent show.[1] But times had changed and the innovation, however distasteful, was a necessity. Samuel, the maker of kings, chose Saul, a tall imposing man—although of the small tribe of Benjamin[2]—as king over the nation.

Saul bears the title of king, but he lacks many of the trappings of kingship. He does not build a palace; instead he governs from under a tree in his home city of Gibeah (1 Samuel 14:2; 22:6). He does not devote his energies full-time to the rule of the land; instead, as we shall see, he continues to engage in the practice of farming. For his successors, David and Solomon, the Bible records lists of cabinet officials; no such list is preserved for Saul, probably because no central administration had developed during his reign. Furthermore, hereditary rule was not a priori an aspect of Saul's kingship (see below). Accordingly, Saul's reign is to be viewed as a type of transitionary kingship. Israel had moved away from the loose confederation characteristic of the period of the judges, but it had not yet achieved the strong central rule that would characterize the reigns of David, Solomon, and subsequent kings.

The Philistine domination of the Hebrews was a great obstacle to overcome. Saul had thus the task not only of uniting disunited tribes but of facing without adequate weapons a well-armed foe. The test came when the Ammonites demanded that the people of Jabesh-gilead submit to the brutal humiliation of having one eye struck out: a punishment now attested also as a curse in Ugaritic. Saul, who was plowing behind a yoke of oxen when the news of Jabesh-gilead came, slaughtered the animals, cut them up, sent the pieces throughout Israel with the ultimatum that any man who withheld himself would have his cattle cut up the same way. (The device is essentially the same as that of the cutting up of the abused concubine. The shocking

---

1. See also Isaac Mendelsohn, "Samuel's Denunciation of Kingship in the Light of the Akkadian Documents from Ugarit," *Bulletin of the American Schools of Oriental Research* 143, 1956, pp. 17–22.

2. Again the theme of elevating the lowly, although here it is also possible that Samuel chose as king a man from a small tribe so that the secular government might not become too strong vis-à-vis the religious forces, whose leader Samuel was.

thing in the case of the concubine was that it happened to be a human being rather than an animal that was dissected and circulated. But both episodes are the same insofar as they were calculated to rouse scattered people into concerted action.) The response saved the day.

Saul's gaining of prestige through his rescue of Jabesh-gilead touched off a feeling of rivalry between him and Samuel, so that the interests of state and church clashed. A series of crises progressively deteriorated the relations between Saul and Samuel until there was finally a rupture. Samuel, who represented the more firmly established theocracy, won out against Saul, who represented the newer and still delicate institution of the crown. Samuel was able to reject Saul and anoint another king in his stead.

Samuel went to the house of Jesse in Bethlehem to find the newly anointed of the Lord to rule Israel after Saul. This time the family was of a large tribe, Judah. But characteristically it is David, the youngest of the sons, who is chosen. Moreover, it is the eighth son who prevails over the other seven, which, as noted above, is paralleled as worthy of saga in Ugarit (compare 1 Samuel 16:1–14 with Ugaritic text 128:II:24–28;[3] cf. III:16).

David becomes not only Saul's armor bearer but also his harper to drive away the fits of melancholia that come over him from time to time. Saul was an impetuous, religious man capable of falling into states of prophetic ecstasy for which he became notorious. The proverb "Is Saul also among the prophets?"[4] was applied to men of high station found behaving disreputably in bad company.

With the anointing of David, inspiration had departed from Saul and gone to David. Or, as the Hebrew text expresses it, "the spirit of Yahwe lit upon David" (1 Samuel 16:13) "and the spirit of Yahwe departed from Saul" (verse 14). The modern reader of the Bible

---

3. In these lines it is predicted to Kret of his bride that
   "She will bear thee seven sons
   And an eighth (daughter) 'Octavia.'
   She will bear thee the lad Yasib (= the eighth son)
   Who will suck the milk of Asherah
   Even suckle the breasts of the Virgin [Anat]
   The wetnurses [of the good and gracious gods]."

4. Ecstatic prophets did not have the stature of the great literary prophets. It is interesting to note that an ecstatic prophet in Byblos is described in the Egyptian tale of Wenamon (eleventh century B.C.E.: Twenty-first Dynasty).

should try to cope with such factors (where the concept, not the event, is the important thing) as within the realm of the history of ideas.

David was gifted, charming, and handsome; a man with the kind of loyalty toward his friends that won in return loyalty toward him. His versatile talents as poet and musician as well as warrior contributed to his becoming the national hero. David, rightly understood in his own context, was no split personality, torn between incompatible artistic and martial impulses. His talents constituted one harmonious whole. He performed for his nation what the elegiac poet and general Tyrtaeus performed for Sparta centuries later.[5] Through song and poetry, David trained the men of his people to fight in unison as a disciplined team on the battlefield (2 Samuel 1:18; Psalm 60:1). Out of national disaster, David established an empire by focusing all his talents on the destiny of his nation.

It may strike the modern Westerner as strange that David and Tyrtaeus used sad compositions to prepare men for battle. Thus 2 Samuel 1:17–27 is a dirge for the slain heroes, Saul and Jonathan. Listening to the stirring poems about the great who perished nobly made the soldiers of Israel, Sparta, and doubtless other East Mediterranean nations want to excel on the battlefield or die like their honored predecessors, whom they heard immortalized in song. In modern times, Turkish soldiers have been prepared psychologically on the eve of battles to fight bravely, and die gladly, by dirges about their heroes slain in battle.

The Goliath episode, which is part of David's history in the mind of posterity, may well have been attached to him wrongly. The Bible gives us contradictory evidence concerning it. According to the main narrative, David killed Goliath. But this account occasions quite a bit of difficulty in that after the reputed episode is over, Saul and Abner forget completely who David is, whereas he is supposed to have been on the court staff for quite some time. Aside from this and other contradictions, the Bible itself contains a more plausible variant tradition: In 2 Samuel 21:19 it is the hero Elhanan who slays Goliath at the town of Gob. Furthermore, the name of Elhanan's father is obviously connected with the weapon used (the weaver's beam), whereas the latter is inappropriate in the case of the account whereby David is credited with the slaying of Goliath. The author of the Books of

5. Cyrus H. Gordon, "The Rôle of the Philistines," *Antiquity* 117, March 1956, pp. 24–25.

Chronicles had before him the Books of Samuel with both variants, which he tried to harmonize. Thus 1 Chronicles 20:5 makes Elhanan the killer of Goliath's brother. Since it is much more natural for a heroic event to be transferred from a minor personage to a great hero, than vice versa, the situation may be summed up as follows: Elhanan slew Goliath but the victory was popularly transferred to David. Both the true and the transformed versions appear in Samuel. The Chronicler, seeing the discrepancy, tried to harmonize them.

An interesting factor in the relationship between David and the House of Saul is that there was a friendship between the crown prince Jonathan and David, although nowhere does Jonathan doubt for a moment that David is going to succeed to the throne. The reason is in part this: The idea of hereditary kingship was not yet firmly entrenched in Israel. Rather the concept of inspirational leadership, not passing from father to son, was still in the minds of the Israelite tribesmen. Therefore, it took no great adjustment for Jonathan to realize that he was outclassed by David and that in the natural course of events, David would succeed to the throne. This feeling was shared by many of the people, including the girls who sang after a battle that while Saul had slain thousands, David had slain tens of thousands. Being less popular than David made a frightful impression on Saul and increased his suspicion of, and enmity toward, David.

David was finally obliged to flee from the court, for while playing for Saul, Saul had heaved a javelin at him with intent to kill. Later, to eliminate David from the scene, Saul had made him a captain of a thousand on a dangerous mission that he hoped would be fatal. When this did not succeed, he said David could marry his daughter Michal at the bride-price of a hundred Philistine foreskins.[6] David got two hundred in less than the time specified, much to Saul's disappointment and embarrassment. Thus David married a princess, which strengthened his claim on the throne (1 Samuel 18:17–27).

His royal wife, to protect David from emissaries sent by Saul to kill him, let David escape but told the emissaries her husband was sick in bed. She had put teraphim in the bed to fool the searching party into thinking David was sick and in no condition to be moved. This

6. Ordinarily proof that enemies were slain consisted of heads or hands cut off from the victims; see above, pp. 179–80. In the case of the Philistines the foreskins were produced, because the Philistines were "the uncircumcised." The circumcised Egyptians counted their slain foes by heads or hands, except in the case of the uncircumcised Libyans, whose phalli were often amputated for counting.

shows that even in the household of David and of Saul's daughter, idols (and, at that, approximating human size) were still on hand.[7]

David, in need of supplies, went to a shrine at Nob, where Ahimelech was the priest. After getting the supplies, he went to a Philistine ruler named Achish, King of Gath. To avoid being hurt, David played insane, and later fled to Adullam, which had had close connections with his tribe since the days of Judah himself, according to Genesis 38:1–2.[8] There David gathered together four hundred fellow tribesmen, all desperadoes who had not gotten along with organized society. Upon becoming their chief, David began his career of leadership among men, on his own; a leadership that was to culminate in the establishment of a long dynasty.

Saul, after hearing about Ahimelech's role in supplying David, had him killed along with eighty-five priests of Yahwe. Only Ahimelech's son Ebiathar escaped, and fled to David. Ebiathar came with the ephod. David retained him and from him sought the oracles of Yahwe that he consulted at every turn, in peace and war. The military use of oracles applied, as we have indicated, to tactics as well as strategy. David began by scoring military successes in keeping with Ebiathar's oracles. When on a subsequent occasion the oracle advised him to retreat, David wisely obeyed.[9]

David was now an outlaw.[10] During his exploits he had a couple of chances to kill Saul but he refrained from doing so because he would not lay a hand on the anointed of Yahwe. This is in keeping with David's character; rarely did he fail to do what would command the respect of the public. David usually treated people as he himself would want to be treated. His refraining from laying a hand on Saul probably had much to do with the fact that no one successfully laid a hand on David, when he attained the throne. (In a society where blood is avenged, bloody usurpation is repaid with bloody usurpa-

7. The institutions reflected in such stories are often more historical than the events that convey them.

8. But see also Gary A. Rendsburg, "David and His Circle in Genesis XXXVIII," *Vetus Testamentum* 36, 1986, pp. 438–46.

9. Obviously a priest giving military oracles would have to understand warfare if he hoped to be of any use. For this reason, priests were sometimes assigned on regular duty with the army in the ancient Near East. For Ugaritic and Mari examples, see Cyrus H. Gordon, *Ugaritic Literature*, Rome, 1949, p. 125.

10. The reader must not conclude that the role was as disreputable as it would be in modern society.

tion; as proved to be the case repeatedly in the northern kingdom of Israel.) David, as distinct from many orientals of the biblical world, and even of later times,[11] was not bent on extirpating the line of his predecessor. On the contrary, he vowed he would not destroy Saul's seed, a vow of which he was later mindful.

The incident of Nabal is interesting because it reflects conditions in the days of David's brigandage. Nabal, a well-to-do citizen rich in flocks, was giving a party. David sent ten of his men to convey good wishes and collect tribute. The argument was that since David was keeping the peace and had never attacked Nabal's interests, David was entitled to Nabal's tribute. In other words, a band of outlaws could be a force to be reckoned with in a given district in Israel and impose the payment of "protection money" on private citizens. Nabal refused to pay and would thereby have brought on himself destruction from David's band had not Nabal's wife Abigail gone to David with gifts to appease him. David accepted the lady's offer and was so impressed with her that they married after Nabal's death.

According to 2 Samuel 17:25, 1 Chronicles 2:16, David had a sister named Abigail. It is conceivable that the two Abigails are one and the same woman, in which case David married his sister (probably a half sister). David also married a woman named Ahinoam, and a woman of this name is listed elsewhere as a wife of Saul. If these two individuals are one and the same person, than part of David's rise to power may have been his having married the wife of the preceding king. This is implied later in the prophet Nathan's words to David (2 Samuel 12:8).[12] In the meantime, David's wife Michal, the daughter of Saul, was taken from him and given to another, an insult that he later rectified.

David complained that Saul's driving him to the Philistines meant that he would be cut off from the inheritance of Yahwe and be forced to worship strange gods (1 Samuel 26:19). David's words reflect the ancient Near Eastern idea, current in Israel then, that each god could be worshipped only on his own soil.

David returned to Achish,[13] King of Gath, who accepted him as a

---

11. The butchery of princes in Turkish and Iranian history is almost unbelievable.

12. Jon D. Levenson and Baruch Halpern, "The Political Import of David's Marriages," *Journal of Biblical Literature* 99, 1980, pp. 507–18.

13. See 1 Samuel 27:2 ff. Our simplified account is not intended to deny the existence of complex literary questions such as whether 1 Samuel 21:11–16 is a variant tradition of David's encounter with Achish.

subject and assigned to him the town of Ziklag. David was careful to
make raids only upon the foes of Israel; he spared his brethren. The
Philistines about this time were arrayed for battle against Saul, whose
desperate plight is described as follows: "And Saul beheld the camp
of the Philistines, and he feared and his heart trembled much. And
Saul sought oracles of Yahwe. But Yahwe would not answer him,
neither in dreams, nor through *urim* [ = cult objects] nor through
prophets" (1 Samuel 28:5–6). To the Israelites, national poverty did
not consist so much of economic, fiscal, or political deficiencies, but
rather of being forsaken by God, who refused to give His precious
words to His people. The word of God was being denied to Saul;
Saul was without inspiration. Samuel was now dead. David, the other
anointed of the Lord, was in a foreign land. Saul in his desperation
resorted to the one means he knew, though it was illegitimate,[14] of
learning God's word on this occasion. That means was witchcraft.

Saul went to Endor, where a woman lived who surreptitiously
engaged in the outlawed[15] art of spiritualism. Saul, by disguising himself, persuaded her to call up the spirit of Samuel from below. The
document describing the meeting of Samuel's ghost with Saul (1
Samuel 28:7–25) clearly mirrors many ideas of the period.[16] Samuel
was indignant that the man who had not listened to him sufficiently
during his lifetime was now disturbing his rest in the underworld.
The prophet told him that God has departed from him (Saul) and
that defeat was a foregone conclusion. Samuel announced that Saul
would soon be entering the underworld, Sheol, where (as we know)

---

14. The three sanctioned means, as stated in the Bible, were dreams, cultic instruments, and
prophets. The fact that priests and prophets refused to give oracles might be interpreted as
meaning that the branches of the clergy had united against Saul. That we must beware of so
simple an explanation is indicated by the including of dreams, which the clergy could not
prevent Saul from having. The psychology of ancient religions, or for that matter of ancient
life in general, will always confront us with elusive phenomena.

15. The reason official religion opposed occult practices is clear from this episode: The Witch
of Endor could surpass the oracles of any living prophet with the oracles of the greatest
prophets of the past. (For, while she only called up Samuel, she and other members of her
craft could equally well call up Moses.) Note, too, that the force suppressing such occultism
was the crown (1 Samuel 28:9; 2 Kings 23:24). Magic persisted sub rosa, and burst into the
open when Jewish kingship was no longer in existence to suppress it. Thus postbiblical Jewish
literature and the New Testament are full of occult practices.

16. E.g., that all the dead resided below, that they could be roused and consulted through the
professional skill of spiritualists, that spirtualistic practices were evil, etc.

the good and evil alike were then believed to go after death. The righteous Samuel and the erring Saul were to be side by side in the roomy underworld of Sheol.

The Philistines preparing for battle against Israel noticed that David with his contingent was to join them. They suspected his loyalty and therefore Achish found it wise to excuse him and send him back home. When he and his men returned to their base at Ziklag, they found it burned, and all their children and womenfolk and property carried off. He consulted Ebiathar to find out whether he could overtake the band that inflicted the disaster. After consulting the ephod, Ebiathar told him to proceed, for he will be successful. On the way, some of the troops had to be left behind because of exhaustion. On returning, the troops that were with David and had gotten back the captives and property, plus spoils, did not want to share the spoils with those that had stayed behind. But David ruled that in the army all must share alike, regardless of whether a man participated in combat or whether he was assigned to guard property in the rear (1 Samuel 30:24). The Davidic precedent may have been coined to lend weight to an army policy of some later generation of Israel.[17]

The wisdom, diplomacy, and generosity of David are again shown in that he sent a share of the booty to the elders of Judah, his own tribe, for it was these elders that some day were to make him king, before the other tribes of Israel would accept his sovereignty.

Saul and Jonathan met their doom in the fateful battle of Gilboa, in which the Philistines crushed the Israelite army. The heads of Saul and Jonathan were cut off and their corpses hung on the walls of Beth-shan.[18] The grateful men of Jabesh-gilead, mindful of how Saul had once rescued them, went by night to the walls of Beth-shan, recovered the corpses of Saul and Jonathan, and buried them with condign rites and mourning. An Amalekite (according to an epic tradition rather than a factual source) bore David what he thought would be welcome news; namely, that he himself had killed Saul, the anointed of Yahwe, so that David could now rule.[19] David did what was in keeping with the heroic representation of his character: He

---

17. We already have noted the Homeric parallel, p. 106.

18. According to 1 Chronicles 10:8–10 the Philistines circulated Saul's head and armor among the Philistine cities and impaled them at Beth-Dagon.

19. This, however, does not agree with 1 Samuel 31:4 or 1 Chronicles 11:4–5.

killed the bearer of the tidings. He had no time for those who specialized in treachery.

David composed a dirge (2 Samuel 1:17–27) on the death of Saul
and Jonathan. Part of it runs:

> "O mountains in Gilboa
> Let there be no dew
> Nor rain upon you!" (verse 21).

It was believed that when heroes were slain, the land on which they
perished would be cursed by drought and sterility. When the Ugaritic
Daniel curses the site of Aqhat's murder, he uses quite similar words.
This unmistakable parallel is of special importance because it provides
the key to the origin of Hebrew historiography. Other nations of the
ancient Near East had annals but not real history in which personal
character and motivation were delineated. Such delineation had been
limited to the epics that dealt with gods and legendary men. We
have observed that historic events (such as Deborah's victory) were
celebrated in poetry as well as prose. David's dirge, as the Ugaritic
parallel proves, is in the epic tradition. Thus the Hebrews achieved
true historical composition by transferring human values from the
epic to current events. In reading the account of the Battle of Gilboa,
we see that while the political and military developments are mentioned, the real interest is in the fate of Saul and Jonathan, and in
how their fate affected the hero David. With the rise of the monarchy, Hebrew historiography comes into its own, for the sense of
national greatness evoked a pride in the story of the nation. The
composition of real history is the greatest achievement of that period.
It antedates Greek historiography by over five hundred years. Prior
to the Ugaritic discoveries, the origin of Hebrew historiography was
a mystery. But now that we know it was created through the application of epic values to current events, it still remains a miracle that not
the large nations (such as Babylonia, Assyria, or Egypt) but tiny Israel
made that momentous contribution to civilization. National, like
individual, genius cannot be explained by analysis in a test tube.
Every nation in the Bible World had epic traditions and experienced
current events. It took the genius of Israel to create historiography
by combining them.[20]

---

20. For another factor in the rise of historiography, see Cyrus H. Gordon, *The Common
Background of Greek and Hebrew Civilizations*, New York, 1965, pp. 96–97.

# CHAPTER XIII

# Israel United under the House of David

**S** aul's fall made it possible for David to return to his own tribal land of Judah, where he settled in Hebron and was chosen as king over the tribe. Israel[1] (as the northern tribes are called in contradistinction to Judah) still remained faithful to the House of Saul and accepted as king his son Eshbaal,[2] whose capital was Mahanaim in Transjordan; because all of Canaan west of the Jordan was at the mercy of the Philistines. David was doubtless a puppet of the Philistines at this point and it is quite possible that the division of the kingdom was favored by the Philistines, who were applying the well-known principle of "divide and rule." However, David was not the man to remain in such a servile state.

Wars between David and the House of Saul were inevitable and at Gibeon the armies of the two factions met. The army of the House of Saul was led by Abner, while David's army was led by Joab. By mutual consent, twelve champions of each army were selected to fight each other. All twenty-four met their death in the fray, thus leaving things as unsettled as ever. Then followed another combat between the two armies. A brother of Joab whose name was Asahel

---

1. In the period of the united kingdom, and during the existence of the divided kingdom as well, the context alone can tell the reader whether "Israel" refers to all the tribes or only to the northern ones.

2. This "Baal" name is usually altered in Scripture to Ish-bosheth ("Man of Shame") out of religious prejudice. Actually, Saul's naming a child Eshbaal no more brands Saul a pagan than our calling a daughter "Minerva" would brand us pagans today. Moreover, it is not out of the question that Baal was then identified with the God of Israel, and was not perceived to be a separate diety, the Canaanite storm god.

chose to pursue Abner, who advised him to desist and instead go
after one of the other lads whose belt he could try to take as a trophy.
Abner, who was a seasoned warrior, was able to cope with Asahel
but he knew that if he slew the youth, it would start a blood feud of
the most dangerous kind with Joab. Asahel, however, would not
desist and Abner was forced to kill him, which sealed Abner's fate.

Abner was soon to fall out with the House of Saul because he
sought in marriage Rizpah, one of Saul's concubines. Eshbaal
upbraided Abner for the presumptuous request,[3] and Abner thereupon decided to transfer his allegiance to David. David accepts his
allegiance on condition that Michal, Saul's daughter, be restored to
David as his wife. So Michal was torn away from her second husband,
who was grief-stricken as she left him to go to David. Abner then
proceeded to win the northern tribes over to David, and he would
have been put in command of David's army had David had his way.
But Joab, although loyal to David, was jealous for his own position.
Through treachery Joab got Abner aside and murdered him, thus
getting revenge for his brother Asahal and at the same time eliminating his rival. David turned all these delicate situations to his own
advantage, through diplomacy and generosity. He fasted and recited
a dirge for Abner, which must have made an excellent impression on
the northerners.

Soon after, Eshbaal was murdered and his head was brought by the
assassins to David (2 Samuel 4). David, instead of rewarding them,
had them put to death as murderers, which again enhanced his reputation; even though this incident (cf. pp. 191–92 above), like so many
in David's narrative, appears to stem from the creation of a bard rather
than a fact recorded by an annalist.

The northern Israelites then transferred their allegiance to David
and came to Hebron to establish a covenant with him and to anoint
him. They quote Yahwe as saying: "You shall pasture my people
Israel." This is the terminology of the old theocratic ideal. The king
is thus like a Sumerian *ensi,* claiming only to be the shepherd who
pastures God's human flock. God is the official ruler; the human head
of the state is only His agent. It is worth noting, too, that a covenant
was made between the king and the people. The people were not
ready to submit to an ancient Near Eastern dictatorship. The Israe-

---

3. Marrying a king's widow could easily suggest designs on the throne.

lites always maintained a sense of tribal and individual dignity and privilege, and so the king had to abide by a covenant that was a sort of constitution he had to grant if they were to accept him.

David's first accomplishment as king over united Israel was the conquest of Jerusalem. Even though the Israelites had successfully established themselves in the mountainous part of the country from Joshua's day onward, Jerusalem remained as a Canaanite (more specifically Jebusite) enclave in Israel's midst. The reason for this is simple: Jerusalem is surrounded on three sides by steep ravines, and through the ages its citizens utilized this natural defense to their best advantage. David's army succeeded nonetheless, but it conquered Jerusalem not through direct military means, but rather through the indirect method again. Apparently, the method of warfare conducted in Joshua's day remained a part of Israelite military strategy, so that a century and a half later David's troops resorted to the same type of tactics. The Bible is not perfectly clear on the matter, but it implies that David's men entered Jerusalem through the *ṣinnor*, i.e., a type of water conduit. Excavations in Jerusalem have uncovered a series of underground water channels and shafts, the purpose of which was to allow easier access to the powerful Gihon Spring lying just outside the city walls. However, all of these installations date to the time of the Israelites, so that none of them should be equated with the *ṣinnor* of 2 Samuel 6:8.[4] Still, it is probable that the pre-Israelite residents of Jerusalem also had some sort of water shaft, still not uncovered by archeologists, and that this conduit was used by Israelite soldiers to enter the city from underneath.

David moved the capital from Hebron in the territory of his own tribe of Judah to the recently conquered Jerusalem. In so doing he was governed by several factors. First, as noted, Jerusalem is very easily defended. Secondly, the city was situated on the boundary between Benjamin (the home of Saul) and Judah (the home of David), so that symbolically it served to unite the two houses and the diverse regions of the realm. Finally, Jerusalem had not belonged to a particular tribe; in forging a united kingdom David was going to have to reduce the importance of old tribal allegiances; a capital that no

4. Yigal Shiloh, *Excavations at the City of David I* (Qedem 19), Jerusalem, 1984, pp. 21–24; Yigal Shiloh, "The City of David Archaeological Project, The Third Season—1980," *Biblical Archaeologist* 44, 1981, p. 170.

tribe could claim as its own was one way of accomplishing his goal.[5] For almost three thousand years now, Jerusalem remains the only conceivable capital of those devoted to the Davidic Line: It makes no difference whether the devotees are Israelis confronted with practical politics, or Christians contemplating the Messianic Age.

David immediately began to build in the city of Jerusalem. He established a wise alliance with Hiram, king of Tyre, that was to last long after David's death. With the assistance of Phoenician skilled workers, and with cedar wood imported from Phoenicia, David built for himself a palace in Jerusalem.

With David now in control of a united Israel governed from a central capital in Jerusalem, he next turned his attention to the country's old nemesis, the Philistines. David routed the Philistines and then exacted tribute from them (2 Samuel 6:17–25; 8:1, 11). Surprisingly, the Bible does not describe David's vanquishing of the Philistines in any great detail. But his defeat of Israel's archenemy must have been a devastating one. Never again in the Bible are the Philistines mentioned as a threat to Israel; instead they were relegated to their five cities along the southern coastal plain.

The ark was transferred to Jerusalem and thus the trend toward centralizing the cult there made its modest start. David, bearing the ephod, danced before the ark. The spirit of the Lord had come upon him and he leaped ecstatically in public. (His well-born wife Michal disapproved of his behavior,[6] so David indignantly decided to neglect her from that time on.) During the celebration David further won the hearts of the people by passing out gifts to them. He was a man who by nature won many friends, who appeased most of his enemies, and who knew how to eliminate what few people were irreconcilable.

David felt, now that he had a house to live in, he should build a temple for his God. He consulted Nathan the Prophet, who later had a dream and reported its message to the king. Nathan represented the conservative element and could not adjust himself to the idea of transforming the shrine from a tabernacle to a temple. Nathan's oracle informed David that a king whose hands were bloody from war was not the king to build God's temple; and that the temple would

---

5. American readers will be familiar with similar factors that governed the choice of Washington, D.C., as the nation's capital.

6. Ecstatic religion, as we have noted, was not approved of in the best Israelite circles.

better wait for the peaceful reign of David's son. The transition was thus postponed for a generation.

David's conquests extended in all directions (2 Samuel 8). He vanquished Philistia, Edom, Moab, Ammon, and Aram up to the Euphrates where he erected a stela of victory (1 Chronicles 18:3). In some cases he was brutal. Moab was conquered and two thirds of the population were put to death. According to 2 Samuel 8:6, the land of the Arameans around Damascus was conquered and governors were sent by David to rule there. The same was done in Edom (2 Samuel 8:14). Also, although the Bible is virtually silent on the issue, Israel must have gained control of large portions of Canaan at this time (not only Jerusalem, but areas such as the coastal plain and the Jezreel Valley as well). Accordingly, in the course of but a few decades, David had transformed Israel from a minor state under the domination of the Philistines into an international empire. Its sphere of influence stretched from the Sinai Desert and the Gulf of Eilat in the south and southwest to the Euphrates River in the northeast, and from the Mediterranean Sea in the west to the Syrian Desert (northern extension of the Arabian Desert) in the east. One of the reasons for the establishment of such an empire at this time was the decline of the traditional powers, Egypt in the one direction, Assyria and Babylonia in the other. Nevertheless, we should take nothing away from David, who exhibited true political and military genius in his forging the international empire.

The nascent empire was equipped with more administration than Israel had ever known before. Joab was commander in chief of the army. There were also the official recorder, scribe, and priests. Sons of David also acted as priests, for there was still some leeway in priestly appointments and also some nepotism in the government whereby sons of the king could be put into responsible positions contrary to the ideals of society. At the head of the foreign troops was Benaiah, who led the Cherethites (= Cretans) and Pelethites: troops of Caphtorian origin. It is worth pondering the desirability of such mercenaries. Natives tend to have family or local loyalties. Foreign mercenaries have no such ties and tend to be well disciplined, loyal to their commander, and interested in his personal welfare, for on him depends their professional welfare. Thus these mercenaries were eventually instrumental in preserving David's life and throne when his own flesh and blood betrayed him.

David, who had vowed not to destroy Saul's family, sought out

Mephibosheth,[7] the son of Jonathan, restored Saul's estate to him, and gave him support at the king's table, that is to say, rations at government expense.

Although David is the hero par excellence of the Hebrew people and the model for all kings to come, and the ancestor of the Messianic Line, there is no attempt in Scripture to exculpate him. He committed a great crime in the case of Bathsheba; not only the crime of adultery but the murder of an innocent man (his loyal soldier, Uriah the Hittite).[8] The narrative makes no attempt to cover David's sin, thus demonstrating one of the Bible's truly unique qualities. In any other society in the ancient Near East, it is obvious that no king's faults could have been portrayed in such an open and public manner.[9] David was soon punished for his sin; the child born of the adultery died (though Solomon, who was also the child of David and Bathsheba, would eventually succeed to the throne).

The personality and loyalty of Joab are borne out clearly in the capture of Rabbath-Ammon (now Amman), where Joab was in a position to conquer the city but called for David to come so that David might deal the final blow and get the glory.

Although David was an effective ruler and natural diplomat, he was a poor master of his own household. The disobedience and misbehavior of his own children shows that his forte was not the role of father. To further demonstrate this point, the compiler of the history of David organized his material around the David and Bathsheba affair. Everything up to 2 Samuel 10 shows David in an excellent light, as he unites the nation and builds his empire. Then follows the adultery in 2 Samuel 11–12. The succeeding chapters, beginning with 2 Samuel 13, depict the disastrous family relationships that tortured David for the remainder of his life.

His firstborn son was Amnon. It is interesting to note that at this period there was a fratriarchal organization of brothers whereby there

7. This is a puritanic distortion of his name; for "bosheth" had replaced "Baal" as the variant Merib-baal (1 Chronicles 8:34; 9:40) shows.

8. For a particularly insightful reading of this episode, see the penetrating study of Meir Sternberg, *The Poetics of Biblical Narrative,* Bloomington, Ind., 1985, pp. 186–229.

9. There is yet another side to this story. Scandal is the spice of epic; all of the many sex scandals in the Hebrew Bible are pre-Solomonic (i.e., from the period when epic, rather than annalistic, treatment, prevailed). See Cyrus H. Gordon, "Homer and Bible," *Hebrew Union College Annual* 26, 1955, pp. 80–82, §§86–92 (= *Homer and Bible,* Ventnor, N.J., 1967, pp. 44–46, §§86–92).

was not only a chief of the brothers but also a second in command. David's son, Chileab, was the prince known as "his second"; i.e., Amnon's second in command. Only after the firstborn and his second in command do the Hebrews number the brothers third, fourth, fifth, sixth, etc. This fratriarchal organization was widespread throughout the East, including Israel.[10]

Amnon conceived a passion for his half sister Tamar and instead of asking for her hand in marriage, which would have been permissible as the biblical text informs us, he seduced her. Her full brother, Absalom, who was the third of the royal sons, slew Amnon to avenge the dishonor. Absalom took refuge, typically enough, in the house of his mother's father, Talmai, the King of Geshur. In polygamous society, where a man has children born by different wives, when strife breaks out among half brothers and half sisters those in trouble will seek refuge with the mother's family.

Joab, who was a powerful figure behind the throne no less than on the battlefield, resorted to a stratagem to effect a reconciliation between father and son. He enlisted the services of a clever woman, called the Wise Woman of Tekoa, who told David that one of her sons had killed the other and now the family was going to kill the slayer with the result that she would lose both her children. (This indicates, incidentally, that the king was the highest court of appeals and could even reverse basic laws of society.) David saw the humanity of her argument and said that the slayer should not be touched. The woman now hints that David should apply the same verdict to his own household and spare his guilty son. David then realized who had put her up to it and she confessed that every word she had uttered had been put into her mouth by Joab. Yet the king was won over to forgiving his son, as his verdict for the woman had indicated. Absalom thereupon came home and although for some time he was not allowed to see David personally, the king eventually relented and permitted him full freedom and the intimacy of the court.

Absalom was a handsome man. We are told that the hair on his head was so luxurious that when he had it cut it weighed two hundred shekels, according to the king's weight. (The existence of a royal standard is of some interest. Each country in the ancient Near East

---

10. See Cyrus H. Gordon, "Fratriarchy in the Old Testament," *Journal of Biblical Literature* 54, 1935, pp. 223–31. Note also the fratriarchal etiquette whereby brothers at a banquet are seated in order of seniority (Genesis 43:33).

had standard weights and measures; but they were not necessarily designed to establish honest weights and measures in the bazaars to protect the public from dishonest merchants. Standards may well have been set up for the benefit of the crown, so that when the king got his taxes he should not be given short weight or short measure. Of course, once the government standard was fixed, private citizens could also resort to it for their own protection.)

The handsome prince played up to the public. His father, who had the responsibility of giving decisions, naturally could not favor all the litigants. Absalom, however, was in a position to do a lot of irresponsible talking; and he gave the impression to the dissatisfied that if he were king, he would give satisfaction to them. He thus built up a following to support him in a revolt. In order to carry out his plans, he went to Hebron ostensibly to pay some religious vows, for the old family shrine was still there. Once in Hebron, however, he mustered enough forces to launch a full-fledged rebellion. His adviser, the wise Ahitophel, came along with him. David could not assemble troops quickly enough to combat those of his son Absalom. Instead he fled with those that were loyal to him. Thus Ittai of Gath, the Philistine in charge of six hundred of David's foreign mercenaries, insisted on going along with David, even though David offered to release him from sharing so precarious a future (2 Samuel 15:18–22). When David's own son betrayed him, and when his own nation rebelled, his best friends included foreign mercenaries, who gladly followed him "whether for death or for life" (verse 21). The fact that these mercenaries were Philistines is in part accounted for by David's Philistine friendships in the days when Saul had driven him into exile.

David left some of his harem, notably the concubines, behind as part of a fifth column in Jerusalem: a fifth column that also included other elements. David insisted that priests should remain with the ark in the capital. He also left behind a counselor by the name of Hushai with instructions to nullify the wise advice that Ahitophel would doubtless give the rebellious Absalom, and to arrange for liaison between the fifth column and the priests so that messages could be relayed to David in his Transjordanian place of refuge.

On his way, while fleeing from Jerusalem to Transjordan, David had some disagreeable experiences. Ziba, a servant of Mephibosheth, the son of Jonathan, offered gifts to David and informed him that Mephibosheth was disloyal to David and favored Absalom's revolt. Another Benjaminite named Shimei came out and reviled David for his treachery against the House of Saul. It is important for us to remember that from the standpoint of the Israelites, particularly of the tribe of Benjamin, David was a usurper who had sinned against the House of Saul. This fact was detrimental to the unity of the Hebrew tribes because the feeling that the Davidic Line was a line of usurpers contributed to the division (never to be mended) after Solomon's death. Abishai, the brother of Joab, wanted to kill Shimei, but again David, with his usual magnanimity toward enemies, insisted that Shimei be spared.

Ahitophel advised Absalom to take over his father's harem that had been left behind, and thus show that he was his father's successor. He further told him to gather the troops that were then available and immediately pursue his father. This practical advice would have granted David no time to assemble adequate forces and Absalom's rebellion would have succeeded. However, Hushai slyly advised Absalom to wait until he could gather an overwhelming force so that David's able generals and veteran troops would have no chance militarily. The deceptive picture painted by Hushai was so attractive that Ahitophel's sound advice was rejected. Ahitophel felt he had lost face so badly that he went home, set his house in order and committed suicide: one of the few suicides in biblical history.

Through the priests, David's intelligence service kept him informed of developments at home. Absalom at last felt ready to move his army under the generalship of Amasa to Transjordan.

David had been well received in the Transjordanian town of Mahanaim. He organized his troops into thousands and then subdivided them into hundreds. The whole army was divided into three; one third under Joab, one third under Abishai, the other third under Ittai. The king, already well advanced in years, was obliged to remain behind because his safety was of great importance to his partisans, and at his age he would have been more of a liability than an asset in the field. His last wish was that his men should deal gently with Absalom if he should fall into their hands.

Absalom's luxuriant hair caught in a low tree while he was riding on a donkey. Suspended in midair he fell into the hands of David's troops. Joab, who later came up, slew Absalom against David's orders. This is typical of Joab who knew what was best for David, even when David's desires went against his own best interests. Instead of being overjoyed at the victory, David went into the most abysmal grief over his son. Again it was Joab's forcefulness that saved the day. The troops felt that, far from having pleased their king and having won the victory, they were guilty of a heinous crime in killing Absalom. Joab therefore reproached the king and forced him to refrain from all expression of grief. David, thus brought to his senses, again sat in the gate as ruler of his people, and the morale of his victorious troops was raised to the height they so well deserved.

Through the mediation of the priests, David made up with the elders of Judah and amazingly agreed to appoint Amasa as general to replace Joab. Like so many despots, David resented the presence of so able and forceful a man as Joab, despite the latter's flawless loyalty.

The tribe of Judah came to the Jordan to welcome the king across. David showed magnanimity to all, to Mephibosheth (who denied any disloyalty), and even to Shimei, who had reviled David in his darkest hour. One of the most touching incidents is that of Barzillai, who had supported David in Transjordan. David now wanted him to come to the royal court where he would live in ease for the rest of his life. But Barzillai replied: "How old am I that I should go up with the King to Jerusalem? I am now eighty years old! Can I distinguish the good from the bad? Or can I taste what I eat or drink? Or can I listen any more to the voice of male and female singers? Why should I be a burden to my lord, the King?" (2 Samuel 19:36). So Barzillai returned home, accepting David's offer to lavish his gratitude on a member of the younger generation, who could make better use of a career at court than could an octogenarian.

The old rivalry between Israel and Judah that was to prove disastrous after the division of the monarchy could be felt even during the united kingdom of David and Solomon. On this occasion the Judeans claimed that they after all were the flesh and blood of the king, while the Israelites claimed that they constituted ten tribes as against the one tribe of Judah. (As we shall soon see, the Hebrews reckoned their tribes as twelve, even though they recognized that there were actually only eleven of political consequence. The twelfth tribe, Levi, was scattered among the others: north as well as south.)

The kingdom was far from firmly established because the appetite of Israel for independence had been whetted by the disruption of David's House in the time of Absalom's revolt. Accordingly, a Benjaminite named Sheba started another revolt that gained support throughout Israel. David designated as commander in chief Amasa, who got off to a bad start by being late. This obliged David to send Abishai, the brother of Joab, to hasten things along. Joab and his men, including the Cherethite and Pelethite mercenaries, proceeded on the march. Joab met Amasa and, with his usual treachery where his honor was at stake, he approached Amasa as if to kiss him, got hold of his beard, drew his sword, and slew him (somewhat as he had gotten Abner out of the way).

Joab lost no time. He pursued Sheba till he cornered him in a small fortress. Joab then threw up earthworks against the wall and would have captured the place except that a wise woman there pointed out that there was no sense in destroying a whole group of people when the head of one man could settle the issue. Joab agreed with her analysis of the situation, whereupon the head of Sheba was cut from his body and tossed over the wall. Joab ordered a blast on the trumpet, and each man went to his tent: the biblical expression for signifying that the war was over and the army demobilized then and there. The formula "each man went to his tent" is a holdover from earlier times. By this time the Israelites did not live in tents but were an agricultural people; yet the old phrase, whereby home was a tent, still lingered on in the language.

Joab went back to Jerusalem and things returned to normal. In 2 Samuel 20:23–26 we get an idea of some of the internal developments in David's time. His reign saw an increase in the organization of the realm. He had carved out the largest empire then in existence. Joab was in charge of the army. Benaiah was over the Cherethite and Pelethite mercenaries. Adoram (otherwise called Adoniram) was director of forced labor; for the empire required taxation in labor as well as in kind. There were also the offices of recorder and scribe. The chief priests of the realm were two in number: Zadok and Ebiathar (together with their families), but it is interesting to note that David had also a private priest by the name of Ira, so that in addition to the so-called legitimate priestly households in the service of the national cult, there were also private priests including one for the king himself.

In 2 Samuel 21 it is related that the land was afflicted with a three-year famine and the people felt that the nation had incurred guilt through the breaking of faith with the Gibeonites by the House of Saul. The Gibeonites required that the crime be expiated by killing the seven sons of the House of Saul. Mephibosheth, the son of Jonathan, was spared by David in order to keep his promise not to exterminate the House of Saul. But David did take seven other descendants of the House of Saul to be slaughtered so as to give satisfaction to the offended Gibeonites. Two of these children were born of Rizpah and five of a daughter of Saul. David, however, was able to salvage part of his popularity by retrieving the remains of Saul and Jonathan and burying them in honor in the tomb of Saul's father, Kish. He also got back for decent burial the seven sons who were slaughtered to appease the Gibeonites. According to the scriptural narrative, God was satisfied and the famine ended.

David was now able to entrust the wars against the Philistines to his heroes whose names we know in considerable detail (2 Samuel 21:15, 17).

The king was impelled to take a census of the realm. This alone was a great tribute to the national organization, for a census requires a great deal of administration.[11] But the census was exceedingly unpopular because the people resented interference in their private affairs. In general, people unused to the compilation of statistics regard census taking as a prelude to conscription and taxation, a viewpoint that was not without justification in the ancient Near East. The census was assigned to Joab, who strongly advised David against it, but then gave in out of loyalty to his sovereign. He started with Transjordan, went up to the borders of Sidon, and then down into the Negev of the south. The totals of the census are given in round numbers: 800,000 men of fighting age for Israel and 500,000 men of fighting age for Judah. Thus the purpose of the count was to estimate military potential. The figures show that Israel was the greater part of the united kingdom.[12]

No historical accuracy should be ascribed to these numbers. Demographic research in recent years has shown that the entire urban population of ancient Israel during the Davidic period was approximately 150,000 with an indeterminate number of people living in small villages and on farms. Cities were very small, and agricultural production and water resources could not have sustained a population much larger than this.[13] How the Bible arrived at its figures is subject to scholarly debate. One possibility is that the Hebrew word *'elef,*

---

11. This is the first serious attempt at a census in Israel. The fact that it met with an unpopular reception confirms that it was an innovation.

12. 1 Chronicles 21:5 attributes still greater numerical superiority to Israel: 1,100,000 fighting men of Israel and 470,000 of Judah.

13. Yigal Shiloh, "The Population of Iron Age Palestine in the Light of a Sample Analysis of Urban Plans, Areas, and Population Density," *Bulletin of the American Schools of Oriental Research* 239, 1980, pp. 25–35.

which means both "thousand" and "fighting unit," was misunderstood. In reality there were 800 fighting units in Israel and 500 in Judah. How many men constituted a fighting unit cannot be established. In time, the scribal tradition reinterpreted 800 *'elef* and 500 *'elef* to mean 800,000 men and 500,000 men. We repeat, however, that this remains just one possibility and we have no proof for this reconstruction of the tradition.

To atone for the sin of the census, David was offered a divine alternative through a prophet.[14] The first choice was a regular phenomenon in the thought processes of the ancient Near Easterners: a seven-year famine. The next was three months of defeat; the third alternative, three days of pestilence. David chose the third alternative. He did not so much as consider the first, for it was the most terrible thing that could befall a country. He chose pestilence rather than defeat because pestilence is dealt out by God; whereas defeat at the hands of one's enemies puts one at the mercy of man, and human foes show far less mercy than God. God was appeased by the erection of an altar and by sacrifices so that the pestilence and other calamities of the realm were brought to an end.

The altar used to curtail the pestilence was constructed on a site that David purchased from a person called "the Araunah." Most translations of the Hebrew Bible interpret this word as a proper name, but in 2 Samuel 24:16 it is used with the definite article, pointing to the fact that it is a title, not a personal name. The word is of Hurrian origin and it means "the lord" or "the king." Note that in 2 Samuel 24:23 Araunah is glossed as "the king."[15] The Araunah, thus, is the former king of Jerusalem who was displaced by David when the Israelites conquered the city. The Hurrian etymology of the title is consistent with the fact that in the Amarna period the ruler of Jerusalem bore the name Abdi-hepa; the latter element is the name of a prominent Hurrian deity.

Related to the question of the identity of the Araunah is the presence of Zadok in the narratives. According to 2 Samuel 8:17, 21:25, he is one of the two main priests in the country; the other is listed either as Ahimelech or Ebiathar (father and son). The latter two are

14. Such narratives are of value primarily for reflecting beliefs and institutions.

15. The attempt by most critics to explain this passage otherwise is uncalled for; see, e.g., the textual emendations discussed by P. Kyle McCarter, *II Samuel* (Anchor Bible), Garden City, N.Y., 1984, p. 508.

mentioned in the story of David's career relatively early (1 Samuel 21:2, etc.; 22:20, etc.), but Zadok appears only after the conquest of Jerusalem. Since earlier priest-kings of Jerusalem bear the names Melchizedek (Genesis 14:18) and Adonizedek (Joshua 10:1), it is probable that the Zedek/Zadok element was a traditional part of the Jerusalem royal onomasticon.

Based on this information, various scholars have suggested the attractive hypothesis that Zadok and the Araunah are one and the same person, who was the former priest-king of Jerusalem before David's conquest.[16] Zadok was his personal name pointing to his sacerdotal authority,[17] and Araunah, "the lord" or "the king," was his royal title. When David occupied the city and proclaimed himself king of Jerusalem, he stripped Zadok of his kingly duties but he permitted him to remain as the high priest of the city.[18] The meaning of this should not be missed by the reader: A pagan priest was retained by David and transformed into a priest of Yahwe in the city of Jerusalem. This will also explain the famous statement by the prophet Ezekiel (16:1) centuries later that the origins of Jerusalem are rooted in paganism.

To return to the story of King David: He was now well advanced in years, so that a Shunamite girl named Abishag was brought to him to nurse him and keep him warm. The latter service means only the physical therapy of keeping the old man warm through the application of young body heat to his body. Sexual implications should not be read into the text.

Like so many despots, David's will became weak in his old age. So now another one of his sons, Adonijah, began to plot another revolt. Adonijah enlisted the help of Joab and Ebiathar, which would seem to be a powerful combination. But he snubbed a still more powerful combination. In giving a feast, he failed to invite his half brother Solomon, who was the son of the favorite queen; he failed to invite Zadok, the priest who was the equal of Ebiathar; he failed to invite Benaiah, who was in charge of the mercenaries; he failed to

---

16. H. H. Rowley, "Zadok and Nehustan," *Journal of Biblical Literature* 58, 1939, pp. 123–32; and C. E. Hauer, "Who Was Zadok?" *Journal of Biblical Literature* 82, 1963, pp. 89–94.

17. The Semitic root *ṣdq*, the base of Zadok/Zedek, means "righteous."

18. The genealogy of Zadok presented in 1 Chronicles 5:29–34, 6:35–38, which descends him from Aaron, was doctored in postexilic times to legitimize the priesthood of Zadok's descendants.

invite Nathan, the leading prophet. Adonijah also snubbed a few other prominent men in military circles. Accordingly, Nathan and Bathsheba decided that this was the time to take matters in hand; and he instructed her to go to the king and remind him of his promise to put Solomon on the throne and to tell him that at that very moment Adonijah was engaging in subversive activities aimed at seizing the throne that was destined for another. Nathan informed her that as soon as she should leave the hall, he would make preparations to have a royal audience and in his own way (independently as far as the king was concerned) confirm the fact. This was done cleverly and the favorite queen and the favorite prophet convinced the old man that this was the time to crown his son Solomon king, while he, David, was still alive.

Once Solomon sat on the throne (c. 965 B.C.E.), he began to eliminate his enemies one by one. Adonijah foolishly requested as a wife Abishag, the girl who nursed David during his last years. The request was indiscreet in that taking over a handmaid of the former king might be an opening wedge to laying claim on the throne, and Adonijah eventually paid with his life for his temerity. Ebiathar, who had cast his lot with Adonijah, was removed from the priesthood. Joab, who had taken refuge at the altar of the Lord where he was entitled to sanctuary, was ordered to leave. Upon stating he preferred to die at the altar, he was killed there in cold blood by Solomon's agents.

Shimei, who was also on the list of personae non gratae, was ordered to live in Jerusalem, where he could be watched, and where he discreetly stayed for three years. At the end of that time he lost a couple of slaves whom he pursued into Philistine territory to retrieve them in the city of Gath. (Apparently relations between the Houses of the Judean David and the Philistine Achish were so good that citizens of one realm could cross the frontier into the other realm, and be accorded sufficient cooperation from the authorities to retrieve fugitive slaves.) On coming back to Jerusalem, Shimei was put to death for disobeying the order to remain in the city (1 Kings 2:36–46).

Hebrew historical writing had, from the literary point of view, reached its height under David. With Solomon, there is already a deterioration in the records, which are excerpted with special reference to his building operations and his material accomplishments. Thus we have correct dates (such as that the building of the Temple began in his fourth year and ended in his eleventh), but Solomon's personality, on the one hand, and the general activities of the realm, on the other, are not portrayed with the fullness of David's history. The exact specifications of Solomon's buildings are small compensation for the lack of the human richness of David's account.

David had shaped a realm, but Solomon could enjoy the fruits of his father's labor. While Solomon was not the empire-builder his father had been, he was enough of a warrior to hold on to distant provinces such as Hamath-Zobah (2 Chronicles 8:3). His construction works in—and exploitation, fortification, and colonization of—points in northern Syria show that his program was imperial, and not limited to the Hebrew homeland (2 Chronicles 8:2–6). Egypt had declined and Israel had grown. Accordingly, at this time we find that a daughter of pharaoh (perhaps the daughter of Psusennes II, the last pharaoh of the Twenty-first Dynasty) is a member of Solomon's harem. Her need to live up to the style of her father's court gave added impetus to Solomon's building program. Solomon built several high places.[19] But the existence of high places around Jerusalem was a necessity in the capital of a king, who married princesses from foreign lands. To extend to his brides the common courtesy of religious freedom, he had to grant them chapels where they could worship their native gods. Also the foreign traders that frequented Jerusalem appreciated the courtesy of access to shrines where they could worship their own gods.

Among the topics included in the history of Solomon are two dreams in which God promised him wisdom and admonished him to adhere to the good way of life. As we have shown, there is no basis for the view that such items must be late accretions. There is no reason to doubt the antiquity of the account of Solomon's dreams any more than the antiquity of Gudea's, which are known to have been recorded, in the form that we have them, in Gudea's reign.

Solomon's regime marked a further growth in administration and accordingly a further weakening of the tribes. In 1 Kings 4 there is a list of Solomon's twelve administrative districts. These districts for the most part do not correspond to the tribes but are new administrative areas set up for the smooth implementing of national policies. The reason for the twelve is explicitly stated: Each district was to maintain

---

19. "High place" came to mean any shrine other than the Temple in Jerusalem. (Shrines were regularly built on heights.)

the royal household and the cost of government for one month of the year. Thus twelveness was still essential in the concept of national administration, although Solomon's districts had replaced the traditional division into tribes.

The boundaries of the twelve administrative districts indicate that Judah fell outside the new system of governance. Probably this is alluded to in the enigmatic words at the end of I Kings 4:19: "one commissioner was in the land," perhaps referring to the land of Judah, which was governed separately from the rest of Israel. The upshot of the new system, then, was a taxation system imposed on the country as a whole for the upkeep of the royal family, whose own tribe in turn received a kind of exemption. If this analysis is accurate, it is no wonder that Solomon experienced unrest in the north, which upon his death eventually seceded and formed its own independent state.

Two of the district governors were sons-in-law of Solomon. It is interesting to note that Azariah, son of Nathan ( = David's son rather than Nathan the Prophet), was in charge of the king's commissioners. Although we were told that Ebiathar had been removed and sent home, we now read that both Zadok and Ebiathar are official priests: a discrepancy showing that the material available to the compiler of Kings had not been edited systematically.[20] Instead of one official scribe there are now two, reflecting how the administration, while following the lines set by David, was increasing. Zabud, another son of Nathan, is a private priest of the king; so through two important appointments (the private priest of the king and the chief of the royal commissioners) the sons of Nathan enjoyed considerable power with the crown. Another official oversaw the Royal House, which required lavish supplies. Adoniram was still over the corvée (or forced labor).

The figure for the Israelites at forced labor is given at 30,000; 10,000 of them worked each month.[21] Quarries had to be operated and trees cut for the building program. A man obliged to render such

---

20. Perhaps at the beginning of Solomon's reign both of the priests were in office; while at the end of his reign, Ebiathar was eliminated. The apparent contradiction in the Bible would then be due to a false arrangement of individually correct facts.

21. Based on the demographic research referred to earlier (p. 204, n. 13), these figures, too, would seem to be inflated.

service for the king would spend two months at home and one away at forced labor. The Canaanite elements of the population were no longer sufficient for doing all the rough work and Israelites were now being reduced to servitude, which was quite unpopular among people who cherished traditions of freedom. Solomon brought glory to Israel, but glory in the form of extensive building programs comes at a great cost, cutting into the living standard of the peasant population. The king's officials were furthermore encroaching upon the prerogatives of local government. Each city had its elders who sat in the gate and gave decisions, but now they had the competition of the king's servants (as officials of the central government were called), who had more power than they. Thus the people's king (as Saul had been) had changed into an oriental despot, which was against the natural inclination of the citizenry. With the growth of wealth in royal and official circles came the growth of poverty among the masses of the people.

Solomon was able to facilitate his construction program by maintaining alliances, notably with Hiram of Tyre. In his message to Hiram, Solomon states: "There is none among us who knows how to cut trees like the Sidonians" (1 Kings 5:20). To the inexperienced reader it might look like a faux pas for Solomon to praise the Sidonians in an appeal to the King of Tyre. But since "Sidonians" is a general term for all the southern Phoenicians, even the men of Tyre are "Sidonians." The famed cedars and other Lebanese evergreens were cut down, brought to the coast, tied into rafts, and floated down to Jaffa, where the rafts were broken up and the trees hauled to Jerusalem. All this had to be paid for and almost the only thing the Hebrews had to give was the produce of the soil; so their wheat and olive oil were shipped in large quantities to Hiram.

The building program of Solomon, contrary to the general impression, was not focused on the Temple. He built a royal complex of which the Temple was only a part. Scripture tells us that the Temple required seven years to build but that the king's palace took thirteen. His house for pharaoh's daughter was quite elaborate, too.

The skilled metalwork was executed by another Hiram, whose father was a master craftsman[22] of Tyre and whose mother was a

---

22. It must have been quite common for sons to follow the trades and professions of their fathers, not only because of environment and natural emulation but because tradesmen and artisans in Canaan were organized into closely knit guilds as attested in the Ugaritic tablets.

widow from the tribe of Naphtali (pointing to the intermingling of south Phoenicians and north Israelites).[23]

The dedication of the Temple and the moving of the ark from Zion, the City of David (1 Kings 8:1–6), into the Holy of Holies of the Temple were solemnly celebrated. The elders of Israel and the heads of the clans were assembled. God is said to have showed His acceptance of the Temple by permeating it as a cloud called "The Glory of Yahwe" that filled the interior. (In the Bible, "The Glory of Yahwe" must often be envisaged as a mist that enveloped the Divine Presence.) There then follows Solomon's dedication prayer, in which divine sanction is regarded as an integral part of justice. It is God's will that justice should be done and in exchange for service to God and the carrying out of His commandments, defeat can be averted, drought can be avoided or terminated, people can be saved from famine, from pestilence, from locusts, and other catastrophes of nature, that so often make life difficult in the land of Israel. God's rewarding His People's devotion will show foreigners all over the world that God's name is really associated with His Temple; for how else could the service in it be effective? The sinning captives from among His People ("for there is no man who does not sin," 1 Kings 8:46) by turning to God will be rescued by Him and brought home again to the only land where they can possibly worship Him[24] and live their national life.

In the second theophany of Solomon (1 Kings 9), it is characteristically noted that the covenant made is conditional: God's protection will continue only as long as the royal line obeys God's will.

The Bible concentrates on Solomon's building of the Temple and of his own palace. Recent archeological work in Jerusalem has not produced evidence of these structures,[25] but other Solomonic build-

---

23. Recent studies in the regional dialectology of ancient Hebrew indicate that northern Hebrew shared many features with Phoenician, but not with Judean Hebrew. The latter is the norm in the Bible, but significant portions of Scripture are composed in the northern dialect. See Gary A. Rendsburg, *Linguistic Evidence for the Northern Origin of Selected Psalms,* Atlanta, 1990 (and the bibliography cited therein).

24. The idea that God could be effectively worshiped by His People anywhere had not yet developed. It was only the destruction of the Temple and the Exile that liberated Yahwistic worship from localism.

25. The reason for this is obvious: The site of the ancient Temple is now occupied by the Dome of the Rock and the al-Aksa Mosque, making archeological work there next to impossible. The exact site of Solomon's palace is unknown, but one day archeologists may succeed in uncovering its remains.

ing projects have been found. The most impressive of these is a very large stepped stone structure; its exact use is still a matter of question, though most likely it served to strengthen Jerusalem's steep slopes and/or it was used as a platform of some sort.[26] It is tempting to identify this structure with the Millo mentioned in 1 Kings 9:24 (see also 2 Samuel 5:9), but the consensus among scholars is that the Millo, whatever it may refer to, still has not been found.[27]

Solomon also expanded other cities in the realm. 1 Kings 9:15 refers to his fortifications at Hazor, Megiddo, and Gezer. At all three sites archeologists have found the remains of these projects, including nearly identical city gates.[28]

Whatever the value of Solomon's constructions, the price was great. King Hiram had to be paid with more than just wheat and oil. Twenty Galilean cities were turned over to him in partial payment for his services.

The pharaoh made an incursion into Canaan and took the city of Gezer away from the local Canaanite population that still occupied and ruled the city. (This shows that, even after David's conquest, there still were small pockets of Canaanites in Israel's midst.) Pharaoh's army killed the Canaanites of Gezer and he gave the destroyed city as a wedding gift to his son-in-law Solomon. Solomon's construction projects at Gezer must have followed soon thereafter.[29]

---

26. Shiloh, *Excavations at the City of David I,* pp. 16–17, 26–27; Shiloh, "The City of David Archaeological Project, The Third Season—1980," pp. 166–69.

27. On this enigmatic term, see Richard C. Steiner, "New Light on the Biblical *Millo* from Hatran Inscriptions," *Bulletin of the American Schools of Oriental Research* 276, 1989, pp. 15–23.

28. For a summary of the evidence, see William G. Dever, *Recent Archaeological Discoveries and Biblical Research,* Seattle, 1990, pp. 102–6.

29. The incorporation of Gezer into the realm brings up the question of the calendars, for a list of local agricultural month names has been found at Gezer. In the Bible there is another such ancient calendar whose spring season opens with ḥodesh ha-abib (Exodus 13:4, etc.) "month of (freshly ripened) barley" (cf. Exodus 9:31; Leviticus 2:14). Moreover the Phoenician calendar (wherein "month" is normally yeraḥ instead of ḥodesh) was also used in official records (1 Kings 6:1, 38; 8:2). Probably many towns under the early Hebrew kings had local cultic agricultural calendars. Centralization under the crown necessitated a uniform calendar for federal administration. Thus was invented the practical though colorless calendar "First Month," "Second Month"—"Twelfth Month" (e.g., throughout Jeremiah starting with 1:3). The inspiration for this development may have come from Egypt where the year was divided into three seasons, each consisting of four numbered months. But even so the Hebrews deserve credit for eliminating seasonal names and streamlining the calendar with simple numbers from one to twelve. After the Exile in 586 B.C.E. the Jews learned the Babylonian month names, starting with the spring new-year month of Nisan; cf. Esther (3:7, etc.) where dates are given both in terms of the numbered Judean and the Babylonian systems.

We are further told that the remnants of the Amorites, Hittites, Jebusites, etc., who were not of the Children of Israel, were reduced to the status of laborers (1 Kings 9:20), whereas the officials and warriors were Israelites (verse 22). However, this can only have been a partly fulfilled ideal. The forced labor actually exacted from among the Israelites made a stronger impression on the people than the pretension that they were exclusively a ruling class.

Solomon included in his ventures a fleet sailing from the port of Ezion-geber (at the head of the Gulf of Eilat) and manned by expert sailors, supplied by Hiram of Tyre. The ships fetched gold, precious stones, and wood (particularly good for the manufacture of musical instruments) from the land of Ophir. Solomon thus had a fleet of Tarshish (which means simply any seagoing fleet) that made a trip every third year bringing back gold, silver, ivory, monkeys, and peacocks. (The statements in 1 Kings 9:26–28; 10:11–12, 22 may well refer to one and the same fleet.)

A queen of Sheba, who visited Solomon, came with a caravan of camels bringing spice, gold, and precious stones from her realm in South Arabia (1 Kings 10:1–3). The historic evaluation of this incident implies that caravan trade bringing minerals and spices was already established with South Arabia. The biblical tradition also reflects the fact that queens frequently ruled among the ancient Arabs: A phenomenon corroborated, as we shall see, in cuneiform records concerning relations between Mesopotamia and Arabia (pp. 251, 254). Furthermore, the trade connections with South Arabia must have continued, at least on and off, for several centuries. From the period of the eighth-sixth centuries B.C.E., we possess three brief, but nonetheless significant, South Arabian inscriptions found in the Jerusalem excavations.[30]

All of this trade by caravan routes and by sea, plus all the new edifices, brought splendor hitherto unknown to the simple Hebrews of the past. The capital and the bigger provincial cities saw more luxury than ever before. But the price paid depleted the resources of the country. The new glamour was for the most part unprofitable. The imported chariots cost 600 shekels of silver apiece. The imported steeds cost 150 shekels of silver each. The royal harem was an expen-

---

30. Yigal Shiloh, "South Arabian Inscriptions from the City of David, Jerusalem," *Palestine Exploration Quarterly* 119, 1987, pp. 9–18. Shiloh also discusses several other South Arabian epigraphic remains from additional sites in Israel.

sive establishment with wives from Egypt, Moab, Ammon, Edom, Sidon, and the Hittites. Solomon's wives led him, especially in his old age, to acts of apostasy including the worship of Astarte, the goddess of Sidon, and Milcom, the god of the Ammonites (1 Kings 11:1–6). Solomon's high places to the gods Chemosh of Moab and Molech of Ammon lasted for three and a half centuries in Jerusalem, until the reign of Josiah (2 Kings 23:13).

What the Israelites (particularly the northerners, who felt abused by the Judean king) had to pay in labor and wealth for Solomon's prosperity, was regarded as plain oppression. The situation was aggravated by the fact that the subjugated provinces of the empire grew rebellious as the warlike qualities of Israel gradually petered out. An Edomite prince named Hadad, who had taken refuge in Egypt and married into the Pharaoh's family, now returned to Edom to regain his country to the chagrin of Solomon, who still wished to keep it in his realm. An Aramean prince named Rezon, who had also taken refuge in Egypt, returned to Damascus to rule over Aram. Thus, while Solomon's Kingdom still held together, the provinces of the empire were being lost, so that his territory toward the close of his reign was considerably smaller than what he had inherited from David. With the loss of the provinces, there grew up a Diaspora of Jews cut off from the main body of their people.

We might ask why the pharaonic family, into which Solomon had married, was allowing his neighbors to dismember his empire. It is well to remember that Hadad the Edomite was also a member of the pharaonic family through marriage. Egypt was at the old game of "divide and rule." Pharaoh was playing politics in Canaan to keep the area as weak as possible. Thus he would play one group against the other, for the weaker Canaan was, the better for Egypt.

An able man named Jeroboam was fatefully chosen by Solomon to be chief of the corvée in the House of Joseph, as the north was called. A prophet named Ahijah of Shiloh met Jeroboam and symbolically tore his garment into twelve pieces, giving ten to Jeroboam and reserving one for the House of David (1 Kings 11:29–32). (The contradiction of ten plus one equaling twelve is obvious; no doubt the biblical author desired to emphasize the singularity of Judah vis-à-vis the rest of Israel, conveniently represented as a round number of ten tribes. However, the historical reality was nine tribes comprising Israel with three tribes [Judah, Benjamin, and Simeon] comprising Judah.) To take the incident out of the prophetic sphere and put it into the sphere of politics: Jeroboam used his opportunity to work with the enslaved masses of Israel to win their support and make things ready for the right moment when a crisis should confront the realm. When his activities and designs became known, he fled to Egypt, where the Pharaoh Shishak protected him. This pharaoh is identified with Shoshenq I (935–14), founder of the Twenty-second Dynasty, well known from Egyptian records. He is the first of all the Egyptian kings mentioned in the Bible to be called by his proper name. This reflects once more the use of annals from the time of Solomon's reign onward, as opposed to the epic traditions that characterize early biblical historiography.

Our Book of Kings cites earlier sources. The compiler here refers us to the Book of the Deeds of Solomon (1 Kings 11:41)—unfortunately now lost—constituting, or at least based upon, the court chronicles of Solomon.

The period of David and Solomon was the golden age of ancient Israel. The country achieved the height of its political, military, and economic power during the tenth century. As numerous examples from world history instruct us (Classical Greece, Imperial Rome, Elizabethan England, Napoleonic France, etc.), a country at the height of its power is also a country with flowering artistic and cultural achievement. The burgeoning of power and the burgeoning of the arts go hand in hand. We know little of Israel's achievements in the plastic arts, and in fact, due to the second commandment, there probably were restrictions to some extent. But in their creativity in writing, the Israelites were unsurpassed in antiquity. Much of this activity no doubt occurred during the time of David and Solomon. The court histories of these two kings, preserved for us in the books of Samuel and Kings, smack of an intimate familiarity with the events narrated.

The Torah, or at least the better part of it, dates from the Davidic-Solomonic period, too. The book of Genesis in particular is filled with all sorts of clues that lead us to date its composition to the tenth century B.C.E. God's words to Abraham and Sarah that kings will descend from them (Genesis 17:6, 16) is a justification for the still recent development of a monarchy. In Genesis 49:10 kingship is to rest with the tribe of Judah, a statement consistent with the Davidic covenant described in 2 Samuel 7. The boundaries of Canaan in God's promise to Abraham (Genesis 15:18) were realized only by David's empire. The manner in which Genesis relates the Moabites,

Ammonites, Edomites, and Arameans to the Israelites reflects the fact that all these people were under the rule of the same king. The episode of Abraham and Melchizedek in Genesis 14:18–20 mirrors the relationship of David and Zadok. Abraham builds many altars but the only place he sacrifices is Mount Moriah, when he substituted a ram for Isaac. This site is traditionally associated with the location of King Solomon's Temple (see 2 Chronicles 3:1), the only place where sacrifices to Yahwe are legitimately to be performed. Even the very wording of the binding of Isaac alludes to Jerusalem, since the story includes a high percentage of words that begin with the consonants yr-, the same two letters that begin the Hebrew word "Jerusalem" (see especially Genesis 22:14, where also "mount of the Lord" is used, an expression used elsewhere in the Bible to refer only to Jerusalem). The biblical portrayal of the patriarchs as merchant-princes, discussed in detail above (Chapter VIII, pp. 114–15), matches the description of Solomon as the king over a large commercial empire. The enigmatic wife-sister motif, which occurs three times in Genesis (12:10–20; 20:1–18; 26:6–11), is a mirror of David's marriage to Abigail, as noted above. The emphasis in Genesis of the motif of the younger son gains a new perspective. True, it is of epic quality, but it also serves to legitimize the succession of Solomon, one of David's youngest sons (if not the youngest), especially since he had to win the right to succeed his father over older brothers, in particular Adonijah. Finally, Jacob's rule over Esau, but the latter's eventual breaking the yoke of the former (Genesis 27:27, 40) reflects Edom's rebellion against Israelite rule at the end of Solomon's reign. The sum of the evidence, then, points decidedly to a tenth-century date for the authorship of Genesis. Similar evidence, though admittedly of not such quantity, is available for the remainder of the Pentateuch as well.

On the death of Solomon (around 935), it is noteworthy that his son Rehoboam had to go north to Shechem[31] for acceptance by the Israelites, who had at best mixed feelings toward the Judean Dynasty and its capital. There was still the feeling that there had to be a covenant between the ruler and the ruled, so that a new king had to lay down a platform acceptable to the people before they would receive him as their sovereign. The Israelites naturally wanted to know

31. The location suggests that the nation as a whole still regarded Shechem, with its shrine at Gerizim, as the true center versus the newer Davidic capital at Jerusalem with its more recent shrine.

whether Rehoboam's rule would be oppressive like Solomon's or whether it would be mild. He consulted the elders, who urged him to reply mildly to the people. As the elders put it: "If you will be a slave today to this people, and serve them and answer them and speak good words to them, they will be your slaves for all the days" (1 Kings 12:7). Instead of following this sound advice, Rehoboam turned to his young friends, who got him to lay down a severe policy and say that he would be even stricter than his father. The dissatisfied northern tribes thereupon deserted him, never to rejoin Judah or the House of David as long as northern Israel was to exist as a national entity. Whatever chance there might have been for the Hebrews to regain political strength, and be masters of their own national destiny, was shattered for centuries.

# CHAPTER XIV

# The Divided Kingdoms
# to Jehu's Purge

Rehoboam failed to grasp fully the seriousness of the situation. He sent Adoram, who was still in charge of the corvée, to exact forced labor from the Israelites. The indignant Israelites assassinated Adoram. Rehoboam fled by chariot to Jerusalem, behind whose walls he found refuge from the hostility of his former subjects in the north.

Thus 1 Kings 12:19 expresses the verdict of the biblical author: "And Israel has sinned against the House of David down to this day." We must bear in mind that the sympathies of the Bible are squarely Judean and therefore against the Israelite North. As long as Israel was detached from the House of David, there could be no virtue in Israel. Moreover, all cults (even for the worship of Yahwe) in Israel will be condemned from this time on, in the Bible, whose authors recognize only the legitimacy of the Temple in Jerusalem. The Bible judges the kings of Judah as good or bad depending on their devotion to the Jerusalem cult; but the kings of Israel were of necessity all bad because they could not adhere to the Jerusalem cult that lay outside their borders.

Above (p. 193, n. 1) we noted that the word "Israel" is ambiguous for much of Israelite history. To alleviate some of the ambiguity, we now introduce a new term "Israelian"[1] to refer to the people of the northern kingdom of Israel. The word "Israel" will remain ambiguous, i.e., it still can refer either to united Israel consisting of twelve

---

1. This felicitous term was introduced by H. L. Ginsberg, *The Israelian Heritage of Israel,* New York, 1982.

tribes or to the northern tribes who broke away and formed their own kingdom. But to distinguish the people of these entities, we reserve the form "Israelite" to refer to the people of all Israel, and we use "Israelian" to refer to the people of the northern kingdom. (Note that the word "Israeli" is used for the people of the modern country of Israel.) Thus during the time of the divided kingdom we will speak of Israelians and Judeans comprising the Israelite people.

The Israelians, after rejecting Rehoboam, summoned Jeroboam to a council in order to interrogate him and oblige him to make a covenant with the representatives of the people. Israel crowned Jeroboam as king and the rupture with Judah was complete.

With the breakup of the Davidic-Solomonic kingdom into two parts, the international empire once ruled from Jerusalem also came to an end. As we have seen, already late in Solomon's reign there was unrest and Edom and Aram probably gained full independence. With the split between Israel and Judah, places such as Ammon and Moab no doubt reestablished their independence as well. The Bible is basically silent on this issue, but the autonomy of Moab, for example, can be inferred from the evidence of the Mesha stela (to be discussed in detail below, pp. 232–33).

Economically the resources of the Hebrews were too limited to secure any continuous or solid prosperity. The tribute of vassal states was no longer present, and the income from Solomon's enterprises were no longer available. The latter were dependent, for example, on control over ports such as Ezion-geber, now once more in Edomite hands presumably. It is unclear how much control the Israelites exercised over Mediterranean ports. Judah probably was landlocked, though Israel may have had access to the sea at a port such as Dor. Otherwise the coast was in the hands of the Phoenicians and to some extent the Philistines. The caravan routes to the east were in the hands of Moab, Ammon, Edom, desert nomads, and Arabian kingdoms, so that the Hebrew could no longer derive income from the toll charges that had been levied under David and Solomon.

The arable land on which the people depended was limited. There was some good land in the "Valley"[2] of Jezreel and a few other narrow plains, and, some less productive hill country, adding up to very little agricultural land to support the population. Furthermore, the sea-

---

2. The Hebrew word ʿemeq is often translated "valley" even when it really designates a plain between two mountainous areas or between mountains and a sea (or lake).

sonal rainfall was precarious, and droughts brought famine as well as thirst. And even in years when the rain was sufficient, locust plagues and blights might ruin the crops. Sometimes the poor land underwent the worst of all calamities: a succession of famine years. All such disasters were regarded as punishments from God for the sins of the people and their rulers[3]; so instead of undermining the faith of His devotees, misfortune simply intensified religion.

Rehoboam was wisely dissuaded by a "man of God" named Shemaiah from launching an attack on Israel. Judah, throughout all its history, never had the means or will to attempt to reconquer Israel.

Jeroboam had problems on his hands. How was he to prevent his subjects from renewing their contacts with Judah? Israel and Judah accepted one and the same God. Furthermore, by this time, the shrine at Jerusalem was considerably more impressive than any other shrine in the land. From political necessity, Jeroboam strengthened the Yahwistic shrines at Bethel and Dan. But he also set up a golden calf as an idol of Yahwe in each of the two sanctuaries. Furthermore, Jeroboam employed non-Levite priests in the northern cult. As discussed above (Chapter X, p. 167), the Levite control over the priesthood must have been, with few exceptions, secure in Judah from Solomon's time onward. But in the North non-Levites still officiated. Jeroboam also altered the traditional calendar. Instead of celebrating the great fall festival of Sukkot on the fifteenth day of the seventh month (as per the Torah), he shifted its observation to the fifteenth day of the eighth month. Calendar differences are a significant way to outwardly distinguish closely related cults, a point that Jeroboam well understood.[4] In light of all this, the Judeans regarded the Israelian cult as spurious, and viewed this brand of Yahwism as apostasy.

Excavations at Dan have uncovered a large sanctuary site, generally dated to the ninth century B.C.E.[5] This is a bit post-Jeroboam, so probably it represents a later expansion of the original shrine established by the first Israelian king. Among the finds on the spot are a

---

3. This was also true of the neighboring people with reference to their national gods.

4. The split of the Qumran community from normative Judaism in postbiblical times was due in great part to their adherence to a different calendar; see Shemaryahu Talmon, "The Calendar Reckoning of the Sect from the Judaean Desert," *Scripta Hierosolymitana* 4, 1958, pp. 162–99. Similarly, Roman Catholicism and Eastern Orthodoxy share much in the way of theology, but their different calendars sharply distinguish them.

5. Avraham Biran, "Dan," in *Encyclopedia of Archaeological Excavations in the Holy Land,* Vol. 1, Jerusalem, 1975, pp. 319–21.

small horned altar, offering stands, and bronze shovels, all of which would have been used in the sacrificial system. To date, however, there still is no evidence of the golden calf placed by Jeroboam at Dan.

Despite the frequent biblical condemnation of Jeroboam, he was in fact not one to flout either the religion of Yahwe or the legitimacy of Yahwe's prophets. When his son Abijah takes sick, he sends his wife in disguise to Ahijah, a prophet of Yahwe, in order to receive an oracle to tell what would happen to the child. The oracle is unfavorable and the boy dies (1 Kings 14). The story is interesting in that it represents Jeroboam as going out of his way to consult a true prophet of Yahwe. While condemning all the Israelian kings, the Bible often lets slip data that show that not all of the condemnation should be left unqualified.

It is to the lasting credit of the Judean authors that they do not whitewash the rulers of the House of David. Judah is repeatedly guilty of worshiping on high places,[6] of setting up monuments (maṣ-ṣebot), of paganizing character, and of worshiping on high hills and under green trees (favorite sites for popular worship). In addition, the qedeshim and qedeshot could still be found in the land, at times even in the Jerusalem Temple.[7]

We have a synchronism taken from authentic chronicles of the kings of Judah for the reign of Rehoboam, in whose fifth year, Shishak, the first pharaoh of the Twenty-second Dynasty invaded Canaan somewhere around the year 930 B.C.E. According to Shishak's records, he invaded both Israel and Judah, and carried off rich plunder from a considerable number of towns. In 1 Kings 14:25–26 nothing is told of these extensive operations other than that Shishak came against Jerusalem so that Rehoboam had to strip the Temple and royal treasury to appease the pharaoh and get him to move on. In 2 Chronicles 12:4, however, Shishak captured the fortified cities of Judah before coming to Jerusalem. Why does the compiler of Kings tell us nothing about Shishak's wide operations throughout Israel and Judah? The reason is that his chief interest is the Jerusalem cult.[8] He cared little

---

6. As noted above (p. 208, n. 19), "high place" comes to mean any shrine other than the one legitimate Temple in Jerusalem.

7. These individuals were discussed earlier, Chapter X, pp. 160–61.

8. Shishak's list may be somewhat exaggerated, for many of the town names therein may have been copied from lists of earlier pharaohs who had invaded Canaan.

about the secular history of Israel; nor was he very deeply concerned about the provincial cities of Judah.[9] His attention was focused on Jerusalem, with special reference to Yahwe's cult in the Temple there.

Alongside the partisan selection of data and the propagandistic attitude of the compiler, the Books of Kings contain many reliable dates and facts from authentic court chronicles; e.g., as we have already mentioned, the dates of the beginning and completion of Solomon's Temple and of Shishak's invasion. Dates are given in terms of the king's reign. Each reign was a unit unto itself. The names and order of all the kings of Israel and Judah are also accurate. Furthermore, the ages at which the kings of Judah ascended the throne, and their mothers' names, are reliable. In the daily life of the people (as distinct from the court chronicles), dating by events was the usual type of chronology.[10] Thus the Book of Amos is dated "two years before the earthquake" (Amos 1:1; cf. Zechariah 14:5).

The canonical Books of Kings have as their sources the annals of the Judean and Israelian kings. A system of chronology was developed, whereby when a Judean king came to the throne his first regnal year was given in relationship to his Israelian counterpart; and when an Israelian king came to the throne his first regnal year was given in relationship to his Judean counterpart. Thus, for example, "In the twentieth year of Jeroboam king of Israel reigned Asa over Judah" (1 Kings 15:9), and "Nadab son of Jeroboam reigned over Israel in the second year of Asa king of Judah" (1 Kings 15:25). By integrating all this information, along with several key synchronisms between Israelite kings and other ancient Near Eastern rulers, we have a very accurate chronology for the entire period of the Israelite kingdoms. It is true that small problems still exist and that no two scholars can agree on how to reconcile the minor discrepancies; nevertheless, especially when compared to the early period of Israel's history, we are on firm ground in the dating of individual reigns and events.

In 1 Kings 15:2, 10 it is shown that Abijam and Asa of Judah are brothers born of the same mother. Accordingly, Asa is not Abijam's son as he is erroneously stated to be in verse 8. Another problem is

---

9. Chronicles often preserves valuable factual data omitted in Samuel and Kings. Thus 2 Chronicles 11:5–12 records Rehoboam's extensive fortifications throughout his realm, including depots for supplies of arms, food, and drink.

10. This is essentially the type of dating used in Mesopotamian tablets of the Third Dynasty of Ur and of the First Dynasty of Babylon. The uneducated people of the Near East still use that method.

raised by the fact that 1 Kings calls the king "Abijam," whereas 2 Chronicles 12:16 ff. changes the name to "Abijah." The older Kings tradition is correct. His name does not contain the divine name "Yah" (for "Yahwe") but the pagan "Yam" (the Canaanite sea-god). Puritanically this was revised to "Yah" by the Chronicler[11] who did not like to see any trace of paganism in the name of a Davidic king. Asa is singled out as one of the good kings of Judah for putting aside pagan images and removing the *qedeshim*. He went to the extent of demoting his mother, who had gotten involved with the Asherah cult, from the queenship. But at the same time we are told that Asa did not wipe out the high places, so that while his virtue was great, it fell short of perfection.

Jeroboam was succeeded by Nadab who warred with the Philistines and, while besieging a city, was assassinated by one of his army officers named Baasha, who usurped the throne. There is a sharp contrast between the histories of Israel and Judah with respect to the continuity of the royal lines. Judah ran its long course under the one Davidic House, whereas Israel experienced a succession of bloody usurpations whereby one line followed another. In total, the Davidic House ruled for 415 years, i.e., from 1000 B.C.E. (approximate date for David's succession) to 586 B.C.E. (end of the kingdom of Judah). There was a short interregnum (under Athaliah, about whom see below, pp. 233, 239), but the fact remains that David's family sat on the throne in Jerusalem for over four centuries. Remarkably, of all the dynasties known to us from the ancient Near East, the Davidic monarchy has the second longest rule. Considering the relative weakness of the kingdom of Judah, this is a singular achievement.[12] And in all of world history a family rule of 415 years is seldom surpassed.[13]

After his usurpation, Baasha proceeded to fortify the city of Ramah, just north of the border, as a defense against Judah and perhaps as a base for making incursions into that country. Asa reacted by bribing the Arameans of Damascus to attack Israel, thus touching off the Israelian-Aramean wars that were to continue for a long time to come. Asa then mobilized all of Judah, so that none was exempt, and

---

11. As the author of the biblical Books of Chronicles is called.

12. The Davidic Dynasty is surpassed by only one Assyrian dynasty, the one that led this Mesopotamian nation to the height of its power, that of Ninurta-apil-ekur (1192–1180) through Shalmaneser V (726–722), for a total of 471 years.

13. David P. Henige, *The Chronology of Oral Tradition*, Oxford, 1974.

proceeded to Ramah, now abandoned by the Israelians who had their hands full in the north. Asa tore down the fortress and reused the building materials to construct Gibeah of Benjamin and Mizpah as strongholds for defense against Israel. Thus 2 Chronicles 14:7–12 records Asa's victory over Zerah the Ethiopian who invaded Judah; verses 13–14 add that Asa plundered the cities around Gerar and, after capturing much livestock, returned to Jerusalem. Asa also seized some Ephraimite cities (2 Chronicles 17:2).

The situation in Israel rapidly deteriorated. Baasha was succeeded by his son Elah who, while with the army, got drunk and was killed by Zimri, a captain of the chariotry, who usurped the throne. However, an able army officer named Omri had himself crowned by his own troops and proceeded against Zimri, who, realizing that his cause was lost, set his palace afire and died in the flames. But another Israelite, named Tibni, set himself up as ruler, so that Israel was divided between two kings, Omri and Tibni. Upon Tibni's death Omri became sole ruler and proved to be one of the ablest kings throughout Israelite history. Fortunately for him and his dynasty he was known as the avenger of his master (Elah) and not as a usurper. Zimri was the usurper as is shown by the taunt of Jezebel in 2 Kings 9:31.

Omri purchased, in a fair and honest way, the site of Samaria and made it the greatest of all the Israelian capitals. It is a good site with an excellent view of the mountains all around, well protected and not dominated by any near height. It is conveniently located near a road down to Dor (a seaport south of Haifa) as well as near the main north-and-south highway of the mountainous part of the country. The Damascenes captured some of Omri's cities, and established Aramean agencies in the bazaars of Samaria (note 1 Kings 20:34). He was wise in his foreign policy, for it was he who also ended the Judean wars so that for a long time to come there was no political or military friction between the two Hebrew kingdoms. Omri's greatest accomplishment (completely omitted in Scripture!) is the conquest of Moab, as we learn from the inscription of the Moabite King Mesha, who relates that Omri conquered Moab so that Moab was suppressed by Israel all the days of Omri and half the days of his son ( = Ahab). This is a good illustration of how the Judean author leaves out data that do not suit his purpose. The chief triumph of a great king of Israel is thus known to us only through a pagan source outside the Bible. Another sign of Omri's greatness is that even long after his death, Israel was known politically to the Assyrians as the "House of Omri."

Possibly Omri was responsible for the wedding of his heir Ahab, who was married to a Phoenician princess of dynamic personality and force of character. Unfortunately those qualities were in the wrong direction. Her name was Jezebel.

The marriage of Jezebel to Ahab meant that the courtesy due to a queen required the building of a Baal shrine with an adjacent Asherah, plus the introduction of the pagan priesthood necessary for the cult. Viewed objectively, it was no worse than what Solomon had done for his wives, although the Bible is far more critical of the Israelian Ahab than of the Judean Solomon.

Ahab was capable. He recovered from Damascus cities lost by his predecessors Baasha and Omri. He established favorable trade relations not only with the kingdom of his father-in-law, who ruled Tyre, but also with Damascus. When he defeated Damascus, he gave generous terms to the fallen foe. At the same time that he retrieved the lost territory of his own people, he established agencies (largely commercial in character) within Damascus, so that Israel now had every advantage. Yahwist fanatics of Israel (whose opinions are given with approbation in Scripture) condemned his restraint and statesmanship as disobedience to God. Actually, his mildness was politically sound because Damascus and Israel were neighbors of comparable size and strength. It was an age when they had to stick together. For Israel to try to reduce Damascus to vassaldom would have exhausted Israel and ended in disaster. To the contrary, circumstances were soon to require Israel and Aram to hang together or hang separately.

It is in Ahab's reign that we have the first absolute date, that can be controlled historically, in the entire history of the Hebrew people. Shalmaneser III of Assyria ended an era when the small nations of Canaan and Syria had only each other to contend with. Assyria had been developing and growing from strength to strength and in 853 B.C.E. Shalmaneser III was ready to attempt to extend his empire into Canaan. In that year he waged a battle at Karkar on the Orontes River in Syria. It was this threat that effected a union of the Canaanite nations including Israel, but with Damascus as head of the coalition.

Damascus was able to throw into the field 1,200 chariots, 1,200 cavalry, and 20,000 infantry. Ahab had the second-largest force, but in a technical sense the strongest of all, for he supplied 2,000 chariots (the most prized of the military arms) and 10,000 infantry. The coalition also included kings from Phoenicia, Que, Musur,[14] Ammon,[15] and camel-riding Arabs.[16] Thus the nations of the west forgot their local animosities and united against their common Assyrian foe. Shalmaneser claims a stupendous victory. In one account he tells us he slaughtered 14,000 of his enemies. Later in his reign, when he rewrote the "history," the number had grown to 25,000. This illustrates how little we can trust statistics meant to glorify monarchs rather than to state sober facts.

Such attacks by Assyria did not incorporate the enemy countries into the empire, as was to happen later, notably under the Sargonid kings of Assyria. Shalmaneser's expeditions cost many lives and enriched Assyria with plunder of gold, silver, slaves, animals, and so forth. But the large walled cities remained intact; and as soon as the invader departed, the local kings reasserted themselves, and politically things were much as they had been before the nightmare. In spite of the great victory claimed by Shalmaneser, he had to return to Hamath and Damascus six years later. In short, the western coalition won the battle; it had succeeded in stopping the advance of the powerful Assyrians.

No doubt Ahab's contribution of 2,000 chariots and 10,000 soldiers was a major factor in the victory of the western kings. And yet once more Scripture passes over this event in the reign of an Israelian king in silence. Just as the Bible fails to mention Omri's subjugation of Moab, so does it fail to discuss Ahab's role in the war against Shalmaneser III. The reason is simple: The Judean author does not want his readers to know that kings of whom Yahwe disapproves can enjoy success nonetheless.

The marriage of Jezebel into the royal house of Israel meant that

---

14. The generally accepted opinion identifies *Gu-a-a* in this text with Que (Cilicia), and Musur with a northern country by that name (not Egypt, which has the same name ["Mizraim"] in Hebrew). See also 1 Kings 10:28–29, where Que and Musur are combined, concerning the sources of Solomon's horses and chariots. An alternative reading views *Gu-a-a* as an error for *Gu-bal-a-a*, i.e., Byblos, and identifies Musur with Egypt; see Hayim Tadmor, "Que and Musri," *Israel Exploration Journal* 11, 1961, pp. 143–50.

15. Gary A. Rendsburg, "Baasha of Ammon," *Journal of the Ancient Near Eastern Society* 20, 1991, pp. 57–61.

16. The absence of Judah shows that the coalition went only as far south as Israel. The fact that Judah (together with Edom, which often was dominated by Judah) was the convenient buffer between the Mesopotamian empires and Egypt explains why Judah bore so much less of the brunt of the Assyrian invasions and why it was spared to the extent that it was.

Baal had a cult in competition with Yahwe's. The Baal worshiped throughout Israel at this time was not a foreign Baal. He was the Baal of the Earth: a universal god who could just as well be associated with the land of Israel as he could with the land of Tyre, Sidon, Byblos, or (in former times) Ugarit. The discrepancy between the "universal" and "local" nature of Baal, or any other god, did not disturb ancient devotees nearly so much as it does philosophically minded modern scholars. In Ahab's reign there was a drought attested not only in the Bible but also in Phoenician history that has come down through Greek channels. In the minds of the Yahwists, particularly of the prophets, there could be only one cause for this prolonged drought and it was that Yahwe, who alone could send rain or withhold it, had been offended; and it was only through the annihilation of the Baal cult and the reestablishment of the cult of Yahwe that rain would come and the nation be saved. The leader in defending the cause of Yahwe is Elijah, whose narratives are among the finest in the Bible. His contest in 1 Kings 18 with the priesthood of Baal is one of the most vivid and moving passages in the Bible. Moreover, the manner in which the Baal devotees and Baal himself are portrayed in the story are accurate, as we now know from the Ugaritic texts. For example, the prophets of Baal mutilated themselves until bloodied in a sign of mourning when they think that their god is dead; in Ugaritic mythology the gods El and Anat perform the same ritual when they learn of the death of Baal. Furthermore, Elijah taunted the worshippers of Baal with his mock that Baal may be absent because he either is defecating or is sleeping; in the Ugaritic texts we have depictions not of Baal, but of El, both sleeping and floundering in his excrement.[17]

The great event that was to be remembered for a long time to come was not so much the wars of Ahab but the affair of Naboth. The latter, a private citizen, who in accordance with Hebrew tradition could stand up for his rights even against the king, had a vineyard adjacent to Ahab's estate. Ahab made every reasonable offer to pay Naboth for the land so that he might enlarge the royal estate, but Naboth stubbornly refused to sell because it was his own inheritance

17. For details see Gary A. Rendsburg, "The Mock of Baal in 1 Kings 18:27," *Catholic Biblical Quarterly* 50, 1988, pp. 414–17. Scholars have noted that what is sometimes attributed to El in the Ugaritic texts is attributed to Baal in the Bible. Obviously there were local variants of Canaanite religion throughout the region, and a certain fluidity needs to be accepted.

handed down from his father. Typically enough from the Israelite viewpoint, Ahab went home disturbed and frustrated because there was nothing he could do against the rights of his subject. Jezebel, however, had a different approach. As we saw above (Chapter X, p. 160), she was guided by Canaanite mores, which saw nothing wrong with a person in such a position exerting one's power.[18] By trumping up a false charge against Naboth and by procuring a few good-for-nothings as witnesses and using the king's seal to authenticate her nefarious case, Jezebel had Naboth convicted of blasphemy and of reviling the king, so that Naboth was stoned to death by the multitude ostensibly in accordance with the law whereby Naboth's property was also forfeited to the crown. The affair made a terrible impression on the people and determined the downfall of Ahab's line because innocent blood had been shed. Israel's institutions of ancient origins required that innocent blood be expiated by blood; and even if Ahab should die a natural death, his descendant(s) would have to pay for the crime, as actually came to pass. A single miscarriage of justice was enough to destroy the most powerful and effective dynasty that northern Israel ever had.

Elijah held himself more or less aloof from practical politics. He stuck to religion and morals in his defense of Yahwism. It was his successor Elisha who gave Elijah's program political implementation.[19] If we strip the narratives about Elisha of their anecdotes, he appears as an important historic personage: a maker of kings and a man who intervened boldly, at the psychological moments, in international affairs.

Some details of the anecdotes about Elisha are often misunderstood. When he counted on the possession of Elijah's cloak for magical powers to show he had inherited his master's inspiration, he says in 2 Kings 2:9 that he wants, not twice the power of his master, but two thirds thereof. The Hebrew fraction is often misunderstood. No disciple of a great prophet would hope to have twice his master's power. The only other possible interpretation is "a double share" such as the chief heir gets in contradistinction to his brothers who

18. In addition, see the interesting light in which the affair is put by H. L. Ginsberg, "Ugaritic Studies and the Bible," *Biblical Archaeologist* 7, 1945, p. 52.

19. The reason the Judean editor is so interested in the northern prophets, Elijah and Elisha, is that they championed the cause of Yahwism against the cult of Baal. The same holds for the lengthy account of Jehu, King of Israel, who later abolished Baalism and vindicated Yahwe.

get a single share. But then the Hebrew idiom could not mean Elisha got twice Elijah's power, any more than an heir could get twice the whole estate.

Another detail in the cycle of Elisha is easily misunderstood to the point of being ridiculous. It is the story of Elisha in Bethel, where he was called "baldy" by local children, upon whom the prophet heaped a hearty malediction so that a couple of bears came out of the forest and ripped open forty-two of the disrespectful youngsters. In traveling through Arab Palestine I [C. H. G.] observed that in certain villages the hospitality toward all strangers (in spite of political tension) was admirable, like Abraham's hospitality to the angels. But at other villages (which had bad, but deserved, reputations) children would without provocation throw stones at strangers. Bethel was a town where there was no respect for strangers or for age. Accordingly, the point of the story is not that just children were punished, but that specifically the children of a bad community were given a punishment they so fully deserved, as everyone in Israel knew.

Among the accomplishments of Ahab was the fortification of Jericho and a number of other cities. He also embellished Samaria and built an "ivory palace" there (1 Kings 22:39). That type of palace soon spread to the upper classes (Amos 3:15). Such palaces were not built of ivory, but as we know from actual ivories found in excavations, houses were adorned with inlays, panels, jewel boxes, and other small objects of artistically carved ivory. Thus the ivory was used for ornamentation and not for construction (which would require more ivory than the supply could meet). Carved ivories and other luxuries were often imported from Phoenicia. Trade with Phoenicia was favored by a pact between Israel and Tyre (Amos 1:9).

Ahab's worst defeat was his loss of the province of Moab. Mesha's inscription dates Moab's successful war for independence in the middle of Ahab's reign. Mesha relates that some of the Israelite tribes, such as Gad, were still in Transjordan. Mesha took those Hebrews captive and forced them to work on his public projects as slave laborers. He visualized his success as a victory of his native god Chemosh over the foreign God Yahwe. Chemosh had been angry with his people but had finally forgiven them and so rescued them out of the hand of Yahwe and Yahwe's subjects. We note that the rivalry of gods was imagined to be the source of warfare. Putting war on a religious plane justified the ever growing brutality in warfare such as we read on Mesha's stela and other documents of the ancient Near East.

Good relations between Israel and Judah were enhanced by ties of marriage between the houses of Jehoshaphat by ties of marriage between the houses of Jehoshaphat and of Ahab. This union gave Judah so much additional strength[20] that it was able to reconquer Edom, which was thereafter administered for a time not by its own king but by a governor stationed there. It should be noted that just as the sign of Israelian strength is its domination over Moab, the criterion for inferring the strength of Judah is its domination over Edom. When Judah has military striking power, it dominates Edom; when Judah is weak, Edom regains independence.

Ahab and Jehoshaphat got together fraternally[21] to try to win back Israelite territory in Transjordan by fighting for the key city of Ramoth-gilead. Before embarking on the campaign, Ahab consulted four hundred prophets available in his court for what passed for the agreeable[22] word of God. One of the prophets named Zedekiah presented a pair of iron horns, which symbolically were to be worn by Ahab to gore Aram and score a victory.[23] This optimistic prophecy did not impress Jehoshaphat who wanted to know whether they might consult some more genuine prophet of Yahwe. Reluctantly Ahab admitted there was one, Micaiah son of Imlah, who in the past had consistently prophesied evil for Ahab. Micaiah was fetched and he at first sarcastically confirmed the agreeable prognosis of the court prophets. But on being prodded to speak the truth, Micaiah declared that God wanted to ruin the House of Ahab and for that very reason He had sent a lying spirit into these prophets. (The point had not yet been reached in Hebraic theology, where a lying spirit sent by Yahwe would be unthinkable. As we have already observed, Yahwe is here represented as acting much like Zeus who intentionally misled Agamemnon by a false dream.) Micaiah finally gives a true prophecy and predicts disaster for the kings in their venture at Ramoth-gilead. He

---

20. In 2 Chronicles 17:2, 11 it is stated that Jehoshaphat retained Ephraimite cities captured by his father Asa, and that Jehoshaphat exacted tribute of silver from the Philistines, and livestock from the Arabs.

21. Though with Judah subordinate to Israel's interests.

22. If agreeableness is demanded of oracles, the oracles soon prove false and become discredited. Furthermore, inspired men never occur in droves. Such prophets as these were simply a variety of court flatterer.

23. Cf. the slate palette of Narmer on which the Pharaoh is in one scene represented as a bull goring the enemy fortifications with his horns. Cf. James B. Pritchard, *The Ancient Near East in Pictures*, Princeton, 1954, p. 93, no. 297 (bottom register).

is sent to jail pending the outcome, but in 1 Kings 22:28 enunciates the test of prophecy, in saying to Ahab: "If you return in peace, then God has not spoken through me." The kings go off to the battle, meet with their defeat and Micaiah is vindicated. Ahab was mortally wounded at Ramoth-gilead. The judgment of Scripture concerning Jehoshaphat is typical of several good kings of Judah: He was good except for one thing; the people were still worshiping on the high places. However, he did wipe out the remnant of the unsavory *qedes-him*. (2 Chronicles 17:6, contradicting 1 Kings 22:44, even ascribes to Jehoshaphat the shutting down of the high places.)

Jehoshaphat felt sufficiently strong, what with his conquest of Edom, to launch a fleet for the purpose of trade on the Red Sea, but his ships were wrecked before they could sail from their home port of Ezion-geber (1 Kings 22:49), in keeping with Judean ineptitude at navigation. King Ahaziah, son of Ahab, offered to cooperate with Jehoshaphat in further naval exploits but Jehoshaphat had had enough and declined (1 Kings 22:50).

Ahaziah consulted the pagan god Baal-zebub. Conversely, Naaman of Damascus turned to Elisha, a prophet of Yahwe, for healing. Often people have the notion that foreign talent is superior to domestic skill. In any case, Naaman came to Elisha seeking to be cured (2 Kings 5:1–19) through powers derived from Yahwe. Naaman was so convinced of the efficacy of the cure and of Yahwe's supremacy that he embraced Yahwism and carried back two mule loads of soil from Israel so that in Damascus he might worship Yahwe on His own earth. (This reflects the belief that a god could only be effectively worshiped on his own soil.) Inasmuch as his official duties included accompanying his sovereign into a pagan temple where he had to bow down, he received in advance an indulgence from Elisha permitting him to do this.

In this period of history the relations between Israel and Judah are quite close and the names of kings reigning simultaneously in the two monarchies may be identical, to the confusion of the reader. We now enter a period where both the north and the south are ruled by J(eh)-orams; one Jehoram is the son of Ahab, the other is the son of Jehoshaphat.

Jehoram of Judah, according to 2 Chronicles 21:1–4, killed his six brothers (who had been granted Judean fortresses by Jehoshaphat) together with some other Judean princes. The purpose of such brutality was to concentrate power in the person of the king. However,

Jehoram of Judah's tyranny stemmed from weakness rather than strength, to judge from the fact that Edom shook off his yoke and proclaimed itself an independent kingdom (2 Kings 8:20–22; 2 Chronicles 21:8–10).

Though Jehoram the son of Ahab, destroyed his father's Baal monument, he is none the less condemned as wicked for the simple reason that as a northern king he could not adhere to the Jerusalem cult. But we discern by his attack on Baalism that the reform of Elijah and Elisha was meeting with a positive response in Israel with the result that Baalism was giving way to the return of Yahwism.

The two Jehorams and the ruler of Edom pooled their resources to march against Mesha and win back Moab for Israel. To understand their relationship it is necessary to bear in mind that the greatest of the three rulers was the king of Israel. Indeed the expedition was for Israel's benefit. Judah was subordinate to Israel; and Edom was Judah's vassal. The three unequal allies proceeded against Mesha of Moab.

Elisha accompanied the armies to give oracles. When an oracle is finally sought of him, he gets into the prophetic mood by listening to music (2 Kings 3:15). (The use of music either to induce the spirit of the Lord, or to drive out an evil spirit are both attested in Scripture.) A water shortage threatened the three armies and Elisha predicted that without observing wind or rain, the dry wadi before them would be filled with water (2 Kings 3:17). The hosts and their beasts were saved by a torrent in the wadi, although they saw no rain to account for it. The phenomenon is not a miracle: It sometimes happens that a sudden heavy rain at a distance in the hills sends a raging torrent through the wadis leaving the natural holes in the wadi bed filled with water for hours, or even days, to come. The only remarkable feature of the story is the timing.

The expedition against Moab was typically destructive and inconclusive. The invaders filled up wells and cisterns with stones, cut down trees and devastated the countryside. Finally, they surrounded the fortified town in which the Moabite king had taken refuge. From the military standpoint, the impregnability of the town wall doomed the expedition to failure, as so frequently happened in ancient warfare. The invaders had plundered and ruined the country but could not win the war. Since Israel did not succeed in its attempt to reconquer Moab, Mesha's earlier war for independence, related on his stela, had not been in vain. Mesha sacrificed to the national god Chemosh his crown prince on the town wall, where everyone could see it. The Israelites and their allies chose this moment to withdraw to their homeland lest the rage of Chemosh should destroy them to their homeland lest the rage of Chemosh should destroy them in his own territory. His pity, aroused by the extreme sacrifice of King Mesha, had brought his "great rage against Israel" (2 Kings 3:27). The incident shows that Israel still shared with her neighbors the national concept of divinity. Just as Yahwe had His land and people, Chemosh had his land and people.

While Mesha's victory over Israel preceded the two Jehorams' invasion, it is probable that the building operations mentioned in his stela were required to repair the damage inflicted during that invasion. The fact that Mesha's program included waterworks as well as buildings and fortifications jibes with 2 Kings 3:25. The question arises why Mesha does not discuss this invasion. The answer is probably that he had very little to boast about in a war where the enemy effected an unopposed withdrawal after devastating Moab. To sum up Moabite relations with Israel: Omri conquered Moab; quite a few years afterward (described as "forty" years by Mesha in accordance with a well-known idiom not meant to be taken literally) Mesha regained independence from Ahab; Jehoram of Israel tried to win back Moab but succeeded only in devastating that land; and Mesha repaired the damage by a building program outlined in his stela.[24]

King Ahaziah[25] of Judah (the son of Jehoram of Judah and of an Israelian princess Athaliah)[26] joined forces with Jehoram of Israel against the usurper Hazael, who had seized the throne of Damascus. Hazael is called in Assyrian annals "the son of a nobody" which means a usurper. In 2 Kings 8:7–15 it is stated that Elisha was instrumental in Hazael's usurpation, for Hazael was viewed as God's tool against the iniquitous line of Israel that had been contaminated with

---

24. See further Gary A. Rendsburg, "A Reconstruction of Moabite-Israelite History," *Journal of the Ancient Near Eastern Society* 13, 1981, pp. 67–73.

25. According to 2 Chronicles 21:16–17, Ahaziah was the youngest son of Jehoram; the other sons had been carried off by victorious Philistines and Arabs after these enemies had inflicted disaster on Judah. The moralistic context in which these facts are stated does not necessarily invalidate the facts themselves.

26. She is called "Athaliah the daughter of Omri" in 2 Kings 8:26 and 2 Chronicles 22:2. However, scholars prefer to consider her Ahab's daughter on account of 2 Kings 8:18, where, nevertheless, it is only stated that Jehoram of Judah married a daughter of Ahab (but not that her name was Athaliah or that she became the mother of Ahaziah); for discussion and a proposed solution, see H. J. Katzenstein, "Who Were the Parents of Athaliah?" *Israel Exploration Journal* 5, 1955, pp. 194–97.

Jezebel and Baalism, and that had polluted the Davidic Line through Athaliah.

The kings of Israel and Judah were wounded in the battle, and went to Jezreel to recuperate. Elisha, with his usual effectiveness and timing, chose that moment to send a prophet to Ramoth-gilead to anoint in secret the army officer Jehu, as king of Israel. (The prophet is referred to as a madman by other officers at Ramoth-gilead because prophetic inspiration and insanity were overlapping concepts; see 2 Kings 9:11.) Jehu, now anointed by a prophet of Yahwe, is hailed as king by his own officers. Having thus secured the support of the army, he proceeds by chariot to Jezreel. Jehoram's scout identifies the impetuous charioteer, for "the driving is as the driving of Jehu the son of Nimshi; for he drives furiously" (2 Kings 9:20).

According to the biblical account, Jehu himself slew the king of Israel and soon after had the king of Judah slain, too. But the recently discovered Aramaic inscription from Dan in northern Israel at once both sheds new light on these events and raises additional questions.[27] Although his name is not specifically mentioned in the text, it is apparent that the author of this royal inscription is Hazael. The text, which needs to be partially reconstructed, states as follows: "I killed Jehoram son of Ahab king of Israel, and I killed Ahaziah son of Jehoram king of the House of David." A difficulty arises because the Bible ascribes the deaths of these two monarchs to Jehu, while the Dan inscription implies that Hazael is responsible. One way to harmonize these apparently contradictory claims is to accept both positions by assuming that Hazael saw Jehu as his agent, though other scenarios also are possible. In any case, this inscription is of singular importance because it provides for us the first attestation of the name David in an extrabiblical text. And while the text refers not to the famous king himself but to one of his descendants a century and a half later, the inscription demonstrates that among the neighboring Arameans the kingdom of Judah was known as the House of David.[28]

After the deaths of Jehoram and Ahaziah, Jehu eventually got around to Jezebel, who with painted eyes looks down from a window

---

27. See Avraham Biran and Joseph Naveh, "An Aramaic Stele Fragment from Tel Dan," *Israel Exploration Journal* 43, 1993, pp. 81–98; and ibid., "The Tel Dan Inscription: A New Fragment," *Israel Exploration Journal* 45, 1995, pp. 1–18.

28. See further Gary A. Rendsburg, "On the Writing *BYTDWD* in the Aramaic Inscription from Tel Dan," *Israel Exploration Journal* 45, 1995, pp. 22–25.

and defiantly calls the usurper a "Zimri who has slain his lord" (2 Kings 9:31). Jehu dispatched two or three of his henchmen who threw her out of the window to her death. The mauled remains of the hated queen were buried by Jehu's orders, because, as he admits, "she is the daughter of a king" (2 Kings 9:34). Few personalities are more colorful or positive than Jezebel. She stopped at nothing—not even murder—to achieve her goals. Her royal husband was like putty in her hands. Born to the purple, she perished without flinching.

One of the most stirring, but also cruel and historically fateful, narratives in all of the Bible is related in 2 Kings 10. Jehu proceeded to wipe out the entire House of Ahab. He also got hold of a party of Ahaziah's kin and slew them in cold blood. Naboth was at long last avenged. There could be no peace in the country until that wrong had been righted and only now could the affair of Naboth be considered closed.

In a still more treacherous fashion, Jehu determined to slaughter the Baalists in fulfillment of his obligation incurred by the circumstances of his coronation. He had been anointed by a prophet of Yahwe to secure the victory of Yahwism and to annihilate Baalism from Israel. He enlisted the help of a puritanical idealist named Jonadab son of Rechab. (Jonadab is the founder of the Rechabites: a group we are to hear more about later in the time of Jeremiah. Their ideal was the God-fearing austerity of the desert. Thus they shunned alcoholic drinks. This prohibition had long been practiced in Israel by individual "Nazirites," who were men destined for particularly holy lives in token whereof they did not shave or drink intoxicating liquor. But the Rechabites extended the prohibition to the whole community. They furthermore lived in tents instead of houses and refrained from agriculture in the true nomadic spirit. They were strict devotees of Yahwe.) Jehu with the help of Jonadab lured all of the Baalists into the Baal temple for a religious celebration; then by stationing eighty well-armed men at the exits, they killed the congregation in cold blood. The House of Baal was destroyed and left as a dung heap. Israel was purged of Baalism, and Yahwism had triumphed.

Jehu's purge was fatal not only for the history of Israel but for all of Western civilization thereafter, for it was a precedent of exclusivism, of fanaticism, where no toleration for any other cult was permissible. This frightful precedent had its reflexes not only on the rare occasions where Jews were in a position to implement such a policy, but more particularly in the history of Christianity and of Islam. Thus the bloody religious wars of Christian Europe in the sixteenth and seventeenth centuries C.E., echo, though indirectly, Jehu's precedent in ancient Israel.

In spite of Jehu's unswerving zeal for Yahwe (and no one can deny that he left no stone unturned in reestablishing Yahwism), Jehu is condemned by the biblical writer (2 Kings 10:31). No amount of Yahwistic devotion could atone for Israel's separation from Jerusalem.

# CHAPTER XV

# From Israel's Largest Empire to the Fall of Samaria

The House of Jehu, founded in usurpation and established in bloodshed, could not be fundamentally strong. After Jehu's accession all of the territory that Israel had in Transjordan was seized by Hazael (2 Kings 10:32–33) and Israel became a vassal state of Damascus. Shalmaneser once more invaded the area in 841 B.C.E., another fixed date in Israelite history. The Assyrian proceeded against Hazael but again failed to capture the well-fortified Damascus. He received tribute from quite a number of vassal kings, including Jehu of Israel, who is mentioned on the Black Obelisk of Shalmaneser III. Whether the portrait in relief given with Jehu's name is supposed to be Jehu or a representative of his, is an open question. The value of the portrait resides more in its worth as a record of authentic costume than of personal physiognomy. This expedition that Shalmaneser claims to have been a great triumph was another one of those ephemeral raids. He did not return to the area until 838, when Jehu did not have to pay him tribute, which implies that Shalmaneser did not menace Israelite territory although he invaded surrounding countries.

At this juncture we may well turn to some of the ideas and institutions of the age. In the realm of theology we note (2 Kings 5:1) that Naaman is regarded as an instrument of Yahwe's plan to grant salvation to Aram. This marks an advance over the older view that made of Yahwe a more narrowly national god, and constitutes a step in the trend whereby God is to become the God of world history. For the first time a Hebrew prophet (Elisha) is connected with the crowning of another nation's king (Hazael of Damascus). The prophets have not yet become literary prophets, that is to say, writers of special biblical books recording their respective messages. They wander about in bands, adhering to a prophetic guild. They made their livings from fees offered for services rendered; for example, the rich gift that Naaman offered to Elisha, and which was accepted in part by Elisha's servant. It is shown in 2 Kings 4:42 that people also gave "the bread of first-fruits" to the prophets, who were therefore partially supported by offerings resembling the gifts given by laymen to priests or Levites.

The most familiar holidays are those of the New Moon and Sabbath, on which occasions people might make a trip to a prophet (2 Kings 4:23). The incident of Naaman is also noteworthy because of his being cured in the Jordan River: the earliest recorded example of baptism in that river for the sake of healing.

The nations of Canaan would be welded into coalitions in the face of Assyrian invasions, but between those invasions Canaan would relapse into small states fighting each other. Intrigue was rife and little nations did not hesitate to bribe a foreign king to attack their neighbors. In 2 Kings 7:6–8 the Arameans abandon their camp, with all their supplies, because of a rumor that the king of Israel bribed the kings of the Hittites and Musur. ("Hittites" do not refer here to Asia Minor, but to the people in some of the Aramean kingdoms of North Syria, which were in some cases relatively powerful in this age.)[1] The same kind of bribery appears in inscriptions of the Aramean kings. Thus around the year 800 B.C.E. King Kilamuwa of the far north Syrian state of Samal relates that he paid the Assyrians to attack his neighbors the Danunites of Cilicia.

With the growth of commerce and wealth, there was a corresponding increase in poverty. The common people frequently fell into debt and were often unable to repay on time. Debtors and their families were often seized as security and thus enslaved. Poverty could oblige people to sell their own children. In a particularly bad state were widows, who had to look after themselves and their children without a man's protection and support; 2 Kings 4:1 tells of a widow whose creditor is about to take away her children as slaves. The old ideal still persisted that every Israelite sat under his own vine and fig

---

1. At times these kingdoms (like Carchemish) used Luwian (sometimes called Hieroglyphic Hittite) for royal inscriptions. Thus they maintained some Anatolian tradition.

tree; but by this time that ideal was little more than a literary cliché, a distant memory, and a vain hope.

In 2 Kings 7 it is shown that lepers were not allowed in the city but were obliged to remain outside. For the history of medicine this is of interest as an early example of quarantine. But the motivation was not identical with that of modern quarantine; the Hebrews abhorred corpses and diseased bodies for reasons of ritual purity. Their instincts were good and were conducive to healthy living but we must refrain from reading into Hebrew civilization modern notions of contagion and of preventive medicine. For the Hebrews, the etiology of disease was the displeasure of the Lord; thus when King Azariah of Judah falls sick it is simply because the Lord afflicted him (2 Kings 15:5).

Jehu, who reigned from about 841 to 814, had weakened the country by his bloody purge. After 838, when Shalmaneser attacked the area and withdrew, there were no more Assyrian invasions for over thirty years. Yet Jehu lacked the resources to emerge as one of the greater powers in Canaan. Instead Hazael reduced Israel and rendered it so impotent that he was able to turn on both the Philistines and Judeans. Hazael destroyed Gath and would have proceeded against Jerusalem had he not been bought off (2 Kings 12:18–19). Accordingly, it was Damascus, not Israel, that became dominant among the local kingdoms.

Athaliah, who controlled Judah from about 841 to 836 B.C.E.,[2] was intolerable to the Yahwists. If the House of Ahab was not acceptable to Israel, it was even less so to Judah. In the tradition of the brutality of the day, she proceeded to wipe out the House of David, but an infant son of Ahaziah, named Joash, was rescued; and some years later, the priest Jehoiada, in concert with the army, staged a revolt which resulted in the coronation of the boy king around 836 B.C.E. and the assassination of Athaliah (2 Kings 11). Joash began his reign under the regency of Jehoiada who was professionally interested in the Jerusalem cult. The boy king, indoctrinated under the priest's tutelage, devoted himself to religious reform. The Temple had fallen

---

2. The statement that the baby Joash was concealed for *six* years and in the *seventh* Jehoiada took action (2 Kings 11:3–4) need not be taken literally. The numbers have an epic ring; cf. the six days of creation climaxed by the seventh day of rest; or the six days of downpour followed by the seventh day when the rains subsided, in the Babylonian Deluge; etc.

into disrepair and the most memorable activity of his reign (2 Kings 12) was his restoration and repair of it. However, his virtue is regarded (verse 4) as not quite up to the idealized standard of his great ancestor David, for the people were still worshiping on the high places. Nor was his reign altogether blessed from a political or military standpoint. His buying off Hazael with the sacred vessels of the Temple and with the treasures of the Temple and palace (verses 18–19) could not escape criticism. Dissatisfaction with Joash led to his assassination about 802 B.C.E.[3]

Jehoahaz, who ruled Israel from about 814 to 798 B.C.E., was a vassal of the king of Damascus. The report that the king of Damascus left to Jehoahaz only 50 cavalry, 10 chariots, and 10,000 infantry (2 Kings 13:7) is probably an authentic statement taken out of the peace treaty. Damascus was making a bid for the domination of all Canaan. Its king, Ben-Hadad, with his allies, marched against the northern Kingdom of Hamath but failed to conquer it. The resulting weakness of Damascus meant a full-fledged revival of small statehood from which Israel could profit. Israel regained its independence under Jehoash (or Joash—not to be confused with the Judean king of the same name), who ruled from about 798 to 783 B.C.E. and scored victories over Aram and regained cities that his predecessors had lost.

The period was not one for bringing out the best in the Canaanite peoples including Israel and Judah. They all took shameful advantage of each other's misfortunes. The state of affairs is vividly reflected in the initial prophecies of Amos, where he lists the countries, enumerates their sins, and justifies their misfortunes.

We learn from 2 Kings 13:20 and Amos 1:13 that there were Moabite and Ammonite raids. This meant the capture of people as slaves, and the Philistines and Phoenicians in the coastal cities gladly profited from the resulting slave trade. This was particularly perfidious in the case of Tyre, which had a pact of friendship with Israel (Amos 1:9). Then, too, Moab turned against Edom, making incursions and desecrating the royal grave there (Amos 2:1). The age was one of unethical and treacherous international relations.

King Amaziah of Judah avenged his father Joash on the actual mur-

---

3. Thus 2 Chronicles 24:17ff. depicts the suppression of priestly influence by the nobility after the death of Jehoiada; the subsequent abandonment of pure Yahwistic worship; the attempt of Zechariah, son of Jehoiada, to regain his father's leadership; Zechariah's assassination on Joash's orders; and an Aramean invasion of Judah followed by the assassination of Joash.

derers but not on their children; which is singled out as a good deed
in keeping with the law of Moses.[4] Amaziah conquered Edom and
took the city of Sela. Emboldened by his victories, he committed the
indiscretion of challenging the more powerful King Jehoash of Israel,
who accordingly invaded Judah, breached the wall of Jerusalem, and
plundered the Temple and royal treasury. Amaziah's costly folly may
well have had something to do with the fact that he, too, was assassinated. He was succeeded by his son Azariah, (also called Uzziah) who
enjoyed a measure of prosperity.[5] and rebuilt the Edomite port of
Elath ( = Ezion-geber) on the Gulf of Eilat. He contracted leprosy
that unfitted him for ruling so that his son Jotham acted as regent.

In 805 B.C.E. Adadnirari III resumed the Assyrian invasions of the
area, overrunning all the surrounding nations but not Judah. Israel,
Philistia, Moab, Edom, Phoenicia, and Aram bore the brunt. When
the Assyrians withdrew with their plunder and captives, things
became much as they had been before, so that Israel was again in
circumstances from which it could profit materially and politically.

Jeroboam II (who ruled from about 783 to 743 B.C.E.) was the most
vigorous member of the House of Jehu and forged by far the greatest
empire ever won by the northern Kingdom of Israel. The biblical
statement that he ruled from Hamath to the Sea of the Arabah shows
that his empire had a huge spread from north to south. In spite of
this phenomenal conquest, his reign is slurred over in the few verses
of 2 Kings 14:23–29. Being wicked, as every king of Israel had to be
from the Judean viewpoint, Jeroboam did not merit a fuller account.
Yet we are thankful for the few revealing facts given in the Bible
about the extent of his realm. The *crux interpretum* in verse 28 we are
inclined to render "he restored Damascus and Hamath from Yehuda
into Israel." Yehuda is not the southern Judah but the kingdom of
the same name in far northern Syria (also known as Samal). The
prepositions are in accordance with uses now fully familiar from the
Ugaritic tablets.[6] The reason there are three apparent anomalies in the

---

4. Whether the reference to the Law of Moses is Amaziah's reason or the exilic compiler's
observation is hard to say. In any case, knowledge of the Law was forgotten until 621 B.C.E.,
when the Law was rediscovered.

5. According to 2 Chronicles 26, Uzziah conquered his neighbors to the east, south, and west,
constructed notable fortifications, and improved the nation's water and agricultural resources.

6. The prepositions *l* and *b* usually mean "to, for," and "in," respectively. But in a number of
instances, as in Ugaritic (and Phoenician as well), these prepositions mean "from." This find-
ing has clarified the interpretation of many biblical passages.

two crucial words ("from[7] + Samal"[8] and "into"[9] + Israel") is due to the fact that, as the verse itself tells, the information is derived from the court "Chronicles of the Kings of Israel." The dialect and history of northern Israel were full of pitfalls for the Judean author, who may well have excerpted his Israelian source without understanding it.[10]

The splendor of the reign of Jeroboam II was ephemeral, both for external and internal reasons. Externally, because any time the Assyrians would put in another appearance, no country in Canaan, no matter how strong, could defend itself effectively. Internally, because society was unsound owing to the cleavage between the rich upper class and the large and ever-growing poor class. The institutions of Israel were such that the royal line (because of the bloodshed in which Jehu had founded it in Jezreel) would have to suffer the same fate as Omri's line (Hosea 1:4).[11]

God's wrath was evident to every Yahwist in the natural ills that befell the land. Locusts, droughts, famines, and other catastrophes could only be the hand of God (Amos 4:6–13). The fact that the people suffered, far from making them turn to another god or abandoning their own God, merely intensified their religion as manifested in cultic fanaticism; but this was not satisfying to the great prophets of Israel. Hosea has very little to say in favor of cultic practices; for example, he points out in 4:14 the abhorrent impurities of sexual rites connected with the qedeshot.

The woes that beset the land evoked a new concept in the prophecy of this time: the Day of Yahwe (e.g., Amos 5:18), the terrible day of reckoning when God would deal out punishment to the wicked

7. Cyrus H. Gordon, *Ugaritic Textbook,* Rome, 1967, p. 92, §10.1.

8. In the Samal inscriptions, the native city-state is called "Yaudi" (= Judean) kingdom. The Hebrew form is *Yehudi* "Judean." Aramaic substitution of *aleph* (not represented in our English transliteration) for *h* is common. Hence the omission of the *h* is linguistically explicable. At a time when northern Judah (= Samal) was the great Syrian power defeated by Jeroboam II, the court chroniclers at Samaria knew that southern Judah was not meant in this context. Bible readers, however, have not had the background necessary to know about the north Judah.

9. Gordon, *Ugaritic Textbook,* p. 92, §10.1.

10. The meaning "from" for the prepositions *l* and *b* was characteristic of Israelian Hebrew (the northern dialect) more so than it was of Judean Hebrew (the norm in the Bible); see Gary A. Rendsburg, *Linguistic Evidence for the Northern Origin of Selected Psalms,* Atlanta, 1990, pp. 21–23.

11. The symbolic naming of a child (here called "Jezreel") is a feature of Hosea that served as a precedent for future prophets; notably Isaiah, whose Messianic prophecy about Immanuel is in line with this tradition.

and inaugurate a godly era. Alongside such severe prophets, there were also the cheerful prophets of victory such as Jonah, son of Amittai (2 Kings 14:25), to bolster the morale of the established regime.[12]

There was a balance of power in the life of the Hebrews that contributed to their strength in the future course of mankind, if not to a spectacular glory in antiquity. Just as the Books of Kings contain elements from court chronicles, from true human histories, and from tales of the prophets, there were the officialdom, the literary men with keen powers of observation, and also the prophets. The prophets were not of one mold; some were optimistic, others gloomy, but none devoid of ultimate hope. The wonder-working or ecstatic prophets continued to exist but they were eclipsed by the new literary prophets such as Hosea and Amos, whose messages were aimed at social reform within the matrix of Yahwism. Religion was represented at radically different levels ranging from priests interested in sacrifices at shrines to a prophet like Amos who attached no value whatever to cultic practices but held that morality and social justice could alone please God. The common people, with traditional rights, retained a measure of their democratic heritage in spite of encroachments thereon. The elders of the people exerted influence in local, and sometimes in national, affairs. Social institutions, such as blood revenge, exacted their penalties of any violator from the king down. Hebrew society had thus many checks and balances and was not subject to the dictatorship of any particular vested interest.

The Aramean wars of Ahab are not the jejune listing of names, numbers, idle boasts, and trivia that one finds in court annals. The account of Ahab's reign is enriched by that magnificent school of historiography that ripened with the United Monarchy. No mere court chronicler would dare record the incident of Naboth's vineyard as we have it in Scripture, on pain of losing his job, if not his life. The fateful affair of Naboth was described by a historian who knew the court well but was not subservient to it. Also Jehu's purge and the triumph of Yahwism is historical writing of a high order and not the formulaic scribbling of a hack annalist. (In Judah, the incident of Athaliah and her removal may be in the same historiographic tradition.) In these accounts there is none of the narrow sectarianism such

---

12. Jonah, son of Amittai, is also the protagonist of the biblical book of Jonah. But the connection between the prophet mentioned in 2 Kings 14:25 and the prophet of the canonical book (written in the postexilic period) is still debated by scholars. See Jack M. Sasson, *Jonah* (Anchor Bible), New York, 1990, p. 344.

as we find in the compiler's stereotyped condemnations of all the Israelian kings.

It is likely that the Hebrew historians (unlike the annalists of other nations) enjoyed prophetic immunity, which would explain their freedom to be critical even of the king. Many of the prophetic books in the Hebrew Bible contain historic as well as prophetic sections. Significantly, Isaiah, whose book contains both types of material, is cited as a historian in 2 Chronicles 26:22; 32:32.

In addition to the historiography concerning royal personages, there is another charming literature about the lives of the prophets, in no way inferior as writing, but different in motivation, atmosphere, and content from the work of the royal historiographers. The lives of the prophets have religious as well as human interest; perhaps the best example is the Elijah cycle (1 Kings 17–19) including the superb account of Elijah's encounter with the Baalists on Mount Carmel (chapter 18). Here again the issue is Yahwism but without any sectarianism (such as propaganda for the Judean or any other cult) or political ax to grind (such as the legitimacy of one particular kingdom or dynasty). Unlike the royal historiography, the lives of the prophets contain legend as well as history. The reader of the Bible must not let the miracles and anecdotes obscure the historic missions of Elijah, who led the Yahwistic reaction against Baalism; or of Elisha, who gave that reaction political implementation.

The Bible, of course, presents for the reader the official position of ancient Israelite religion. It is true that from stories such as Saul's visit to the Witch of Endor, or from the contest between Elijah and the prophets of Baal, we learn a lot about popular beliefs in ancient Israel. But the overall message of the Bible remains the official outlook of Israelite religious leaders: prophets, priests, and others who adhered strictly to the worship of the one God, Yahwe, without an admixture of pagan customs. Exactly what percentage of the population followed this position, in, let us say, the eighth century B.C.E., cannot be stated with any accuracy. But scholars today are in a better position to study the problem due to the recent discovery of two epigraphic remains.

The first comes from Khirbet el-Qom in Judah, and the second comes from Kuntillet 'Ajrud, a caravan station in the eastern Sinai (just west of the current Israeli-Egyptian border). Both date to the eighth century; both mention Asherah in connection with Yahwe. The el-Qom inscription is carved into a pillar in a tomb, and while it is both difficult to read and subject to varying interpretation, a translation such as "Blessed be Uriyahu by Yahwe, and from his enemies save him by his Asherah," is acceptable. The ʿAjrud material includes several inscriptions and accompanying drawings on vessels. The most interesting of them reads "I bless you by Yahwe of Samaria and by his (or its) Asherah," alongside of which is a depiction of Yahwe and, at least according to many scholars' view, Asherah. There is a debate among scholars as to whether Asherah in these inscriptions refers to the Canaanite goddess by this name, or to a cultic wooden pole or tree (perhaps a phallic symbol). So while there is still uncertainty in the specific meaning of the words of these inscriptions, there is no doubt of their importance. They serve as an excellent witness to the manner in which Canaanite religious ideas were easily mixed with the worship of Yahwe syncretistically.

With the prophet Amos during the reign of Jeroboam II there emerges into history a creative individuality in spiritual life, the like of which is not attested earlier anywhere in the world. Amos was a herdsman from Tekoa in Judah. All we know of his ministry is limited to his fearless preaching in Bethel on an occasion "two years before the earthquake." He left his land of Judah because of an inner urge that he was unable to resist. Crossing the border, he went to the royal shrine at Bethel, enumerated the recent historic sins of all the nations round about, culminating with a terrible indictment of Israel: the chief target of his message. He predicted the fall of Jeroboam by the sword and the exile of the Israelians for their iniquity. This was hardly popular with the authorities, but the priest of Bethel, Amaziah, could not have Amos killed because the latter enjoyed prophetic immunity. Prophets could be unpopular but normally their lives were spared, whether their divine message was agreeable or not. Amaziah reported the affair to Jeroboam and came back to tell Amos to go home to Judah, where he could eat bread and prophesy all he liked, but not to bother Bethel: a royal shrine where his ranting was not welcome. Amos denied the implication that he was professional; he was not preaching to earn his bread. "I am neither a prophet nor the son of a prophet" means he did not belong to any prophetic guild. He was a shepherd[13] who had left his flocks in Tekoa because God had sent him

---

13. It might seem strange for a shepherd to be so well informed of international events. However, the watering holes frequented by shepherds were often the best places to gather foreign news from caravan personnel.

to Bethel. As is typical of the great prophets, Amos remained fearless and proclaimed that Amaziah, whose family would suffer the worst disgraces and bloodshed, would himself be taken captive to an unclean land. Amos was not concerned with the establishment of a cult in Jerusalem or anywhere else, nor does he stress idolatry as one of his grievances against the Bethel community or the Israelites in general. He was against all cultic practices, which, insofar as they do not go with good living, are meaningless and offer no pleasure to God. He spoke of the unethical practices of the day: how the merchants sit around waiting for the end of the Sabbath or the New Moon when they could again cheat the public "making small the *ephah* (measure) and making large the shekel (weight)"; that is to say, selling short quantities but overcharging the customer, who pays with weighed silver. Amos hated hypocrites who frequented the shrine and altar but accumulated ill-gotten gains and abused the poor. He had no time for the rich who were living in "houses of ivory" with both summer and winter homes, in luxury all year, while the poor who were ground down under them had to pay for that luxury and groaned under the oppression. For Amos, God has no concern with the cult but only with ethics. The following passage (5:21–24) will suffice to sum up Amos's attitude toward what God wants of men:

> "I hate, I loathe your pilgrimages,
> Nor will I inhale the odors of your convocations.
> Though you make sacrifices to Me
> I shall not accept your offerings
> Nor shall I regard the peace offering of your fatlings.
> Take away from Me the noise of your songs
> For I will not listen to the music of your harps.
> But let justice roll on like the waters
> Even righteousness like a mighty stream."

Note that Amos parallels "justice" with "righteousness" in this passage. The word "justice," as used by the Hebrew prophets, does not usually mean what the word signifies in English. To the Hebrew idealist, "justice" required that, in any conflict of interests, the poor were always right and the rich were ipso facto wrong. It would be unthinkable, in prophetic or wisdom literature throughout the Bible World, to call for an investigation to find out whether a widow or the creditor about to foreclose on her was legally in the right. The widow is by definition in the right and the creditor in the wrong.

(The popular dichotomy between the God of Justice in the Hebrew Bible and the New Testament God of Love is unjustified. In each Testament we find both strict justice and charitable love, with the latter prevailing.)

Amos pronounced the doctrine that things have gone so far that Israel must be destroyed except for a remnant. Certainly the upper class, whose members reclined on couches in Samaria and Damascus (Amos 3:12),[14] were doomed to destruction. As for the shrines, Amos (7:9) declares:

> "The high places of Isaac shall be destroyed
> Yea the sanctuaries of Israel, laid waste."

For what pleasure could a righteous God have in shrines frequented by hypocrites?

In 8:11 Amos predicted that the physical hunger and thirst experienced by the people are nothing compared with the impending hunger and thirst, not for bread and water, but for Yahwe's word. Thus persisted the old[15] idea that national bankruptcy came only when God stops talking to men. Such would be the culmination of the period of disaster that must precede the Day of Yahwe when things will be righted.

Amos had risen above the narrow idea that God could only be interested in His own Chosen People. For Amos, God's concern for all mankind was equal; and in 9:7 He asks:

> "Are ye not to Me as Ethiopians
> O children of Israel?
> Have I not brought up
> Israel from the land of Egypt
> And the Philistines from Caphtor
> And Aram from Kir?"

Thus Israel's Exodus from Egypt is not unique in history. God, who has also arranged an exodus for the uncircumcised Philistines and for the Arameans, cares not a whit less for the black Ethiopians than for Israel.

---

14. This confirms the statement in Kings that Jeroboam's empire included Aram.

15. It will be recalled that national bankruptcy in Saul's reign came when the oracles of God could not be obtained through any of the legitimate channels.

But the destruction that is to come will not strike the remnant, small though it be, because those devoted to Yahwe must not disappear from the earth. Yahwe's religion must continue; but it is to be an ethical, not a cultic, religion. Amos (9:14–15) ended his book with an undying message of hope:

> " 'And I shall return the captivity of My people Israel
> And they shall rebuild desolated cities and dwell therein
> And plant vineyards and drink their wine
> And make their gardens and eat their fruit.
> And I shall plant them on their land
> And they shall not be separated any more from the land
>     which I gave to them'
> Saith Yahwe
> Your God."

These are great words that make history. Centuries later, in the time of Ezra and Nehemiah, people thought that these words were being fulfilled. But history has shown that the Second Commonwealth[16] was not the fulfillment of Amos's prophecy. Yet Amos's immortal words will continue to cry out for fulfillment until every promise comes true. His words are inseparable from the vigor of Israel down to the present time; and his message of hope has encouraged Israel to survive millennia of disaster. It was by warning the Hebrews that before their remnant could be saved, they would undergo devastating vicissitudes, that their morale was prepared for withstanding the blows of destiny that have wiped out the historic continuity of nearly all their ancient contemporaries. Jewish suffering, instead of proving fatal, thus became an assurance of the truth of the promise that the remnant will survive. Amos and the other immortal prophets of Israel will continue as a vital force in the unfolding of human history as long as men dwell upon the earth.[17]

During the reign of Azariah (also called Uzziah) of Judah, many changes took place in the Kingdom of Israel. Zechariah, son of Jeroboam II, succeeded his father, but lasted only six months. He was

16. This designates the period of the Second Temple, from the late sixth century B.C.E. to the late first century C.E.

17. Cf. H. Orlinsky's evaluation of Hebrew Prophecy in his *Ancient Israel,* Ithaca, 1954, pp. 142–68.

assassinated by Shallum, who reigned only one month, to be assassinated around 742 B.C.E. by Menahem, who seized the throne and perhaps enjoyed the reputation of an avenger of his sovereign (Zechariah) rather than that of usurper. Menahem was doubtless confronted with a civil war and his atrocities in quelling it included the ripping open of pregnant women in the city of Tiphsah (2 Kings 15:16).

In Menahem's reign, an Assyrian king sometimes called Pul, but more often called Tiglathpileser[18] III, who began to rule in 745 B.C.E., made changes throughout the entire Near East, including Israel. Tiglathpileser was a vigorous monarch who inaugurated new administrative policies. Hitherto the incursions of the Assyrian kings into the West meant that they would strike, make off with as much booty and as many slaves as possible, exact as much tribute as they could collect, and go home; whereupon the old dynasts would reassert themselves. Or, if the old dynasts were too unpopular or too weak to regain control, a native opposition party or native usurper would take over. To reconquer the state, Assyria would have to begin all over again in another campaign. Tiglathpileser began the policy of incorporating the conquered territory into the empire as provinces. The Assyrian kings before him had done this with territory nearer at hand, so in a sense Tiglathpileser's policy was the extending of an old principle to Syria, Babylonia, and Anatolia. Brutality was justified from the Assyrian viewpoint on religious grounds. The god Assur had willed that his country and his king should achieve world domination; and all other gods, kings, and peoples had to be subservient to Assur's will. Any resistance meant rebellion against the great god and was put down with condign severity.

Tiglathpileser also put into greater effect than had ever been known before, the efficacious but cruel policy of transplanting conquered populations.[19] This did not mean simply exiling people from their homeland; it meant also putting other exiles from distant areas into the evacuated territory so that there would be no continuity between the old population and the new. Moreover, any hope the old population might have to return would be shattered by the pres-

18. As king of Assyria he was Tiglathpileser; but as king of Babylonia, he took the name Pul. The Bible confusingly uses both names without explanation.

19. See the detailed study of Bustany Oded, *Mass Deportations and Deportees in the Neo-Assyrian Empire,* Wiesbaden, 1979.

ence of the new population that would forbid their homecoming.[20]

The transplanting of populations reduced rebellions to a minimum and explains why the northern Kingdom of Israel has not had any effective continuity in Jewish history. Men will fight for their own, but not for a strange, country. Tiglathpileser and his successors transformed the East permanently. The shifting of populations meant a leveling-out process that terminated the individuality that had once characterized the nations of the Near East. One aspect was linguistic; Aramaic displaced other varieties of speech with accelerated tempo throughout the area.

The Assyrian regime had to have as its backbone the army that was progressive, and mastered, as it went along, all the new techniques of warfare. It developed siege warfare to a greater extent than ever before; battering rams and other devices for breaching strong city walls reached an unprecedented degree of development.

It is of interest to add here a few words about Syrian rulers of this period with Yahwistic names. The annals of Tiglathpileser III refer to a king named Azriyau, and while the exact locale of his rule cannot be determined, it is clear that he was a local king in Syria.[21] Similarly, later, during the reign of Sargon II, Assyrian records refer to a ruler of Hamath named Yaubidi (about whom see further below, Chapter XVI, pp. 257–58). Presumably, Hamath had fostered some sort of Yahwism for at least several centuries, to judge from Joram of Hamath (2 Samuel 8:9–10) who was an envoy to Jerusalem in David's day.[22] If we go further back in history, to the second millennium B.C.E., it will be recalled that Yahwistic forms also appear among the Amorite personal names from Syria. The picture that emerges is that Yahwe was worshipped not only in Israel, but to some extent in Syria as well. Probably the Syrian version of Yahwism differed from the Israelite version of a monolatry focused on Yahwe, but still it needs

---

20. This is one important reason why Israel (conquered by Assyria) was wiped out; while Judah (whose Babylonian conquerors did not repopulate the land with aliens) survived. Exiled Israelians therefore joined the subsequently exiled Judeans to share in a common restoration on Zion, and in a common Diaspora.

21. At one time scholars tended to identify Azriyau with Uzziah (also called Azariah in the Bible). See Hayim Tadmor, "Azriyau of Yaudi," *Scripta Hierosolymitana* 8, 1961, pp. 232–71.

22. The later author of Chronicles, apparently unable to entertain the idea of a non-Israelite with a Yahwistic name, modified Joram's name to the more pagan-sounding Hadoram (1 Chronicles 18:10).

to be recognized that the worship of Yahwe persisted in areas of the Near East outside of Israel.[23]

In 738 Tiglathpileser again struck at the West and collected tribute from Asia Minor, Syria, the Phoenician cities, and from King Rezin of Damascus, King Menahem of Israel, and Queen Zabibe of an Arab tribe. According to 2 Kings 15:19–20, the tribute Menahem paid was a thousand talents of silver. The sum was raised by imposing fifty shekels of silver on each tax-paying citizen,[24] implying that there were 60,000 such citizens in the Kingdom of Israel. Upon the payment of this tribute, Pul (= Tiglathpileser III) withdrew from Israel.

Menahem's son and successor, Pekahiah, was assassinated in 735 B.C.E. by one of his charioteers, Pekah, who was accompanied by a group of fifty Gileadites. Pekah combined with Rezin to attack Judah around 734 B.C.E. but none of their specific operations are known from the brief statement in 2 Kings 15:37. Tiglathpileser had conquered and exiled the populations of Transjordan and the northern part of Israel west of the Jordan to Assyria as is related in 2 Kings 15:29; cf. 1 Chronicles 5:6, 26.

The inevitable disaster that faced the people of Israel (and doubtless, too, the surrounding countries) was one of the major factors leading to rampant pleasure seeking and immorality. This immorality evoked the appeal for moral reform from the earliest literary prophets.

Prophetic reform in Israel (unlike Judah) stopped short of demanding the removal of the golden calves at the northern shrines.

Amos had set a new precedent: His work was put in a book. His example may have inspired the writing of Hosea's prophecies as a permanent record. Hosea's, unlike Amos's, was not a broad mind with worldwide horizons. Amos introduced his prophecy to and against Israel with a survey of the entire surrounding world, mentioning the misdeeds of the individual kingdoms as the reason for the punishment that was to descend upon them. Hosea's is a much smaller spirit. He knew only Israel well, plus Judah incidentally. The

---

23. For full treatment see Stephanie Dalley, "Yahweh in Hamath in the 8th Century B.C.: Cuneiform Materials and Historical Deductions," *Vetus Testamentum* 40, 1990, pp. 21–32.

24. The term, *gibbore ha-ḥayil,* means the aristocrats who, in theory at least, were descended from the warriors who had conquered Canaan under Joshua and received land grants in perpetuity. This class had to help the king economically as well as militarily in times of crisis.

world beyond was outside his interests. He realized of course that Israel and Judah were related people worshiping the same God; but Hosea's country was his beloved "Ephraim." He cried out against the moral evils of the cult in Israel, and against Israel's ignorance of God. He pictured Israel's betrayal of God in terms of marital infidelity because God had, so to speak, accepted Israel and Judah as His brides but they were unfaithful to Him.

It is impossible to understand the literal meaning of Hosea's prophecy without knowing some of the background in terms of daily life and social institutions. In Hosea 2:4–5 the following words are addressed to children:

> "Take action against your mother
> Take action!
> Because she is not my wife
> And I am not her husband. . . .
> Lest I have her stript bare
> And set out as the day she was born."

The first part of this declaration ("she is not my wife and I am not her husband") is a legal divorce formula. The penalty whereby a reprehensible wife is to be prosecuted by her own children and driven out naked is attested in earlier cuneiform tablets and in later Jewish Aramaic texts.[25]

Hosea was a religious spirit and not a practical politician. He envisaged a return to the covenant, when God would reaffirm His relationship to His People through a second Exodus from the land of Egypt.

Hosea, unlike most of the biblical authors, was a northerner, not a Judean. Before the fall of Israel (722 B.C.E.), his book was transplanted and adopted in Judah, where for linguistic and psychological reasons it was misunderstood; with the passing of time that misunderstanding has increased. Its linguistic and psychological obscurities have facilitated scribal errors in transmission. The conjectural methods used to correct those errors have (as usual) led to fallacious results. The Book of Hosea is a parade example of the rule that while an individual

---

25. For the cuneiform and Aramaic parallels, see Cyrus H. Gordon, "Hosea 2:4–5 in the Light of New Semitic Inscriptions" *Zeitschrift fuer die alttestamentliche Wissenschaft* 13, 1936, pp. 277–80; and Cyrus H. Gordon, "Zu *ZAW* 1936, 277ff.," *Zeitschrift fuer die alttestamentliche Wissenschaft* 14, 1937, p. 176.

correction may conceivably be an improvement, a hundred corrections invariably lead us further from the truth than does the traditional text, no matter how many difficulties be in it. (This holds even when the emendations are made by profound Hebrew scholars gifted with ingenuity. When unqualified Hebraists emend the text, their corrections are impossible as compositions in the Hebrew language. Unfortunately new Bible translations often palm off such impossibilities on the unsuspecting reader.)

Tiglathpileser's departure from Syria in 737 B.C.E. was the signal for the small states to reassert themselves. It was then that Rezin and Pekah attacked their neighbors, including Judah, to strengthen themselves in the area while they were free from Assyrian pressure. The king of Damascus took away the port of Elath from Judah and cleared out the Judeans so that the vacuum was filled by the nearby Edomites who became firmly entrenched as the population of Elath (2 Kings 16:6).

When Ahaz succeeded Jotham[26] to the throne of Judah, Jerusalem was surrounded by the forces of Rezin and Pekah. Ahaz consulted the prophet Isaiah, who had already received his call around 740 B.C.E. (Isaiah 6) via a vision in which he had beheld the Lord of Hosts enthroned between the cherubim. (Such visions are related to the art of the times. Just as Gudea in his visions sees Imdugud, the divine storm-bird, as it is portrayed in Sumerian art; Isaiah sees God on the throne between cherubim in the manner of the royal throne as illustrated on the Megiddo ivories and elsewhere in Canaanite art.) On this occasion, Isaiah's answer to Ahaz is described in Isaiah 7. The prophet comes with a child who bears the symbolic name "A-Remnant-Will-Return." (Isaiah's device of giving symbolic names to children had already been practiced by Hosea.) Isaiah tells King Ahaz not to fear, for all will end well. Isaiah (7:14), then comforts the king with a reference to a child Immanuel ("God-is-with-Us") just, or about to be, conceived; for before that child is old enough to reject evil and to choose good (by which the prophet must have meant at least the age of two), Aram and Israel will be desolated.

To give further comfort to the harassed Kingdom of Judah, Isaiah (8:3) goes home to the prophetess (which suggests that "prophet" was a professional term to the extent that even his wife was automatically

---

26. Jotham's most notable achievements were his fortifications and his conquest of Ammon (2 Chronicles 27:3–5).

accorded the title of "prophetess"), who is to bear a child called "Hasten-Plunder-Hurry-Spoil." Before that child will be able to say "father" or "mother," Assyria will plunder Damascus and Samaria. It was probably the military and political impracticability of Isaiah's message that drove Ahaz to the desperate step of sacrificing his own son (2 Kings 16:3) and to the practical expedient of bribing Tiglathpileser to attack Aram and Israel and thus to save Judah from them (2 Kings 16:7). In any case, Tiglathpileser conducted military operations in Syria from 734 to 732 B.C.E.

Ahaz, a vassal of Tiglathpileser, visited the victorious Assyrian monarch in the captured city of Damascus. There Ahaz saw an altar that appealed to him. He had the specifications of the altar recorded and sent to Jerusalem where the priest Uriah executed the specifications to duplicate the pagan altar for Yahwe's Temple.

Tiglathpileser's invasions, as we have noted, resulted in the conquest of the northern and eastern territory of Israel and in the exile of the captured inhabitants to Assyria (2 Kings 15:29). Pekah could not retain the confidence of his subjects after his military fiasco. The last king of Israel, Hosea, usurped the throne by killing Pekah, and became Tiglathpileser's vassal over a truncated state of Israel without Transjordan or the northern provinces west of the Jordan. Tiglathpileser's annals, however, give a slightly different version to the effect that the Israelites ousted Pekah, whereupon Tiglathpileser made Hosea king over them. No contradiction is involved but only a difference in emphasis and interpretation.

After the capture of Damascus, Tiglathpileser marched against some Arabs who were ruled by Queen Shamsiyya. The Arab tribes, however, were willing to come to terms with Assyria because they depended on caravan trade for their prosperity. It was only by fitting into the Assyrian Order that they could live in peace and carry on their vital commercial pursuits.

Tiglathpileser assigned the tribe of Idibail (mentioned in Genesis 25:13)[27] to guard the Egyptian frontier against Pharaonic interference in the Assyrian sphere of influence that now included Canaan. Tiglathpileser then went to conquer Babylonia. In addition to his conquests, he is also known for his constructive activity. He built up ruins and converted badlands into cultivable tracts. His reign marks a

27. On this tribe, and related peoples from the desert regions south and east of Israel, see Israel Eph'al, *The Ancient Arabs*, Jerusalem, 1982.

considerable refinement both in art and in the writing of annals. He made one fatal mistake. He took away the privileges of the two sacred cities of Assur and Haran. The people there had been exempt from taxation and military service. By rescinding these privileges he caused the downfall of his dynasty at the end of his son's reign. Tiglathpileser was followed by Shalmaneser V (726–722 B.C.E.), who warred against Israel and in whose reign Hezekiah, whom the Bible commends as a righteous king of Judah, sat on the throne in Jerusalem (about 726–697 B.C.E.).

King Hosea, who started out as a vassal, turned out to be unfaithful to his Assyrian overlord and rebelled. He found numerous anti-Assyrian allies ready to join hands with him, notably the Egyptian king who is referred to in the Bible as "So" (2 Kings 17:4). The exact meaning of this form is debated by scholars, because there is no pharoah of the period (or of any period) who bears this name. The most likely possibility is that it represents a Hebraized form of "the Saite," referring to the king who ruled from Sais at the time, namely, Pharaoh Tefnakht.[28]

Egypt, Israel, and a number of small potentates around Canaan joined forces in the uprising against Assyria. Hosea was captured and carried off in chains. However, Samaria continued its resistance and it was three years before the city fell in 721, whereupon the inhabitants were exiled to Assyria and Media. According to the annals of the Assyrian usurper Sargon II, who finished the war, 27,290 inhabitants were carried off from the Kingdom of Israel. Thus, 2 Kings 17:3 specifically mentions Shalmaneser V, who started the siege of Samaria; but 2 Kings 17:6, where the expression "king of Assyria" is used, refers to Sargon II, who completed the destruction of Israel and exiled its population.[29] Fragments of victory stelae of the latter king have been discovered in Israel at two sites: Ashdod and Samaria.[30]

Many scholars view the Assyrian exile of the Kingdom of Israel as a complete transfer of the entire population. This view is incorrect. As is often recognized, some of the population no doubt fled southward to Judah. Less widely recognized is the fact that a certain per-

28. See further Mordecai Cogan and Hayim Tadmor, *II Kings* (Anchor Bible), New York, 1988, p. 196.

29. Cogan and Tadmor, *II Kings*, pp. 198–201.

30. For convenient pictures of the fragments, see Cogan and Tadmor, *II Kings*, pl. 11 (between pp. 228–29).

centage of the population never left the land of the northern kingdom of Israel.[31] Stories such as Jeremiah 41:5 and 2 Chronicles 30 attest to the fact that Israelians continued to live in their native land. We possess at least one of their literary remains, namely, Nehemiah 9,[32] and the residents of one village in Israel, called Peqi'in, have retained into the twentieth century the tradition that they are descended from the Israelians who never were exiled from their land.

The story of what happened to the Israelian exiles in Assyria and Media is of special interest. Probably a good percentage of them, especially those with paganizing tendencies, simply assimilated into the greater Assyrian Empire, never to be heard of again. Thus develops the famous legend of the Ten Lost Tribes of Israel. However, we must also reckon with the fact that a good percentage of the northern exiles retained their Israelite identity. Various Jewish communities of the Near East possess the tradition that they are descended from the northern exiles, and there is no reason to question the veracity of these beliefs.[33] Furthermore, the Bible contains a good deal of evidence pointing to the reunification of Israelians and Judeans once the latter were themselves exiled to Mesopotamia by the Babylonians a century and a half later.[34]

31. Sara Japhet, "People and Land in the Restoration Period," *Das Land Israel in biblischer Zeit*, Göttingen, 1983, pp. 104–5.

32. Gary A. Rendsburg, "The Northern Origin of Nehemiah 9," *Biblica* 72, 1991, pp. 348–66.

33. The exception being Ethiopian Jews who claim descent from the tribe of Dan. From a critical historical view, this is quite unlikely.

34. Cyrus H. Gordon, "North Israelite Influence on Postexilic Hebrew," *Israel Exploration Journal* 5, 1955, pp. 85–88.

# CHAPTER XVI

# Judah Alone

S argon, though a usurper, enjoyed the role of avenger for the god Assur, from whose city Tiglathpileser had taken away time-honored privileges.

Sargon blamed King Yaubidi of Hamath for stirring up the rebellion in Syria and Canaan. The coalition had many members besides Hamath, Damascus, Israel, and Egypt. For example, Hanno, the ruler of Gaza, who had escaped to Egypt, came back to lead his city in the rebellion.

Sargon's reprisals were severe. Israel was put under a governor and had to pay permanent tribute. Samaria was strengthened as an Assyrian stronghold and the land was settled by an alien population.

After the fall of Israel, one Merodach-baladan, aspiring to the throne of Babylonia, went to Babylon for the New Year (= the first of the month of Nisan) 721 B.C.E. and grasped the hands of the Marduk idol there. This was the way to claim kingship over the country for the year to come. He found allies in the Elamites and in tribes that had been suppressed by Assyria.

Hamath was sacked in 720. Babylon was crushed in 709, although Merodach-baladan escaped and lived to stir up future rebellions indefatigably. Exiles from Hamath and Babylon were sent to Israel (2 Kings 17:24). So not only were the deported Israelians being punished for their rebellion, but the new settlers were being punished for theirs. The new population in Israel accounts for the founding of the Samaritan nation, which was to play a considerable role in local history and to figure prominently in both Testaments. The new settlers reacted to difficulties in the land by turning for protection to the local authentic religion, which they recognized to be Yahwism. They shared the widespread idea that only the god of a particular area could be effective in that area. Accordingly, they requested a genuine Yahwistic priest to teach them the religion of Yahwe. Such a priest was sent by the Assyrian government and he set up headquarters in Bethel. But the fact that numerous other priests were appointed from various strata of society constituted one of the offenses of the Samaritans, according to the Bible. Yet the adherence of the Samaritans to Yahwe has been constant throughout their subsequent history, although at this early time the accusation is made in Scripture that they mixed their Yahwism with the cults they had known before their advent to Israel.

The treatment that Sargon meted out to the whole area was typically Assyrian in its cruelty. Yaubidi was flayed; Hamath was incorporated into the empire; the people were exiled; the land was resettled. Sargon's victory was complete. Siwi of Egypt was defeated. Hanno of Gaza was sent in chains to Assur. But other sovereigns who were allowed to pay tribute and live in peace included the rulers of Philistine cities, Judah, Edom, and Moab. Both the Cypriots and Arabs paid tribute and made peace with Sargon; the Cypriots because of the necessity of maintaining sea trade with the mainland, and the Arabs on account of caravan trade. Sargon built the new capital of Dur-Sharrukin for himself, not far from Nineveh. It was excavated first by the French and then by the Oriental Institute of the University of Chicago, and has yielded rich finds. Dur-Sharrukin, which was never quite completed, was abandoned after Sargon's death.

Sennacherib, son of Sargon, came to the throne in 705 B.C.E. The change in sovereigns was the sign for Merodach-baladan to return from exile in Elam and stir up a rebellion in his bid for the throne of Babylon. It might have been then that he sent his delegation to King Hezekiah of Judah (2 Kings 20:12). Merodach-baladan was able and enterprising. Nothing discouraged him. As long as he lived, he was ready for a comeback and it is probable that his mission to Hezekiah was not merely one of banal diplomacy and the extending of kindly wishes, but rather part of a bold attempt to found a great alliance for ridding the world of Assyrian tyranny.

The verdict of the Bible on the character of Hezekiah is exceedingly favorable. In 2 Kings 18:3ff. we are informed that he was the best of the Judean kings and was like his ancestor David. He put an end to the high places, the paganizing monuments, and Asherah. He went so far as to destroy a bronze serpent called Nehushtan; it was used as a cult object and was believed by the people to have been manufactured by Moses (see Numbers 21:9). There is new archeological evidence that greatly illuminates the Nehushtan. As discussed earlier (Chapter X, p. 166), archeologists working at the site of Timna in the southern Negev found a portable tent shrine remarkably similar to that constructed by the Israelites in the desert. At the same excavation was found a bronze serpent, about five inches long.[1] Most likely, Moses' Nehushtan was modeled after such a bronze serpent.

In 2 Kings 20:20 we read that Hezekiah constructed a tunnel to bring water into the city. This watercourse, known as the Siloam Tunnel, was found by early explorers in Jerusalem in the nineteenth century, complete with a Hebrew inscription telling how the tunnel was hewn. The workers began at separate ends, eventually they heard each other through the stone, and then they joined their two sections as water flowed through the tunnel. The watercourse, moreover, is not a direct line; instead, it cuts through the rock in an S-shape course. It remains a marvel of ancient engineering, and scholars still debate how the two crews of workers met one another.[2] The tunnel was necessary because the Gihon Spring, Jerusalem's main water source, lies outside the city walls. (An earlier watercourse constructed by the Israelites brought some amount of water into the city, which could be accessed by a vertical shaft, but apparently this amount was insufficient to meet the needs of Jerusalem's growing population.) In times of peace, this was not a problem. Water carriers simply went through the city gates and brought back water into the city via buckets. But with an Assyrian siege of the city on the horizon, Hezekiah knew that he had to insure a constant water source for the people of Jerusalem. The tunnel thus was constructed, with water now flowing under the city walls into a pool in the center of the city, and the spring was stopped up at the surface so that the advancing Assyrian army would not know of its existence. The project clearly was a major factor in the ability of Jerusalem to withstand the Assyrian siege.

Hezekiah took the lead in organizing a regional rebellion against

---

1. See Suzanne Singer, " 'From These Hills . . .'," *Biblical Archaeology Review* 4:2, 1978, pp. 16–25 (with photos of the bronze serpent on p. 18 and on the journal cover).

2. The most likely hypothesis is that they followed the natural fissures in the rock. This would have made their task of hewing the rock easier, and it also assured them that they would meet somewhere in the middle.

Sennacherib.[3] He smote the Philistines unto Gaza (2 Kings 18:8) to force them into the anti-Assyrian camp. This was done in concert with Egypt, whose dominant figure was to be Tirhakah (who had not yet become pharaoh), and with the Philistine city of Ashkelon, the Phoenician city of Tyre, and perhaps also with Babylon under Merodach-baladan. The result was that in 701 Sennacherib invaded Judah and took all the walled cities except Jerusalem (2 Kings 18:13). Sennacherib's annals record that he took forty-six walled cities and carried off 200,150 Judeans (or so he claims) as captives. All that was left to Hezekiah was his capital. Excavations at various Judean sites, e.g., Lachish, reveal the destruction wrought by Sennacherib. The Assyrian king then parceled out the captured Judean territory to his Philistine vassals at Ashkelon, Ekron, and Gaza.

Egypt had tried to relieve Ekron but was defeated by Sennacherib. By this time Hezekiah felt obliged to send emissaries to sue for peace from Sennacherib, whose headquarters were at Lachish. He had to release Padi, a Philistine vassal of Sennacherib, and pay (according to the Assyrian annals) 800 talents of silver and 30 of gold. According to the Bible, however, he paid 300 of silver and 30 of gold. Outside of the discrepancy between the figures 300 and 800, there are no contradictions between the two versions, although the viewpoints naturally differ and each version supplements the other.[4] Sennacherib declares that he shut up Hezekiah in Jerusalem like a bird in a cage, but he never claims to have conquered the city. This confirms the biblical account to the effect that Jerusalem escaped the fate that Sennacherib had planned for it.

One of the purple passages of the Bible is 2 Kings 18:17ff., in which an Assyrian official, called by his title Rabshakeh, is sent to

---

3. In 2 Chronicles 30 it is related that Hezekiah attempted, with partial success (verses 11, 18), to reunite (cultically, at least) Israel and Judah, from Dan to Beersheba, by inviting northern Israelites to celebrate the Passover in Jerusalem.

4. There is no doubt that the biblical and Assyrian accounts refer to the same invasion. What has misled some scholars into assuming two invasions is the fact that the Bible mentions Hezekiah's tribute at the beginning of the narrative, whereas Sennacherib's annals state that the tribute was paid in Nineveh after Sennacherib had gone home. Hezekiah offered tribute during the invasion but on condition that Sennacherib first withdraw. Since the offering of the tribute occurred early in the episode, the editor of Kings decided to finish the subject before going on to other items; especially since the tribute was recorded in the royal chronicles, while the Rabshakeh speech hails from a different historiographic source. Aside from desiring to keep his word, the reason Hezekiah paid tribute after Sennacherib had withdrawn was that the Assyrian should not have cause to return to Judah in future campaigns.

Jerusalem to get the city to capitulate by breaking down public morale. He addressed the representatives of Hezekiah within the hearing of the people crowded on top of the city wall. He started out with advice against Judah's laying any reliance on that "broken reed" of Egypt, which was in no condition to render any effective help. He furthermore pointed out that trust in Yahwe is without justification because Yahwe is angry at Hezekiah for closing Yahwe's shrines all over the country and forcing the people to come to the one shrine at Jerusalem. This ties in with the statement that Hezekiah abolished the high places of the land, which must have been an unpopular act for those who did not live in Jerusalem. The weakness of Judah is then highlighted by a sarcastic wager that the king of Assyria would provide 2,000 horses for Hezekiah if the latter could supply the men to ride them. Rabshakeh then stated it was Yahwe who ordered Sennacherib to destroy Judah. This agreed with what certain prophets had been proclaiming for a long time. The Assyrian envoy probably was sincere in believing that Yahwe was the God of the land who presided over its destiny.[5]

Hezekiah's representatives, worried about the effect Rabshakeh's words would have on the people, requested him to continue in Aramaic, the diplomatic language, which the common people could not understand. But Rabshakeh cleverly insisted on speaking "Judean" (= Hebrew), because he said his message was vital not only to the king and officials but especially to the common people who have to bear the consequences of official policy. He then proceeded to tell all the people within earshot not to let Hezekiah deceive them, that Yahwe will not save them and that Yahwe's will is being carried out by Sennacherib, not by Hezekiah. Then he promised that, if they surrender, they could go back home outside the city to their own vineyards and groves and drink water from their own cisterns, until the king of Assyria saw fit to deport them to good territory, just as good as their own, where they could enjoy a successful life with all their needs gratified. He observed that all of the gods had failed to save their lands from the hands of Assyria; and he significantly included Samaria, which Yahwe Himself had not saved from Assyria.

---

5. Several scholars have proposed, in a very original hypothesis, that Rabshakeh was a former Israelian who had joined (or had been forced to join) the Assyrian cause. See Chaim Cohen, "Neo-Assyrian Elements in the First Speech of the Biblical Rab-šaqê," *Israel Oriental Studies* 9, 1979, pp. 32–48.

This was psychological warfare of a high order. The Assyrian annals, by their very nature, tell us nothing of such factors. It was the Judean historiographers who had the interest to preserve the account of Rabshakeh, even though what he said was hardly agreeable to Judean sensibilities. That the episode is authentic cannot be doubted.[6]

It is a tribute to the Judeans that their morale was not broken. They kept perfect discipline and clung to their faith in Yahwe and remained loyal to His anointed one, who ruled over them.

In 2 Kings 19 it is related how Hezekiah, on receiving the news of Rabshakeh's ultimatum, expressed his grief and sent for Isaiah, who consoled him with the prediction that Sennacherib would hear a rumor of trouble in his realm and depart. Hezekiah, in his prayer to Yahwe, expressed the conviction that the gods Sennacherib had destroyed were simply the creations of human hands out of stone and wood but that Yahwe is alone the God and that therefore Rabshakeh's claims were vain. Isaiah's prediction (verses 20–34) was followed by a plague that smote the camp of the Assyrians so that, according to the biblical figures, 185,000 men perished (verse 35). This catastrophe is independently attested in variant form via an Egyptian source in Herodotus, so there is no reason whatever for doubting its authenticity. Although Isaiah had not correctly predicted the cause of Sennacherib's departure (a rumor is not the same as a plague), the sudden salvation of Jerusalem had vindicated Isaiah's optimism and his reputation was established.

The biblical statement that Sennacherib returned to Nineveh and was murdered by his sons (2 Kings 19:36–37) is true, but we know from Assyrian records that the assassination took place years later.[7]

Isaiah has come down in tradition as the greatest of the writing prophets. In the spirit of Amos and Hosea, he proclaimed that God does not want ritual and sacrifices, but rather justice and morality. In particular, the people are called upon to "uphold the rights of the orphan, defend the cause of the widow" (1:17). These individuals are

---

6. In 2 Kings 19:9b–14 it is stated that Rabshakeh's oral message was followed up by a written one delivered to Hezekiah. We take this to reflect actual military usage rather than parallel literary traditions. Isaiah 37:30 informs us that the invasion of 701 was timed so as to strike Judah at the most vulnerable point in the Jubilee Cycle: when the forty-ninth and fiftieth years (during which the land was to lie fallow) created a food crisis. This makes Rabshakeh's threat of famine in 2 Kings 18:27 the more pointed.

7. For details see Simo Parpola, "The Murderer of Sennacherib," *Death in Mesopotamia,* Copenhagen, 1980, pp. 171–82.

the underprivileged in society; without a male figure in the household they are defenseless and easily can be taken advantage of (in a
socioeconomic sense). This line appears virtually verbatim in the two
Ugaritic epics dealing with the legendary Kings Daniel and Kret.
Isaiah's wording, therefore, is not absolutely original; instead, it harks
back to Canaanite epic literature. But there is a crucial difference that
should not be missed. In the Canaanite sphere, the defense of the
orphan and the widow was the duty solely of the king (and even with
the king, these may be only empty words). According to Isaiah, this
was to be the duty of every Israelite, regardless of station. In other
words, while one would not want to call ancient Israelite society a
democracy in the later sense of the word, there are incipient democratic ideals built into the messages of the prophets.

Isaiah enunciated prophecies concerning foreign nations as well as
Judah. Here he is following the precedent of Amos. Far from being a
practical, down-to-earth politician, militarist, or statesman, Isaiah is
concerned solely with morals and religion. For him, God is the cause
of everything that happens. It is obvious that Isaiah was not the spirit
of resistance. We have every reason to believe that it was Hezekiah's
own idea to start the rebellion against Sennacherib; in no case was he
aided and abetted by Isaiah. For Isaiah, Assyria is simply God's tool
for meting out punishment to the nations of the world and particularly to Judah. But Assyria in turn is to be destroyed, though by God
and not by man (Isaiah 10:5 and especially 31:8). Assyria, incidentally,
is portrayed with great accuracy in the prophecies of Isaiah. The Jeru-
salemite prophet was fully conversant with Assyrian literary propo-
ganda. For example, when Isaiah quotes the king of Assyria as
boasting that he cut down the cedars and junipers of Lebanon (Isaiah
37:24 = 2 Kings 19:23), he is echoing, almost verbatim, the inscriptions of the Neo-Assyrian monarchs.[8]

According to Isaiah (3:1–7; 24:2)—and this is in the tradition of
Egyptian prophecies of the second millennium B.C.E.—there is to be
an upheaval of society,[9] with chaos and distress, when the respect of
the young for the old will go by the board, and when the distinction

---

8. Peter Machinist, "Assyria and Its Image in the First Isaiah," *Journal of the American Oriental
Society* 103, 1983, pp. 719–37. See also Gary A. Rendsburg, "*Kabbîr* in Biblical Hebrew:
Evidence for Style-Switching and Addressee-Switching in the Hebrew Bible," *Journal of the
American Oriental Society* 112, 1992, pp. 649–51.

9. Cf. also Hesiod, *Works and Days,* 180–201.

between master and slave, priest and layman, ruler and ruled, will be reversed or obliterated. Only after that unbearable upheaval will salvation come. In the spirit of all the Hebrew prophets, Isaiah urgently tells his people to mend their ways so that there may be national salvation. For the biblical prophets, salvation is national, not personal.[10]

In spite of the fact that national salvation is so important, there is no chauvinism in the total picture of Isaiah's message. In 19:24–25 he mentions three nations that are to turn out to be blessings: Egypt, Assyria, and Israel. It is thus through all of mankind that God's plan is to unfold. The disaster that confronts the world, and particularly Judah, is to be followed by a glorious and happy future. Thus Isaiah shares with his predecessors the conviction that after all the many woes that are in store, a wonderful and eternal age lies ahead. Isaiah incorporates the concept of the End of Days, which was to grow into the eschatology that figures so prominently in later Judaic development.[11]

In the End of Days there will come into its own a remnant that will include not only Judeans but Israelians. The remnant will have to be assembled from the ends of the earth, when God will show His majesty in leading the remnant back to Zion, even as He showed His divine power and purpose when He led Israel out of Egypt. The whole world will then accept Yahwe who will reign alone as God over a perfect world (18:7).

Long before Isaiah there had been, as we have noted, a school of Egyptian prophecy that dealt with a punishment to Egypt for offending the gods. The punishment was to be in terms of foreign domination, widespread destruction, and in social upheaval whereby classes would no longer retain their former relationships. These woes would be terminated by a godly king who would be victorious in temporal and spiritual affairs, so that he would inaugurate the divine order. These elements plus ethical Yahwism (such as we find in Amos

---

10. This is still prevalent in Judaism, where the continuity of the People is important, but where very little emphasis is placed on personal salvation.

11. Eschatology is the school of thought devoted to the idea that the historic process with all its dislocations will come to a close at the End of Days toward which all history moves. At that time an eternal era of static perfection will be inaugurated for the righteous. Birth, growth, death, wars, all types of change will then be unknown. The more the Jews suffered, the more they cherished their eschatological dream. It is obvious that this static idea can have little attraction for modern westerners who cannot conceive of a desirable order without progress.

and Hosea) add up to the Hebrew prophecy such as we find in Isaiah. The Messiah or king who will inaugurate the golden age at the end of days, must be of the Davidic Line. That Messianic Age will be a perfect world, a kingdom without end, in which justice and peace, but not violence, will be the determining factor. In Isaiah 11:5 it is stated that righteousness or faithfulness will be the girdle on the loins of the Messiah. That is to say, he will not be a hero of physical combat whose strength is symbolized by the wrestling belt;[12] instead he will be symbolized by morality and virtue. He will inaugurate eternal peace and right, replacing all the world empires.

There are still other elements in Isaiah; for example, his innovation that the animal kingdom will change its nature in order to fit in with the ideal age. According to 11:6–9, the lion will have to give up eating meat and turn to eating straw, because in that perfect world all the beasts shall live together in peace with a little child leading. This turn to vegetarianism is a reflection of the paradise that was when God created the world. According to Genesis 1:29–30, 2:9, man and the animals were created as vegetarians. According to Isaiah, they will return to this diet in the Messianic Age.

The reconciliation of man and beast fits into a pervasive aspect of the Bible World, where beasts were accorded almost human status. God's covenant is made with man and beast (Genesis 9:9). Animals, as well as people, are accountable for their crimes (Genesis 9:5). Domestic animals have to keep the Sabbath (Exodus 20:10) and may be obliged to observe special fasts and public mourning (Jonah 3:7–8; 4:11). In the plague of the slaying of the firstborn, Egyptian cattle as well as men (but not Hebrew men and cattle) were doomed (Exodus 11:5; 12:29).[13]

Many of Isaiah's contemporaries had complete conviction that Zion was inviolable. Samaria could fall but not Zion; for how could Yahwe abandon His holy city and His holy Temple? Sennacherib's invasion had strengthened the doctrine of Zion's inviolability, for

12. The terminology harks back to the heroic age of the Near East (illustrated on seal cylinders) when combat took the form of belt wrestling. Cf. C. H. Gordon, "Belt-wrestling in the Bible World," *Hebrew Union College Annual* 23, 1950–51, pp. 131–36.

13. While the Hebrews forbade carnal relations between man and any kind of animal, the Hittite Code permits human copulation with certain animals but not with others. Thus some of the people in the Bible World felt varying degrees of kinship with the different animal species; some ruled out but others permitted carnal relations with animals; much as our laws of incest spell out the permitted and forbidden degrees in terms of human kinship.

every surrounding nation had fallen, every city in Judah had been captured, but not Jerusalem and its holy shrine. History enabled the Judeans to adhere to this doctrine for some time to come. Prophets like Micah (3:12) and later Jeremiah were to oppose it, but the majority of the people in and around[14] Jerusalem cherished the illusion until Jerusalem fell in 586 B.C.E.

Micah, in chapter 4, enunciates the doctrine of the End of Days, when all nations will flock to Zion and enjoy an eternity of peace, and thus follows Isaiah in the idea that all nations will participate along with the remnant of Israel in the golden age. Micah, like nearly all of the prophets, holds that God is not interested in ritual and sacrifices. His outcry against sacrifices of the fruit of the womb (6:7) may have been evoked by the atrocity of Ahaz, who sacrificed a son in his misguided concept of Yahwism. Micah (6:8) points out that Yahwe wants only justice, uprightness, and humility with God; all the rest is unessential. In Chapter 7, Micah (like all the other prophets) preaches faith in ultimate salvation from Yahwe. There will always be a remnant (7:18) that God will spare and to this remnant God will carry out the promises He made to the patriarchal fathers of the Hebrew people (7:20).

Hezekiah's brave struggle for independence had resulted in loss of land, people, and livestock. The Judeans had suffered materially in consequence of his policies. Isaiah's optimism might have made a favorable impression on the Jerusalemites, who heard his message and witnessed the salvation of the capital; but there was little consolation for the inhabitants of the rest of the country. It is only natural, then, that there should have been a reaction to the era of Hezekiah and Isaiah.

Around 697 B.C.E. Hezekiah's twelve-year-old son Manasseh became king of Judah. He reacted against the prophets toward cultism, hand in hand with the priesthood throughout the country. This does not mean that he abandoned Yahwe as the national God but only that Yahwe was now the chief of a group of popular deities (largely astral) that had a great appeal at local shrines and among the common people. He revived institutions that the biblical authors always regard with abhorrence. Thus there reappeared male and female sacred prostitution in the shrines, a usage that was widely practiced in the surrounding countries. Manasseh's reactionary brand

14. The people in the nearby villages and fields took refuge in Jerusalem from invading armies.

of religion was also expressed by his sacrificing his firstborn, which, to the biblical authors who judge him, is not piety but the shedding of innocent blood. We have very few facts from the long reign of Manasseh (about 697 to 641 B.C.E.). Probably the facts are so few because very little happened in his peaceful reign. He represented a reaction against the spirit of resistance as well as the spirit of prophecy. He was, throughout most of his reign, discreet enough to stage no revolts, to pay his tribute promptly,[15] and to keep out of mischief as a vassal within the world empire of Assyria. His were days of economic prosperity and political tranquillity, for after the suppression of Hezekiah's revolt of 701, Canaan enjoyed peace and trade under the *Pax Assyriaca*.

In rebuilding the high places destroyed by Hezekiah (2 Kings 21:3), he gained the support of most of the people outside of Jerusalem, especially the priesthood and other leaders at the various centers, who had strong feelings in favor of their own shrines as against that at Jerusalem. In bowing down to all the host of heaven, he was following the trend of the times, because in the Assyrian empire the importance of astral worship was great, for the Mesopotamians were among the most star-conscious people of history.

The altars he set up in the spirit of paganism were even erected within the Temple itself in Jerusalem. The sacrifice of his son may have set a fashion that gave rise to the charge that his reign saw Jerusalem gorged from end to end with innocent blood. He also revived the popular religious institutions of divination and spiritualism that had been suppressed in the preceding reign. Accordingly, the Bible condemns him as exceedingly wicked and as having misled the people into being worse than the nations God had expelled to make room for the Hebrews. Therefore, the fate of Samaria would have to

---

15. He is listed as Minashi among the vassals who paid tribute to Assyria. Assurbanipal's campaigns encompass Judah but do not touch it, showing that Manasseh (at least at that time) behaved himself to Assyrian satisfaction. In 2 Chronicles 33:11–16 is mentioned an Assyrian invasion (unsupported by Assyrian annals or the Kings account), the deportation of Manasseh to Babylon, followed by his reform and return to sound Yahwism. Some scholars regard his deportation and reform as unhistorical midrash (to teach the moral that wickedness is punished but a sinner can always repent). On the other hand, his otherwise unattested defense works in verse 14 have a true ring and may well go back to authentic annals. Moreover, the kings of Assyria from time to time carried off rebellious chieftains to Mesopotamia for instructions and indoctrination, and then sent them home to rule. Assurbanipal did just this with the Egyptian Necho I of Sais. It would not be unparalleled, then, if Assurbanipal first deported and then restored the king of Judah, too.

befall Jerusalem. However, it is likely that the tradespeople who enjoyed better business than usual were in favor of Manasseh. It is likely, too, that he had the support of the provincial priests in a way that Hezekiah could not have obtained. But the Jerusalem faction and the prophetic movement, which could not tolerate his policies, reacted against them and crushed them shortly afterward.

Amon followed his father Manasseh not only on the throne but in his policies. After a short reign of two years, Amon was assassinated and the reaction had asserted itself. Amon was succeeded by his eight-year-old son Josiah, who reigned from 638 to 608 B.C.E. and effected a tremendous impact on all subsequent history. The Bible approves of him and compares him with David. There is also the statement (2 Kings 23:25) that no king before or after him was as good.

It was during the reign of Josiah that the Assyrian Empire tottered. In 626 B.C.E. Babylon broke away and the collapse of Assyria was just a matter of time. This gave the signal for independence movements and national restorations all through the Assyrian Empire.

In his eighteenth year Josiah sent the scribe Shaphan to the Temple to investigate the progress made in repairs. The situation is reminiscent of that in the time of Joash, who also was a boy-king under priestly tutelage, in whose reign the Temple was repaired.[16] The terminology is largely the same; e.g., in the repetition of one fact that appears important to the biblical writer, namely, that there was no bookkeeping in financial matters because everyone could be counted on to work in good faith.

The High Priest Hilkiah had found in the Temple a book, which he turned over to Shaphan, who, on reporting to the king, read the book to the king. On hearing the text, Josiah rent his clothes in grief because he and his predecessors had not been following this Book of the Law that had just been found. To know what to do, he sought an oracle from the Lord so as to avert the wrath of God that would befall him in accordance with the message of that Book, since the Law had not been followed. For the oracle he turned to the prophetess Huldah, who announced a favorable prognosis for his reign, although the ultimate wrath of God for previous disobedience was to bring on

---

16. The similarity is due not only to the fact that history was repeating itself but also that the historiographic style is the same.

destruction thereafter. The religious reform was stepped up without delay.

It is worth noting who backed the reform. It was supported by the priesthood of Jerusalem, notably Hilkiah, by the officialdom of Jerusalem such as Shaphan, by the crown, and by the prophetic movement, if we are to infer that the individuals who took part in the basic stages of the reform represented, as men often do, the interests of the groups from which they came (2 Kings 22).

Josiah then convokes all the elders of Judah and Jerusalem (2 Kings 23). The division is no longer that of Israel and Judah; now the factions of the Hebrew people are the Jerusalemites and the provincial Judeans. Already in the time of Hezekiah, Rabshakeh, in his oration, had spoken of the people of Jerusalem and those of Judah. That is the cleavage that lasted down to the end of Judean independence. Josiah convokes not only the elders but also the common people of Judah and Jerusalem. Furthermore, two other categories of leaders are specified: the priests and prophets. It was before this impressive aggregation of leaders and citizens that Josiah had the Book of the Law read in public.

The traditional view is that the Law, discovered by Hilkiah and now read before the nation, was the entire Pentateuch. Obviously it would take hours to read the entire Torah aloud,[17] and since an ancient scroll is generally much smaller than the Pentateuch, it is conceivable that the scroll covered only a part of the Pentateuch. However, the view that the scroll was forged shortly before its alleged discovery in 621 B.C.E. is based on false premises. Throughout the ancient Near East, law codes were disregarded in actual life. At the very time when the codes were promulgated, the actual business contracts disregard the codes. The judges regularly omit any reference to codes in their court decisions in Mesopotamia. They are instead guided by tradition, public opinion, and common sense. This is also true of Israel, where Solomon's suggestion to divide the harlot's baby was not prompted by any code. This does not prove that the Law did not exist. In Israel, as in Mesopotamia, judges and rulers did not refer to codes or keep law books on hand for consultation. There were

---

17. But this does not make the custom impossible. To this day the Samaritan elders read the entire Torah at the funeral of the Samaritan high priest. See *Jerusalem Post,* January 27, 1987, p. 4.

two distinct currents: (1) practice and (2) written law. Attempts to codify law naturally reckoned with custom and past experience, but once such codes were written, they were at best studied by a few scholars and had little or no direct influence on legal and social practice. Accordingly, the fact that neither Josiah nor his immediate predecessors had known anything of the Law does not prove it was a forgery by Hilkiah or Shaphan. The rediscovery of Hammurapi's Code would have come as a complete surprise to most kings of Babylon after Hammurapi. It is the consensus of conventional scholarly opinion that Josiah's scroll was a composition of his reign and resembled Deuteronomy, though it was not coextensive with Deuteronomy. Scholars call that hypothetical document D (= Deuteronomic Code) and while no two scholars agree on exactly what it includes and excludes, virtually all scholars agree on its actuality. The circumstances of the Josianic discovery fit in with what we know of the ancient Near East so well that we may take it at its face value. A forgotten book was rediscovered. Since only a few scholars studied such books, law codes (whose practical value was quite limited) were generally forgotten in the Bible World. The significance of 621 B.C.E. is not that a great forgery was foisted on a gullible world. The significance of that date is that for the first time in human history a written document was *actually* adopted *for all time* and *without interruption* as the permanent guide of a nation. The fact that it was regarded as divinely inspired lent it the necessary authority. Hitherto in Israel and Judah divine guidance had been sought by oracle. Josiah himself resorted to an oracle when he was jolted by the discovery of the scroll. But after 621, oracles have been on the way out, and written scripture holds the field for most of mankind.[18]

The covenant reaffirmed in 621 bound God, king, and people for all time.

The order of events as narrated in Kings implies that Josiah's reforms followed the discovery of the Law. However, 2 Chronicles 34:3–7 presents an alternative chronology; it states that he began his reforms in his twelfth year (627), six years before the Law was found in his eighteenth year (621; note verse 8ff.). In any case, Josiah destroyed cult objects that were not within the orthodox repertoire.

---

18. The pattern of development follows three stages: (1) oracles, (2) canonical scripture, and (when the changing needs of life are no longer met by the antiquated scripture) (3) interpretation of scripture. We are of necessity in the third stage.

He burned a number of them and transported their ashes to Bethel (2 Kings 23:4). Josiah then put an end to the priests of the high places who worshiped Baal and the various solar deities. He also destroyed the houses of the *qedeshim* (on whom see above, Chapter X, pp. 160–61) in the Temple itself, where women, too, used to weave cult objects called "houses for Asherah." We may note in passing that to the Jerusalem devotees of Asherah, the goddess was the wife of Yahwe, just as she is the spouse of El in the Ugaritic pantheon.

Josiah also defiled the high places; his usual method of defiling was to scatter bones upon them. The priests from outlying districts were allowed to come to Jerusalem and eat unleavened bread along with their brothers, but they were not allowed to sacrifice in the Temple. This means that while they were stripped of important sacerdotal functions and graded down to subservient positions, they were not liquidated economically. Josiah also defiled the Tophet: the place where the sons and daughters of Judeans had been burned as Molech offerings: human sacrifices. Solar worship had become established under Manasseh and Amon so that Josiah had to put an end to the solar horses and chariots, which were doubtless regarded as chariots of the solar god identified with Yahwe in the reigns of Manasseh and Amon. Not only Manasseh's but also Solomon's constructions had to be destroyed in the Jerusalem vicinity, for in verse 13 we read that Josiah devastated the shrines of Solomon's Sidonian Astarte and Moabite Chemosh and Ammonite Milcom. Josiah also put down the witchcraft and spiritualism that had flourished in Manasseh's reign.

The excavations at Arad, in southern Judah, revealed evidence that may relate to Josiah's reforms. A small temple stood at Arad and was used by the Judeans there from the tenth century through the seventh century, at which point it was abolished.[19] Most likely the end of the Arad temple came as a result of Josiah's defilement of the high places throughout the land.[20] The Passover had either fallen into disuse or lost its importance. So, in accordance with the Law, a great Passover such as had not been celebrated since the days of the Judges was now celebrated under Josiah's orders. (The Exilic compiler of the Books of Kings adds [verse 26] that inasmuch as God could not forget the

19. Yohanan Aharoni, "Arad," *Encyclopedia of Archaeological Excavations in the Holy Land,* vol. I, Englewood Cliffs, N.J., 1975, pp. 85–87.

20. There are some scholars, however, who date the abolition of the Arad temple to the eighth century, in which case this action should be connected with the reign of Hezekiah.

unspeakable evil of Manasseh, the city and Temple eventually had to face destruction although not in the days of the good Josiah.) The reform of Josiah amounted to the inauguration of a divine order whose neglect had occasioned the wrath of God and had brought the nation to such low estate.

The question as to what part of the Law was discovered in 621 has been much debated. One of the most applicable parts of Scripture is Deuteronomy 17 and 18, which map out the proper duty and conduct of a king of the Hebrew people. The fact that hitherto the kings had not been living up to this standard because of their ignorance of this Law intensified the reaction of Josiah. Deuteronomy 18:3ff. specifies the rights and privileges of the priests and Levites, who were to occupy such an exalted position that they are compared with judges in the dignity they were to enjoy (Deuteronomy 17:9; 19:17). Deuteronomy 18:6 outlines the rights of the countryside Levites; but this is significantly contradicted in 2 Kings 23:9, and even more so in the later writing of Ezekiel (44:15), in which only the Zadokite priests are to enjoy the full rights and privileges of priesthood. Such difficulties show the futility of facile, schematic solutions.

Also applicable to Josiah's reform might be Deuteronomy 18: 15–22, where it is stated that the prophets are to be obeyed if their messages prove to conform with objective truth. Also 18:10 might be applicable because of the prohibition against human sacrifice and magic, both of which Josiah abolished. However, the legislation calling for the freeing of Hebrew slaves in the sabbatical year was not even attempted by Josiah. The first recorded attempt to enforce it was in the reign of Zedekiah (Jeremiah 34:12–16).

To be effective in Josiah's program, the Book embraced in 621 should have included the Patriarchal narratives and the Exodus, for it is those traditions on which the unity of the tribes is based. Josiah (like Hezekiah before him) aimed at reconstituting the entire nation, envisaged as the Twelve Tribes. The Passover was appropriate for rallying the nation, because all the tribes figure in the Exodus epic as equals.

The reform whereby the cult and residence of God was limited to one city was appropriate to and feasible in a small city-state. Aside from cultic matters, the actual enforcement of the Law came as a result of the Exile, and we find it in effect only after the Exile when it becomes an integral part of Judaism down to modern times.

The growing emphasis on the Law meant in the long run a curbing of the prophetic spirit; and ultimately the establishment of the Law did away with the acceptance of prophecy as a living institution. However, it is a mistake to shut our eyes to the prophetic spirit in many parts of the Law such as the Ten Commandments, the section beginning "Hear, O Israel," and in admonitions such as those to treat neighbors and foreigners as we would be treated.

Above we noted that Josiah removed the pagan cult objects from the Temple in Jerusalem, burned them, and then carried their ashes to Bethel. The latter city, it will be recalled, lay outside the territory of Judah. In fact, Bethel had been one of the principal cities of the cult of northern Israel, and the temple that Jeroboam I had constructed there was still standing in Josiah's day, a century after the northern kingdom's downfall. Accordingly, Josiah did not stop at the boundaries of Judah. He pursued his program into former Israelian territory. He destroyed the Bethel site (2 Kings 23:15), and then advanced even farther northward into the region of Samaria proper, where he destroyed other high places still in existence (2 Kings 23:19). Since the year 721, this territory had been part of the Assyrian Empire, but, as we shall see below, the great power now was beginning to crumble. Thus, we assume that Josiah took the opportunity of Assyrian weakness to move into previously Israelian territory. Since the Bible is silent about any Assyrian opposition to his advances, Josiah must have been successful in his operation. His ultimate goal, no doubt, was to reestablish the entire traditionally Israelite territory (i.e., of the original twelve tribes) under one throne in Jerusalem, just as had been the case in the days of David and Solomon. This also is evident in the account of Josiah's unsuccessful attempt to prevent Egyptian troops from passing through Canaan near Megiddo (on which see below).

A number of prophets flourished during the reign of Josiah. One of them was Zephaniah who predicted God would wipe Baalism and astral worship out of the land of Judah. Thus the prophetic movement helped lead up to the reform. Zephaniah also stressed the Day of Yahwe and prophesies against all the nations round about, including Assyria, which was the most hated of all, because it was the most powerful and oppressive. Zephaniah 3:9 states the ideal whereby in the End of Days all nations would have one language and one God. Since that God is Yahwe, the Judean ideal would be extended to all mankind. Universality was triumphing over narrow nationalism, at least in the highest strata of Judah's prophets.

Zephaniah 3:12 predicts that the sole survivors who were to have a happy future in Zion are the poor and humble who trust in Yahwe. The emphasis on "in Zion" had grown since the year 701 and there was a strong feeling among the people and among most of the prophets that Zion would be spared and be the scene of the happy future. It was on this point that the prophets and Jerusalem priesthood could agree, however much they might differ on other matters. This agreement between two groups of religious leaders contributed to the success of Josiah's reform. Few were bothered by philosophical problems such as the conflict between Yahwe as the local God of Zion and Yahwe the World God. And if we examine the question, we shall see that the conflict does not really exist; for the ruler of a great empire can reside in a localized capital. Just as the Assyrian king resided in Nineveh or a Babylonian king resided in Babylon, while claiming world dominion, why cannot Yahwe, who rules the Universe, choose as His capital the Davidic city of Zion?

Since 701 B.C.E. things had been generally quiet throughout the Assyrian Empire. The most notable exception was Babylon, which felt that it should be the center of world dominion and hence it was unfitting in the eyes of gods and men that it should be subservient to Assyria. When Sennacherib was slain, his son Esarhaddon came to the throne and decided to rebuild Babylon and appease the population. His policy went hand in hand, as was usually the case, with a theology. He held that the gods had been angry with Merodach-baladan for transporting the treasures of the Babylonian temples to Elam; but now that they could be recovered and the city reestablished, the gods might be conciliated and Babylon might enjoy prosperity again. It is interesting to note that he resettled the remnant of Babylon in their old city and restored all their old privileges. Thus we witness a forerunner of the restoration to Zion.

During Esarhaddon's reign, the Phoenicians, the Edomites, the Arabs, and the Egyptians staged a revolt, from which Judah remained aloof and therefore suffered no Assyrian retribution.

Esarhaddon did what none of his predecessors had done: He conquered Egypt and took the title of King of Lower Egypt, King of Upper Egypt, and King of Ethiopia. His victories made him head of a world empire including Egypt, Syria, and islands such as Cyprus.

The Phoenician cities of Sidon and Tyre revolted in concert with Tirhakah of Ethiopia, who again came to the fore and struck for the independence of the Nile Valley. This obliged Esarhaddon to return to Egypt in 671. His Arab allies helped him with water and supplies en route, especially in the dry Negev south of Judah. He reached Memphis where the local princes willingly yielded to him, partly because they disliked the rule of the Ethiopian, who, according to Egyptian prejudices, was a barbarian.

There was still more trouble in Egypt in 669, when Esarhaddon headed for that land but died on the way. His successor Assurbanipal is one of the most interesting kings in world history. He was too civilized to concentrate his efforts on war. His father Esarhaddon had already shown signs of reluctance to take part in battles and stayed home much of the time. Assurbanipal left much of the fighting in Egypt to generals with heavy forces to be further reinforced by Syrian contingents. The Egyptians by this time had learned that the Ethiopians, even though they were Negroid, belonged to the same general culture as the Egyptians and were preferable to the brutal and completely alien Assyrians. Upon the invasion of Assurbanipal's army, Tirhakah fled south. Assurbanipal pursued a policy of appeasement toward Egypt. After summoning the Egyptian prince Necho as a captive to Assyria, he sent him back to the city of Sais where Necho assumed the throne (Twenty-sixth Dynasty).

Tirhakah died in 664 B.C.E. to be succeeded by his elderly nephew Tenuatamon, who managed to reach Memphis but upon the approach of the Assyrian armies, retreated southward to Thebes. The Assyrians pursued him and destroyed Thebes in 660 B.C.E., which made a deep impression on the ancient Near East. Thus when the prophet Nahum (3:8), who predicted the downfall of Assyria, wants to point out that Assyria deserves the fate that was in store for her, he asks rhetorically: "Are you better than No-Amon (= Thebes)?"

The defeats that the Egyptians suffered under their Ethiopian leaders had meant the end of the Amon World Empire, which had been a fiction for a long time but was now reduced to such limited territory on the Upper Nile that it had to relinquish its pretensions. Vestigially, however, it held on for some centuries as a local religious state in its remote southern refuge.

Assyria was mistress of a famed world empire and was universally hated for that reason. Nahum is the best example of a writer in this period who expresses that hatred and predicted the fall that everyone wished Assyria.

At heart, Assurbanipal, who was anything but a warrior, loved peaceful pursuits. He was from early youth a scholar. He was trained as a scribe and his fondest project may well have been the establishment of his great Nineveh library, which was unearthed by the British in the nineteenth century, and whose tablets provide us with much of what we know of Babylonian and Assyrian civilization. He sent scribes around to copy ancient texts of all kinds so that their transcripts have been preserved for us.

Assurbanipal considered himself divinely appointed by Assur, the god of Assyria, to rule over the world. Therefore anyone who rebelled against him was guilty of heresy as well as treason and so was treated in the cruelest fashion.

His building operations were extensive and of fine quality. The art of this period was enriched by contacts from the West and from Egypt. Greater compositions, especially in relief, were now attempted than ever before. These reliefs have several levels set on different horizontal lines, so that the figures convey a feeling of depth unequaled in earlier Assyrian reliefs. The animals of this period are particularly fine when they do not hark back to a stereotyped tradition. Thus the wounded animals expressing pain in the hunting scenes are among the finest representations in world art, comparing favorably with animal representations at their best in Egypt.

With Assurbanipal Assyrian civilization reached its apex. There was Egyptian influence, but within the canons of Assyrian drawing and manner. Moreover, Assyrian conceptions of composition were bolder than the more traditional Egyptians would attempt. But it is also interesting that this high point of refinement in Assyrian civilization came just before its downfall.

Assurbanipal died around 631, and by 626 the Babylonians had shaken off Assyrian domination. The new dynasty in Babylon is called Chaldean or Neo-Babylonian; its first great figure is Nabopolassar. In 616 B.C.E. the Babylonians and Medes, under their respective kings Nabopolassar and Cyaxares, united to crush Assyria. The union was solemnized by the marriage of the Babylonian crown prince, Nebuchadnezzar, and the daughter of the Median king. The united armies vanquished the city of Assur in 614; and Nineveh, after bitter resistance in 612. All four historic capitals (Assur, Calah, Nineveh, and Dur-Sharrukin) were soon in ruins, never to be resettled. The mightiest nation the world had ever known was annihilated. The cruel fate of Carthage at Roman hands was only the destruction of a single city. But Assyria had been a whole nation dominating the world and now it was gone without any survival. Thus Xenophon saw the ruins of Calah two centuries later without realizing it had been the capital of a great nation. Never was a dire prediction more literally fulfilled than Nahum's prophecy against Assyria.

Hatred of Assyria made the rejoicing universal. The spoils were divided. The Medes got the Upper Tigris country; the Babylonians won West Mesopotamia and Syria so that the civilized Semitic areas fell to them.

Media, with its share of Assyrian territory north, east and west of the Tigris became for a time the world's greatest empire. Media remains among the least known of the large empires of the ancient East, but its contribution to the later Achaemenian Empire of the Medes and Persians was enormous. It had already absorbed a considerable degree of Assyrian civilization that it integrated with its native Iranian heritage. The synthesis of Median and Assyrian culture was incorporated into the Achaemenian Empire, when Cyrus of Persia created that empire through his conquest of Media. The capital of Media was Ecbatana, the site of the modern city of Hamadan in Iran. The ancient citadel is fortunately an unoccupied mound overlooking the city and accessible for excavation.

The Median Empire extended into Asia Minor, where it came to grips with the kingdom of Lydia. The latter had made a contribution of wide practical significance for commerce. Around the middle of the seventh century B.C.E. coinage was introduced in Lydia. Prior to coinage, business transactions were by barter. While gold and silver bars and rings had long been known, the seller always had to check their weight and purity to avoid being "shortchanged." Accordingly, the metal was more nearly akin to a commodity than to currency.

Early coinage was not the prerogative of the emperor alone. The kings and governors of the component parts of the empire could also issue coinage.

The advantages of coinage to trade were considerable. Coinage placed the responsibility for the value of the metal on the ruler, thus relieving the merchant. Moreover, since the ruler established his coinage as a compulsory medium of exchange in his territory, business practices were simplified. Coined currency did not however oust the older system of barter in the East. Both systems continued to exist side by side.

In addition to the monarchs of Babylonia and Media, another king made a bid for power upon the collapse of Assyria. That was Pharaoh Necho II (609–595 B.C.E.), who wanted Canaan and Syria as his share. The Judeans, however, wished at long last to have their independence and not to be part of another empire. Necho marched through Canaan on his way to the Euphrates, to aid Assuruballit II (612–609 B.C.E.) the Assyrian who was trying to reconstitute the shattered empire from a temporary capital in Haran. The situation is reflected, though with insufficient detail, in 2 Kings 23:29.[21]

The Syrian provinces yielded to Necho but the Judeans under Josiah would not submit. In trying to block Necho at the city of Megiddo, Josiah lost his life.[22] His successor Jehoahaz was anointed king by "the people of the land" (2 Kings 23:30), attesting the tradition of democracy whereby the common people had a say in the highest policies including the coronation of kings. Jehoahaz lasted only three months; for Necho arrested and dispatched him to Egypt, crowning another prince in his stead as Egyptian vassal over Judah. That prince was Eliakim, whose name the Pharaoh changed to Jehoiakim on the occasion. A moderate tribute was imposed on the country: a hundred talents of silver and one of gold, which Jehoiakim raised by taxing citizens, each according to his ability to pay (verse 33).

Jeremiah (46:2) records that Necho opposed Nebuchadnezzar at Carchemish in the year 605–4 B.C.E., but Nebuchadnezzar won and proceeded to the Egyptian border so that Judah was now within the confines of the Neo-Babylonian Empire (2 Kings 24:7).

Jeremiah's (25:9) prediction that the kingdoms of Syria would be destroyed did not have to be fulfilled. They yielded to Nebuchadnezzar without a struggle. (It may not be out of place to note here that it is not the fulfillment but the nonfulfillment of a prophecy that establishes its historic authenticity; though fulfillment does not prove the reverse.)

Fortunately for the exact chronology of the later kings of Judah, Jeremiah gives double datings as in 25:1 where he informs us that the first year of Nebuchadnezzar is the fourth year of Jehoiakim. Jeremiah's ministry began in Josiah's reign and ended after the destruction of Jerusalem, which took place in 586 B.C.E. His synchronisms put

---

21. The Hebrew text means that Necho was going to help the Assyrian king against the Babylonian menace. It is commonly misunderstood to mean that Necho was opposing the Assyrian.

22. It is interesting to compare the account in 2 Chronicles 35:21–22, which surprisingly represents Pharaoh Necho as speaking the word of God but blames the virtuous Judean King Josiah for failing to listen to "the words of Necho from the mouth of God."

the period from Josiah to the end of Judean independence on an exact chronological basis.

Jehoiakim, in a reign of eleven years, was a vassal of Nebuchadnezzar for three years and then rebelled (2 Kings 23:36, 24:1) in the spirit of independence and defiance wherewith the Judeans wanted to be masters of their own destiny.

Jeremiah began to preach in 626 upon hearing his call in Josiah's reign. The prophet tells us he would gladly have evaded his unpleasant mission if he possibly could, but the urge was irresistible. As we can see in Jeremiah, Chapters 7 and following, the prophet took a view opposed to that of the majority. He felt that only ethical Yahwism, and not the Temple or the cult, could save the country. It was for that reason that he saw dismal destruction in store not only for Judah but for Jerusalem and the Temple. Corruption pervaded the nation. Trust in the outer forms of the cult could not mend this for the simple reason that God wanted what Amos had told the people, not what the priests of the Temple, or any other sanctuary, desired.

Jeremiah was not alone in predicting the downfall of the capital. There was another prophet, Uriah,[23] who had fled to Egypt, fearing the consequences of his doctrine; but the Egyptians turned him back to Judah[24] where he was put to death (see Jeremiah 26:20–23). Jeremiah saw that Nebuchadnezzar would prevail and was politically realistic enough to state that vassaldom was the only practical course and that the idea of independence was an illusion.

Because the book of Jeremiah includes a wealth of historical and biographical information, we know more about the life of Jeremiah than we do about the life of any other biblical prophet. We learn, for example, that the prophet had a scribe, named Baruch, who was responsible for the written version of Jeremiah's messages. The names of all sorts of Judean dignitaries of the period are known to us from the book of Jeremiah. Once more we have a good match between the textual evidence and the archeological remains: Seals and bullae of a number of people mentioned in the book of Jeremiah have been found at Jerusalem and at other Judean sites. These include Baruch

---

23. Like most Hebrew prophets, Uriah has not left writings behind him.

24. The extradition of political refugees (which is included in the treaty between Ramses II and Hattusil) may have been according to a pact between Judah and Egypt, which were now allies.

the scribe (Jeremiah 32:12, etc.), Jerahmeel son of the king (Jeremiah 36:26), and Gemariah son of Shaphan (Jeremiah 36:9).[25]

Jeremiah (11:13) proclaimed that the number of Judean cities was the number of the Judean gods; that is to say, the Yahwe worshiped at the high places was not Yahwe at all, for such Yahwism was no different from the Baalism of the Canaanites whereby each town had its Baal.[26] Cult objects meant nothing to Jeremiah; in 3:16 he claims that even the holy ark was no source of protection. For him, true religion was ethical and moral. He finds that Judah was worse than Israel (3:11) and therefore a just God would see to it that Judah shared the fate of Israel. But for the common people, the greater their distress, the greater their hope. When Assyria was at its height, Nahum confidently predicted that Assyria would perish but that Judah would be saved. Subsequently, Habakkuk, when Babylon ruled, predicted that God would destroy Babylon and save Judah.

Jeremiah's contemporary, the prophet Hananiah, prophesied in 593 the imminent fall of Babylon. Jeremiah took the unpopular viewpoint and contradicted him. But with all the prophets, we meet with the common theme of ultimate hope; an unshakable belief in a remnant that would be saved for the Messianic Age; a conviction that Judeans would survive their temporal masters.

To return to the march of political and military events: Egypt was in no condition to aid Jehoiakim in his move for independence, for all Canaan was in Nebuchadnezzar's hands down to the Egyptian border (2 Kings 24:7). Jehoiakim is reported to have died (2 Kings 24:6),[27] leaving his eighteen-year-old son, Jehoiachin (also called Coniah and Jechoniah), on the throne to face Nebuchadnezzar's besieging army. After a reign of only three months and ten days (2 Chronicles 36:9), the young king capitulated and was carried off into exile to Babylon in 597 B.C.E. Although Nebuchadnezzar set another member of the Davidic House (Mattaniah, whose name Nebuchadnezzar changed to Zedekiah) on the throne of Judah, Judeo-Christian tradition considers Jehoiachin the legitimate king through whom the

---

25. Nahman Avigad, *Hebrew Bullae from the Time of Jeremiah*, Jerusalem, 1986; Yigal Shiloh, "A Hoard of Hebrew Bullae from the City of David," *Eretz-Israel* 18, 1985, pp. 73–87 (in Hebrew).

26. Jeremiah thus realized the distinction between strict monotheism and local pluralism.

27. But 2 Chronicles 36 may be right in stating that Jehoiakim was carried off in chains to Babylon by Nebuchadnezzar who at the same time pillaged the Temple of some of its vessels.

Messiah must come (see Matthew 1:11–12). In 597 the Temple treasures were taken to Babylon as booty. The cream of the population
was skimmed off and exiled to Babylon. Seven thousand warriors and
one thousand artisans were among the ten thousand Judean exiles (2
Kings 24:8–16).

Tablets from Babylon have come to light containing memoranda
of rations issued to Jehoiachin and other Judean princes. These documents are of particular interest because they also record rations for
artisans of other Canaanite nations. Thus the Judean Exile fits into
Nebuchadnezzar's policy of transporting talent from conquered areas
to aid in the building program he energetically pursued in Babylonia.
His father, Nabopolassar, had begun to repair the damage that Sennacherib had wrought in Babylonia—damage that Esarhaddon had
only repaired in part—and that Assurbanipal had aggravated in suppressing the Babylonian insurrection under his own brother Sha-
mash-shumukin.

Nebuchadnezzar boasts very little of his conquests and empire. In
his own inscriptions he stresses his constructive work in his homeland. By irrigation and building, he enriched and embellished his
country. Prominent among his pious works were the restoration of
Esagila, Marduk's temple in Babylon, and Ezida, Nabu's temple in
Borsippa. His energy was amazing for any age, including our own.
The fact that he erected a palace in fifteen days is not only claimed
in his own texts but corroborated in the Greek writings of Berossus.
The Hanging Gardens of Babylon (one of the Seven Wonders of
antiquity) were his work (rather than Queen Semiramis's, as Herodotus reports). He fortified Babylon with two walls. A stream ran
through the city dividing it into two parts connected by a bridge
whose beams could be removed by night so that if one half of the
city fell into hostile hands, the other half could be defended. The
stream was walled for some distance from the city to enhance the
defenses. The farthest canal to the north, joining the Tigris and
Euphrates rivers, was also walled against Median invasion.

Nebuchadnezzar experienced comparatively little opposition from
his empire, whose people had long been accustomed to subservience
and for whom the new regime meant only a change of masters. Trade
was the better because of the empire. When any of the nomadic
Arabs grew restive, Nebuchadnezzar knew how to quell them (Jeremiah 49:28–33) so that they were brought back into line. Armenian
merchants came down the rivers to trade in Babylonia. Ships on the

Persian Gulf carried goods between Babylonia and East Arabia. Nebuchadnezzar so established Babylon that it (or its local successor) remained more or less the commercial capital of the world until the Mongol invasions.

In foreign affairs Egypt came after Media as a source of concern for Nebuchadnezzar. The pharaoh could not view with complacence the loss of Canaanite trade, with which Egypt's prosperity was linked. Therefore Egypt incited the states of Canaan to revolt against Babylonia. Nebuchadnezzar wisely extended his empire to the Egyptian border but did not exhaust his resources by attempting to absorb Egypt as Sargonid Assyria had done.[28]

The removal of the aristocracy and talented elements of Judah had produced a social revolution. The poor who had been left behind were able to buy the abandoned land and other possessions of the exiles cheaply. Nebuchadnezzar might have speciously reasoned that the nouveaux riches of Judah would be satisfied with the economic and social advantages they had come by so easily because of his policies. But one factor nullified such a view: The Judeans still trusted in Yahwe, who unlike the other gods of the conquered nations could not be bodily carried off because He alone of the gods had no image. Optimists like Hananiah predicted the early return of the exiles including Jehoiachin. Many of the exiles shared this optimism; but not Jeremiah (chapter 29), who wrote to Babylon assuring the exiles that their stay would be long and that they should settle down to a sound communal life as loyal Babylonian subjects.

Pharaoh Psammetichus II (593–588 B.C.E.) directed most of his foreign activities to Ethiopia, not Canaan. But when Pharaoh Hophra, who was crowned in 588, resumed a policy of interfering in Canaanite affairs, Nebuchadnezzar returned to Canaan in 587. Syria yielded to him to avoid a hopeless war. Jeremiah advocated surrender to Nebuchadnezzar, whom he regarded as the instrument of Yahwe's wrath. The Jerusalemites looked upon Jeremiah as a defeatist and would have killed him had not King Zedekiah rescued him from their hands. It is possible that the king's kindly feelings toward the prophet were in part prompted in gratitude for Jeremiah's discouragement of those who looked to Jehoiachin's return, which would have meant Zedekiah's dethronement.

---

28. Not realizing Nebuchadnezzar's moderation in foreign policy, Jeremiah and Ezekiel incorrectly prophesied the ruin of Egypt.

There is a contemporary source for the last days of Judah. Eighteen ostraca, mostly military letters, were found in 1935, and three more in 1938, at Lachish. The texts were written for units of the Judean army around Lachish and Azekah, the last provincial cities to hold out against the Babylonian invaders. The documents show that Yahwism was firmly entrenched. Not only are the personal names Yahwistic but the officers swear "by the life of Yahwe" as is prescribed by orthodox biblical religion. The Lachish letters mention the activity of prophets, since oracles were still sought for guidance in military tactics. The texts deal tersely with signal communications and intelligence reports. Some of the ostraca reflect the eternal situation of officers in the field trying to square themselves with headquarters. That Egypt had a hand in the Judean revolt is reflected by a reference to a Judean mission to Egypt.

Lachish and Azekah fell leaving Jerusalem alone to resist. The Babylonians at last breached the walls of the capital and Zedekiah attempted to escape through the gap. He was overtaken, captured, and blinded, and many of his followers were killed. Between thirty and forty thousand additional exiles were carried off to Babylon leaving little besides the poorest in Judah. Jerusalem and the Temple were destroyed. All that was left to the Judeans was a hope for the future, eloquently expressed by Jeremiah (30:18): "the city will be rebuilt on its mound." This statement reflects an awareness among the Israelites (and others, too, no doubt) that cities constantly were destroyed and then rebuilt. This is the heart of field archeology, which endeavors to reveal the strata of ancient mounds (the technical word is a *tell,* the very word used by Jeremiah).

Jeremiah, whose peaceful policies were regarded with favor by the conquerors, was allowed to remain in Judah. The Judean Gedaliah was made governor of the province by Babylonia. Reading between the lines of the Bible, it is clear that Judean patriots regarded him as a collaborationist. Ishmael, a member of the Davidic House, who had been harbored and helped by the king of Ammon, treacherously slew Gedaliah and his followers. Fearing reprisals for his violence and rebellion, Ishmael and his men fled back to Ammon.

A remnant of the Judean army and civilian population, fearing Babylonian reprisals for Ishmael's treachery, was inclined to flee to Egypt (Jeremiah 41:16ff.). They sought oracular guidance from Jeremiah but after getting it, refused to abide by its dictum to remain in Judah. Persisting in their plan, they fled to Egypt carrying the prophet off with them. He continued to prophesy in Egypt, where he presumably spent the rest of his days.

Few of the other Canaanite states resisted Babylonia. King Ithobaal II of Tyre withstood a long siege lasting from 585 to 573 B.C.E. and while the city island was not actually captured or occupied by the Babylonians, the Tyrians came to terms with Nebuchadnezzar, surrendered their royal princes as hostages, and became part of the Babylonian system.[29]

29. For a detailed study of the events surrounding the year 586, see Abraham Malamat, "The Last Kings of Judah and the Fall of Jerusalem," *Israel Exploration Quarterly* 18, 1968, pp. 137–55.

## CHAPTER XVII

# Exile and Restoration

Amasis, who became pharaoh in 569 B.C.E., again stirred up the Canaanite states to revolt against Nebuchadnezzar, who was thus obliged to return to the West, where he restored order and reestablished his boundary at the Egyptian frontier.

Babylonia had long depended on the personality of Nebuchadnezzar rather than on well-balanced national strength. Therefore, when he died, collapse set in relentlessly. He was succeeded by his son Evil-Merodach, who reigned only from 561 to 559. The latter's brother-in-law, Nergalsharezer, then came to the throne but lasted only until 556. Labashi-Marduk (son of Nergalsharezer) was crowned but was soon deposed by the courtiers who placed on the throne Nabonidus, who was not of royal extraction. For the most part Nabonidus's reign was peaceful. He spent most of his career rebuilding cities other than Babylon, including the northern Haran, where he restored the temple of the moon-god Sin. The propaganda of Cyrus the Great, who vanquished Babylon in 539 B.C.E., is of interest for the view it expresses about Nabonidus. Cyrus accuses Nabonidus of having neglected Marduk, the great universal god. Furthermore, Nabonidus, in the course of Cyrus's invasion, had offended the pantheon by exiling the various gods to Babylon. (From Nabonidus's viewpoint, the step had been taken to save the gods from falling into the hands of the enemy and to keep the gods on Nabonidus's side.) Marduk therefore summoned Cyrus to restore the gods to their rightful shrines. Aside from the way this explains Cyrus's restoration of Yahwism on Zion, it shows the monotheistic undercurrent of the times: Marduk is identified with the supreme deity that governs world history.

Meanwhile there had been developments in Egypt. Hophra had been solicited by the Libyans west of the Delta to rescue them from the Greeks who had founded Cyrene in 630 B.C.E. and had ever since been enlarging their coastal holdings. The Egyptian army fared badly, although the Greek mercenaries in pharaoh's service remained loyal. The disgruntled army chose Amasis as pharaoh (in 569, as we have already noted). It is to be observed that although he was fighting the Greeks of Cyrene, he was an admirer of Greek culture. The emergence of the Greeks was destined to terminate the history of the ancient Near East within two and a half centuries.

The faith of the Jews[1] in Yahwe had been strengthened by the Exile and concomitant misfortunes because Yahwe's prophets had predicted them. Down to the Exile the rank and file of the Judeans adhered to a localistic religion, for the orthodox view maintained the exclusive legitimacy of the Jerusalem cult. Exile, however, had forced upon the Jews the belief in the universality of Yahwe, who would follow them wherever they might wander. Thus their loss of land and Temple had forced the Jewish people as a whole to embrace a universal concept of God that had formerly been the concept of only a few select leaders.

The Jews and the other national groups that were now part of the Babylonian Empire no longer had any political power. They were even losing their national languages and adopting Aramaic. Exile, trade, and service in the Babylonian army and government also resulted in some intermarriage. Yet people tended to call themselves by their ancestors' nationality. Thus there were still the Judeans, albeit without political power, without their own soil, without their own spoken language. Such nationalities resolved themselves into religious communities.

The theological universality of the age ran parallel with the theological individuality of each nation. All national groups tended to identify their particular god with the one and only cosmic deity who ruled the universe. The conflicting pretensions of all the national groups led to missionizing for the propagation of one's own national cult or theology. Zoroastrianism, though it started in Iran, was a missionizing religion from the start. But Judaism first became missionizing in the sixth century B.C.E. under the impact of the Exile.

---

1. It is convenient to call the people "Jews" (derived from "Judeans") after the Babylonian Exile changed their status into a predominantly international folk.

The age of propagandizing ideas may have given an impetus to wisdom literature, whereby the god-fearing sages of Egypt and Western Asia set forth the principles of the good life in the form of proverbs. Although there is a timelessness and transcendence of national boundaries in wisdom literature that often makes it difficult to localize and to date, it is possible that some of the wisdom literature in the Bible was composed or recast in this era.

Exile had replaced the physical bonds between men and god with a personal bond whose incorporeal character made it indestructible. It is the latter quality, fully attained by Judaism in the sixth century, that has imparted lasting vigor to Judaism and its daughter religions: Christianity and Islam.

As all the gods tended to be identified with Re in Egypt since the Old Kingdom, now in the sixth century all national gods throughout the Near East tended to be identified with the divine World Ruler. Thus in Syria, Baal Shamen ("Lord of Heaven"), so identified, was fostered more than ever before. In Mesopotamia, the Jews and their newly won converts so identified Yahwe. Since all great or national gods were thus identified, the cultic practices became more and more important to the masses who lacked the sophistication for appreciating lofty ethical concepts and theological refinements. The cults had not only their own distinctive sacrifices but also their own codes of purity.

The oppressed victims of exile and dislocation turned more and more to eschatological ideas whereby they would enjoy personal salvation in paradise. The preexilic prophets had not been concerned with salvation for the individual but rather for the nation. Weary from the vicissitudes of cruel history, people sought comfort in eschatology that offered the welcome illusion of the end of the historic process. Zoroastrianism made a contribution to eschatology in the basic tenet that the present conflict between good and evil would be resolved in the End of Days by the eternal victory of the good.

It is against the above background of the sixth-century scene that all the religions of the East are to be evaluated down to the Greek period. Judaism happens to be not only historically the most important but also the best recorded of those religions.

A return to Judah would at best be most difficult. Not only would the Jews have to experience the miracle of getting back from afar, but the land had been occupied by encroaching neighbors who partially filled the vacuum left by the exiles. (The extent of the vacuum is attested not only by the biblical account but also by the numerous mounds never resettled since 586.) And yet, despite all the discouraging odds, the Jews could not regard their exilic status as permanent. Just as the prophets had foretold their defeat and exile, they had also predicted the return of the remnant. The fulfillment of the one guaranteed that of the other. Besides, if God would not restore this remnant as He had promised, that would mean the triumph of the heathen over Yahwe—which was unthinkable.

The historic cultic religion of Yahwe had ceased because sacrifice was legitimate only in the Jerusalem Temple. Accordingly, prayer, the Sabbath, and circumcision received added prominence. The institution of the decentralized synagogue, in which prayer took the place of sacrifice, grew in this period. Yearning for Zion while exiled by the waters of Babylon evoked some of the finest psalms in the Psalter.

The first political sign that encouraged the exiles was in 561 B.C.E. when Evil-Merodach elevated Jehoiachin and treated him with respect.

The great prophet of the Exile is Ezekiel, the architect of the Restoration. The first verse of his book contains a date in terms of Jehoiachin's exile. The fortieth chapter opens with a double date in terms of the first exile (597) and the destruction of Jerusalem (586). Ezekiel, mindful of his nation's plight was not merely looking back at past woes. Chapters 40 to 48 are the blueprint for the New Jerusalem of the Restoration. With Ezekiel, Jewish Apocalyptic comes into its own. The exposition of extravagant visions as keys to the future had modest origins in the remote past. Ezekiel made Apocalyptic a major form of religious expression in Judaism. It was to become the essence of books in both Testaments—such as Daniel and Revelation—let alone a host of books among the noncanonical writings known as Apocrypha and Pseudepigrapha.[2]

Like the former prophets, Ezekiel was concerned with spiritual values and divine justice. Many of his contemporaries explained the destruction of the Temple and the loss of Jerusalem through the old theology of the sins of the parents being visited upon the children. This is built into the Ten Commandments (Exodus 20:5; Deuter-

2. See R. H. Charles, *The Apocrypha and Pseudepigrapha of the of the Old Testament,* Oxford, 1913; and James H. Charlesworth, ed., *The Old Testament Pseudepigrapha,* 2 vols., Garden City, NY, 1983. Another major source of material of this nature is the Dead Sea Scrolls, found in the caves above Qumran. For a basic introduction, see Geza Vermes, *The Dead Sea Scrolls: Qumran in Perspective,* London, 1977.

onomy 5:9), and 2 Kings 23:26 clearly states that Yahwe inflicted His wrath upon His people in 586 because of the sins of Manasseh two generations earlier. Ezekiel realized the errancy of this belief, and instead began to speak about personal responsibility.

In a famous chapter (Ezekiel 18), the prophet states that no longer will the sins of the parents be visited upon the children, and conversely no longer will the merits of the parents save the children. He referred to the three great worthies, Noah, Daniel, and Job (Ezekiel 14:14), who would no longer be able to save their children through their own righteousness. Noah, of course, is the hero of the biblical Flood story, who saved not only himself through his righteousness, but also his three sons. Job is the protagonist of the biblical book that bears his name; in the beginning of the book his children die, but by story's end they come back to life due to Job's unswerving faith in God.[3] Daniel in Ezekiel 14:14 is not, however, the same as the hero of the biblical book that bears his name. Instead, he is the Daniel of Ugaritic fame, whose son Aqhat was slain by the goddess Anat, but who, presumably, was restored to life at the end of the epic. The end of the tale is not extant, but there is a consensus among Ugaritologists that the story ended happily with Aqhat's return to the land of the living. Accordingly, we conclude that the great Canaanite epic of Daniel and Aqhat was known to Ezekiel and his readers. The story was part of the literary heritage of the land of Canaan. So while the Israelites reacted against Canaanite religion, they continued to appreciate the literary creations of Canaan. In all societies, great epics transcend denominational boundaries.[4]

In short, for Ezekiel, the loss of Jerusalem could not be accounted for solely by the sins of previous generations. The living, too, were guilty for the plight of the Judeans. Salvation was coming but not for the sake of the guilty living or the guilty dead. Salvation for Judah was inescapable for the sake of God's own name. The heathen had to be shown that God was supreme and looked after those who believed

---

3. Most scholars interpret Job 42:13 to mean that he gained a new family of seven sons and three daughters. But since a) his children are not doubled, unlike his other possessions, and b) Ezekiel groups Job with Noah and Daniel, we conclude that the children at story's end are the ones from the beginning brought back to life.

4. Long after Christianity became the dominant religion in the West, the great Greek poets (Homer, Hesiod, etc.) and dramatists (Sophocles, etc.) continued to be read and enjoyed, regardless of the polytheistic character of the society that produced these writers. Similarly, Homer was known to the rabbis of the Talmud.

in Him. The return to Zion was thus a necessary consequence of God's nature.

Ezekiel mapped out the construction of the Second Temple and the regulations of its priesthood, which was limited to the descendants of Zadok. Other priestly families, such as those that had been associated with the high places, were to be lowered in rank to Levites. While the Zadokite priests were to serve God, the Levites were (so to speak) to serve the priests. (This subordinate role of the Levite made it hard to round up levitical volunteers when the restoration came.) Ezekiel laid great stress on the Temple rituals and laws of purity, particularly the purity of the priests, who had to be pure for their sacred duties. Unlike the other prophets, Ezekiel emphasizes the cult as well as ethics and morals. Postexilic Judaism, whose architect he was, was destined long to remain a religious community rather than a political entity.

The age was one of restorations. Nabonidus was restoring ancient cults all through his Mesopotamian Empire. The Twenty-sixth (or Saite) Dynasty in Egypt was devoted to reviving the glories of the great Eighteenth Dynasty. Into this pattern fit the Judeans who aimed at restoring the Davidic Dynasty on Zion.

The restoration came sooner and more suddenly than any one expected. There would have been no restoration under the Neo-Babylonian Empire. But in 539 Cyrus the Great conquered Babylon without shooting a single arrow. The Babylonian Empire disappeared and the Achaemenian Empire ruled the East down to the Egyptian frontier. Cyrus's policy of restoring exiled men and gods fulfilled the Jews' desire to return home. In 538 Cyrus issued an edict that Jewish exiles could return with the sacred vessels (taken from the First Temple by Nebuchadnezzar) and with royal permission to construct a Second Temple on Zion (Ezra 1). Dreams had come true. Now 42,360 Judeans, plus 7,337 slaves and 200 singers,[5] and livestock[6] returned to Judah (Ezra 2:64–67). Sheshbazzar, the Prince of Judah (Ezra 1:8), was made the Persian governor of Judah and the predicted restoration was at hand.

---

5. The low status of the Temple singers is reflected in their being listed after the slaves. The gatekeepers and *netinim* were also petty Temple personnel of low status (note their position in Ezra 2:70).

6. Domestic animals are often included in ancient censuses; e.g., Ugaritic texts 305:4; 329:18–19.

The prophet of the return is the author of chapters 40–55 in
Isaiah.[7] He offered consolation with such buoyancy of spirit that he
is the most blithe author in the Bible and perhaps in all religious
literature. Earlier prophets had scolded the people for their backslid-
ing. But Deutero-Isaiah (as the prophet is called in scholarly literature) offered only a joyous message. Israel's mission is to convert all
the Gentiles. The whole world including Cyrus (whom he calls the
anointed of the Lord in 45:1) will know that Yahwe is supreme and
has alone shaped history. For Deutero-Isaiah there is no issue of
Yahwe versus other gods, but only of Yahwe versus lifeless idols made
by man's hands. Deutero-Isaiah, thus, is the first Israelite writer to
proclaim the doctrine of pure monotheism.

The factors that brought about a shift from monolatry to monotheism at this time can be reconstructed along the following lines.
The provincialism of an earlier Israel had given way to an era of
internationalism. Whereas Moses told pharaoh that the Hebrews
could not worship Yahwe in Egypt, and whereas David told Saul that
he would have to worship foreign deities once he left the land of
Israel, by the 500s B.C.E. the nation of Israel had entered a new age.
Israelians and Judeans had become accustomed to life in international
settings. Under David and Solomon, Israel had ruled an international
empire, and Israelites were stationed in foreign lands (see 2 Chronicles 8:2). With the growth of the Assyrian and Babylonian Empires,
it was not unusual for peoples to be uprooted from their lands.
Accordingly, the politics of the time, with the breakdown of traditional territorial boundaries, influenced the theology. Yahwe could
now be worshipped outside the land of Israel. So, once Judean exiles
arrived in Babylonia, they continued to worship Yahwe. Of course,
the method of worship had to change, because sacrifices no longer
could be performed with the destruction of the Temple in Jerusalem.
But new modes of worship, especially prayer, developed. Exemplars
are to be found in the Bible, such as Psalm 137.

The shift to monotheism requires that Yahwe, the God of Israel,

---

7. Different compositions by different authors were often combined by the Hebrews. The
different collections that make up the Book of Proverbs are fortunately supplied with titles.
Frequently, however, titles are omitted (e.g., Genesis 1:1). It may be that Isaiah 40–55 was
attached to 1–39 because of the Messianic theme they have in common. Chapters 56–66 of
the Book of Isaiah reflect a slightly later period, after the Temple was rebuilt. They may be
the work of Deutero-Isaiah, whose career could have spanned several decades; or they may
be the work of still another individual whom scholars call Trito-Isaiah.

must become the God of all mankind. If this is the case, then the question arises: Is Israel still special in any way? Deutero-Isaiah's response is yes, as he redefines the covenant between God and Israel. True, Yahwe is to become the God of all people, but it is His special people Israel who will spread the message of monotheism to the world.[8] Jewish missionizing had presumably already won converts, some of whom went to Zion with the returning exiles. Among such folk would have been former Israelians, now reunited with their Judean cousins.[9]

The change from national entity to religious community inevitably brought with it disappointment to those who had looked for a glorious restoration of a Judean Kingdom that would be the center of world affairs, and to which all the nations of the earth would submit, and whose people would be the one people that all the others would join.

The returning exiles found Judah badly run down in the half century of desolation that followed the catastrophe of 586. Remnants of clans in the south gladly attached themselves to the returnees, not just for the help they could give, but more especially for the protection they would thereby receive. There had encroached upon Judean soil squatters from the surrounding peoples such as the Edomites, Moabites, Ammonites, Philistines, and particularly the Samaritans. The latter were specially hostile, partly in reaction to Judean exclusiveness that prevented the returnees from embracing the Samaritans into the orthodox fold. The prophesied remnant that was to usher in and preside over the Messianic Age did not have to be large, but it did have to be pure and consist of the select few of the Chosen People who had remained true to Yahwe. While this ideal was not adhered to strictly, it did contribute to the Judean rejection of the Samaritans. (There were, indeed, some *gerim,* that is, people who, although not

---

8. According to the view of most scholars, the book of Jonah, usually dated to the sixth century B.C.E., also fits into this picture. The prophet Jonah represents Israel, whose job now is to preach the message of God to the pagans of the world. Jonah is reluctant to do so, just as a segment of the Jewish people may have felt uncomfortable with this new role.

9. We even possess linguistic evidence that bears this out. Postexilic compositions include northern Hebrew elements, the result of former Israelians mingling with Judean exiles in Mesopotamia and in the return to Zion. See Cyrus H. Gordon, "North Israelite Influence on Postexilic Hebrew," *Israel Exploration Journal* 5, 1955, pp. 85–88; and Gary A. Rendsburg, *Linguistic Evidence for the Northern Origin of Selected Psalms,* Atlanta, 1990.

of Judean extraction, identified themselves with the Judeans, by whom they were accepted.)

The towns had each a group of elders with authority in local affairs. These elders could on occasion convoke popular assemblies. One tenth of the men were drafted by lot for service in Jerusalem, to shoulder the onerous duties of soldiering as well as building. Their numbers were augmented by gallant volunteers,[10] so that in all about three thousand men devoted themselves to the important task of restoring unhappy Jerusalem to a fitting capital.

The High Priest in Jerusalem was Jeshua, the grandson of Seraiah who had served as the last High Priest in the First Temple prior to the destruction in 586. Building operations went ahead in spite of the havoc wrought by drought and famine (Haggai 1:6, 10ff.; 2:16ff.). The painful difficulties that confronted the returned remnant made it obvious that salvation was not yet at hand. Patience may have been inspired by the view that seventy years (Zechariah 1:12; 2 Chronicles 36:21) would intervene between the disaster of 586 and the real Restoration, which would therefore first come around 516. Such was the state of affairs on Zion. Meanwhile important developments had taken place on the international scene.

Shortly after Cyrus conquered Babylon in 539, he installed his son Cambyses as governor in Babylonia. Thus Cambyses, as crown prince, gained valuable experience in administration. When Cyrus lost his life in 528 during a military campaign, Cambyses became king and in keeping with the customs of his land and people, he married his own sisters Atossa and Roxana.

Cambyses set himself to execute the great unfinished project of his father: the conquest of Egypt. Amasis had been succeeded by Psammetichus III, who had many Greek allies. However, Greek loyalties were divided and some Greeks gave aid to Cambyses. The Phoenician cities were brought effectively into the Persian sphere and the Nabatean Arabs supplied water for Cambyses' troops in the hazardous desert that separated Judah and Egypt.

The Judeans probably cooperated with Cambyses and in no case placed obstacles in his way. Indeed Cyrus may have facilitated the

---

10. Unless the word "volunteers" (Nehemiah 11:2) is a euphemism for "draftees," much as we call soldiers "enlisted men" even though they be drafted. (The reconstruction above is composite for about 530–430.)

Restoration to Zion with a view to setting up a friendly state on the Egyptian border that would some day aid his armies in conquering the Nile. Relations between the Achaemenian government and the Jews were always good; certainly at this time, as we shall soon see. Yet no reference to Cambyses exists in the Bible or in Jewish tradition. The reason is probably that he did not affect Judean welfare.

The decisive battle was fought at Pelusium in the northeast part of the Delta. The end of Egyptian autonomy came in 525 when Cambyses captured Memphis. The conqueror wanted to push on to Carthage but his Phoenician allies refused to turn against their daughter colony.[11] Instead, Cambyses marched to Ethiopia. Through his conquest of Egypt, Cambyses became a pharaoh and is so depicted on Egyptian monuments. He also left hieroglyphic texts in the Egyptian manner. Though he favored some Egyptian temples, he reduced the income of many others, thus incurring the hatred of their priests and devotees.

With Persia's conquest of Egypt, it is appropriate to speak of the Jewish community resident there. When the Babylonians advanced on Jerusalem, some Jews fled in the opposite direction toward Egypt. The prophet Jeremiah actually counseled against such action, but in the end he himself was taken there and most likely he died in Egypt. Most of these Jews settled in the northern area of Egypt, in places such as Migdol and Memphis.

But a unique community of Jews existed in far southern Egypt, at a place known alternatively as Syene (see Isaiah 49:12), Elephantine (its later Greek name), or Yeb (the native Egyptian name). Elephantine is an island in the Nile River at the first cataract of the great river, close to modern day Aswan. The origins of this community are not clear, but since there are connections between it and northern

---

11. Friction between a mother country and its offshoots does not mean that one would be willing to attack the other. Frequently the awareness of kinship is stronger than all other considerations. It was probably for such a cause that Jeroboam II (like several other strong kings of Israel) never harmed Judah, although he vanquished his neighbors on virtually every side and could easily have conquered Judah, as far as military considerations went. Friction between Britain and her English-speaking dominions does not mean that the dominions will not stand by the mother country in a crisis. Nor does the accumulation of differences between Britain and the U.S.A. mean that they will not support each other with blood in any serious war for the foreseeable future. Only ignorance of this basic historical fact could have misled the Axis into trying to secure United States' neutrality early in World War II by offering the United States a free hand in (i.e., the conquest of) Canada, Australia, and New Zealand. One does not stab his mother in the back even for material advantage.

Israel, it is very possible that the Jews of Elephantine descend from former inhabitants of the northern kingdom.[12] The most unique aspect of the Jews of Elephantine is that they constructed a temple to Yahwe on the site, a temple that was built before the arrival of the Persians and that stood until 410 B.C.E. (when it was destroyed by zealous Egyptian priests of the god Khnum).[13] Furthermore, the community was syncretistic, as indicated by references to Anat-Bethel and Anat-Yahwe alongside Yahwe alone. The Jews of Elephantine eventually served as garrison troops for the Persian rulers, defending the southern extremity of the realm. Our knowledge of the Jews in this remote corner of the ancient world is greatly enriched by the dozens of Aramaic papyri discovered at the site.[14] Most of the texts deal with basic administrative and legal issues, but there are also important religious issues that arise (such as a letter to the priesthood in Jerusalem requesting information on the proper observance of Passover). In addition, an important Aramaic literary text, the story of Ahiqar, was discovered among the papyri at Elephantine.[15]

In 522 B.C.E., Cambyses' kinsman Darius, then only twenty-eight years old, served Cambyses as a spear bearer in Egypt. In that eventful year Cambyses left Egypt for home. His brother Smerdis (really the Magian Gaumata who impersonated Smerdis whom Cambyses had slain—according to Darius's account) revolted and seized the throne. By canceling three years of taxes and levies, Smerdis won some popular support. On the other hand, his centralizing of the cult occasioned the hostility of those devoted to local shrines. Cambyses died in 521 leaving the rebellious Smerdis as king, but Darius boldly returned to Persia where he gathered a following and proceeded to Media, where he slew Smerdis. Down to 519, Darius had to quell a whole series of revolts throughout the empire; for in time of central weakness, empires tend to disintegrate into their component parts under local nationalistic leadership. Darius's account of the rebellions and his vic-

12. Cyrus H. Gordon, "The Origin of the Jews of Elephantine," *Journal of Near Eastern Studies* 14, 1955, pp. 56–58.

13. The Jews of Elephantine naturally sacrificed sheep, which was an anathema to the devotees of the ram-headed god Khnum.

14. These texts date mainly from the fifth century B.C.E. A standard work on the subject is the series by Bezalel Porten and Ada Yardeni, *Textbook of Aramaic Documents from Ancient Egypt,* Jerusalem, 1986– .

15. The poetic sections of the text, a collection of proverbs, are treated by James M. Lindenberger, *The Aramaic Proverbs of Ahiqar,* Baltimore, 1983.

tories over them is told in his large autobiographical inscription on the rock walls of Behistun. The text is the most extensive and important of the royal Achaemenian inscriptions. It is, like so many of those inscriptions, trilingual, with versions in Old Persian, Elamite, and Babylonian. The decipherment of the Old Persian, which is closely related to Sanskrit and the sacred texts of the Zoroastrian Parsees in India, was the key to the Babylonian version, which in turn opened up all of Akkadian and eventually Sumerian literature. Elamite, being unrelated to any well-known language, is still only partially deciphered. For interprovincial purposes, Aramaic was used, especially west of Iran. Thus part of Darius's autobiography has been found in Aramaic among the Elephantine papyri.

The religion of the Persians was Zoroastrianism, which recognizes a single supreme god, Ahura Mazda (later Ohrmazd).[16] The chief characteristic of Zoroastrianism is an extensive dualism that views world events as the setting for the great battle between the forces of good and the forces of evil. The former are led by Ahura Mazda, while the latter are led by the evil spirit named Angra Mainyu (later Ahriman). The dualism of the Persian overlords had an effect on Jewish theology. Biblical writers of the period make a point of distinguishing between Persian dualism and Jewish monotheism. In the former system, as noted, different entities are responsible for good and evil, thus providing a simple solution to the vexing problem of their simultaneous existence in the world. In a monotheism such as Judaism, however, a different solution to this question must be found. In a reaction to the Persian view, Jewish writers state that Yahwe is responsible for both good and evil (see most importantly Isaiah 45:7). This is an unsettling theological stance, especially for Jews accustomed to viewing their God as the purveyor of good (this is one of the key messages of Genesis 1:1–2, where evil is preexistent and God is responsible for only the good in the world). Accordingly, it did not necessarily remain a dominant position in Judaism.[17] But the whole issue well illustrates an important point to consider: The Hebrew Bible is an anthology, with texts by diverse authors from different

16. The founder of the religion is the great prophet Zoroaster. His exact date still is undetermined, though Iranicists place him very roughly in the period 1000–700 B.C.E. However, there is no reference to Zoroaster in any of the Achaemenian inscriptions.

17. Indeed, the aforecited passage, Isaiah 45:7, is incorporated into the Jewish prayer book, but when it is cited the words "creator of evil" are changed to "creator of everything."

times and different places. We need not expect and of course we do not find in the Bible a monolithic view on theological issues. As we have seen on other occasions (e.g., Ezekiel's discussion of personal responsibility), Jewish writers were constantly grappling with the issues and were subject to the political, historical, and theological developments of the general world around them.

The nature of the Persian Empire made it appropriate for the emperor to have the title "King of Kings" (continued into the most recent past by the last Shahin-Shah "Of-Kings the-King" in modern Iran). It is to this period that Yahwe's title "King of the Kings of Kings," still used in the Jewish prayer book (e.g., in the Alenu prayer), dates.

The Jews took no part in the revolts described above, but many Jews must have regarded those revolts as the disintegration of the World Empire that would be replaced by their own Messianic Kingdom. It may have been such a line of thought that induced the prophet Haggai to instruct Zerubbabel, grandson of Jehoiachin, to begin constructing the Second Temple on the first of the month of Elul 520, while the rebellions were in progress. But whatever illusions of glory any Jews may have cherished, they were rudely dispelled when Iran won and every spark of revolt was extinguished. The gentile World Empire was more firmly established than ever and common sense showed that Judah, far from being the center of the world, would have to remain a little province in a great gentile order. Darius, to be sure, upheld his predecessors' policy of permitting the Jews to reestablish their commonwealth with a Temple. Indeed the only tangible result of the Restoration was the completion of the Temple (and a modest one it was!) on the third of Adar 515.

External conditions were good. The empire provided the basis for trade and public security. But such blessings were small consolation for a frustrated people, whose dreams of their own Messianic World Order had vanished into thin air.

# CHAPTER XVIII

## The Passing of
## Near Eastern Antiquity

When Cyrus the Great issued his decree allowing the Jews to return to Judah to rebuild Jerusalem and the Temple, only a minority of the people responded to the offer. Jews now had been living in exile, either in Babylonia or in Egypt, for at least two generations. Probably they were accustomed to life in these countries, and at least in the case of the Babylonian community, we have evidence that there was some measure of prosperity. Accordingly, only a minority of Jews decided to return to Judah when the opportunity to do so arose.

The Judean community did not possess the power to extricate itself from its poverty and impotence. Its piety went unrewarded (Isaiah 58:3) and even wicked pagans fared better than God's people (note Malachi 3:14–15). But help was to come from the richer Jewish community of Babylonia. There in the East many Jews prospered and some entered government service in which they achieved high positions close to the king. Since the eastern Jews lived among gentiles, they clung all the more tenaciously to their religion. Some doubtless made pilgrimages to Jerusalem (cf. Zechariah 6:10). However, their devotion to the Jewish religion did not blind them to the reality of a great, stable World Empire in which there could be no real restoration of the Jewish nation or state. Thus they were loyal citizens of the Achaemenian Empire and as Jews were interested in Jewish religion rather than Jewish statehood. They used their influence effectively with the Persian government so that Artaxerxes I in

458 authorized Ezra to proceed to Judah to establish the Law of the God of the Heavens (Ezra 7:12, 21, 25).[1]

Ezra, on his mission to stabilize the Judean community, was accompanied on the long road to Jerusalem by some 1,760 Babylonian Jews including not-too-enthusiastic Levites (8:15ff.) and other Temple servitors like the *netinim* (verse 20). The community they found in Judah was pious but badly off. The few well-to-do were concerned with worldly affairs and were entirely too intimate with those outside the fold, including the Samaritans. Ezra decided on a reform that included the putting aside of foreign wives and their children. This brought on the hostility of the non-Judeans, notably of the Samaritans. Thus it became imperative to rebuild the walls of Jerusalem (cf. Ezra 4:13, 21) against the possibility of attack. But Rehum, the governor of Samaria, together with his associates and subjects, convinced Artaxerxes that the walls were preparative to rebellion and to the cessation of paying taxes to the king. The upshot was that the walls of Jerusalem were wrecked anew and Ezra lost his prestige and efficacy as a leader. (See Nehemiah 1:3.)

Late in 446 (?), Nehemiah,[2] a Jew highly placed in the Persian court, heard of the sorry state of affairs in Jerusalem. He appealed to the king, who dispatched him there as governor of Judah. Ezra had been a rather impractical cleric lacking the personality for effective leadership. Nehemiah, on the other hand, was a practical, clearheaded, and model layman with the desire and power to help the Jewish community. He reached Jerusalem in 445 (?) and, after examining the dilapidated walls, summoned the leaders of the people and inspired them to begin enthusiastically the arduous task of reconstruction. Rich and poor responded. Even men like the High Priest Eliashib, who had opposed Ezra's reform, responded to Nehemiah's call. Nehemiah gained considerable popular support among the poor

---

1. That Achaemenian kings took such steps affecting minority religions is also known from Darius II's permit in 419 for celebrating the Passover in Elephantine.

2. We follow the traditional view that Ezra's mission preceded Nehemiah's. However the sequence and chronology of the two leaders have been hotly contested by inconclusive arguments on both sides. The subject is covered with objectivity and full documentation by H. H. Rowley, "The Chronological Order of Ezra and Nehemiah," *Ignace Goldziher Memorial Volume*, I, Budapest, 1948, pp. 117–49. Our adherence to the older view is not prompted by tradition alone. More cogent are considerations arising from the fact that the practical administrator Nehemiah would be needed to straighten out the failure of the impractical scribe Ezra, rather than vice versa.

by proclaiming a remission of debts. Again the Samaritans tried to block the rebuilding program. Thus Sanballat and Tobias (both of whom had connections through marriage with influential Judean families) and Geshem the Arab tried to incite an attack on the builders and capture Nehemiah, but all such machinations were foiled and the task of reconstruction was energetically completed in fifty-two days.

Nehemiah resisted the attempt of Judean fanatics to revive Messianic pretensions for which there could be no place in the Persian Empire. Neither Nehemiah himself, nor any scion of the Davidic House (such as Zerubbabel of whom we hear no more) emerged as the anointed of the Lord. Tactfully Nehemiah (12:38) remained in the background at the popular convocation that he assembled, for as governor he did not want his presence to create an atmosphere of government pressure. His aim was fulfilled by the decision of the people to prohibit business on the Sabbath and holidays, to enforce the sabbatical year with its remission of debts (a boon for the poor debtor class), to contribute each a third shekel head tax to the Temple, to render first fruits and other emoluments to the priests and tithes to the Levites. These decisions on the twenty-fourth of Tishri 445 (?) were in a sense the foundation of the Judaism that lasted till recent times. National aspirations, which had proved unrealistic, were deferred to the far-off golden age of the Messiah. For the time being, Judah would content itself with its life as a religious state, which Josephus (*Contra Apionem* 2:165) later termed a theocracy. No more pretenders to the Davidic throne appeared on the scene. Tribute was paid to the empire that attended to external politics, military affairs, and the security of life and property. But autonomy in religion (and in other internal affairs such as justice) had been secured for Judah by the religious party, whose most influential leaders were Babylonian Jews.

In the ecclesiastical state of Judah, where the Temple was the raison d'être, the priests soon became the wealthy elite who assumed the leadership over the council of elders for administration and justice. The High Priest, who alone was acknowledged to have direct contact with Yahwe, mediated between God and the people. (Prophecy came to an end during this period; the last of the biblical prophets is Malachi.) The function of the laity was to support the Temple so that its service should be kept up. Laymen had to be content with the role of spectators and worshipers obedient to the divine Law.

Nehemiah's work of 445 (?) proved to lack sufficient momentum. After the distinguished layman departed, public laxity set in. Accordingly, he returned to Judah in 433 (?). This time he ordered the gates of Jerusalem closed on the Sabbath to prevent merchants from entering to profane the holy day. Intermarriage, some of which was unpreventable, had led to some Jews no longer being able to speak Hebrew (13:24). Priests were illegally taking the tithes that were the Levites' due. The High Priest was much too closely allied with Samaritan chiefs including Tobias, whom he invested with the collection of priestly income and to whom he assigned a room in the Temple. A grandson[3] of Eliashib married the Samaritan Sanballat's daughter and preferred to leave Judah rather than to give up his wife and Samaritan contacts. In any case, Nehemiah (13:28) expelled him but tactfully refrains from giving his name. It has been plausibly suggested that he was none other than Manasseh, the first High Priest in Shechem in accordance with a tradition (Josephus, *Antiquities* 11:302ff.) containing a kernel of historic truth. In any case it was in that period that the rupture between Samaritans and Jews became irreparable and that the Samaritan heresy became firmly established. As often happens in sectarian splits, close neighbors like the Samaritans and the Jews, with very similar beliefs, rituals, and laws, became mortal enemies.

The major difference, of course, was the identification of God's Holy Mountain, with the Jews recognizing Mount Zion in Jerusalem and the Samaritans claiming Mount Gerizim near Shechem (modern day Nablus). Though the Samaritans were numerically significant for centuries (as is implied, for example, in the New Testament), they could have no real future, because their religion was that of the Jews, and withal they were not Jews.

Other factors also played a role in the continuity of the Jewish people versus the rather sad later history of the Samaritans. Judaism to a great extent began to depend on its communities in the Diaspora (i.e., the dispersal of the Jews beyond the limits of the land of Israel) and not on the homeland community. This factor is heightened in Jewish history in the era after the destruction of the Second Temple by the Romans in 70 C.E. The Samaritans, by contrast, remained very

---

3. A son of Jehoiada, son of Eliashib.

much a people singularly devoted to their holy site. But as the land of Israel no longer held center stage in world history, again, largely in the post–70 C.E. era, the Samaritans themselves began to disappear.

Still another factor is the developing canon within Judaism and among the Samaritans. The latter canonized only the Torah (and held also the book of Joshua in esteem), but never increased the size of their Holy Scriptures. The Jews, by contrast, added the prophetic corpus to the Torah (and eventually a third grouping as well, the Writings). The prophets, as we have seen, imbued the religion of ancient Israel with an optimism and a hope for a better future unparalleled in world religion. Jews devoted to the reading of the Prophets alongside the Torah grasped that optimism and saw reason for continuing. The Samaritans, alas, without the prophetic view of world history, were doomed to the extinction now confronting their tiny remnant (recent estimates suggest no more than one thousand Samaritans today, in the two cities of Nablus and Holon).

The Judean high priesthood did not have a model record. Eliashib's grandson Johanan murdered his own brother Jeshua (or Joshua) in the Temple to hold on to the high priesthood which Jeshua wanted to take away from him with Persian help. As a punishment the Persian governor Bagoaz laid a tax of 50 drachmas on the daily sacrifice of a lamb.

The incorporation of new blood from the outside, although against the professed policy of the Commonwealth, was instrumental in strengthening the Jews to the extent that they could surmount the early obstacles that beset them. Gradually the Jews expanded into Philistia and later, in Greek times, into Transjordan and Galilee. The official view prohibited the admission of Moabites and Ammonites into the congregation of God (Nehemiah 13:1) but there was a more liberal view against such discrimination (Isaiah 56:3). The expansion of the Jews meant that the High Priest, presiding in Jerusalem over the assembly of ecclesiastical and civil leaders, was growing in importance with the spread of his followers.

As the end of the Book of Nehemiah shows, Judah was set up strictly as an ecclesiastical entity. The community there was not the main body of Jewry. The Diaspora was ever widening. From Babylonia, Jews spread to Susa, Media, and westward to all the provinces of the World Empire (Esther 3:8; 8:17; 9:2–3, 16). Those Jews, no matter how separated they were, retained their Jewish identity so that they were different from the rest of the population (Esther 3:8). As is sometimes the case with minorities,[4] the Jews were enterprising and successful both in private business and in government service.

The prime evidence for enterprising Jews in the business world comes from the Murashu texts, a set of cuneiform documents found at Nippur, in southern Mesopotamia, dated to the fifth century B.C.E. The texts record the activities of a large Babylonian banking firm. In the employ of this company were many Jews, present not only in Nippur but in about two dozen other communities in the area.[5]

The success of various Jews in government service is to be explained as follows: since the Jews were not bound by close ties to their gentile neighbors, they were free to serve the king without conflicting loyalties. Thus men like Nehemiah or Mordecai[6] were in a position to serve their king well, to attain positions of influence, and to secure royal protection for their coreligionists when necessary. This, of course, stirred up jealousy and hatred so that with the Diaspora appears anti-Semitism. As long as the Hebrews were a nation on their own soil, they had normal feuds and friendships with their neighbors, like all other nations. But anti-Semitism is a product of the Diaspora, as exemplified by Haman, the villain in the Book of Esther.

While it lies beyond the scope of our investigation to give a detailed account of the Achaemenian Empire,[7] it is fitting to outline its origins, culture, and history in order to fill in in greater detail the environment that existed toward the end of the biblical period.

Indo-Europeans appear on the Near East scene shortly after 2000 B.C.E. While their chief representatives are the Hittites, the Mitannian kings and gods often bear Indo-European names. The Hyksos hordes included Indo-European warriors. With the Indo-Europeans the horse, effectively used for pulling the war chariot, entered the Near

4. The Friends and Mormons in America, and the Parsees of India, are modern examples of such minorities.

5. Michael D. Coogan, "Life in the Diaspora: Jews at Nippur in the Fifth Century B.C.," *Biblical Archaeologist* 37, 1974, pp. 6–12.

6. Regardless of the historicity of the story of Esther, the book is reliable as a mirror of Achaemenian times. We have every reason to believe that Jews like Mordecai who attained high positions at court (like Nehemiah) were not rare.

7. A very valuable book on the subject is A. T. Olmstead, *History of the Persian Empire,* Chicago, 1948. For the Jewish aspect, see Elias Bickerman, *From Ezra to the Last of the Maccabees,* New York, 1962; and the individual essays in W. D. Davies and L. Finkelstein, eds., *Cambridge History of Judaism,* vol. I, Cambridge, 1984.

East and revolutionized the art of warfare. The Iranian plateau was to become a great stamping ground of the Aryans (as we may call the segment of the Indo-Europeans to which the Iranians belong).

As is the case with so many countries, the earliest written records on Iran are cuneiform. In 836 B.C.E. Shalmaneser invaded the mountains of western Iran and subdued, among others, a few Median tribes.[8] The height of Assyrian power in western Iran came under Sargon, who in 715 exiled the Median chief Dayuku and forced over twenty Median city-states to pay tribute in Nineveh. By 713 those tributaries increased to forty-odd. The Sargonid kings continued the Assyrian grip on Media until the decline that set in toward the close of Assurbanipal's long reign (668–631?), when Media first emerges as a great power. Under Cyaxares, Median sovereignty extended from Iran to Asia Minor and had a rival on the world scene only in Babylonia. Cyrus of Persia upset the equilibrium when he rebelled against his Median master Astyages, the son of Cyaxares, and within three years defeated him at Pasargade (in Persis) and later captured the Median capital of Ecbatana. Since Cyrus disregarded the treaties made by Media, he was opposed by a coalition that included Nabonidus of Babylon, Amasis of Egypt, Croesus of Lydia, and the Spartans. By vanquishing Croesus in 546 B.C.E., Cyrus's borders were extended to the Mediterranean. His victory over Nabonidus in 539 made him master of Western Asia down to the Egyptian border. Cambyses in 525 added Egypt to the empire and pushed up the Nile into Africa until his expedition against the Ethiopian Kingdom of Napata and Meroe came to grief but not before he established the span of the Achaemenian realm "from India to Ethiopia" (Esther 1:1).

The phenomenal success of the Iranians was due in part to strong leadership and to the effective use of archers, whose shower of arrows kept the enemy at a distance. Iranian infantrymen carried lances and daggers for engaging the foe at close range, while the cavalry, skilled by the long attachment of the Aryans to the war horse, supplied maneuverability when it was needed. Iranian military successes were first checked by the Greeks at Marathon. The Greek phalanx proved to be fatal to the Iranians whose hail of arrows was at last answered; for with the phalanx Alexander the Great ended the Achaemenian Empire.

While Darius I and to a lesser extent Xerxes I made minor exten-

8. The Medes (like the Persians) are a division of the Iranians.

sions in the imperial borders, the limits of the empire were basically established by Cyrus and Cambyses.

The Achaemenians had the majestic plan to rule rightly over a united world. The mild treatment they accorded their conquered subjects is admirable. The Persians of the homeland enjoyed a privileged position. They offered "first fruits" and other gifts to the king, but not outright taxes. In exchange for those offerings, given on holidays, the king would present his fellow Persians with gifts. To be sure, the privilege of being Persian went hand in hand with the duty to render military service.

The number of Achaemenian capitals seems at first confusing. In the district of Pasargade, Cyrus built a town, palace, and tomb; the tomb is still standing almost intact near the modern village of Murghab. Upon the conquest of Babylonia, however, Babylon became the real capital of the Achaemenian Empire and it was from there that the kings generally ruled the empire during the winter months. Darius I and Artaxerxes II erected great palaces at Susa (in Elam), which was also used as a capital during the winter months. The story of the Book of Esther is set in Susa. Darius I, however, replaced Cyrus's Persian[9] capital at Pasargade with a new capital of unprecedented splendor at Persepolis.[10] There the king celebrated and received homage on the New Year, which until very recently was the greatest occasion on the Iranian calendar (at times celebrated for no less than thirteen days). Other kings, notably Xerxes I, embellished and augmented the buildings of Persepolis. Ecbatana was also a capital, probably in the hot summer when Babylon and Susa are unbearable[11] but Ecbatana, at an elevation of over 6,000 feet, is comfortable. It was by Mount Elvend, south of the city, that Darius and Xerxes

9. By Persian we here mean pertaining to Persis (= the modern province of Fars), the homeland of the Achaemenians.

10. Persepolis was the "home" residence of the king in his native province. It was too remote to serve as a capital of the empire, for which a more central location (such as Babylon's) was called for.

11. Well-to-do natives keep cool by seeking refuge in deep cellars. American veterans of the World War II Persian Gulf Command (of which the author [C. H. G.] is one) do not have to be convinced of the summer heat in the area. Around Dizful (near Susa), there are flies in winter but none in midsummer when the heat is too much for them. More than one army doctor, on his first day of duty there, took a patient's temperature, set the thermometer down for a minute (not realizing the room temperature was between 110° to 120° Fahrenheit) and when looking at it, fearfully marveled at how the patient was alive with a temperature in excess of what the thermometer is made to indicate.

built residences. Both monarchs lavished much effort on constructing the royal residences at Persian Persepolis and Median Ecbatana, perhaps with a view to cementing the union of the Medes and Persians on which Achaemenian power was based.

The king had seven counselors (Ezra 7:14; Esther 1:14). Under Darius I the realm was divided into twenty satrapies each of which was subdivided into administrative provinces; note the 127 provinces ascribed to Xerxes in Esther 1:1. We have seen in the case of Judah how such districts enjoyed a great measure of autonomy, often under native sons. Yet at the same time there was an atmosphere of despotism because there were occasions (however rare they might be) when the central government or the satraps would strip the helpless subjects of their rights and privileges.

Court officials and the troops were paid in kind and were fed at government expense ("they ate at the king's table" as the idiom goes). They also received land grants and other royal gifts as a reward for meritorious service. Greek mercenaries, however, were paid in coinage. Thus for them and certain other enterprises the king had to have money. The governors took contributions for their table at which officials ate (Nehemiah 5:14). Gold was minted only by the king, but less precious metal could be cast into currency by local rulers such as satraps.

The Book of Esther is a valuable mirror of the Achaemenian court and times. The scene is laid in Susa the capital, during the reign of Xerxes (Esther 1:1–2). The author knows of the seven nobles who enjoy the intimacy and confidence of the king (Esther 1:14). He also knows that in Iran the Law was immutable (8:8).[12] He is familiar with the channels of empire administration (8:9). The book is full of Persian words. But it has escaped the attention of scholars that Esther gives the earliest evidence of a distinctively Iranian institution that has survived down to modern Islamic times in Iranian Shiism, as the doctrine of *kitmân* or *taqiyya* that we may translate as "dissimulation." This doctrine permits one to deny his religion and pose as a member of another religion to avoid personal danger. Thus, Iranian Shiites are allowed to pose as Sunnites when they make the pilgrimage to Mecca, which is in the hands of Arab Sunnites who on occasion

---

12. As we have noted above, the Judeans began their unbroken tradition of regarding the Law as final only in 621 B.C.E. Among the Gentiles, the Achaemenian kings of the Medes and Persians are the first on record to regard the Law so strictly.

show violent antipathy toward Shiites. In Iran itself religious minorities often pose as Shiites for self-preservation. Thus sometimes Jews and Christians, and frequently Bahais, parade as Shiites. Westerners who have been raised to admire martyrdom and to frown upon denying one's faith consider "dissimulation" contemptible, but in Iran it fits into the regulated mores. Esther (2:10) hides her Jewish affiliations without any qualms very much in the spirit of Iranian dissimulation; and when the tables are turned and the Iranian majority have reason to fear the Jews, the Iranian gentiles pretend to be Jews (8:17).[13] The doctrine of dissimulation, instead of being an Islamic innovation, may well be an Iranian survival in Shiism.

Darius commissioned a Carian captain named Scylax to explore the Indus River. After doing so, Scylax circumnavigated Arabia and sailed to Suez. He wrote the narrative of his itinerary in Greek. Darius completed the canal from the Nile to Suez and celebrated the feat in texts pointing out that it had become possible "for ships to sail direct from the Nile to Persia via Saba ( = South Arabia)." Thus the Indian and Egyptian extremities of the World Empire were connected by water.

We have noted how tolerant the Achaemenians were in matters of religion. This secured local support throughout the empire for the government through the various priesthoods. With slight lapses, Iranian favor toward the Jews can be traced from reign to reign. Cyrus authorized the Restoration; Darius I confirmed it; Artaxerxes I in sponsoring Ezra and Nehemiah enabled them to bolster it.

Zoroastrianism was geared to tolerance, for it made a place for foreign gods as helpers of Ahura Mazda. This, to be sure, resulted in other religions influencing Ahura Mazdaism. Although Zoroastrianism from the start was a missionizing religion, it was checked at the Iranian borders by the fact that its sacred writings were not available in translation. Judaism, on the other hand, developed a facility for translating the Hebrew Scriptures, into Aramaic Targumim (as the Aramaic versions are called) and, under the Ptolemies, into Greek. While Judaism eventually gave up its missionary work, it provided Christianity with a ready-made apparatus for reaching the gentiles through translation, first in Greek, then in Latin, and finally in innumerable modern languages. Zoroastrianism, in spite of its failure to

13. Rather than "became Jews" as the English translations would have it. The verbal conjugation (known as "hithpael") can convey the meaning of pretending.

become a world religion, has many features that look like developments in postbiblical Judaism, Christianity, and Islam. The effective dualism, whereby the good god Ahura Mazda is now battling, but in the end of days will conquer, the evil deity Ahriman is if anything clearer cut than New Testament or Qur'anic dualism, where God's influence is prominently opposed to Satan's. Furthermore, Zoroastrianism had the motif of the Savior, who in the end of days will help Ahura Mazda triumph over the forces of evil. Yet it can be shown that Christianity inherited such features from Judaism, not from Zoroastrianism. Specifically there is evidence that Jewish, Christian, and Islamic dualistic trends did not originate in, but may have been heightened by Zoroastrianism.[14]

As so often happens in religion, minor gods become more popular than the head(s) of the pantheon. Just as the young Baal eclipsed the old El and the maiden Anat eclipsed the mother goddess Asherah; in Iran Anahita, the goddess of the springs,[15] and Mithra, the sun-god,[16] grew in importance so that Artaxerxes II and III (unlike the earlier kings) mention them in addition to Ahura Mazda.

A World Empire must be international. This is reflected in Iranian art. Cyrus's constructions at Pasargade are relatively national Persian; whereas those of Darius and Xerxes at Susa and Persepolis have incorporated more Babylonian, Greek, and Egyptian elements, plus elements from Asia Minor in the rock sculptures around Persepolis. The fusing of these elements into an organic unity make Persepolis one of the greatest accomplishments in world architecture. The Achaemenians followed Babylonian precedent not only in architecture and design but in the policy of employing foreign craftsmen. Since the art and artisans were those of a World Empire, when the empire collapsed, its art perished with it.

Although the Persians controlled the empire, their success depended in great measure on Greek armies and Greek generals. Not

---

14. See Cyrus H. Gordon, "Near Eastern Seals in Princeton and Philadelphia," *Orientalia* 22, 1953, pp. 243–44; and David Winston, "The Iranian Component in the Bible, Apocrypha, and Qumran," *History of Religions* 5, 1966, pp. 183–216. For general discussion see also Edwin Yamauchi, *Persia and the Bible,* Grand Rapids, Mich., 1990, pp. 458–66.

15. On the Iranian plateau the scarcity of water naturally favored her rise to prominence.

16. Love of the sun is common enough in many parts of the world but nowhere more than in Iran down to the present. Iranian students abroad have been known to become so depressed by rain and fog, and miss their native Iranian sunshine so much, that in extreme cases they have committed suicide.

only Greek mercenaries but also Greek traders and artisans spread Greek civilization. An index of what was taking place in the empire is supplied by the coins of Phoenicia and Asia Minor, where the art and inscriptions on the coins witness the impact of Hellenism. Greek leaders became increasingly aware of the shame whereby Greek talent was being exploited for maintaining an empire for Iran. The Greeks, talented though they were, were cursed with disunity. By playing off one Greek faction against the other, Iran neutralized Greek potentialities.

Darius I (521–485) and Xerxes I (485–465) came to grips with Greece and failed, so that the Aegean Sea became the focal spot of the world scene. Corruption and intrigue grew apace in Iran to the detriment of the empire. Thus Xerxes I was murdered by his Vizier Artabanus. Artaxerxes I (465–425) has been alluded to as probably the king of that name in whose reign Ezra's and Nehemiah's activity took place. The ephemeral reigns of Xerxes II and Sogdianus fell in 425–424. Darius II (Nothus), who ruled from 424 to 404, is of special interest since many of the Elephantine papyri date from his reign. It was he who authorized the Jews of Elephantine to celebrate the Passover in 419. In his fourteenth year (410) some Egyptians and Persians attacked the Jews of Elephantine. They destroyed the temple there and carried off the sacred cult objects. Jedoniah, the head of the community, and his associates wrote a long letter in 407 stating that the destroyed temple dated from before Cambyses' conquest (525) and that they had written to the Jerusalem High Priest Johanan (cf. Nehemiah 12:22, 23) but had gotten no reply. It is probable that the Jerusalem High Priest did not favor the existence of rival temples, but did not dare say so because a government tolerant in religious affairs could scarcely be expected to allow a religious community to suppress its adherents in other parts of the empire. Besides, the Samaritans, whose leaders were also influential in Persian circles in the land of Israel, had a temple. What was most important, however, was the undeniable fact that Jerusalem depended on the exiles of Babylonia for support, so that the High Priest could scarcely afford to deny the right of Jews outside Israel to have a place of worship. Disapproving of the Elephantine temple, but not daring to maintain the principle of Jerusalem exclusivism, perhaps the best way out was to leave Jedoniah's letter unanswered. Jedoniah also wrote to Deliah and Shelemiah, the sons of Sanballat, which shows that, as seen from Egypt, the Samaritans no less than the Judeans were reckoned as coreligionists of the Elephantine Jews, who had left Israel before the irreparable break in Judeo-Samaritan relations had developed. From 410 to 407, when the letter was written, the Elephantine Jews were in mourning for their demolished temple. Finally the permit came from Deliah and Bagoaz, the Persian governor in Judea, to rebuild the Elephantine temple.

In the reign of Artaxerxes II Memnon (404–359) the empire faced dissolution[17] but Artaxerxes III Ochus (359–338) reunited the empire and restored it to its full limits. His barbarism led him to exterminate nearly all of his own family before he himself was poisoned by the eunuch Bagoaz. After the short reign of Arses (338–336), who resented Bagoaz's power and was therefore poisoned by him, Darius III (336–330) came to the throne. It was in the same year (336) that Philip of Macedon, who had united some of Greece, set out to liberate the Greek cities from Iranian domination but was assassinated before he could fulfill his plan. Philip was succeeded by his brilliant son, Alexander, in the same year that Darius III became king. In 334 Darius reconquered Egypt, which had revolted. An eyewitness might little have realized that the great Achaemenian Empire that had dominated the world for over two centuries was about to vanish. In that same year of 334 Alexander set out with his army, and a staff of scientists and authors, to conquer the Persian Empire. His father had begun his plan to strengthen Macedonia by incorporating his immediate neighbors. Then he launched on the crusade so dear to the hearts of all Greek nationalists: to free the Greek cities. Alexander not only fulfilled his father's plan but proceeded on the grander project of conquering the Achaemenian World Order. After subjugating Asia Minor, he pushed on through Syria and captured Tyre in 332. Tyre, on a fortified isle just off the coast, had resisted every earlier attack and siege; but Alexander joined it to the mainland by a causeway so that it is now a little cape instead of an island. Thence he moved south to Gaza and to Egypt, which he annexed to his rapidly growing empire. At Gaugamela, near Erbil in Assyria, he defeated Darius's army in 331. As a finishing touch he burned Persepolis in 330 and thus avenged the Persian burning of Greek Athens. It lies beyond our subject to go into the details of Alexander's short-lived empire. Judah seesawed between the Ptolemaic and Seleucid kingdoms in what had

17. For example, Egypt regained its independence under Nekhtenebef (378–360) and his son Jedhor (360–359) and the latter's nephew, Nekhtharhebi (359–340).

been Alexander's empire. Greek Europe and the Near East fused more intimately than ever before, and the union was destined to produce glorious results, ranging from the science of Alexandria to the Christianity modestly born in Judaism but sensationally spread among gentiles on all three continents of the Old World.

The Hellenistic Age, ushered in by Alexander, wrought profound cultural changes throughout the East.[18] Greek influence on the art and science of the Near East is unmistakable. Entirely Hellenistic cities were founded in the Near East (most notably Alexandria in Egypt). One minor point may serve to illustrate the extent of Hellenistic influence. In the Near Eastern tradition authorship of texts typically was anonymous; this will explain why the authors of the books of the Hebrew Bible are not mentioned by name.[19] The first Jewish author whom we know by name is the man known as Ben Sira, the author of the book known to Christians either as Sirach or Ecclesiasticus (one of the Apocrypha, canonical in the Roman Catholic and Eastern Orthodox traditions), who lived c. 180 B.C.E. Another result of Hellenistic influence may be seen in the sphere of writing. Alphabetic scripts replaced the old native systems of writing, with the result that Babylonian cuneiform died out in the first century C.E. and left the burden of literacy to Aramaic. Egyptian eventually began to be written in Greek letters and entered the Coptic stage of the Egyptian language. Knowledge of the hieroglyphs persisted into Roman times, but then lapsed into oblivion. Both cuneiform and hieroglyphic texts remained closed books until they were deciphered in the nineteenth century.[20]

During the Hellenistic period the uppercrust of Near Eastern society began to speak Greek. In the Bible, specifically in the Aramaic portion of Daniel, written c. 165 B.C.E., there are several examples of Greek loanwords, specifically names of musical instruments (*sumponya, psanterin,* etc., in 3:5, 7, 15). In Hebrew compositions from the following centuries, we encounter dozens of loanwords from Greek (as well as from Latin). But the masses in the Near East retained their

18. The Hellenistic Age may well be regarded as the pivotal era of Western civilization. Into it funneled the main streams of the past: Babylonian, Jewish, Iranian, Egyptian, Greek, Roman, etc. Out of it came Late Roman, Byzantine, Islamic, and Medieval civilization.

19. Apparently, even the individual prophets did not ascribe their names to their works. Instead, superscriptions (introductory verses) were added later to identify the compositions.

20. On the decipherments of these and other Near Eastern scripts and languages, see Cyrus H. Gordon, *Forgotten Scripts: Their Ongoing Discovery and Decipherment,* New York, 1982.

native languages: The Semites of Asia spoke mainly Aramaic; the Egyptians spoke Coptic; and the North Africans spoke Berber and Punic (in contrast not only to Greek but also to Latin).

With the coming of Islam in the seventh century C.E., this picture changed dramatically, for the Arabs of the Arabian peninusla brought with them not only their religion but also the Arabic language. In time, languages such as Coptic and Punic died out as spoken languages. On the other hand, small islands of Aramaic speakers remain to this day in Syria, Iraq, Iran, and Turkey; and across North Africa Berber (akin to the ancient language of the Libyans with whom the Egyptians fought) is still spoken by millions. Furthermore, the Christians of the Near East more often use Syriac (a branch of Aramaic) rather than Greek in their liturgies. And Coptic continues to the present as the liturgical language of the Christians of Egypt. These exceptions aside, Arabic has been the dominant language of the Near East for more than a millennium.

But while the languages of the ancient Near East gradually have given way to Arabic, the spirit of the ancient Near East lives on in the Islamic East of today. Without knowing why, the Arab in Canaan still calls rain-fed land *baal* after the fertility god of ancient Canaan, a testimony to the tenacity of Near Eastern tradition. Much more important is the fact that much of old Mesopotamian law eventually was incorporated into the legal systems of Judaism and Islam, as evidenced by the Babylonian Talmud of the former and the *Fiqh* (legal system) of the latter.[21] Many other manifestations of the persistence of antiquity could be pointed out; perhaps the most important (and most elusive) survival lies in the realm of social psychology.

By the Hellenistic Age, the period of the Hebrew Bible is virtually over.[22] The Jews, in admitting books to the Canon, regarded the Achaemenian Age as the last in which books could be divinely inspired. Daniel, by claiming to have been written by a man whose career spanned Nebuchadnezzar's and Darius's reigns, managed to enter the Canon even though it is of the Greek age. The book contains such grotesque errors concerning the Neo-Babylonian and

21. The influence of Greek and Roman law on Jewish and Islamic jurisprudence should be tempered with an awareness of the impact of ancient Near Eastern law.

22. The Hellenization of Judaism is abundantly evident not only when it is in Greek dress, such as in the writings of Philo or Josephus. Even in normative rabbinic Judaism, the wisdom of the sages, in form and to a lesser extent in content, is more nearly akin to the teachings of Epictetus than to the wisdom literature of the Bible.

Achaemenian empires that as a historic source for those periods Daniel is of quite limited value. One of the faux pas is that Belshazzar (erroneously called the son of Nebuchadnezzar) was the king of Babylon when Cyrus conquered it. Actually the Babylonian king was Nabonidus but since Daniel is widely read as a biblical book, there are probably more people who think Prince Belshazzar was the king than there are people who have ever heard of Nabonidus.

While it had been in vogue to date various parts of the Hebrew Bible to Hellenistic times, there is really very little that can be convincingly attributed to any time after the passing of the Achaemenians. The big exception is Daniel which, as noted above, has Greek words and references to Greek history. The book, which is a unity as it stands, follows the ABA pattern; starting in Hebrew, continuing in Aramaic, and ending in Hebrew.[23] To separate the Hebrew and Aramaic portions of the book, as some scholars are wont to do, is to shut our eyes to the stylistic plan of the book in ABA form. The King of Greece (Daniel 8:21) refers to Alexander the Great, and the Four Kingdoms (8:22) refer to the major parts into which his empire was fragmentized after his death. The purpose of the book is eschatological: to discover what will happen in the end of days (2:28) when God's incorruptible Kingdom, which He will never forsake to the gentiles, shall smash the tyrants of the earth and abide forever (2:44). In Daniel, the latest book of the Hebrew Bible, appear phenomena not to be found in early Hebrew literature. The anonymity of angels (as we have noted in the periods of the Patriarchs and Judges) has given way to the beginning of a complicated angelology destined to take hold in Judaism, Christianity, and Islam. Thus Michael is the guardian angel of Israel (12:1). The early idea that all men went alike to spend eternity in a dreary Sheol has now given way to the idea that the worthy will be resurrected for life eternal while the wicked are destined for everlasting damnation (12:2). The frustrations of the Jewish people had evoked these new developments. Apocalyptic extravagances were fostered to perpetuate the hope that earthly tyranny would be replaced by the Kingdom of God on earth. Men had so little satisfaction in a world full of dislocations that a personal afterlife was created to help them bear the agony of this world.

23. The Aramaic of the book of Daniel is virtually identical with what scholars call Imperial Aramaic, the international form of the language used throughout the Persian and Greek Empires.

The merging of the Near East with classical Europe brings us to the close of Near East antiquity, including the end of ancient Israelite history. The last of the native empires (namely, the Achaemenian) was the largest of the ancient Near East. But it was the small Jewish minority in that empire that was to exert profound and ever renewed influence on the world of the future.

# CHAPTER XIX

# The Hebrew Bible
# in the Making

Tribal and illiterate people are often prompt to celebrate current events in song. When I [C. H. G.] first visited Palestine in 1931, I heard Arab villagers already singing ballads about the Muslim-Jewish riots of 1929. In antiquity, epic celebration of history often preceded prose accounts. The Greeks had their Homer long before their Herodotus and Thucydides. The King of Battle epic proclaimed the conquests of Sargon of Akkad before there were any prose annals of the Assyrian kings. Even after a nation gets scribes to transform speech into more permanent records, there is often a long lag until the urge arises to supplant epic history with the more factual prose history. The epic precursors leave their mark on prose historiography; the origin of poetic literature therefore impinges on the origin of historic writing.

The ancient epics of which we have actual transcripts embrace notably those in cuneiform and those ascribed to Homer. As we have noted in Chapter VII, the impact of cuneiform tradition was brought to bear on the Ionians via the Hittites and other Asianic[1] people. This influence is in keeping with the general trend of cultural progress from east to west in antiquity. But there is an important exception to this trend: The Sea Peoples from the Mediterranean invaded the Asiatic mainland and so constitute a cultural movement from west to east during the latter half of the second millennium.[2] The Caphtorian

1. "Asianic" refers to Asia Minor.

2. The Sea Peoples movements may be related in part to the Indo-European migrations from the East. The Indic epics called the Ramayana and Mahabharata have close ties with ancient

impact on craftsmanship is universally recognized[3]; but it is equally true that the Caphtorians made literary contributions to Canaan.[4] Moreover, the close connections between the literature of Ugarit and Homer are due in large measure to the Caphtorian element that spans them. Also, the fact that Ugaritic, of all known literatures, lies closest to the Bible is due not only to the circumstance that both are products of the land of Canaan, but also in part because Caphtorian influence bridges Ugarit and Israel.

That not only the poetry but even the prose of the Bible betrays epic antecedents has been evident from formal considerations.[5] The advanced literary stage of even the earliest Hebrew literature is due to the fact that the Hebrews on entering Canaan adopted the already highly developed literary tradition of the land. Naturally, the Ugaritic corpus of literary texts is poetic, whereas the biblical narratives are in prose. But snippets of early epic poetry have been preserved in the Bible, for example, Exodus 15 and Judges 5 (each of which has a prose parallel, Exodus 14 and Judges 4, respectively). Accordingly, at some point Hebrew literature shifted from the earlier poetic epics to the canonical prose narratives (perhaps under the influence of Egyptian literary convention, in which prose narrative is well developed).

To illustrate the vestiges of epic form in the transformed prose Hebrew version, we need cite only a single example. The Bible preserves a dual tradition that David was the seventh son of Jesse (1 Chronicles 2:15) or the eighth (1 Samuel 16:10–11). This points to a poetic origin with the device of climaxing "7" with "8" parallelistically, a usage attested in both Ugaritic and Hebrew poetry.

That the epic forerunners of the Hebrew prose narratives are attested formally is too well known to require further demonstration here; but that they are attested also in content is sufficiently new to warrant some documentation.

East Mediterranean epic. Hebrew history and literature, from the Patriarchal beginnings, are products of the Canaan that had been transformed by the Indo-European migrations. See Cyrus H. Gordon, "Indo-European and Hebrew Epic," *Eretz-Israel* 5, 1958, pp. 10–15.

3. For example, the Hebrew word for the capital of a column is *kaptor.*

4. "Caphtorian" is the Canaanite term for "Aegean." Both the Bible and the Ugaritic tablets refer to the cultural center in the East Mediterranean as "Caphtor" (though possibly in some instances the word refers specifically to Crete). The Egyptians likewise used the same term, though typically it is rendered as "Keftiu" (probably reflecting loss of final -*r* in Late Egyptian especially).

5. For an excellently documented statement, see U. Cassuto, *The Goddess Anath,* 2d edition, Jerusalem, 1953.

The interrelations of the surviving expressions of ancient epic are evident not only from the details (cf. Chapters VI–IX, XI) but also from basic motifs. Gilgamesh, Achilles, and Kret are, though of at least partly divine extraction, destined to die. Moreover, their anticipated death is the subject of epic regret. Gilgamesh and Achilles (whose actual deaths are suppressed with artistic restraint) are compensated with immortal fame. Kret's mortality, however, is compensated with the continuance of his line through progeny. The latter solution of the classic tragedy of man's futile quest for personal immortality is already hinted in the Gilgamesh Epic, where Gilgamesh (X: iii:1–14) is told to give up his wild-goose chase for divinity and content himself with the comforts and realities of wife and child. Furthermore, the twelfth and last tablet of the Gilgamesh Epic stresses Enkidu's message from the underworld to the effect that a man's welfare postmortem is in direct proportion to the sons he has left on earth.

The Ugaritic treatment of the topic of progeny can be outlined in some detail: There may be difficulty in securing the right bride (thus in Kret). The progeny is promised by divine annunciations and blessing (Kret and Aqhat). The biological process is supplemented with religious rites: incubation, direct divine revelation to the prospective father as to the necessary sacrifices. After sons are born, there is a preference for the youngest at the expense of the firstborn (in Kret). We are thus confronted with the fact that the Ugaritic legends of Aqhat and Kret reflect a pervading element of the patriarchal narratives; to wit, the divine promise of progeny. Difficulty in securing the right bride is overcome by Isaac and Jacob. Annunciations start with Hagar before Ishmael's birth. Divine blessings with promise of progeny typify the narratives of all three Patriarchs. Abraham (quite like Kret and Daniel) receives direct instructions from God as to the proper rituals, which are combined with incubation (Genesis 15:1–12). And after the birth of sons, the junior may be preferred to the senior; thus Jacob is preferred to Esau (as subsequently Perez to Zerah, Ephraim to Manasseh, and David to all his brothers). However, all claim to divine ancestry or to personal immortality is lacking in the Patriarchal narratives. The quest for immortality is realistically and completely solved through progeny. Preoccupation with the birth of a son remains a theme in the history of notable men down to the end of the Period of the Judges. In the case of Samson, the annunciation is still via a divine entity; in the instance of Samuel, the prediction is through the priest Eli, reflecting the development whereby direct communion between laity and God became supplanted by mediation of divine messages through priests and prophets.

The direct mingling of men and gods is of a piece in Ugarit and the patriarchal narratives. Thus Abraham and Sarah, quite like the Ugaritic Daniel and his wife Dnty, entertain god(s) for dinner in natural fashion. When we come to Moses, the contact is shrouded in a supernatural aura. Samson's parents, to be sure, serve a sacrificial meal to a deity but it is consumed supernaturally and not like the dinners served to the divine guests of Daniel or Abraham. In the Bible, crass personal contact between men and God is gradually eliminated so that even His words must be mediated by His special human representatives, the prophets. The earlier direct relationship between men and gods is common to all the epics: Mesopotamian, Ugaritic, Greek, and "Proto-Patriarchal." The later barriers grew hand in hand with factual historiography and religious vested interests.

If the Patriarchal cycle is the epic of The Birth of a Family, the Exodus is that of The Birth of a Nation. The historic kernel of the Exodus should not be questioned. It fits into the general framework of Egypto-Asiatic relations, whereby famine in Canaan impelled Semites repeatedly to seek bread in the Nile Valley regardless of the price. The end of any famine in Canaan might be the signal for many an exodus. That *the* Exodus is handled in an epic manner no more disproves its historicity than Homer's epic manner disproves the historicity of the Trojan War. Often the epic manner calls for elaborating specific details whose historicity is banal rather than marvelous. What could be more commonplace than a supply of bread before a planned mass movement? Yet this is singled out for epic celebration in Kret: 79–84, 171–75. Accordingly, the prominence given to the baking of *maṣṣa*,[6] "unleavened bread," in the Exodus was evoked by the repertoire of the epic tradition in which the Exodus was celebrated.

Of course there are epic features that do not fit into the matrix of reality. Thus when we read that the clothes of the Israelites did not

---

6. This word appears in Greek as *maza*. The spread of such words over the Northwest Semitic speech area as well as Greece may be attributed to the Northwest Semites who dominated Minoan civilization on Greek soil and who continued to write inscriptions in their own Semitic language as late as Hellenistic times on Cyprus and Crete.

wear out for the forty years they wandered in the wilderness, we are dealing with the same motif we meet in the Gilgamesh Epic (XI:244–45, 246), whereby Gilgamesh is equipped with a garment that will remain new and show no sign of wear throughout his long and arduous journey from the abode of Utnapishtim to his native city Erech. Once we get a feeling for these epic features, it is easy to single them out of the biblical narrative. For example, the Ten Plagues have an unmistakable epic ring. However, it is not our purpose to set up criteria (no matter how sound) and base thereon a hypothetical system for analyzing the Hebrew text so as to detach the epic features. It is rather our aim to confine our observations to specific elements controllable from extrabiblical sources.

The Conquest, which must have some historic basis, has also epic features. We shall note only one that happens to contain nothing supernatural: the ruse whereby the Gibeonites use stale bread (Joshua 9:12) to convey the impression of a long lapse of time in their supposed wanderings. This reechoes an old motif. Gilgamesh (XI: 200–28) is convinced that he has slept a week, by a loaf baked for him on each successive day; the seven loaves displaying the signs of age ranging from mold to freshness.

The crowning epic cycle in biblical historiography is the Hebrew "Shahnameh," the Epic of Kings celebrating the rise of the monarchy that under Saul stood up against Philistine tyranny, and under David shook off the yoke of tyranny and achieved the glory of empire.[7] David's greater accomplishment and his founding the first and only enduring dynasty explain why he and he alone merited epic treatment par excellence. Like Kret (:9), David was one of eight brothers (1 Samuel 16:10–11). Moreover, the fact that David is the youngest who eclipses all his elder brothers is an epic motif we have already discussed but which we may briefly amplify by pointing out that it is particularly applicable in Ugaritic epic to royal succession (128:I–II). Furthermore, as noted above, the Bible retains two traditions, marking David as either the seventh or the eighth son, again pointing to

7. It is likely that the Book of Jashar was the poetic epic that told of the Hebrew Conquest (Joshua 10:13) culminating in David's reign (2 Samuel 1:18). Most likely, its tribal Judean emphasis rendered it unfit for uniting all the tribes. Therefore the Exodus, in which all the tribes have a more or less equal share, became the national epic and so remains in Jewry to the present day. The acceptance of the Exodus has resulted in the almost total loss of the Book of Jashar, whose two surviving excerpts indicate that it would have ranked high in world literature.

epic treatment. No one will question David's historicity, but neither will any open-minded scholar fail to see that the *manner* of recounting his annointment in 1 Samuel 16 reflects dramatic epic form.

Like Kret who must win the hand of a princess by war, David must slay many a Philistine to win the princess Michal as his bride. Furthermore, the fact that David loses her and has to regain her (2 Samuel 3:14) suggests that when the Ugaritic bard tells that Kret's (:12–14) rightful bride departed, it does not mean she died but that his destined wife has somehow or other left him and must be rewon. (In other words, Kret's marital history, as far as the story goes, is monogamous.) The epic of King Kret also relates his suffering in consequence of sin. We may compare David's suffering for his sin with Bathsheba. That the child's fatal illness lasts for the epic number of seven days (2 Samuel 12:18) reflects a poetic original. Kret's disaster involves the welfare of his realm which faces famine (126:III); David's errors confront his realm with a choice of disasters including famine (2 Samuel 24:13).

With David the nation comes of age. Genuine triumph makes epic exaggeration less necessary. The institution of government scribes makes possible annalistic records with heavy inroads on less accurate popular epics. Moreover, the consciousness of historic significance evoked among the Hebrews a historiography not to be equaled anywhere in the world until half a millennium later under the fifth-century Greek historians Herodotus and Thucydides.

David's narrative combines earlier epic with later historiography. With Solomon the epic elements diminish and annalistic elements increase. After the division of the kingdom, many of the traditional epic features disappear. Schematic numbers for the reigns become quite rare after the forty years each of David[8] and Solomon. Preoccupation with the birth of a son and heir, though it must have remained common enough in real life, is no longer considered worthy of inclusion in the history. Romantic marriage[9] (which certainly could not have died with David in Israel) is no longer mentioned. Annunciations are eliminated from secular life and confined to the sphere of

8. Epic round numbers may be broken down in the course of prosification. Thus David's epic "40" is broken down into his 7 years at Hebron plus 33 at Jerusalem. Similarly, the epic "70" members of Jacob's household are broken down into 66 + 2 + 2 in Genesis 46:26–27.

9. Since romantic marriage is absent from pre-Ugaritic epics (e.g., Gilgamesh), its presence in Ugarit, the Bible, and Homer points to Indo-European influence. Cf. Cyrus H. Gordon, "Notes on the Legend of Keret," *Journal of Near Eastern Studies* 11, 1952, p. 213.

religion.[10] Post-Davidic history is virtually devoid of the old Canaanite epic content, however much the language continues to reecho
the epic tradition in expression and style.

To sum up, the earliest Hebrew literature was no doubt of poetic
epic form and had much in common with Ugaritic literature. In
time, these epics were transformed into prose narratives. The most
likely period when this transformation occurred was the reign of
King Solomon. During his reign there was contact with Egypt, and
the cultural influence from Israel's neighbor may have led the Hebrew
literati to adopt Egyptian prose narrational style (witness, for example, the Romance of Sinuhe, the Shipwrecked Sailor, the Eloquent
Peasant, the Tale of Two Brothers, various Tales of Wonder, and others, all written in prose). Furthermore, as we saw in Chapter XIII,
there is much in the Genesis narratives that points to a tenth-century
date of composition. With the establishment of a large bureaucracy
in Solomon's day, royal scribes became the recorders of the nation's
history and the style of writing became annalistic. Accordingly, epic
treatment of Israelite history is much more prominent in the early
books of the Bible and is much less a factor in the later books of the
Bible.[11]

The catastrophe of 586 did not strip the Jews of their conviction
that their history had eternal significance and hope. For it was during
the sixth century that the comprehensive work of Genesis through
Kings achieved its final form. The Genesis-Kings account cannot be
a haphazard, unedited collection. Each successive book takes up
where the preceding one leaves off. The last event in Kings was the
hope-inspiring event of Jehoiachin's elevation (see below). Since the
Genesis-Kings account begins with the creation of the world, the net
result is all of history (or all of history germane to the experience of
Israel) presented in one continuum. This creation of linear history is
an innovation of ancient Judaism and it is directly related to its unique
understanding of God. Since Yahwe is a God of History, interacting
in human affairs, the telling of history becomes a sacred act.[12] Among

10. The first purely religious annunciation in Canaan occurs in Ugaritic text 77:7.

11. However, the Elijah and Elisha cycles retain some features of epic proportion. Possibly,
the northern kingdom, with its lack of stability in royal administrations, retained the ancient
epic literary tradition more so than did Judah.

12. Continued in many ways in Judaism down to the present day, the most famous example
of which is the Passover Seder with the recounting of the Exodus (along with midrashic
embellishment).

the other peoples of the ancient world, whose gods were gods of nature, the creation of historiography or of a document such as the Genesis-Kings account is nonexistent. Israel's neighbors had all the features of this large collection (creation stories, flood stories, epics, law collections, tales of wonder, royal annals, etc.), but it took Israel to put it all together into one unified work.

In the postexilic period another comprehensive history was created, the books of Chronicles. This work, too, begins with the start of human history (the first word is "Adam"). The last event in Chronicles is the Edict of Cyrus authorizing the return to Zion. By this time the international situation had ruled out all practical prospects for real national independence. The restoration could be in religious terms, but not in terms of Davidic sovereignty. Hence the Chronicler's history took on a religious orientation, while at the same time it looked back with great pride upon the Judean kings of old. The latter factor led to a glorification of these kings, even when undeserved, so that the kings of Judah are portrayed in Chronicles in a more positive light than they are in Samuel and Kings. The most striking illustration of this feature: David's sin of adultery with Bathsheba is mentioned not at all.

The fact that Ezra and Nehemiah are supposed to follow Chronicles must have been obvious to the men responsible for the present Hebrew order in which Chronicles follows Ezra and Nehemiah. For Ezra opens with a repetition of the last statement in Chronicles thus picking up the narrative before going on. May it not be that the present arrangement resulted from a desire to close the Hebrew Bible on a hopeful note: the Edict of Cyrus?[13] Ezra ends with affairs of Zion in a sorry state. Nehemiah ends his book on the middling note that while all was not rosy, he had done his best. Nehemiah would be an uninspiring "finis"; Ezra, a quite hopeless one. The choice of Chronicles with which to close the Hebrew Bible made for a happy ending even though chronological considerations call for the order Chronicles-Ezra-Nehemiah.

In like manner, note that while the last chapter of the great narrative of Genesis through 2 Kings describes the disaster that befell Jerusalem in 586 B.C.E., the very last paragraph is optimistic. It relates how

13. It was Joan K. Gordon who called this to our attention. Her view is substantiated by the fact that in the traditional editions of the Hebrew Bible, the last felicitous verse is repeated at the end of any biblical book (such as Lamentations or Ecclesiastes) whose final verse is unpleasant.

the Judean king in exile, Jehoiachin, was released from prison in 561 B.C.E. by his Babylonian captors, and how he received royal rations for the rest of his life (2 Kings 25:27–30).

The optimism that permeates the Bible undoubtedly is a major factor in explaining the continuation of the Jewish people as a nation to the present day. Whereas all the other entities of antiquity (Sumer, Babylonia, Assyria, the Hittites, the Canaanites, Egypt, etc.) fell by the wayside, only tiny Israel persisted through the millennia. The hope expressed in the literature of the Bible, coupled with an eschatology pointing toward a Messianic Era, go a long way toward explaining this remarkable phenomenon.

To evaluate the historical books of the Hebrew Bible the student would do well to bear in mind the whole as well as the parts. Both the Genesis-Kings and the Chronicles-Ezra-Nehemiah "Histories of the Hebrew People" have embraced many a transformed epic, such as the Epic of Creation, the Deluge, the Birth of a Family, the Birth of a Nation, the Epic of Kings, etc. Why and how the transformations were effected should be among the questions foremost in the minds of biblical students today.

Before the Hebrews had conceived of the idea of a Bible, they possessed both oral and written literatures. Oral literature is not so fickle (nor is written literature so stable) as one might suppose. Poetic form helps preserve oral literature from excessive change. Moreover, once oral recitations become part of the repertoire of priests, as well as of minstrels and other professional entertainers, the recitations tend to be frozen in fixed form. These forces affected the oral literature of Israel and her neighbors. Parts of the Bible may have been transmitted orally long before they were written down. Thus, folktales such as the exploits of Samson are of popular oral origin. Also the tales of the prophets, such as the miraculous stories about Elijah and Elisha, arose orally and had to achieve credence and sanctity among the people before they were written down.

The writers of the Hebrew Bible drew on earlier written sources and frequently cite them by name; e.g., The Book of the Wars of Yahwe, The Book of Jashar, The Chronicles of the Kings of Judah, The Chronicles of the Kings of Israel, and the plethora of sources (in part midrashic) cited by the Chronicler. These early sources used by the biblical writers have been doomed to destruction because of the exclusive status won by Scripture.

The evidence of the Bible itself helps us understand how some books came to be written down. Jeremiah 36 tells us that the scribe Baruch wrote down what the Prophet dictated. After the resultant scroll happened to be destroyed, Jeremiah redictated the text, with additions, to Baruch (v. 32). But Jeremiah 36 is replete with the narrative explanations of a later editor about Jeremiah and Baruch.

Some of the biblical books are of an international rather than Hebraic character. This is particularly true of Wisdom Literature, which lays no stress on cult and is of universal applicability. The Egyptian composition called The Wisdom of Amenemope is from the same source as, or may well be the source of, the section of Proverbs containing the long-misunderstood "Have I not written for you the thirty"? (Proverbs 22:20). Amenemope, which is divided into thirty sections, and parallels the contents of this part of Proverbs, leaves no doubt that the Hebrew word is the numeral "30."

The Book of Proverbs is a compilation of several collections of different origins. Proverbs (1:1) opens with a section attributed to Solomon. Proverbs 25:1 introduces more so-called Solomonic wisdom, but this time the contents are said to have been transmitted by "the men of Hezekiah, King of Judah." Other sections are not even Israelian or Judean. Thus "the words of Agur" (Proverbs 30:1) and "the words of Lemuel, King of Massa" (31:1), are ascribed to personages not directly associated with the Hebrew tribes.

Another piece of Wisdom Literature with a truly international flavor is the book of Job, set in the land of Uz in the desert regions to Israel's southeast. None of the characters is Israelite; the language of the book is not standard Hebrew, rather it reflects the dialect of the Transjordanian desert fringe; and the main theme, the problem of why righteous people suffer, is universal. On the other hand, an exilic or postexilic Jewish author probably adopted this well-known story to suit his own needs. The book of Job thus appears as a message of faith to Israel, whose experiences in the sixth century B.C.E. still were in need of explanation. As we saw earlier (Chapter XVII, pp. 288–89), the author of Kings blamed the events of 586 on the previous generation of Manasseh; while the prophet Ezekiel pointed the finger directly at the generation of 586 as being a sinful one. Some time later the author of Job offered his theological explanation: There is such a thing as righteous suffering. That is to say, Israel is a righteous nation, though the people have suffered nonetheless. But if you have faith in God, He will restore your fortunes, just as God restored Israel in 538 B.C.E.

Other books in the Bible are also compilations. The Book of Habakkuk now consists of three chapters; the prophecies are in the first two chapters, while the third chapter is a psalm. Scholars had long suspected that the third chapter was added to the original book of two chapters. This supposition is confirmed by the Dead Sea Scroll called the Commentary of Habakkuk, which stops at the end of the second chapter, even though there is room for continuing with a third chapter, if there had been one.

The Dead Sea Scrolls are of great interest in clarifying what happened between biblical times and the fixing of the Hebrew Bible as we have it today. Fragments of all the biblical books (save Esther) have been found in the caves around Qumran that have yielded the scrolls (and, in the case of Isaiah, we possess a complete book). The texts were written in the last two centuries B.C.E. and were used until roughly around the destruction of the Second Temple in 70 C.E. Qumran-type scrolls were also found at Masada, the last stronghold of the Zealots that fell to the Romans in 73 C.E.

The Qumranites possessed quite a few writings that are not in the Bible today. Some of these extra writings, like the Pseudepigraphical books called Jubilees and Enoch, have long been known in Greek,[14] Latin, and other languages (such as Ethiopic), but now we have parts of them in Hebrew and Aramaic. Moreover, the Dead Sea sectarian Jews possessed other writings hitherto unknown to us, notably the Manual of Discipline. The rabbinical authorities were confronted with the need of specifying which writings were sacred and which were not. But in so selecting the books that were to be regarded as sacred, they eliminated the others thereby threatening them with destruction. Many writings were in circulation during the battle for recognition and survival. Canonization was a selective process that preserved some books but destroyed others.

The Dead Sea manuscripts[15] of the Bible have many variants diverging from the Masoretic (i.e., traditional, authorized) Hebrew text. Some of these variants go with the Septuagint; others go with

14. The Greek translation called the Septuagint was made in Alexandria, Egypt, during the third and second centuries B.C.E. It embraces the Canonical and Apocryphal (and, in some editions, parts of the Pseudepigraphical) books of the Bible (excluding the New Testament, of course).

15. We refer specifically to the Qumran scrolls, not to the Murabbaʿat texts, used by normative, rabbinite Jews during the Bar-Kokhba rebellion (132–135 C.E.), which conform closely to our Masoretic text.

the Samaritan Pentateuch, or with Bible quotations in rabbinic literature.[16]

What we have just noted about text and canon is typical of all
classical and sacred literatures. During the precanonical period of
transmission, the text and repertoire are full of variations. Then there
comes a time when order must replace the chaos, for neither synagogue nor church can maintain authority if every individual has his
or her own text and his or her own list of sacred writings. Thus
diversity precedes uniformity in such matters. Where there had been
several variant readings, one reading is accepted as correct and the
devout are warned against, and protected from, the other readings.

The work of establishing text and canon was entrusted to able and
conscientious men. By and large they preserved the best books and
the best readings. In textual matters they used good and old manuscripts. The system of spelling in the Dead Sea Scrolls is later than the
spelling in the Masoretic text. In other words, though our Masoretic
manuscripts may have been written long after the Dead Sea Scrolls,
they are based on exemplars typologically older than the Dead Sea
documents.

Our Bible is but a fragment of the writings of the Bible World. To
understand that precious fragment, we need all the collateral information we can get and digest. If this Introduction has helped the
reader to grasp the nature of the problem and has showed him or her
how specific gaps in our knowledge are filled, this book has fulfilled
a useful service.

---

16. The variants also tell us much about the history of the Hebrew language. For an excellent
work on this subject, devoted to the aforementioned Isaiah scroll, see the majesterial work of
E. Y. Kutscher, *The Language and Linguistic Background of the Isaiah Scroll (1QIsaᵃ)*, Leiden,
1974. For a more general introduction to the subject, see E. Y. Kutscher, *A History of the
Hebrew Language,* Jerusalem, 1982, especially pp. 87–114.

# INDEX

Aaron, 144, 145, 150, 165, 206n
Abdi-hepa, 205
Abel, 37–38
Abigail, 189, 216
Abijam, 84n, 222–23
Abimelech (son of Gideon), 180
Abimelech of Gerar, king of the Philistines, 118, 119, 122
Abishag, 206, 207
Abishai, 201, 202–3
Abner, 186, 193–94, 203
Abraham (Abram), 41, 50, 83, 101, 109, 111–16, 119–20, 122, 130, 140, 164, 176, 215–16, 229, 317, 318
  in Amarna Age, 112
  Aramaic background of, 113–14
  in Canaan, 114
  God and, 116, 117–18
Absalom, 199–202
Achaemenian Empire, 18, 25, 277
  administration of, 305–6
  Alexander's conquest of, 310–11
  art of, 308
  Babylon and, 290, 305
  Babylonian Jews and, 298
  capitals of, 305–6
  dissimulation doctrine and, 306
  Egypt conquered by, 294
  Greeks and, 308–9
  inscriptions of, 296
  Jews and, 294
  origins of, 303–4

  religious tolerance in, 307
  Zoroastrianism of, 307–8
Achilles, 105, 317
Achish, king of Gath, 188, 189–90, 207
Adadnirari III, 241
Adah, 38
Adam, 37
Adapa Legend, 51
Adonijah, 206–7
Adoniram (Adoram), 203, 209, 218
Adonizedek, 206
Adoram (Adoniram), 203, 209, 218
Aesop, 126
afterlife concept, 60
Agamemnon, 104, 130, 230
Ahab, 103, 160, 224, 225–27, 229, 230, 231, 232, 233, 235, 239, 243
Ahaz, 253–54
Ahaziah, 231, 234, 235, 239
Ahijah of Shiloh, 214, 221
Ahimelech, 188, 205–6
Ahinoam, 189
Ahiqar, 295
Ahitophel, 200–201
Ahriman, 308
Ahura Mazda, 296, 307, 308
Ai, 150, 170–71, 172
'Ajrud inscription, 244–45
Akhenaton (Amenhotep IV), 84–85, 141
alcohol, prohibition against, 235
Alexander the Great, 27, 304, 310–11, 313